Making Policy in B
Education 1945–20

Making Policy in British Higher Education 1945–2011

Michael Shattock

 Open University Press

Open University Press
McGraw-Hill Education
McGraw-Hill House
Shoppenhangers Road
Maidenhead
Berkshire
England
SL6 2QL

email: enquiries@openup.co.uk
world wide web: www.openup.co.uk

and Two Penn Plaza, New York, NY 10121–2289, USA

First published 2012

A catalogue record of this book is available from the British Library

ISBN-13: 978 0 335241866 (pb)
ISBN-10: 0 33 5241867 (pb)
eISBN: 978 0 335241873

Library of Congress Cataloging-in-Publication Data
CIP data applied for

Typesetting and e-book compilations by
RefineCatch Limited, Bungay, Suffolk
Printed in the UK by Bell & Bain Ltd, Glasgow

Fictitious names of companies, products, people, characters and/or data that may be used herein (in case studies or in examples) are not intended to represent any real individual, company, product or event.

"In the last 30 years Britain has experimented with some of the most innovative higher education policies including academic quality assurance, research assessment, income contingent loan financing, tuition policy, information for students, and other efforts to stimulate competitive market forces. In this highly enlightening, meticulously researched, and fascinating history, university administrator and scholar Michael Shattock examines the individuals and financial policy drivers that have shaped British higher education from World War II to the present day and explores the impacts of these policies on the university sector."

David D. Dill, Professor Emeritus of Public Policy,
University of North Carolina at Chapel Hill, USA

"Michael Shattock's important new book could not be better timed. He offers a detailed, nuanced and (above all) intelligent account of policy making in British higher education over the past 60 years ... This book reminds us that novelty is more often in the eye of the beholder than the historical record. It also warns us that those who have forgotten past events are often fated to relive them – and that second (or third) time round is rarely an improvement."

Peter Scott, Professor of Higher Education Studies,
Institute of Education University of London, UK

The past which a historian studies is not a dead past, but a past which is in some sense still living in the present

R.G. Collingwood, *The Idea of History*

Contents

List of figures

List of tables

Acknowledgements

Any author trying to cover an extended period of post-War history, where such a wealth of archival material exists, is bound to rely heavily on the published research of others. I would wish to express my appreciation of Philip Gosden's *Education in the Second World War* (1976) and his *The Education System since 1944* (1983) and Paul Sharp's *The Creation of the Local Authority Sector of Higher Education* (1987) which are both models of how research based on a detailed scrutiny of archival evidence should be presented. The 30 year rule restricts access to material in the National Archive and for the 1980s and 1990s a parallel source to Gosden and Sharp is provided by Maurice Kogan and Stephen Hanney's *Reforming Higher Education* (2000) based on an extended programme of interviews of leading players in the higher education scene. Too much has been written by scholars of and actors in higher education to mention all the persons on whose work I have drawn but mention must be made of two doctoral dissertations, the first by C. D. Godwin, summarized in an authoritative article, The origin of the binary system (1998) and the second by G. J. Taggart, *A critical review of the role of the English Funding Body for Higher Education in the relationship between the State and Higher Education in the period 1945–2003* (2004) which provides a valuable account, from the advantage of also being written from the front line as it were, of the Higher Education Funding Council for England (HEFCE). I have, of course, greatly benefitted from access to the National Archive at Kew particularly in relation to Treasury and University Grants Committee (UGC) files.

None of the above, and only one of any of the scholars I have cited, as far as I am aware, have had access to the specifically higher education archive material on which I have been able to draw. These are: the archives of the Committee of Vice Chancellors and Principals (CVCP) up to 1988 deposited in the Modern Records Centre, University of Warwick together with the Committee's/Universities UK (UUK) files 1988–98 held in Woburn House; the archives of the Committee of Polytechnic Directors deposited at the Modern Records Centre, University of Warwick; the archives of the Association of Commonwealth Universities (ACU) in respect to the Home

Universities Conferences, held by the Association; papers deposited by Vanessa Walsh arising from the interview programme carried out by her husband James Walsh, in association with Geoffrey Lockwood, in the 1970s, deposited in the Brotherton Library, University of Leeds; the Toby Weaver archive held in the Library of the Institute of Education; and the T. R. McConnell papers deposited in the Bancroft Library, University of California-Berkeley. (T. R. McConnell was a professor of higher education at Berkeley who visited Britain in the 1960s and 70s to conduct interviews with senior figures in British higher education.) Of these, the CVCP/UUK archives offer an indispensable record of events and issues, and access to documents which were only available within higher education. I should like to express my thanks and appreciation to all the archival/library staff who gave me access to and helped me in identifying relevant material, to the staff of the ACU's office who took special steps to retrieve the material I needed from an archive some distance from the ACU's office and to the staff of UUK who allowed me access to and gave me assistance in working through their 'dead' committee files.

Above all I should like to express my gratitude to Dr Stephen Hanney and Professor Mary Henkel for giving me access to the unique interview material associated with the Kogan and Hanney book, referred to above, and particularly to Mary for writing personally to the interviewees to seek permission for me to read the material. I should also like to thank those persons who I interviewed myself in the course of the research. Since many of these were civil servants I have chosen not to list their names to protect their identity.

I should like to thank my colleagues for assistance and advice: Nick Crafts and Wyn Grant, professors of economic history and politics respectively at Warwick, and Vincent Carpentier, Paul Temple, Gareth Williams and Celia Whitchurch at the Centre for Higher Education Studies at the Institute of Education. My special thanks go to Ian McNay at the University of Greenwich for reading and commenting so thoroughly on the manuscript. However, this manuscript would not exist, at least in readable form, but for the efforts of Pam Bate and Caroline Steenman-Clark to whom my final thanks must be given.

Michael Shattock

Acronyms

AAU	Academic Audit Unit
ABRC	Advisory Board of the Research Councils
ACC	Association of County Councils
ACU	Association of Commonwealth Universities
AEC	Association of Education Committees
AFE	Advanced Further Education
AMA	Association of Metropolitan Authorities
AMC	Association of Municipal Authorities
APR	Age participation rate
ATTI	Association of Teachers in Technical Institutions
ATCDE	Association of Teachers in Colleges and Departments of Education
AUT	Association of University Teachers
BIS	Department of Business, Innovation and Skills
CAT	College of Advanced Technology
CATS	Credit Accumulation and Transfer Scheme
CDP	Committee of Polytechnic Directors
CIHE	Council for Industry and Higher Education
CIPFA	Chartered Institute of Public Finance and Accountancy
CLEA	Council of Local Education Authorities
CPRS	Central Policy Review Staff
CUC	Committee of University Chairmen
CVCP	Committee of Vice Chancellors and Principals
C and AG	Comptroller and Auditor General
CNAA	Council for National Academic Awards
DES	Department of Education and Science
DFE	Department for Education
DfES	Department for Education and Skills
DIUS	Department for Innovation, Universities and Skills
DSIR	Department of Scientific and Industrial Research
DTI	Department of Trade and Industry

EHE	Enterprise in Higher Education
ELQs	Equivalent or lower qualifications
ESRC	Economic and Social Research Council
EUA	European Universities Association
FE	Further Education
FTE	Full time equivalent student numbers
HEC	Higher Education Corporation
HECS	Australian Higher Education Contribution Scheme
HEFC,	Higher Education Funding Council,
HEFCE	Higher Education Funding Council for England
HEIF	Higher Education Innovation Fund
HEQC	Higher Education Quality Council
HESA	Higher Education Statistics Agency
HMI	Her Majesty's Inspectors of Schools
ILEA	Inner London Education Authority
IRC	Interdisciplinary research centre
LAHEC	Local Authorities Higher Education Committee
LCC	London County Council
LEA	Local education authority
LSE	London School of Economics and Political Science
MIT	Massachusetts Institute of Technology
MRC	Medical Research Council
NAB	National Advisory Body for Public Sector Higher Education
NACEIC	National Advisory Committee for Education in Industry
NACTST	National Advisory Council for the Training and Supply of Teachers
NAO	National Audit Office
NATFHE	National Association for Teachers in Further and Higher Education
NCIHE	National Committee of Inquiry into Higher Education
NCTA	National Council for Technological Awards
NEDC	National Economic Development Committee
NERC	Natural Environmental Research Council
NIC	National Incomes Commission
NPM	New Public Management
NUS	National Union of Students
NUT	National Union of Teachers
OFFA	Office for Fair Access
OIA	Office of the Independent Adjudicator for Higher Education
OPCS	Office of Population and Census Surveys
OU	Open University
PAC	Public Accounts Committee
PAR	Programme Analysis Review
PCAS	Polytechnics and Colleges Application System
PCFC	Polytechnics and Colleges Funding Council
PES	Public Expenditure Survey

PESC	Public Expenditure Survey Committee
PSHE	Public Sector Higher Education
QAA	Quality Assurance Agency
RAC	Regional Advisory Council
RAE	Research Assessment Exercise
REF	Research Excellence Framework
SCOP	Standing Conference of Principals
SED	Scottish Education Department
SERC	Science and Engineering Research Council
SISTERs	Special Institutions for Scientific and Technological Education and Research
SRC	Science Research Council
SRHE	Society for Research in Higher Education
SSRC	Social Studies Research Council
STEAC	Scottish Tertiary Education Advisory Council
THES	*Times Higher Education Supplement*
TRAC	Transparent Approach to Costing
TQA	Teaching Quality Assessments
UCAS	Universities Central Admissions System
UCCA	Universities Central Council on Admissions
UCL	University College London
UFC	Universities Funding Council
UGC	University Grants Committee
UKCOSA	UK Council for Overseas Students Affairs
UMIST	University of Manchester Institute of Science and Technology
UUK	Universities UK

1

Higher education and the policy process

The aim of this book is to show how policy has been made in British higher education and how policies, and often their unintended consequences, have determined the shape of higher education, nationally and institutionally. The book covers the period from 1945 and the assumption that higher education, or perhaps more specifically, university education had become the responsibility of the state, to the 2011 White Paper, *Higher Education: Students at the Heart of the System* (BIS 2011b), when the state, nominally at least, took a significant step towards handing the development of higher education back to the market. The decision to attempt to trace major policy decisions over such a long period was deliberate in order to illustrate how far the roots of policy in modern higher education, that is from 1992, reach back into the 1950s and the post-Robbins settlement. The length of the period, and the political changes which it has seen, render generalizations about a policy process dangerous. Policy drivers varied at different points over the period depending on changing political, economic and structural contexts but two stand out consistently over the whole period: the increasing demand for places in higher education and the implications of financing the expansion. Taken together, in the context of competition with the claims of the rest of the public services, where costs were also rising in total faster than the rate of GDP, the conjunction of these two drivers has proved to be the prime forcing house for policy change.

Viewed from the perspective of policy process theory, higher education represents a somewhat aberrant field of study. Policy was not consistently made top down or bottom up (Sabatier 1986). In the first place, 'the top' is hard to define because it comprised a network of interrelated bodies: not only the responsible government minister but also the Treasury, the intermediary bodies (University Grants Committee (UGC), National Advisory Body (NAB), Universities' Funding Council (UFC), Polytechnics and Colleges Funding Council (PCFC) and the Higher Education Funding Councils (HEFCs)) and, between 2001 and 2004, the Prime Minister's Office. 'The bottom' might seem easier to define as most obviously the institutions (universities, polytechnics and colleges) but their interests certainly did not always coincide. It also comprised their powerful representative bodies (chiefly the Committee of Vice-Chancellors and Principals (CVCP), the Committee of Polytechnic Directors (CDP), Universities UK (UUK), and the Russell Group) together with, on significant occasions, the National Union of Students (NUS). All these bodies had separate entrées into the policy process. And, of course, there were other bodies as well, ranging from the Royal Society and the research councils to trades unions and other institutional representative bodies.

'The top' might appear to be represented by a draconian letter of guidance from a secretary of state to a funding council but policy hardly ever sprang fully developed from a secretary of state. It may have been virtually dictated by the Treasury after a gruelling series of public expenditure round interviews; it may have been prepared in the Department by officials who, from 1990 onwards, were almost certainly more influential in policy matters than ministers and who themselves would have tested out issues with the UUK and the funding council. By convention, any such letter would also have been shown in draft to the funding council for comment and, occasionally, modification. Policies emerged as a result of 'a bargaining process' (Minogue 1983) or from 'partisan mutual adjustment' (Lindblom 1965). Sometimes a decision emerged out of an entirely separate decision-making process as, for example, the new tuition fee arrangements in the 2010 Comprehensive Spending Review.

Occasionally, particular policy interests played a prominent role in policy formation such as, for example, the Royal Society on the science budget in the 1990s and the Russell Group on top up fees in 2001 or the Council for Industry and Higher Education (CIHE) on two particular occasions, on expanding student numbers in 1987 and on teaching quality in 1988. But unlike other public policy areas higher education rarely found a place in political party manifestos and the ideological divisions between the major political parties, at least until 2010, were not great. Political parties bickered about higher education policy but in many of the major decisions such as the creation of the polytechnics, the establishment of the National Advisory Body and the merger of the two sectors in 1992 their policies were almost bipartisan. Ideologies were certainly present in the formulation of policy: ideology played a significant role in the rejection of the Robbins recommendations and the establishment of the binary line (though other considerations played a part) but the evidence is clear that, although Sir Edward (later Lord) Boyle, the Conservative Party spokesman, would not have committed himself to the sentiments of the Woolwich speech, he supported the practical implications; Sir Keith Joseph was influenced by the Institute of Economic Affairs and the public choice school of decision making, but the Blair Government was equally at home with neo-liberal policies as addressed to the public services. New public management approaches were first adopted under the Conservatives but were continued and further developed under Labour.

Policy theorists distinguish between the rationalist and the incremental process of decision making (Smith and May 1980). The former presupposes a tidy process where objectives are formulated, alternative strategies are reviewed and, once selected, a decision is executed and the outcomes evaluated. With the possible exception of the 1991 decision to merge the two sectors, where officials did review formally the options, there is little evidence that major policy changes ever followed this process. Because the main forcing house for policy changes was the growth in demand for higher education and the funding requirements necessary to meet it, and because the decision-making process for determining the response to these issues took place through formal mechanisms like the quinquennial planning system, or the public expenditure survey process, policy making was largely incremental. Policy makers had to begin their consideration of any given issue with reviewing the policies already in force, eventually taking decisions which were essentially at the margin rather than challenging basic assumptions. There were few dramatic departures: even the most far reaching decisions on the Robbins settlement can be viewed in this light as a reinforcement of the *status quo*, and, indeed, this is how Crosland presented them in his 1966 Lancaster speech rather than as a revolutionary switch of policy as in his more famous speech at Woolwich. The development of higher education, therefore, fits Lindblom's definition of 'disjointed incrementalism' (Lindblom 1965) far more closely than any rationalist planning perspective. Higher education policy development also illustrates Minogue's description of 'the sheer messiness of real-world political and organisational life' (Minogue 1983). A good illustration of this is the statement by a senior policy maker interviewed by Kogan, referring to events in the 1980s:

> My experience of government was shocking for me. I had expected that the nearer one got to the commanding heights, the more rational it would all be. The more calmness, the more rationality, the more careful consideration, looking at evidence. I discovered the opposite. Ministers were in a constant state of mild panic rushing from one thing to the next, never having time to grasp any issue, needing to make a decision in extraordinary short periods of time and often trying to make decisions without having grasped the issues. Then officials tried to rush around to clear up the mess.[1]

Kogan and Hanney concluded that: 'Policy making followed no rational model. Policies were created largely on the hoof and were . . . the product of a complex interplay of context, ideologies, ministers and bureaucracies' (Kogan and Hanney 2000: 235).

A further important factor in reconciling higher education policy processes with theoretical perspectives is that except in rare instances, such as the Parliamentary debate over top up fees in 2004, higher education policy was seen as peripheral in terms of British politics at large. Education ministers were much more concerned with issues about pre-16 education than higher education; higher education was much more a technical area which had to be argued about by intermediary bodies, research councils and representative bodies behind closed doors than the more high profile issues affecting schools policy, which occupied a great deal more of a minister's time. Alistair Darling describes how at an early stage in his Parliamentary career he turned down an invitation to be shadow spokesman for higher education because it offered so few opportunities to shine in the House of Commons where an opposition spokesman's reputation is made (Darling 2011). Most secretaries of state saw Education as a stepping stone to something else, the exception being Keith Joseph, and their turnover was rapid, giving very little opportunity to comprehend underlying issues in higher education policy. Again, the exception was Joseph who spent four years in office (as also did David Blunkett) and was genuinely interested in policy questions intervening, often unproductively in quite minor issues, but who, as a consequence, left a larger mark on underlying policy matters than many of his more obviously dynamic successors. One result was that higher education policy was largely in the hands of civil servants who, with the exception of Toby (later Sir Toby) Weaver, took an administrative, less strategic and certainly less ideological approach to policy questions than committed ministers might have done. Thus Richard Bird, the senior official responsible for higher education in the Department of Education and Science (DES), writing of the 1980s, a period of significant change, argued that:

> most of the significant developments of the decade happened in a piece-meal and pragmatic fashion. There were certainly overall trends in policy, though these could by no means be assembled into any kind of grand strategy. Indeed in my judgement, the creation of an embracing strategy was always beyond reach because of the Government's refusal to appoint royal commissions . . . and the usual insistence that certain actions could 'brook no delay'.
>
> (Bird 1994: 84)

Except in very rare cases like the Crosland/Weaver binary line policy, and even here a counter argument as in the Lancaster speech could be advanced, higher education policy evolved and emerged out of the interactions of a network of bodies and organizations, mostly over long periods of time. Thus we tend to think of 'the Robbins principle' that all those qualified to enter universities and wishing to study in them should be permitted to do so, as being the product of the Committee's Report in 1963 but, in fact, it represented the tacit principle for which the Government had sought to make provision since 1945. Questions of widening access, a potentially divisive issue with the creation of the Office for Fair Access (OFFA) in 2004, reach back to Tawney in the 1940s, the Kelsall Report in the 1950s and the joint statement between the UGC and NAB which substituted 'to be able to benefit from' for 'qualified for' in the Robbins principle, in 1984 (UGC 1984 para 8). It has been argued that since the mid-1980s higher education policy has been increasingly subordinated to economic needs and the demands of industry (*cf* Salter and Tapper 1994) but the need to invest more in science and applied science to match national and industrial needs were key issues for the Barlow Report target set in 1946, the investment in applied science and technology in the universities and the colleges in the 1950s and for the UGC in the balance of its allocation of student numbers in the 1970s. While the Joseph Green Paper (DES 1985) re-emphasized the issue, it was the combination of an apparent emphasis on the economic view with the funding implications that sprang from its pessimistic forecast of student numbers which generated its unpopularity. From the re-structuring of the university system in the immediate post-War period the Treasury always put the economic argument high on its agenda.

All these issues, however, were subordinate to the financial question as to how growth in higher education was to be funded when its growth rate exceeded the growth in GDP. An indication of the scale of the problem can be drawn from Halsey's observation that staff numbers in universities in 1990 were as large as student numbers in 1950 (Halsey 1996). From 1962 onwards the Public Expenditure Survey demanded that the universities and, after 1981, the whole of higher education, competed for additional funding, over and above inflation, against the demands of defence, infrastructure (roads etc.), health, social security and the rest; within the Education budget higher education also had to compete with further education and the demographic led needs of schools and colleges. One result of this has been that the formulation of policy in higher education has been much more closely integrated with the government's financial decision-making machinery than in many other countries. Policy more often emerged from the interactions and dialogues within and between different parts of Government than specifically from the department formally charged with responsibility for higher education.

One should not assume that policy was not also driven from below. Of course, in the period up to the late 1970s the UGC's position meant that university policy was, to a significant extent, protected from external intervention, except in regard to the overall funding allocation that was made available. But even after the Thatcher Government had imposed its 1980 budget and Joseph had expressed the intention to assert the Government's role to direct policy there are convincing cases of policy in critical areas being driven from the institutions themselves. One example was the CDP pressure which led to the 1988 legislation releasing the polytechnics from the control of the local authorities; another was the campaign for 'top up' fees by the CVCP which led to the setting up of the Dearing Committee, while a third would be the Russell Group's persuasion of the Prime Minister, Blair, that tuition fees had to become part of the higher education funding package. Although British higher education institutions are rightly regarded internationally as having a high degree of autonomy the findings of this book suggest that the higher education system is enmeshed in the machinery of government at many levels and that the formulation of policy results much more from a complex web of organizational relationships rather than from any single source. That those organizations that sit on the Government's side of the line have become more dominant since 1992 is unquestionable, but the line remains blurred in practice with personalities, informal links and interlocking networks all contributing to decision making.

In reviewing policy decisions over nearly 70 years it is important to pay attention to the period context. However, defining periods in the development of the higher education system depends a great deal on what theme one wishes to pursue. The first issue of the *Universities Quarterly*, in 1946, opened with Ernest (later Lord) Simon's words 'There is no university "system" in Britain. There are 16 self governing universities each of which has developed in its own way' (Simon 1946). Periods defined by system structure might then be developed beginning with 1945 to 1965, recognizing the rejection of the structure proposed by Robbins that was effected by the Woolwich speech as the break point, followed by 1965 to 1992 when the two sectors, the university and the public sector, co-existed across the binary line and concluding with a last and continuing phase from the merger of the sectors in 1992. A second exercise in periodicity might be to define the break points around the life of intermediary funding agencies. This would give a period of 1945 to 1989 when the universities were funded (and their strategies steered) through the UGC and the public sector institutions through the Advanced Further Education (AFE)/Futher Education (FE) pooling system, (where steering only began with the creation of NAB in 1982), followed by a second period of funding through funding council mechanisms (Universities Funding Council (UFC)/Polytechnics and Colleges Funding Council (PCFC), HEFCs) a period which came to an end with the introduction of the new tuition fee based funding system in 2012, and the translation (in England) of the funding council into a regulator rather than a funding body.

A third approach would be to define periods by government departmental responsibilities so that the years 1945 to 1964 would cover the period when the UGC came under the Treasury, 1964 to 2006 would represent the period when higher education was the responsibility of the DES/DfES, and from 2006 a new period would begin when the Department reverted to its pre-1964 role and higher education was transferred to a Department of Business, Innovation and Skills (BIS) with a brief stopover in a Department of Innovation, Universities and Skills (DIUS). This transfer, in itself suggests another break point, the introduction of the first research assessment exercise in 1985–86, the beginning of the long running attempt to restructure the higher education system by concentrating research in fewer institutions and separating the funding for the research function from the teaching function. Other equally important break points might be identified from changes in funding methodologies: from 1945 to 1962 when the university sector was funded direct by the Treasury on the basis of forecasts of student demand; from 1962 and the introduction of the Public Expenditure Survey Committee process, to 1976, which saw the change from volume planning to Cash Limits; to 1981 and the cuts in public expenditure; and finally to 2006 when the Labour Government introduced 'top up' fees to be paid for through income contingent loans.

Lastly, one might distinguish between what I have described elsewhere as the 'inside out' and the 'outside in' periods of British university policy making, the former being the period when policy for the universities was largely conceived and implemented by the university system itself (the UGC, the CVCP and the institutions themselves) and the latter when policy was substantially created outside the university system (Shattock 2006 and 2008). Identifying precise dates for this change can be a controversial exercise. My own preference is to draw the line at 1981–2, regarding the UGC's re-allocation exercise in 1981 (the 1981 cuts), with its reliance on subject criteria, its commitment to restore the unit of resource to 1970 levels and its decision to base its judgements on quality indicators, as representing a last hurrah of the 'inside out' regime. Many contemporary commentators saw the UGC's implementation of the budget reductions as indicating that it had become an agent of Government, rather than as I read its actions, as being an unsuccessful attempt to preserve the university system by drawing on traditional university values which owed nothing whatever to the Department's priorities (see pages 226–38).

One important result was Joseph's decision to assume a more pro-active role in determining policy than his predecessors. This, over time, fundamentally altered the balance of power and authority over higher education policy making. On this reading, although the UGC continued for the next eight years, it could no longer be described in Carswell's phase as acting as 'a collective Minister' (Carswell 1980: 12). 1981–82 was also a break point for the public sector in the decision to set up NAB and begin the process of removing it from the control of the local authorities. The later creation of the funding council system and the devolution of funding to Scotland and Wales served to accelerate the 'outside in' process. It could be argued that the 2011 White Paper, with its substitution of fees for grant, brings this period to an end because it potentially offers institutions greater freedom to pilot their own future. However, the evidence of the trends in government behaviour does not suggest that the change in funding regime will encourage a less interventionist style of policy making.

One interpretation of the whole period from 1945 to 2011 could be that it represents a long march from a fully subsidized higher education system to a substantially privatized one; another could be that the long march has been from an age participation rate of around 3 per cent to one around 43 per cent; and another might reflect the growth of universities themselves from small inward looking institutions to large international organizations. The truth of the matter, however, is that the development of higher education has not been in a straight line. As March and Olsen wrote: 'Institutions and their linkages coevolve. They are intertwined in ecologies of competition, cooperation and other forms of interaction . . . The complications turn history into a meander' (March and Olsen 1996: 256). Perhaps the most reliable interpretation is that the development of British higher education closely mirrors the development of post-War British history, political, economic and social. In other words, its development should not be seen as a progression, as such, but as a reflection of wider currents of economic and social change: the 2011 White Paper simply marks another twist or turn in a longer narrative.

The difficulty in assigning hard and fast periods to the context of policy making was one reason for presenting its development in this book in terms of general themes: structure, financial drivers, research policy, accountability and the part played by institutional policy interests. One important benefit of this approach is to illustrate the persistence of certain underlying policy issues in the conduct of higher education. Policy issues apparently settled in one era recur in new contexts, and some like tuition fees have extraordinary longevity. For the historian and policy analyst the interest in the development of higher education lies in the complex of forces, at every stage, that have determined change, and the extent to which external and internal pressures have interlocked to generate decision making. This can, I believe, be best studied by following how major policy questions were worked out in an environment of continuous general political, economic and social change under the pressure of a persistent growth in demand which had to be addressed by governments whose financial resources were almost always overstretched.

2

Determining the structure of higher education

The post-War settlement

In many ways the universities had had a good War: their recurrent grants through the UGC had been maintained at 1938–39 levels in spite of the absence of many of their staff on War duties, and as a consequence some universities had been able to build up quite substantial reserves, a change of fortune from the lean years of the early 1920s. Indeed in 1936 the CVCP had minuted that thanks should be conveyed to the Chancellor of the Exchequer for 'the generous and sympathetic consideration he had given to their appeal for an increase of the quinquennial grants'.[1] When, in 1942, Beresford, the then Secretary of the UGC, had a meeting with Tribe, his opposite number in the Treasury, to discuss the continuation of the peace time level of funding he was able to write to Sir Walter Moberly, his Chairman, that his plea might have received sympathy: 'I well realised My Lords' [of the Treasury] propensity for trampling the weak [museums, art galleries and music were all cut] but that the Universities stood for Civilization with a capital C and appealed to him as an Oxford man. I think this somewhat immoral shaft went home'.[2] British university scientists had played a prominent role in the War, academics had occupied senior positions in Whitehall, and in 1945 Lord Keynes and the future Lord Robbins were critical to discussions in Washington on the ending of Lend Lease. The academic community commanded both respect and deference.

Beresford was echoing a more general sentiment fostered by Flexner in his 1928 lectures in Oxford where he criticized vocationalism in universities, particularly in the US land grant universities and advocated their intellectual role to 'give society not what society wants but what it needs' (Flexner 1930: 5). A.N. Whitehead had criticized specialist studies as lacking 'fertility of thought' (Whitehead 1929) and in the War years themselves the debate about the function of universities stimulated by Truscot in *Redbrick University* and *Redbrick and These Vital Days* (Truscot 1943 and 1945) had emphasized their important liberalizing influence and the role of the humanities in a civilized society. Lowe makes the added point that as the full horrors of Nazi domestic policy became clear in 1945 there was a growing belief that universities had a duty 'to inoculate future political leaders against the danger of unbridled scientism' (Lowe 1988: 57). Such ideas were to have a powerful influence on policy in regard to technological education in the 1950s and on the perception that university education had a cultural value which transcended mere education as a discipline. A manifestation of this was a demand for halls of residence to provide opportunities for social and intellectual exchange amongst students.

Perhaps the high point of the elevation of the universities as a kind of intellectual conscience of the nation came in the publication of Moberly's *The Crisis in the University* (1949). As a respected Vice-Chancellor of Manchester and Chairman of the UGC throughout the War years, Moberly spoke with unique authority. Although today his apologia for the Christian mission of universities might fall on deaf ears it resonated with a society emerging from the War. 'Our generation,' he wrote, 'is confronted with a stupendous intellectual task [so that] a heavy responsibility rests on the universities as the chief organs of the community for sifting and transmitting ideas' (Moberly 1949: 294). He was passionate about the importance of building halls of residence as quasi colleges to encourage a cultural corporate life: 'an opportunity for the free and unfettered intercourse of seniors and juniors which has played so large a part in the older English universities' (p. 221). An essential element in this almost sacerdotal view of the university was the preservation of its intellectual freedom and autonomy. (Again the unspoken reference was to the collapse of German universities under the pressures of the Nazi regime.) Such freedom demanded a special kind of organization: 'Any sort of regimentation is unfavourable to the creative thinking which is the highest task of a university' (p. 230) and he quoted Hutchins, the revered President of the University of Chicago: 'Academic freedom is simply a way of saying that we get the most out of education and research if we leave their management to people who know something about them' (Hutchins 1952: 21), and even Gladstone:

> The universities are bodies of the highest rank and dignity in the kingdom and, whatever you do with regard to them you must do with the most scrupulous respect not only for their position but even for their prejudices, and above all with a scrupulous respect for the fond and fervent affection of the community for them.
>
> (Gladstone 1850: 1495 *ff*)

Moberly thus firmly linked universities' value to society with a minimalist role for the state:

> Direct state action, like surgery, should be occasional and rare; its function is negative rather than positive, it is to remove otherwise immovable obstacles.
>
> (Moberly 1949: 241)

Such thinking set a background for university: state relationships. Coming out of the War universities' financial requirements were, of course, considerable. The colleges of the University of London had been dispersed around the country: The London School of Economics and Political Science (LSE) had resisted an attempt to locate it half at Glasgow and half at Aberdeen and, at the last minute, had secured a comfortable billet attached to Peterhouse College, Cambridge (Dahrendorf 1995) while University College London (UCL) had been scattered over the colleges of the University of Wales, and some other institutions. (Some staff showed a marked reluctance to return to the metropolis after lengthy sojourns in Aberystwyth and Bangor.) LSE's buildings were taken over by the Ministry of Works, the University Senate House by the Ministry of Information; some universities had suffered from enemy action, and all had generated a considerable maintenance backlog. Moreover, they were all faced with the pressure of demobilization and the enlightened arrangements for the admission of ex-servicemen to the universities under the Class B priority scheme. As early as June 1943 the CVCP had recorded in their minutes that 'it will be physically impossible for some of our universities to deal adequately with the influx of students now planned by the Government'.[3] The universities naturally turned to the Government for support, and received it on a generous scale in spite of the parlous position of the government's own finances: eight days after the cease fire in the Far East the country was facing what Keynes called 'a financial Dunkirk' (quoted in Hennessey 1992: 90), with the withdrawal of Lend Lease. In fact, discussions between the UGC and the Treasury regarding post-War policy for universities had begun earlier in late 1943 under the impetus of Lord Hankey's Inter-Departmental Committee on Further Education and Training whose task was to make recommendations on the future needs of those currently in war service. In the spring of 1944 it had recommended that there would be a 50 per cent increase in demand for places above the 50,000 recorded in 1938–39 (they actually reached over 85,000 in 1949–50). This figure was also independently called for in an Association of University Teachers (AUT) Report on University Development Part 1 in the same year (AUT 1944). Hankey's estimate was immediately supported by Attlee, then Deputy Prime Minister (Gosden 1983).

The UGC asked the Treasury to provide 75 per cent of the cost of the additional numbers on the grounds, urged by various university deputations, that this would be less injurious to academic independence than to have to be dependent on local authority contributions (Gosden 1976). The Chancellor, Sir John Anderson, responded sympathetically with an increase in recurrent grant from £2.149m to £5.950m over the next two years, and in 1946 his Labour successor, Dalton, further increased it to £9.450m. Under Dalton, a first allocation of capital support was also made available, the Treasury having accepted that the universities' needs over the next decade was some £18.750m (it actually allocated £35m over the period 1947–52). These injections of state resource via the UGC brought sharp changes in the composition of university budgets (see Table 2.1).

Table 2.1 Comparison of sources of university income 1935–36 and 1949–50

	Endowments	*Donations and subscriptions*	*LEAs*	*UGC*	*Fees*	*Other*
	%	%	%	%	%	%
1935–36	14.5	2.5	8.7	34.3	32.5	7.5
1949–50	5.7	1.7	4.6	63.9	17.7	6.4

Source: Dodds *et al.* (1952), Table 4.

By 1952 the UGC recurrent grant had risen to 66.5 per cent of total income and was due to go on rising till the 1980s; the local education authority (LEA) contributions, which had reflected both pride in a local institution and the fact that a significant proportion of the students came from the locality, continued to decline. Fees, as we shall see in Chapter 4, oscillated in their proportionate contribution to the total budget.

The publication of the Beveridge Report in December 1942 unleashed a national appetite for reform and post-War planning: the Hankey Inter-Departmental Committee formulated views on the training capacity of universities, the Percy Committee on Higher Technological Education, the Barlow Report on Scientific Manpower, the Goodenough Report on Medical Education, the Teviot Report on Dentistry, the Loveday Report on Higher Agricultural Education, the Scarborough Report on Oriental, Slavonic, East European and African Studies, the Clapham Report on Social and Economic Research, the McNair Report on teacher training, sponsored by a range of government departments, all bore testimony both to the enthusiasm for new developments and to the demands that were to be placed on the universities and their finances.

The CVCP responded to these pressures with two important policy documents, the first a Memorandum to the Chancellor dated 5 January 1945, addressed to the universities' immediate financial needs and the second *A Note on University Policy and Finance in the Decennium 1947–56* issued on 6 July 1946. A commentary on the Memorandum spelt out what was to be a crucial point of university policy throughout the pre-Robbins period, the preservation of existing standards in a period of expansion: 'The first duty of the universities is to maintain and improve the level both of their teaching and of their research: and they would ill serve the national interest if they were to allow a quantitative enlargement to imperil the quality of their service'.[4]

The CVCP was looking for support for the projected increase in student numbers, an increase in the duration of some studies, the provision of new courses for new categories of students, the provision of more generous staff:student ratios to free up time for research, higher salaries, greater provision for research and the need to undertake the necessary building programme in which residences must be included as they were 'convinced of [their] great educational benefit'.[5] We might see this as an almost timeless agenda except for one or two qualifications: it accepted that the 1944 Education Act would bear fruit not just in increased student numbers but also in a new clientele; it emphasized what it saw as its 'Imperial duty' to provide places for undergraduates from the colonies, postgraduates from the dominions, and for the education of students from further afield like China and Turkey. (That this was a principled concern and not just a bid for numbers was demonstrated by the fact that the theme of the first Home Universities Conference to be held after the War was the staffing of the colonial universities (University Bureau of the British Empire 1946).) Finally, on salaries, while it accepted that a university career offered 'attractions and compensations greater than those of any other calling' universities must be able to provide 'a reasonably adequate livelihood' to their staffs. All these themes were due to come back to haunt higher education. The Memorandum emphasized that there was nothing fundamentally new in the programme but 'an intensification and enlargement' of what had gone before. It sought to link universities firmly to national economic development, manpower needs for professionals in key fields and to research partnerships with industry. The commentary concluded with a statement that would have delighted a later Secretary of State, Sir Keith Joseph: 'They agree that they must look to other sources of income as well as the National Exchequer. They have no desire to become wholly dependent on the state'.[6]

A Note on University Policy was published some 18 months later and was clearly aimed at influencing a wider public opinion than simply the Treasury. Moreover there had been a change of government and a new Chancellor, Hugh Dalton, potentially even more sympathetic to universities' needs, was in office. The Committee set the scene by recognizing the changing needs of the economy and tacitly reacting to the explosion of reports calling for the redress of professional manpower shortages in key fields:

> The universities themselves have been, both individually and collectively, fully alive to the facts, first that the incidence of total war has revealed chinks in the armour and shortages of intellectual manpower, often where that manpower is most needed, and secondly that the aftermath of war presents a field in which old methods, the methods of gradual, piecemeal and laboured development are not enough.[7]

However, it was quick to add the qualification by quoting from the Barlow Report, which had been published two months earlier that 'whatever happens the quality of our university graduates must not be sacrificed to quantity. Academic standards once lowered are not retrievable; and Greshams Law applies to them' (Committee on Scientific Manpower 1946 para 25). The document went on to strike a distinctly concessionary note:

> [T]he universities entirely accept the view that the Government has not only the right but the duty to satisfy itself that every field of study which is in the national interest ought to be cultivated in the university system

> . . . The university may properly be expected not only individually . . .
> but also collectively to devise and execute policies to serve national
> interest and in that task, both individually and collectively, they will be
> glad to have a greater measure of guidance from the Government than
> until quite recent days they have been accustomed to receive.[8]

There has been a tendency for scholars (notably Berdahl 1959; Shattock
1994) to read into this a general willingness to sacrifice some aspects of
autonomy to the state but I now believe that it was intended to refer to the
earmarking of Government funding for the development of particular fields
(£1m was made available for the implementation of the Goodenough Report
in 1945, the total of earmarked funds rising to over 30 per cent of total recurrent funding by 1951–2 (Berdahl 1959)). The UGC was later to criticize
these injections of funding as uncoordinated and leading to distortions,
piecemeal development and idiosyncratic prioritizations of certain activities.
What the passage was actually saying was that while the universities were not
going to resist investment in such activities they would be glad if the UGC,
which had 'never used methods of prescription',[9] were to be formally authorized to undertake a survey of all the main fields (UGC 1948). Later in the
same month, the timing clearly suggesting some orchestration of policy, the
UGC's terms of reference were amended to add:

> and to assist, in consultation with the universities and other bodies
> concerned, the preparation and execution of such plans for the devel-
> opment of the universities as may from time to time be required in order
> to ensure that they are fully adequate to national needs.
>
> (UGC 1948: 82)

However, the CVCP had shifted its position somewhat on the question of
finance. It urged that to meet national needs universities' annual revenue
would need to be multiplied by a factor of three. Tuition fees could not be
increased in the present climate and local authority contributions could not
be expected to grow so that this meant accepting the implication that UGC
funding would grow from about 30 per cent to 75 per cent of university
budgets. With a realism that they were later somewhat to renege from they
accepted that 'an increase of Government finance may require a corresponding increase in direct Government control'.[10]

The key, however to this shift lay in the confirmation of the UGC as
the vehicle through which this increased resource was to be routed to the
universities. The CVCP's support for the UGC's continuance of its role as
'the central and authoritative coordinating body'[11] had been confirmed at
a joint meeting with the UGC in May 1944. Indeed it had been driven by
the CVCP. Gosden (1976) provides evidence from 1943 of pressure from
Sibly, then Chairman of the CVCP, on a reluctant Moberly who wanted the
UGC to become a rather different body which wielded 'moral authority of a
kind resembling that of the scholar and scientist rather than that of government'.[12] The CVCP's view was reinforced by the Barlow Committee's Report

published in May 1946 which said that while the UGC had in the past been 'somewhat a passive body . . . circumstances now demanded that it concerned itself with a more positive university policy than it has in the past' (Committee on Scientific Manpower 1946: 21). Henceforward this was to be a cardinal point of CVCP policy right up to the UGC's dissolution in 1989 in spite of the shocks to the system in the 1980s.

It was the Barlow recommendations which proved to be the catalyst for the reform of the UGC not the CVCP's. In March, Ellen Wilkinson, the energetic new Minister for Education, raised with Morrison, Lord President of the Council and effectively deputy Prime Minister for domestic affairs, the need for a better coordination of university policy and in June a joint Education and Treasury meeting of Wilkinson, Dalton, Maud, the Permanent Secretary of Education and Barlow, second Permanent Secretary at the Treasury, had agreed that Government must play a more active role in university development policy than in the past.[13] Wilkinson then urged the Cabinet to implement Barlow. Later in that month Wood, from the Ministry, put a paper to Cabinet, supported by notes from Wilkinson and Morrison to obtain authorization for the reform.[14] The Government had decided in 1943 to expand the UGC's membership from 10 members mostly retired from university posts to 15, a preponderance of whom were to be serving academics, and the widening of its terms of reference in July 1946 established machinery that was sufficiently robust to carry through what undoubtedly represented a watershed in relations between the universities and the state.

The transition was assisted by the existence of a common 'Oxbridge' culture built up particularly through the War years which bound together senior university figures, the UGC, Treasury officials and (some) politicians. Three American observers (Dodds was President of Princeton) capture it well:

> The connections between the universities and the government have been very close during the last two generations, at least. University people have gone into the universities, into government offices and back into universities. This was particularly so during the two world wars. Government officials were the pupils of university dons; they worked side by side in government offices during the wars; they went to the same public schools and belong to the same clubs. In effect officials, university leaders and teachers are members of the same group.
>
> (Dodds *et al.* 1952: 63)

Moberly saw relations between government and universities as 'partners in a common enterprise' (Moberly 1949: 238), and paints what even then must have been an idealized picture:

> When their representatives sit down at table together, both parties recognise the special function and character of the university and are determined to preserve it. So as their discussions go forward, mind is stimulated by mind and ideas flash to and fro. When a conclusion is reached the question where it first originated is usually unanswerable.

When this spirit prevails the precise machinery of cooperation is of secondary importance.

(Moberly 1949: 240)

Dodds and his colleagues wrote in confirmation: 'Socially and intellectually they [Treasury officials] and the university dons are cut from the same cloth [Oxbridge]. They understand what a university is and why it should be free from interference from amateurs' (Dodds *et al.* 1952: 112). Berdahl, whose immensely influential book *British Universities and the State* cast a somewhat rosy glow over the governance of higher education, on the basis of research conducted only some two or three years later, claimed that: 'It is inconceivable that, short of a major economic or political crisis . . . these people [Treasury officials] should ever initiate any action hostile to the universities' (Berdahl 1959: 168) (the traumas of 1962 lay only four years ahead, see Chapter 3). Dodds and his colleagues almost apologetically refer to one of the legends of this period: 'The facetious observation that the Committee [the UGC] succeeds only because its members, the Treasury officials and the vice-chancellors are all members of the Athenaeum Club really expresses a deeper truth' (Dodds *et al.* 1952: 112). Berdahl might seem to confirm this in that five of his interviews with vice-chancellors took place in the Athenaeum. However, the Athenaeum's role in university affairs was probably greatly exaggerated. The Athenaeum was clearly a good watering hole for vice-chancellors from out of town coming to London for CVCP meetings and Sir Keith (later Lord) Murray, Chairman of the UGC, for the decade 1953–63 used always to dine in the Club on the night before these meetings 'just to see the chaps'. Conversation was often just about the wine, Sir James Mountford told Walsh, but it was useful for vice-chancellors to give them an opportunity to talk about their own university.[15]

Relations between the CVCP and the UGC were extremely close, not just in this period, with frequent meetings between chairmen and subsets of members and almost daily communication between officials. At the level of their principals such meetings were invariably conducted on a high level of colleagueship: Hector Hetherington, Principal of Glasgow and Chairman of the CVCP 1943–47 and 1949–52, for example, used, according to his biographer, to proceed straight from the night train from Glasgow to see Moberly at 9 o'clock at the UGC to pick up the latest relevant news before the CVCP meeting starting at 10 o'clock (Illingworth 1971). Moberly was an old friend and they had been neighbours as vice-chancellors of Liverpool and Manchester respectively.

The apparent commonality of view about the development of the post-War university system concealed, however, some significant tensions. One can be summed up in the opening sentence of Simon's introductory article in the new *Universities Quarterly* (Simon 1946): 'There is no university "system" in Britain'. The British university world was highly heterogeneous: in 1945–6 Oxbridge still took about 20 per cent of the total UK student population and many of what we would now regard as stalwarts amongst the civic universities – Exeter, Hull, Leicester, Nottingham and Southampton – were still university colleges teaching for London degrees. Truscot writing in 1943 described 'our modern universities' – a phrase unconsciously appropriated later by post-1992 universities in somewhat similar circumstances – as being 'half strangled' by Oxford and Cambridge (Truscot 1951: 31); Moberly, on the other hand, thought Oxbridge embodied 'the idea of the university' in the eyes of the nation and that the civic universities were still looked on as the poor relations'. However:

> They were not designed to be inferior imitations of Oxford and Cambridge. They were to excel them in seriousness of purpose, in range of studies, and as befitted 'a nation of shop keepers', in intimacy of relation to a commercial community. That those hopes have not been fully realised has been due, in the main to causes outside their control. Their chief handicap has been their relative poverty and for some, the backwardness of secondary education in their areas.
>
> (Moberly: 19–20)

(Moberly did not take much cognisance of the separate university tradition in Scotland.)

Snow, writing in the 1930s, puts into the mouth of one of his characters: 'Universities will get more and more specialised in this generation. We shall concentrate on original work in a few centres . . . the minor universities will cease to exist as research institutions' (Snow 1934: 79). The investment in defence related scientific research during the War had tended to confirm this forecast. Within these divisions we see the difficulty of the CVCP (and later UUK) in finding a common voice. The CVCP in its *A Note on University Policy* may have committed universities to 'playing their own part in the cooperative planning of the whole university system' and 'to devise methods of working together to ensure the complete fulfilment of their common task'[16] but translating that into practice when institutional agendas were so different represented a difficult, if not impossible, task.

The second area of tension lay in the rate of expansion that the universities were prepared to tolerate. The *Note on University Policy* had reiterated the need for student residences following arguments deployed by Truscot in *Red Brick University* but the case for major capital grants was reinforced by the overall state of university buildings which Simon argued in his *Universities Quarterly* article quoted above would require the Chancellor to find at least £75m. In 1944, in response to a request for development plans from the UGC, stimulated by the Hankey Inter-Departmental Committee's forecast, the universities had only offered 9,000 places, some agreeing to expand by 40 per cent–50 per cent but three offering an increase of only 30 over the next decade. Hankey thought that the universities were making no serious effort to grapple with post-War problems and Attlee, still Deputy Prime Minister, sought to make clear to Anderson, the Chancellor, and Butler, the President of the Board of Education, the need for trained personnel. Institutional caution at the thought of expanding without adequate financial support could all too easily be interpreted as a failure to respond to national need.

A third tension lay in the heart of government itself. In 1919 when the UGC was established an important technical reason why it was not placed under the Board of Education was because the Board had no remit in Scotland. However, as post-War planning began to take shape in Government the Board's dependence on university graduate output for its supply of teachers raised awkward questions of coordination. Gosden highlights Butler's frustration at his isolation from influence over universities as early as 1942 (Gosden 1976) and describes him suggesting to his permanent secretary in 1943 that responsibility for the universities could be transferred from the Treasury to the Lord President of the Council with the UGC coming under Education. Wood, the civil servant, who headed the teachers branch of the Board was asked to prepare a paper but concluded prophetically that while it was impossible to envisage a transfer of the UGC at that time 'the time will come when a responsible minister of education – though shunned by those he desires to help – will wish to discuss with his colleagues the question of the future of the universities, for whom he is so busily supplying candidates'.[17]

The Board (it became the Ministry in 1944) had a low reputation in Whitehall and although it had launched what became known as the Green Book on *Education after the War*, which was a reaction to widespread criticism of the Board's failure in the 1930s to think about the state of education, its reception was vitiated by a very public row over the fact that it had been issued as a confidential document (in 'a blase of secrecy' according to one Director of Education (quoted in Browne 1979: 49)). Because it was supposed to be confidential the CVCP chose not to respond to it and when a meeting with vice-chancellors did take place it resulted in no more than a 'desultory' discussion around secondary school examinations.[18] Two reports published in 1944 and 1945, however, the McNair and the Percy Reports, raised more significant overlaps. After the change of government Wilkinson, who did not trust the universities' commitment to meet post-War manpower needs, tried yet again to assert the Ministry's interest in universities on the grounds that 'any supervision of universities should be carried out by a Ministry whose primary concern was education'.[19] The CVCP's explicit statement of a willingness to accept guidance, quoted above, was probably a key element in spiking her guns, although Dalton would not have given the universities away willingly. The Cabinet committee that was created to consider the issues never met.

The post-War settlement confirmed that the universities should remain under the Treasury and that their development and funding was the responsibility of a revamped UGC which had itself been armed with a wider set of terms of reference which embraced the national interest. Action to push the UGC into a more pro-active role had been driven by the state – initiated by a senior Treasury official, Barlow and his Committee, and the Minister for Education, Wilkinson – though the CVCP was in strong support. The UGC became what Carswell was later to describe as 'a collective minister' (Carswell 1985) with the Treasury adopting an ostensibly strictly non-educational policy role. The Government, in spite of the extreme financial problems of the immediate post-War years had accepted responsibility for the expansion of universities at more or less pre-War financial levels to meet the demands for places presented by demobilization together with the implication that the growth of government funding that this would require would effectively 'nationalize' the universities (along with the rest of the services to be provided by the Welfare State). It also tacitly accepted the principle of an essential linkage between university autonomy and freedom from direct intervention by the state and the social and intellectual role expected of them in the post-War world. The McNair and Percy Reports, however, represented unfinished business and the issue of what later became known as 'the seamless robe' remained outstanding.

The structuring of technological and technical education

The War had demonstrated the need to invest more heavily than had been done in the 1930s in scientific, technological and technically trained manpower. The Board of Education responded to this in April 1944 by the establishment of a Committee on Higher Technological Education under the chairmanship of Lord Eustace Percy, Rector of the Newcastle Division of the University of Durham and a former President of the Board of Education in the inter-War years. The Committee was broadly representative of the relevant interests – in particular the local authorities, but including the UGC – but its four assessors were all appointed by the Board of Education. Its report, published in 1945 (Ministry of Education 1945), raised fundamental issues about the development of higher education and the power to award degrees which were not resolved in a formal sense until the abolition of the binary line in 1992; the Report's actual implementation dragged on for more than a decade. The Percy Committee's analysis that the output of universities and technical colleges in science for industry was inadequate was entirely accurate but where the Committee split was over the right of non-universities to award degrees, with the Committee's majority arguing that, without the right to award a B.Tech. degree through a national council of technology, colleges would be stamped 'as institutions inferior to universities' (Ministry of Education 1945 para 59), while the minority argued that a diploma, if awarded by a state authority 'would soon win national and international acceptance' (para 62). The diploma qualification was condemned by the other side as likely 'to be regarded merely as a substitute for university degrees made available to students who for any reason have failed to gain admission to a university' (para 62).

The statistical background to this disagreement reflects the fluid situation which had emerged in the immediate post-War years. On the university side there were 11 full universities and two university colleges providing technological education (both university colleges were on the UGC funding list and were given full university status in the next decade) while on the local authority side there were 150 technical colleges already doing engineering of whom 27 were providing full time higher technological courses of three years duration. To make matters more complicated well over 100 colleges had students working for University of London external degrees. Indeed by 1947–48 of 8,977 students registered in the Faculties of Science and Engineering in the University of London 3,846 were students of local authority colleges in London, 38.1 per cent in Science and 58.1 per cent in Engineering, and one college had more students in engineering than any of the colleges in the University of London. Moreover there were a number of institutions which occupied indeterminate positions: the Manchester College of Technology, a municipal college, owned by the Manchester Corporation, which had Faculty of Technology status of the University of Manchester; the Royal College of Science and Technology, Glasgow, which came under the Scottish Office (and which Sir Hector Hetherington was vigorously resisting awarding its own degrees); Sunderland Technical College, which was taking internal degrees up to pass degree level of Durham in conjunction with the Newcastle Division and taking a fourth year for honours via the London external degree; and Bradford and Huddersfield Technical Colleges which were under invitation to affiliate with the University of Leeds in technological fields.

The root of the problem (setting aside attachments to status and self interest) lay in the perception of how degree awarding status was linked to the concept of what constituted a university. The CVCP in its evidence to Percy said:

> a single Faculty institution cannot be a University ... Only a multi-Faculty society, housed at one place, where every day its staffs of different faculties may educate one another, and its students of different faculties may likewise educate one another, can begin to come within the description 'University'.[20]

Lord Percy echoed this thinking in a personal note at the end of his committee's report:

> Government policy has been based on the principle that a university should be a self governing community of teachers and students, working together in one place, with substantial endowments of its own, mature enough to set its own standards of teaching and strong enough to resist outside pressures, public or private, political or economic.
>
> (Ministry of Education 1945, Note para 4)

If, he went on, colleges were to be upgraded to university status they must have these powers and privileges but, he warned:

> if it is intended that they shall remain municipal colleges with only such autonomy as is compatible with financial control by the representatives

of rate payers the privilege of thus exercising collectively university powers [the national council of technology proposal] which cannot be entrusted to them individually could not be confined to them alone.

(Ministry of Education 1945, Note para 7)

In other words disciplines other than higher technological education would seek similar status.

That this was not just a concern of university leaders can be illustrated by the response of the AUT to the draft report of the National Advisory Committee for Education in Industry and Commerce (NACEIC) five years later:

> The fundamental business of a university is not to teach this or that but to train minds . . . it is in the universities that a young man finds the inspiration that is kindled by contact with brilliant minds and, whatever his subject finds it handled with the strict intellectual integrity, the searching inquiry and criticism and the contagious enthusiasm which shape one for life.[21]

Discounting the tendency to hyperbole implicit here the general argument that all these statements sought to convey was the concept embodied in Truscot's *Red Brick University* (1943) that the award of a degree implied a broader education than could be acquired from a one off vocational or professional programme.

At the heart of these concerns lay the controls exercised by the local authorities. The CVCP in its evidence to the Committee, quoted above, suggested that the colleges' desire for university college status was 'in some cases . . . prompted by a national desire to escape from local, lay, control'.[22] Walsh quotes a letter from a professor of physics at Leeds to Tizard, chairman of the Advisory Council on Science Policy, commenting on the proposed affiliation of Bradford and Huddersfield with Leeds (neither of which were to occur) that the colleges were 'under the heels of the local authority and the Ministry of Education' where their staff were treated like teachers, paid under Burnham conditions of service, and lacked adequate measures of self government, and where good academics would not stay (Walsh 1996). In 1950 the UGC put its own seal on the divisions illustrated by the Percy Report in *A Note on Technology in Universities:*

> There is a difference . . . not in status or grade but in kind . . . In general the university courses should be more widely based in higher standards of fundamental science and contain a smaller element of training related to immediate or special work . . . This corresponds with a distinction between two types of recruit required by industry . . . While there may be some degree of overlapping in the functions of universities and of some technical colleges, the distinction between the technology proper to universities and that of technical colleges ought to be recognised more clearly in planning future change.

(UGC 1950)

The serious differences of view expressed in the Report about the academic machinery for recognizing degree level performance in technological subjects made the recommendations virtually impossible to implement. However, the Ministry's powers to push matters along were strictly limited. The universities lay outside its responsibility and, under the terms of the 1944 Education Act, it could only fund developments in further education against LEA plans to be submitted by 31 March 1948. By the end of 1948 only 59 out of 146 had been put in and, by the end of 1949, 37 were still outstanding (Gosden 1983). The Ministry's reputation for ineffectiveness was to persist for another two decades.

Faced with this inaction the Lord President of the Council set up the Barlow Committee on Scientific Manpower in January 1946 and packed it with active scientists, including Blackett and Zuckerman, with C.P. Snow as a scientific assessor. The Committee reported back with commendable speed in May recommending both an increased role for the UGC in the planning of university development (see above), a doubling of graduates in science and technology within ten years and, more controversially, the establishment of a new technological university along the lines of Massachusetts Institute of Technology (MIT). Such was thought to be the urgency of the manpower problem that at a meeting with the CVCP in February Barlow asked vice-chancellors to consider the expansion 'on the assumption that "the Treasury purse was wide open" and that all necessary priorities in buildings and staff would be accorded'.[23] Nevertheless the university response, as we have seen above, was cautious although in the event the Barlow target was met in five years.

The proposal for early consideration to be given to the foundation of at least one new university, however, caused great concern within the CVCP. It appears to have been originated by Blackett who wrote to the Lord President of the Council suggesting that Vannevar Bush's *Science – The Endless Frontier* provided a model for Britain (Bocock *et al.* 2003) but it was soon taken up by Professor Lindemann (later Lord Cherwell), Churchill's influential advisor on science policy, who became a public proponent of the proposal when Churchill returned to power in 1951. The CVCP's response was immediate and was contained in its *Note on University and Finance* referred to above: the proposal would not help the expansion issue for some years, it was 'not much impressed by the necessity for the sentimental gesture'; such an institution would only attract second rate teachers or would drain staff from existing universities where they were needed to meet Barlow targets; and if funds, constructional material and equipment (still subject to heavy restriction and licences from the Ministry of Works) were indeed available for a new university they 'had much better be spent in expanding existing institutions'.[24] The UGC privately agreed.

In the meantime two further bodies which were to have important policy roles were created. The first, in 1947, was the Advisory Council on Science Policy, to be chaired by Sir Henry Tizard, who had been Rector of Imperial College but resigned to play a significant role in defence policy during the War. The Council's role was to advise the Lord President of the Council and to be the top scientific policy-making body in Government. The second, in 1948, was the NACEIC, established by the Ministry of Education to carry forward the Percy recommendations. This was a large and unwieldy body comprising 72 members, 52 nominated by the new Regional Academic Boards (established following a Percy Committee recommendation to coordinate university and college contributions to local industrial and commercial training needs) and 20 nominated by the Ministry itself.

The debate which these bodies had, together with the UGC, the CVCP and the Government itself, while important in laying down arrangements for the development of technical and technological education, was critical in influencing the shape of higher education not just up to the Woolwich speech in 1965 but, one could argue, right up to 1992. Questions of principle as well as self interest were involved. As we have seen, the post-War university concept was that a body qualified to award degrees required institutional autonomy and a form of self governance where there was a high level of academic participation in decision making. Institutions should not be narrowly specialist and science and technology should be taught in a liberal environment where students were not isolated from humanities and the social sciences. This integration also presupposed that institutions were significantly residential in character where social mixing and intellectual interchange was more easily facilitated. Such beliefs conflicted, however, with an alternative tradition deriving from local authority efforts to build up local institutions, primarily attended by local, home based students where vocational education was, at least in theory, closely linked to local employment. Advocates of locally based technical education argued the desirability of providing a 'top storey' on these institutions where higher technological education could be built seamlessly on to technical training. Of course self interest was also involved: universities were anxious to protect their unique degree awarding status; local authorities were ambitious to grow their institutions within their own new extensive set of social and economic responsibilities. Funding and student numbers were closely wrapped up in the arguments: universities wanted to grow and to compete with one another and American universities; the local authorities knew that their level of funding would increase if they could mount higher level courses. The pre-War links between civic universities and local authorities, which were represented by local authority rate contributions to university budgets, seemed to have broken down in the post-War period, reflecting the interests and ambitions of a new brand of local politicians, and the greater financial independence conferred on universities by the government's assumption of a comprehensive funding responsibility. University pride in their independence and autonomy was equalled if not surpassed by local authority ambition to play an increasingly powerful role in the running of the Welfare State.

The NACEIC's report in 1950, *The Future Development of Higher Technological Education*, had been preceded by a joint committee with the UGC, where the UGC had continued to maintain the line of argument in its 1950 *Note* referred to above, and by a Steering Committee of its own, reporting in 1949, which was much more sympathetic to the position of the colleges. (It had received a furious letter from the Principal of the Northern Polytechnic, who had been a member of the joint committee with the UGC, arguing that the strength and breadth of major technical colleges was being ignored). The Steering Committee recommended that a National Institution of Technology be established which would have considerable support from LEAs 'on the grounds that it is vitally important to create an Institute whose award should quickly enjoy parallel status with existing university qualifications'.[25] It was concerned that the government would move to establish a series of MIT type institutions along Lindeman lines which would compete for student numbers with the colleges.

The NACEIC's report was, therefore, heavily influenced from several sides: it accepted the UGC's position in its *A Note on Technology in Universities*

> that the universities have a specific function to perform in the develop-
> ment of technological education, and that their work should be much
> more closely related to fundamental science than that of a technical
> college, their courses in general containing a smaller amount of training
> related to immediate or special work in industry.
>
> (NACEIC 1950 para 4)

But it went on to press strongly for the development of high level teaching in selected colleges to a standard equivalent to that of a first degree and called for a new 'high prestige' award at what it carefully put in inverted commas 'first degree level' and the creation of a national body to approve and moderate courses. It accepted that the universities would object to the award of a degree and proposed instead the creation of a self governing Royal College of Technologists which would have power to award Associateships, Memberships and Fellowships. It went on to suggest that an evolutionary approach should be undertaken 'in the development of higher work and research' and that the selection of colleges qualified to undertake it should be made after consultation with the Regional Academic Boards. One possibility was that colleges could be affiliated to their local universities under whose auspices they might award degrees. It said it would have recommended that such colleges be funded centrally through a Technological Grants Committee but had had to reject the idea because it would have required legislation. This was a radical response to local authority ambition and drew immediate protests from the local authorities concerned that their control over colleges would be weakened, if not removed altogether. A White Paper which followed, *Higher Technological Education* (Ministry of Education 1951) was careful not to commit itself to this but promised further details about higher grants for advanced work and that arrangements for the College of Technologists would be begun. It also committed the Government to an expansion of technology in existing universities but did not respond to the proposal to found a new technological university.

Implementation of the White Paper was delayed by a dispute between the Ministry and the Treasury over the level of grant to be awarded for advanced technological courses in the colleges (Gosden 1983) and was then overtaken by a change of Government which brought Churchill back to power and Cherwell into the Cabinet where he immediately began campaigning for the creation of a new technological university. The debate about the future development of technical and technological development spun out into the press, particularly *The Times* and *The Times Educational Supplement* and caught the attention of the Parliamentary and Scientific Committee, an occasionally influential body comprising some 200 peers, MPs and representatives of scientific bodies chaired by Sir John Anderson the former Chancellor of the Exchequer. This body took evidence, invited the President of MIT to address it and supported the proposal for a new institution. It followed this with a report arguing that some 25 colleges should be freed from local authority control and come under a central funding body similar to the UGC. These ideas were to form part of the desiderata of the next stage of policy making.

Walsh, in an authoritative account (Walsh 1996) describes how within Government the assault by Cherwell and fellow Cabinet member Lord Woolton (initially Lord President of the Council, and later Chancellor of the Duchy of Lancaster), on Butler, now Chancellor of the Exchequer and responsible for the universities, to support and finance a new prestigious technological university was resisted. Lord Woolton's position was complicated, though not it seems in his mind, by the fact that as Chancellor of the University of Manchester he had a strong interest in the Manchester College of Technology, already the University's Faculty of Technology, being removed from local authority control and put under the UGC and being regarded as a contender for designation as the new technological institution. Another player was the Secretary of State for Scotland, Sir James Stuart, on behalf of the Royal College of Science and Technology, Glasgow, then in dispute with Glasgow University over the right to award its own degrees, who again had ambitions for the Scottish College being seen as a contender.

Butler turned to the UGC for advice. The UGC was not sympathetic to the idea of founding a wholly new technological institution on grounds similar to the CVCP's, that it would be detrimental to the university building programme and could only be staffed by withdrawing people from technology departments in existing universities. As early as May 1950 its Technology Sub-Committee, of which Tizard was a member, pronounced itself not in favour of a wholly new institution but asked Moberly to talk to Imperial College. However, this raised a new set of problems. The University of London Senate supported the expansion of Imperial but also pressed the claims of Kings and Queen Mary Colleges. Even when the University was eventually persuaded that the funds would only be available for concentration on a single site it became apparent that the Imperial site would be exceptionally expensive to develop unless it were to be moved to land available at Selwood Park, Sunningdale where an expansion of up to 4,000 students would be possible. The initial estimate for redeveloping the College on its Prince Consort Rd site was £6m, already a figure which Butler had told Woolton and others could not be afforded[26] but the move to Selwood Park would break the entrenched UGC principle that developments in techno-logical education should only occur where it could be associated with other disciplines, a principle which, with a stretch of the imagination, could be maintained by retaining Imperial on its present site.

The UGC had won the argument and in June 1952 Woolton and Butler reported to the two Houses of Parliament to confirm the Government's intention to build up at least one institution of university rank devoted predominantly to the teaching and study of various forms of technology. In February 1953 Boyd Carpenter, the Financial Secretary to the Treasury, announced to Parliament the intention to invest in the development of what was to be a 17 acre site for Imperial College on the Prince Consort Rd site with a plan to raise student numbers from 1,650 to 3,000 between 1957 and 1962 and to 4,000 by 1967. While the Treasury and the Ministry of Works offered their best support in removing the Imperial Institute and other occupants from the site the total cost was eventually to reach over £25m (Walsh 1996). One reason for the additional cost was the public outcry at the proposed removal of the Imperial Institute buildings and the placatory decision to incorporate Colcutt's great tower into the new development plan (Harte 1986). The Manchester case was also recognized and in 1955 it moved from local authority control to join the UGC's grant list. The Royal College in Glasgow, having turned down a UGC proposal that it become a Faculty of Technology of the University of Glasgow, did not, however, secure independent university status as Strathclyde University until the Robbins Report of 1963.

The Chancellor had sought advice from the UGC on how the funds promised in the 1951 White Paper should be spent, and the Committee's response, while accepting, as it had already done, the case for Imperial (which was to be funded out of a separate pot of money), argued that: 'Whatever may ultimately be possible in the way of concentration, it will be many years before the need for technologists can be met without recruiting them from a wide range of institutions' and that it was essential to do something for universities working in overcrowded and out of date science and engineering accommodation and with obsolete equipment.[27] As a result 13 institutions: Birmingham, Cambridge, Leeds, Liverpool, Queen Mary College and University College London, Kings College Newcastle, University of Durham, the Manchester College of Science and Technology, Nottingham, Oxford, Sheffield, University College Swansea and the Glasgow Royal Technical College, shared a distribution of £43m for building starts in 1957. This was to be a crucial investment for many institutions, and had the effect of determining the character of the 'civic' university with its solid commitment to science and technology and the provision of a widening base for student recruitment. It represented a decisive endorsement of what one must now begin to call the 'university sector' of higher education and was a key factor in shaping it over the long term.

The UGC showed no inclination to support the NACEIC proposal to link colleges to universities for the award of degrees (except in the case of

Strathclyde), a proposal for which the CVCP also showed little enthusiasm. (In May 1950 before the publication of the NECEIC Report the Principal of the South West Essex Technical College had published a letter in *The Times Educational Supplement* suggesting that up to 20 technical colleges should be recognized as university colleges and linked to adjacent universities.)[28] The UGC did recognize the Manchester and Glasgow bids for support but, as the Chancellor reported to the House of Commons in 1954, it would not offer support to other institutions because they did not have adequate facilities for the teaching of basic sciences. The decision not to follow the NACEIC proposal up represented another step in the separation of the two 'sectors'. On the 'public sector' (more properly called 'the local authority sector') side events moved more slowly. Failure to take forward the NACEIC 1950 report led to threats by W.M. (later Lord) Alexander, General Secretary of the Association of Education Committees (AEC) to lead a delegation to the Ministry. In response the NACEIC was asked to look again at its proposed College of Technologists and in 1954 it responded with a proposal for a National Council for Technological Awards (NCTA) which would simply be an awarding body (later determined to be a Dip.Tech) with no policy functions. This was finally appointed in 1955 and in 1956 the White Paper on Technical Education (Ministry of Education 1956), which finally pulled together the threads of the Percy Report, was published.

In many ways this White Paper was as formative of future structures in higher education as the much higher profile Robbins Report published seven years later. On the universities side, the White Paper noted that they had fully met the Barlow expansion target for science and technology numbers and that the designation of Imperial College, instead of a wholly new institution, had fulfilled the other main Barlow recommendation. On the college side, the White Paper proposed that the output from advanced courses should be raised from 9,500 to 15,000 over the next five years, to be supported by £70m of capital investment, with the programmes to be concentrated in 24 colleges, to be selected on the basis of the volume of advanced work already being undertaken, the number of staff who were sufficiently qualified to teach them, the adequacy of their premises, and of their facilities for research, and arrangements for governance which conformed to the Ministry's recommendations. Finally, the White Paper announced that a subset of institutions, ultimately nine, were to be selected to become a new category of institution, a College of Advanced Technology (CAT), which must be strong in the fundamental sciences where the opportunity to conduct research was essential and which must have 'the independence appropriate to the level of their work' (Ministry of Education 1956 para 69), tacitly accepting some of the universities' conditions for degree awarding powers. In 1952 the Ministry had finally reached agreement with the Treasury that advanced work would attract 75 per cent funding rather than the 60 per cent applied to most college courses. This had unleashed an explosion of bids from local authorities prompting Eccles, the Minister, to say at the AEC annual conference in 1955: 'I shall use the resources of the law to prevent the local authorities putting their prestige above the national interest' (quoted in Gosden 1983).

The White Paper represented a triumph for the Ministry, therefore, because in the face of a great deal of local authority pressure it produced a hierarchy of colleges of advanced technology, regional colleges and other colleges which for the first time imposed a structure on the local authorities. It was also a triumph for the civil servant who drove the structure. Anthony (later Sir Anthony) Part had to contend not just with the local authorities but also considerable resistance within the Ministry on the grounds that the designation of colleges created artificial distinctions within the sector. Part, however, was supported by the professional bodies and by Eccles, his Minister.[29] The list of designated colleges provided a significant contribution to the long term institutional development of higher education in England and Wales: Birmingham, Bradford, Brighton, Lanchester (Coventry), Leicester, Liverpool, Nottingham, Salford, North Staffs, Sunderland, Rugby, West Ham, Cardiff, Glamorgan Colleges and Battersea, Chelsea, Northampton (Finsbury), Northern (Islington), St. Marylebone, Southwark, Woolwich, Middlesex polytechnics, the Brixton School of Building and Sir John Cass College. In various forms this group of institutions were to become the polytechnics of the Woolwich speech and the new universities of the 1992 legislation.

Bradford, Cardiff, Battersea (later to become Surrey University), Northampton (later to become City University), Loughborough, Bristol (later to become Bath University), Birmingham (later to become Aston University), Salford, Chelsea and Acton (later to become Brunel University) Colleges were selected to be CATs. Initially the CATs remained under local authority control but as they developed this became increasingly anomalous. Part in his interview with Walsh said that over the first four years while they made considerable progress they were handicapped by being under LEA control which prevented them from attracting good staff, by the absence of degree awarding powers and by the fact they were engaged in a considerable exercise in upgrading their programmes. In 1961 the Ministry removed them from local authority control and funded them directly. It seems likely from the Ministry's and the Treasury's evidence to Robbins that the Ministry would have set up a technological grants committee, picking up on ideas first voiced by NACEIC and then by the Parliamentary and Scientific Committee, had Robbins not recommended that the CATs be given full university status and be funded through the UGC.

The White Paper also covered developments in Scotland and drew attention to the marked difference in the development between England and Wales and Scotland which 'began not with a large number of local technical colleges as the broad base of a pyramid on which higher institutions would later be raised but with a small number of central institutions as pioneer centres' (Ministry of Education 1956: 114). These were listed as: Robert Gordons Technical College, Dundee Institute of Art and Technology, Heriot Watt College, the Scottish Woollen Technical College, the Royal Technical College, Glasgow, Leith Nautical College and Paisley Technical College. The

White Paper suggested that these were all of CAT status, with Heriot Watt and the Royal Technical College Glasgow already doing degree level work. As with the colleges designated in England and Wales, these institutions were to form the basis for the long term development of higher education in Scotland.

The evidence points strongly to the fact that, in the policy debate about the development of technological and technical education, university argument largely carried the day. Whatever the strengths and weaknesses of the Percy, Barlow and NACEIC proposals, the university sector, as it was to become, successfully resisted the extension of degree awarding powers outside the university sector (although one of the first actions of the CATs on becoming universities was to offer their past students conversion of their Dip.Techs awarded by the NCTA to B.Techs), resisted a powerfully backed proposal, which had even received Cabinet blessing in principle, to found a new technological university in favour of the development of Imperial College (a decision which was to prove immensely costly to the Treasury) and secured new investment in technological facilities which provided a significant reinforcement to the standing and reputation of a substantial part of the sector. The educational arguments for all this were strong as was the case for a concentration rather than a dispersal of scarce resources of finance and manpower but their successful deployment did not endear them to some civil servants and politicians. Part, for example, looking back from a vantage point in the 1970s felt that universities were very ignorant of the technical college sector and did not appreciate how dismissive of it they appeared to be. He thought that universities should have done much more to help the colleges.[30] Similar comments were made by two other Walsh interviewees one of whom, a former senior civil servant, emphasized that universities' attitudes to technical education had had a considerable affect on officials like Weaver who was also very much opposed to the transfer of the CATs away from the Ministry's control. Strathclyde was able to sidestep Glasgow's hostility to its receiving degree awarding powers as a result of Robbins, but when Sussex and Warwick tried to merge with local authority institutions in the immediate post-Robbins period the Ministry/Department stepped in to prevent it. Although the CVCP in its evidence to Robbins urged the granting of university status for the CATs its aloofness at earlier stages in the debate did it no favours with the colleges, the local authorities or the Ministry. It can be argued convincingly that the development of the CATS, as steered through the 1956 White Paper, represented in the long term a more effective and responsible use of resources but it did not seem that way to ambitious local authorities and frustrated college principals.

In the light of subsequent events it is worth analysing who and what were the policy drivers that protected the universities' pre-eminent position. The first and most obvious card which they held was the extent to which they were so heavily enmeshed in the upper levels of Whitehall where decisions were made. The Advisory Council on Science Policy was chaired by Tizard, a former Rector of Imperial College, and had in its membership the Deputy

Chairman of the UGC (Trueman) a former professor, two leading scientific professors (Todd and Zuckerman) a future Principal of Edinburgh (Appleton) and Barlow from the Treasury. The other two members, the chairman of ICI and the Director of Kew were not likely to take a very different view on most university questions to their colleagues. Tizard was, as we have seen, a member of the UGC's Technology Committee which was the chief architect of UGC policy in this area. It was the Technology Sub-Committee which first proposed the development of Imperial College and it is impossible to imagine that Tizard, a former Rector, was not aware of the potential site difficulties which were so to escalate the costs of the development. In adopting the Imperial College option Tizard was reprising the feud with Lindemann over bombing policy during the War years described in Snow's *Science and Government* (1962) and he triumphed in this conflict as he had done on the previous occasion. Links between the CVCP and the UGC, as we have seen, were exceptionally close, as they were with the Treasury. When Henry Brooke, Financial Secretary to the Treasury, met the vice-chancellors for their pre-1957–1962 quinquennial funding meeting in 1956, Brooke opened the meeting by saying:

> From the Treasury point of view, of course, it is one of the redeeming features of the lives of Treasury Ministers that we have contact with the universities. I feel that very keenly myself. We have to be constantly dealing with figures and saying 'No' to our colleagues in the Government and yet here is something of a warm and young and constructive character into which we can throw ourselves.[31]

At a subsequent meeting in 1962 he noted that one of the vice-chancellors present had been his tutor and another had played in the same college hockey team.[32] When Butler was put under pressure by three hostile Cabinet Ministers, Cherwell, Woolton and Stuart, he made it clear that he would take no decisions without the UGC's advice:

> We should ask them to pay particular attention to the question of concentration and to be sure that our resources are expanded as economically as possible, having regard to the paramount importance of quality. They should re-consider carefully the proposition that our efforts should be concentrated in, say, two or three places beside Imperial College; though I am bound to ask them also to report to me on the effect of such a policy on other universities.[33]

The letter containing these words was drafted by Playfair who had succeeded Barlow as the senior Treasury official responsible for university affairs and one can infer that Butler was fully aware of the UGC's likely response. There was a kind of circularity in the communication between the three parties about policy issues which ensued that the universities' interests were protected.

The Ministry of Education was not in this loop. It had been indecisive in its implementation of the Percy recommendations, largely because until the arrival of Anthony Part it had been in thrall to the local authorities. There was a strong case to be argued for closer links between the colleges and the universities but it was never put by the Ministry. The one positive move in this direction, the creation of regional academic boards, was not a success. Although in the Attlee Government Wilkinson had sought some decision-making role in relation to the universities, this was not pursued and Labour ministers seemed in general to be no more sympathetic to local authority views than their Conservative Party opposite numbers. Indeed Michael Stewart, the Shadow Education Minister intervened in the House of Commons debate on the 1956 White Paper to suggest that the CATs should be given their own grants committee, the effect of which would be to remove them from local authority control. The Labour Party's *The Years of Crisis, Report of the Labour Party's Study Group on Higher Education* (1962) published six years later was strongly orientated towards a university based view. It wanted the CATs to be given university status but it described the work of the colleges as 'an essential service to society. But it is not a university activity' (Labour Party 1962: 33). However, the exceptional university influence on policy over this period depended on the existence of a tripod of CVCP, UGC and Treasury inter-relationships; once one of these legs was knocked aside, the universities' position was to become less decisive.

The universities and teacher training

Teacher training and the future of the college of education sector served to bring policy divides to the fore like no other issue in higher education in the period between 1944 and 1964. In many ways the colleges of education represented a turnkey for decisions on wider policy issues and their resolution brought sharply into focus the perceived responsibilities of the state, exercised through the Ministry/Department and the local authorities, on the one hand, and the autonomy of the universities on the other. Godwin argues that if the UGC advice against the Robbins recommendations on teacher training had been different 'the binary concept would have been still born' (Godwin 1998). This may overstate the case but certainly it can be said that if different decisions had been taken on the structural issues involved, the higher education scene would have looked profoundly different.

Teacher manpower forecasts for the post-War era were a matter of critical concern to the Board of Education, especially after the passage of the 1944 Education Act so much so that 50 additional, emergency teacher training colleges were established to help meet expected needs. Training courses that led to certified teacher status were only of two years duration and in 1947 only 16 per cent of the teaching profession were university graduates (Gosden 1983). Butler, as President of the Board of Education, was keen to involve the universities much more closely in teacher training (in the 1930s a number of the university colleges had depended on teacher training numbers allocated by the Board to justify their appearance on the UGC grant list) in order to raise its quality; he was sympathetic to the idea that courses should be extended to three years (they had been in Scotland since 1931) even with the manpower implications that this entailed. In this he was strongly supported by the head of the Teachers Branch of the Board, S.H. Wood, although Wood was worried that universities might make teacher training too academic (Gosden 1976). In 1942 Butler had appointed a Committee, under the Chairmanship of Dr Arnold McNair, Vice-Chancellor of Liverpool, on Teachers and Youth Leaders which reported in 1944 (Ministry of Education 1944). Many of the Committee's recommendations for an improvement in teachers' pay and conditions and for the extension of the Certificate course to three years were widely welcomed but the Committee was split on the issue of structures and the extent of university involvement.

One proposal, Scheme A, supported by five members including Wood, Sir Philip Morris (a former Director of Education and later Vice-Chancellor of Bristol and a key member of the Robbins Committee) and Sir Fred Clarke (Director of the University of London Institute of Education and Chairman of the Association of Teachers in Colleges and Departments of Education (ATCDE) wanted all universities to establish Schools of Education which would approve training standards, influence appointments by laying down standards of qualifications to be a recognized teacher of a School of Education (along the lines of the 'recognized teachers' for the London External Degree), establish a library and run teachers' refresher courses. Clarke's speech to an education conference shortly after the Report was published, as summarized by Browne, captures both the flavour of the thinking of the period and the academic argument: 'only the universities had the power and prestige to enhance educational standards. The historical stigma of the colleges had to be removed. The political issue had also to be faced . . . it was not beyond the bounds of imagination to realise this country might have to meet the problem of strongly developing totalitarian tendencies. The teaching profession would be the first that supporters of such a regime sought to capture. The universities were the only body that could stand against excessive centralisation' (Browne 1979: 71). Public opinion, at least in the shape of *The Times* and *The Guardian* supported Scheme A.

The second proposal, Scheme B, was that a Central Training Council should be established to be responsible for a national system of training and to redevelop the existing regional Joint Board scheme between universities and colleges to secure a closer cooperation with LEAs (who were the main employer of teachers), thus retaining a university involvement but rebalancing it with local authority and central government influence. Unlike the Percy Committee this division of view did not reflect a clear university orientated, local authority and college split. McNair himself and Mary Stocks, Principal of Westfield College, University of London were among the five members who voted for Scheme B. According to Aldritch, Stocks 'believed that it would be impossible to raise the training colleges and their students to university status; they were different entities with different origins and different functions' (Aldritch 2002: 127). McNair opposed Scheme A on administrative grounds that the number of students involved would over-whelm the 'absorptive capacity' of the universities and that the burden would fall unequally on universities in large industrial cities (Gosden 1976). Another difference was that where the technical colleges and their local authorities were keen to develop an alternative route to degree awarding powers, the training college principals and the dominant representatives of staff, the ATCDE and the National Union of Teachers (NUT), were strongly in favour of the Scheme A structure, as of course were the Ministry through Butler and Wood. On the other hand, the local authorities supported Scheme B and the influential London County Council (LCC) thought that universities were too academic in their orientation and not interested in the training of primary school teachers. The university reaction to the two Schemes was distinctly mixed. The CVCP's immediate reaction was to reject both Schemes and to want to see local forms of association between colleges and universities worked out.[34] A small delegation met Butler as President of the Board of Education and according to Gosden (1976) washed their hands of responsi-bility for teachers with the Vice-Chancellor of Cambridge arguing that universities should have no responsibility for professional education. When Ellen Wilkinson became Minister she wished to impose Scheme A on univer-sities but had to be reminded by Wood that the Ministry had no statutory control over the universities (Gosden 1983).

In their defence the universities could argue that the demand that they respond to McNair came at a time in 1944 when they were under pressure to embark on a raft of new initiatives urged on them by government sponsored committees (see above). The CVCP's response to McNair was undoubtedly coloured by the evidence it gave to the Percy Committee where it had supported the idea of regional academic boards but argued the importance of degree work only being undertaken in multi-faculty institutions. As far as the teacher training colleges were concerned Scheme A left the manage-ment of the colleges in other hands: governing bodies contained no teacher representation and were often merely sub-committees of the local authority education committee; academic boards, where they existed, were not effec-tive; the colleges were managed by the LEAs with the Director of Education serving as the clerk to the governors. If the universities were to be responsible for the award of academic qualifications they had to be involved in decisions about staffing, facilities and equipment. Some five years later when, at the instigation of the Chairman of the UGC, the CVCP was debating its relations with the technical colleges it drew analogies with the view it had taken on the McNair proposals and confirmed its opinion that: 'To suggest that they should simply regulate the standards of examination without having a powerful and constant say in those other matters would be to misconceive the needs of the situation and the nature of a University, and the supposed academic cachet of the qualification (whatever its title) would be a sham'.[35] This, of course, was precisely the position the University of London adopted in respect to the award of its External Degree! Stewart (himself a professor of education) suggests that lying behind some vice-chancellors' attitudes lay a consciousness of the low regard within universities in which departments of education were held and, by implication, their ability to represent appropriate academic standards to colleges (Stewart 1989). This is given substance by the Principal of Kings College, London, speaking at a conference in November 1944:

> In Kings College, the Department of Education is one department and not the most important in the College. So that we look at the matter . . . from the point of view of the University rather than that of the teachers. Our view is that though in the past the training of graduate teachers has happened to fall upon the University, the training for the professions is not primarily a university business . . . The universities are going to be asked more and more to do jobs which we do not regard as university jobs, and quite frankly we would rather see the training of teachers go out of the University altogether than the training of teachers coming within the University.
>
> (Halliday 1944, quoted in Aldritch: 129)

He was not alone in these views within London but perhaps fortunately in 1945 the Senate of the University was won round by Jeffrey, Clarke's successor as Director of the Institute of Education, to support the principles of Scheme A, although it was another four years before the machinery was set up to implement it (Aldritch 2002). At the CVCP level, Hetherington, the Chairman, had worked out a compromise, effectively a Scheme C, which left universities individually to work out arrangements at local level under Institutes of Education, thus keeping education departments functionally separate from the management of the university/college relationships. Manchester followed London in 1947 and 10 more universities joined Scheme A in the next year leaving only Cambridge, Liverpool and Reading outside, though Liverpool and Reading were later also to join Scheme A.

There may have been some substance in the universities' concern about extending their responsibilities for teacher training qualifications without the formal power to create an environment within colleges where work of an appropriate quality could be carried out but the grudging attitudes expressed, which were paralleled in the 1960s, when universities were encouraged to award BEd degrees for extended four year courses, which many institutions resisted or would only award without classified honours, testified to an unwillingness to respond flexibly to the wider training needs of the teaching profession. Such views fed the concerns of otherwise sympathetic officials in the Ministry like Woods that universities needed to be shaken out of their hidebound attitudes (Gosden 1983) and strengthened the hand of those who believed that education as a whole should come under one department rather than the universities being able to stand apart, protected by the UGC and the Treasury. Although the universities were under great pressure to support new government initiatives of various kinds they were being well funded for doing so – there were even earmarked grants for universities with departments of education between 1947 and 1952 – and their reluctance to accept responsibility for college programmes confirmed in many minds a sense of exclusivity and academic self interest. Relatively few certificated teachers found their way into grammar schools or independent schools, where teachers if they had any teacher training qualification had PGCEs from university education departments, and were mostly confined to primary and to secondary modern schools which did not produce many candidates for university places. The universities could afford to ignore them.

These suspicions undoubtedly coloured attitudes when the future relationships between universities and colleges came up for scrutiny again at the time of Robbins. By this time the University Institutes of Education were securely founded but the prospective raising of the school leaving age to 16, the pressures of demography, the prospect of extending the three year qualification to a four year BEd and the growing interest in the comprehensivization of grammar schools led to a need for a more or less doubling of the numbers of students in colleges over the next decade. Lord Robbins, according to Carswell, who as the Treasury assessor on the Committee and who therefore came to know him well, 'knew little about schools and their problems, still less about local education authorities or the realities of teacher training' (Carswell 1985: 28) but Morris, who had been on McNair, Elvin, who was Director of the London Institute of Education, Shearman, who had been Chairman of the LCC Education Committee, and a head teacher from the state sector, certainly did. Any examination of the depth with which Robbins cross examined the National Advisory Council for the Training and Supply of Teachers (NACTST) does not suggest that he had not mastered the problems of the sector.

The NACTST which, from an official point of view, was the most influential group giving evidence on these issues offered the Committee three scenarios. The Ministry had tended to concentrate growth in those colleges which had had the closest contact with universities through the McNair Institutes, and the Council's first option was that there were some colleges which were 'ripe to become parts of universities and take internal degrees'.[36] (The Chairman of NACTST, the vice-chancellor of Sussex had one such college just across the road from his University.) A second scenario was that where there was no university in close proximity there might be the possibility of a federal solution of linking a college with strong local art and technical colleges to form an institution that might in time award its own degrees. This was the option put forward by local authority members, led by Alexander, and might be classed as a first public exploration of the later polytechnic idea. The third possibility was where a college was isolated from a university or art or technical colleges it might be encouraged to accept a sponsorship arrangement, such as Oxford, Birmingham and Manchester had entered into with the University College of North Staffs (Keele), to enable it to develop and eventually become a degree awarding body.

Neither the second or third options were acceptable to the four Directors of University Institutes of Education on the Council who wrote a minority report urging a reinforcement of the Institute system. The ATCDE, the group traditionally most anxious to enhance college/university relationships, went further in its evidence and recommended, largely out of considerable dissatisfaction with institutional governance arrangements under the local authorities, that the Institutes should extend their role to be responsible for the financial and administrative affairs of the colleges with local authority oversight being restricted to membership of their governing bodies (Browne 1979: 113). This was obviously completely at variance with the views of the local authorities and seems to have commanded the support of the great majority of college principals as well as their staffs.

By contrast the CVCP evidence echoing its original response to McNair, was lukewarm: it did not think there was much evidence of universities wanting to take over colleges (in this it was to be proved wrong because in the next decade or so colleges merged with Durham, Exeter, Loughborough and Warwick, and would have done with Sussex if it had been permitted); it supported closer academic links through the McNair Institutes; but a majority of vice-chancellors opposed the granting of degree awarding powers to colleges unless through universities.[37] The CVCP sights were locked on bigger game – the rate of expansion, relations with Government, defending autonomy, resources – to which taking on responsibility for teacher training was an incidental.

Perhaps most interesting was that the Ministry in its oral evidence was careful to avoid committing itself to a clear position. In its first appearance before the Committee, Part, who led for the Ministry, stuck closely to the NACTST scenarios, supporting both college/university mergers in appropriate cases and the federal college option moving towards degree awarding powers, but making no comment on the proposal to transfer financial and administrative powers to the universities. In its written evidence, however, the Ministry had laid down a new argument which was to cast a long shadow over wider issues that came out of Robbins. Under the heading 'The Comprehensive University', an 'Aunt Sally' because the evidence did not put forward a case for such an institution nor had the CVCP sought it, it argued that: 'Whatever the theoretical merits of this proposal it is not practical politics to change British higher education so radically as to substitute for the present varied pattern of institutions a complete network of comprehensive universities . . . where a university would "throw its cloak over all such institutions in its area"[38] and take over budgetary authority for them. It went on to argue that the higher education system was best run along the lines of a homogeneity of interests and that universities, preoccupied with the major problems of their own growth, might damage either their own or the interests of institutions coming under their possible control if this principle was ignored. This led to two alternative structures being proposed. The first was for a single Ministry which coordinated a group of committees modelled on the UGC: the UGC itself, a second committee for the College of Aeronautics, the Royal College of Art, the CATs and the Scottish Central Institutions and a third for the technical colleges and teacher training colleges. The second alternative was for a structure where there would be only the first two committees and the technical colleges and teacher training colleges would be left with the LEAs. Either alternative would have allowed the LEAs which had developed the institutions 'to assist the further development of these colleges up to a point where a college is ready to become a university college or a part of a university'[39] but the second alternative, which reflected the Alexander model, was obviously the preferred one: it was more practicable and it involved less radical change.

This represented perhaps the most conservative stance which the Ministry could have adopted and was demolished by Robbins' recommendation that the CATs should become full universities and be transferred to the UGC. This removed them from direct Ministry control leaving the College of Aeronautics and the Royal College of Art remaining directly responsible to the Ministry, and the Scottish Central Institutions responsible to the Scottish Education Department, which would in any case have strongly resisted their transfer. However, underneath the bureaucratic jockeying for control a further consideration can be seen in the Ministry's written evidence that: 'It would benefit both the country and the universities if the universities, by assuming wider responsibilities were to identify themselves more closely with the higher education system as a whole'.[40] In their response to McNair and in their evidence to Robbins the universities had shown little appetite at vice-chancellor level (though there was quite a lot at lower levels in the institutions) for playing a major role in teacher education. The Ministry had after all pushed for an expanded university role in teacher training through the Institute model but the CVCP, at least, had shown little sign of wishing to have a more positive engagement with teacher training issues and a decided reluctance to encourage the development of colleges towards full BEd degree awarding status even in association with the universities themselves.

The Robbins response was a robust reassertion of the McNair Scheme A, with a School of Education with its own academic board responsible, under a university senate, for the award of degrees and certificates. But it also went further by accepting the inhibitions to autonomy implicit in control by the local authorities and recommended that responsibility for finance and administration be transferred to the universities leaving college governing bodies answerable to university councils. This represented a radical shift in organizational thinking, although the Committee was clearly concerned that universities might be unwilling to take up the administrative responsibilities implied. Robbins saw the new relationship as not just a matter of the colleges wanting the opportunity to develop degree programmes but as involving 'the whole standing of the colleges in the system of higher education in this country' (Committee on Higher Education 1963 para 360). It would, moreover, 'give the universities a major responsibility for direct leadership in a vital sector of higher education that has so far been only marginal to their main activities' (para 347).

The ATCDE was 'frankly jubilant' (Browne 1979: 117) about the recommendations which exactly matched their own views on the future of the colleges. The CVCP was more restrained and more interested in questions such as the distribution of Government departmental responsibilities, the future of the CATs and student numbers. At its first meeting after the publication of the Report with Boyd Carpenter, Chief Secretary to the Treasury, and Hailsham, Lord President of the Council, its Chairman, Mansfield Cooper, Vice-Chancellor of Manchester, was cautious and was concerned about the two Minister problem (that is the Education Ministers' statutory responsibility for the training of teachers and the effects this might have on whether the universities might be moved from the Treasury to Ministry). Logan, however, Principal of London, which had 22 colleges linked to it for academic purposes was entirely positive: 'the sooner we can bring teacher training more closely into relations with the universities the better for all' but the CVCP could not commit itself without vice-chancellors consulting their senates.[41] Hailsham, however, warned them that 'you will find almost hysterical opposition from the local authorities to the transfer and strong opposition within the Ministry itself'. They resented the loss of the CATs and they would very much resent the loss of the colleges. His advice was that since the CVCP had expressed support for the Robbins proposals for Ministerial responsibility (that is for the transfer of responsibility from the Treasury to a Minister for the Arts and Science) it should see that as its priority and, 'Talking as a politician I am quite sure this is rendered more difficult by pressing the transfer of the colleges'.[42]

Almost simultaneously the Association of County Councils, the Association of Municipal Councils and the Association of Education Committees led by Alexander wrote to the Prime Minister arguing that there had been a four-fold increase in teacher training numbers since the War, the result of close cooperation between the Ministry and the local authorities, and, while it was appropriate that the colleges should be given more independence, no change in their status should be contemplated at least for the next phase of expansion.[43] Sharp suggests that there may have been a further element in the local authorities' case, that they had not been impressed by the perform-ance of the Institutes of Education and that the lack of interest which the universities had shown in their institutes 'does not really give most of them a very strong case now' (Haynes 1963, quoted in Sharp 1987). It is clear that the location of Ministerial responsibility was central to the internal debate: moving the control of teacher training away from the Ministry of Education to a Minister of Arts and Science – a 'Minister for the Intelligentsia' as Carswell called it (Carswell 1980: 53) was for some a step too far. Crosland, in an interview with the American researcher McConnell in 1966, exemplified this attitude saying that it would have been intolerable for the colleges to have gone with the universities: 'it was essential for the Ministry to keep full control of the education of teachers if enough were to be trained to meet demand'.[44]

But within the Ministry views were divided. Responsibility for teacher training was split between two branches, Teacher Training and Teacher Supply: the former supported a transfer to the universities, the latter opposed it (Boyle 1979). Shearman's *Note of Reservation on Administrative Arrangements* seems to have been the crucial public corrective to the Robbins vision. In arguing that education was 'one and indivisible' he believed that responsibility for the universities should be transferred to the Ministry of Education and that coordination in raising standards of work in the colleges and improving their status should be the responsibility of a single Minister. The Robbins recommendations would mean that the colleges would 'have no immediate contact with those who have major responsibility, central and local, for the schools'. It may well be he wrote 'that some local education authorities have not shown a sufficiently liberal attitude to the colleges' but 'if Training College students have rarely been recognised for degrees, that has not been the fault of the education authorities' (Committee on Higher Education 1963: 293–5). But within the Ministry defensive moves were already afoot. Godwin describes how two months before the Report was published the officials, led by Toby (later Sir Toby)Weaver who had now taken over as deputy secretary for further and higher education, had decided to advise Ministers not to give an immediate positive response to the Report's structural recommendations because those affecting teacher training raised issues about whether a transfer should take place when a major expansion was in progress, whether the local authorities would withdraw their cooperation, whether the Ministry would lose control over the numbers and types of trainees and whether the colleges would no longer be accountable if they came under the universities and were, therefore, not subject to scrutiny by the Comptroller and Auditor General (Godwin 1998). When Boyle, the responsible Minister, presented a paper to the relevant Cabinet Committee in October he stressed that the less radical option was to encourage universities to continue to validate college qualifications and to avoid upsetting the local authorities by taking further steps, after their loss of the CATS to remove them from an effective share in the running of higher education.[45]

A further important element in the decision was the attitude of the UGC. Murray, Chairman of the UGC 1953–63 had been an assessor on the Robbins Committee and was a powerful influence on the Committee. It is inconceivable that he would have allowed the Committee to recommend the transfer of the colleges had he been opposed to it, if only because of the elaborate bureaucratic hurdles that would have had to be overcome. His successor, Wolfenden, former Vice-Chancellor of Reading, a much less committed figure, took over within days of the Committee reporting. Having consulted the universities on their views, and finding that 14 supported the proposals, seven would implement them if it became Government policy and only two, Kent and Sheffield, were opposed, he found himself in the position where he could confirm the universities' support. Godwin provides authoritative evidence why he did not: first he was leant on by Sir Herbert Andrew, the Permanent Secretary at the Ministry and second, accepting responsibility for the colleges threatened the long standing fear of the universities being made subject to the scrutiny of the Comptroller and Auditor General (C and AG) (Godwin 1998).

The Ministry's position had hardened: Part had left the Ministry and his place had been taken by Weaver. Godwin describes how in January, shortly after he had taken over from Part, Weaver gave a lunchtime talk within the Ministry outlining his criticisms of Robbins. In March he drafted a second Cabinet Committee paper for Boyle in which he argued that 'whatever decisions are taken about the training colleges will go far to determining the future shape of the whole of higher education' and criticized the implications of a unitary system which would place over 80 per cent of higher education under the universities. His solution was to expand the colleges in association with the regional and other technical colleges (the NACTST, local authorities option) and utilize the new CNAA degree awarding powers 'which might eventually cater for a quarter of a million students' (Godwin 1998). Andrew had talked Wolfenden round sometime in April and Wolfenden prepared draft advice to the Secretary of State designate, Hailsham, which was discussed and approved by the full UGC, with Andrew present, in June. This advice became in Godwin's words 'the cornerstone' of the Government's rejection of the Robbins proposals on teacher training. However, Godwin believes that the UGC's minutes suggest that a clinching argument was the fear that taking over responsibility for the colleges would tip the argument over subordination to the Comptroller and Auditor General which members agreed 'was a very serious danger'.[46] This was later rationalized in the UGC's Quinquennial Report that 'it would [have been] unwise to introduce comprehensive changes which were bound to result in prolonged argument and upheaval' (UGC 1968). Of course, by the time that was written the universities had lost the argument over the Comptroller and Auditor General's access to their accounts.

Meantime there had been a change of Government and a new Labour Secretary of State, Michael Stewart, was in post. Stewart had been a member of the Labour Party's *The Years of Crisis* Study Group which had supported the transfer of the colleges from local authority to university control and had given evidence to the Robbins Committee. According to Sharp a crucial meeting with the local authority associations took place with Stewart on 30 November 1964. Sharp provides a clear account of the meeting from the AEC files. Alexander argued that college independence could only be achieved outside the supervision of the universities. The acceptance of the Robbins recommendation for the creation of the Council for National Academic Awards (CNAA) meant that there was an alternative route for colleges to obtain recognition of the four year BEd degree, which was still being resisted in some universities. Clegg, the Chief Education Officer for Yorkshire joined in with the view that university orientated courses would be disastrous for low ability streams in the schools. Stewart in response sought assurance about reforms in college governance but within a few days the AEC was making plans on the assumption that their case had been accepted (Sharp 1987: 21). On 11 December Stewart confirmed this in a statement to the House of Commons, quoting the UGC's view and stating that there would be a review of the colleges' governance. According to Crossman he had 'quietly accepted the departmental line because there was nothing in the Party policy about committing us to repeal it' (Crossman 1975: 326).

According to Boyle, Hailsham said he would have acted in the same way (Boyle 1979).

In a speech in the House of Lords (1 December 1965) Robbins expressed his criticism of the UGC for its failure to provide leadership over the college issue (a clear sign that he would have expected support from the UGC under Murray). His Committee he said was concerned at the colleges' 'sense of remoteness from the rest of the higher education system' and of 'ultimate dependence on the shaping of policy upon the whims and wishes of the LEAs sometimes, though not by any means always, quite out of sympathy with the requirements of academic institutions of this kind' (Robbins 1966: 142). Their main concern was that in order to redeem the inferior status of the colleges it was desirable that their administration should be transferred from the LEAs and that they should become 'federated members' of universities (Robbins 1966: 144). In a wider attack on the binary policy, which had just been announced by Crosland in his Woolwich speech, he said 'we are now confronted with the prospect of an educational caste system more rigid and hierarchical than before' (Robbins 1966: 153).

It is undoubtedly the case that the Robbins recommendations on the future of the colleges, inextricably enmeshed as they were with decisions on the role of the Ministry of Education in relation to higher education, were bound to be difficult for Government to swallow. In this sense the future of teacher education acted as a trigger for wider decisions about the shape of higher education. Even a change of Government seems to have had little impact: the technical issues seemed to predominate so that Boyle and Hailsham were as much influenced by arguments put forward by officials as were Stewart and Crosland. Robbins' concern, as was that of the Teacher Training branch of the Ministry, centred on the need for the universities to exercise maximum influence on the academic training of teachers, especially as the teaching profession sought to move to a graduate entry. To achieve this fully LEA influence in the management of colleges needed to be sharply reduced. But Robbins went further in wanting to raise the status of the colleges to enfranchise them in some way into the university sector. The Committee had seen how in the Soviet Union and elsewhere teacher training institutions could have parity of esteem with universities. The weakness of this case was that the universities themselves had been historically ambivalent in their attitudes to the colleges. From McNair through to the approval of BEd degrees the university system had been conservative in its attitude towards upgrading the colleges, though individual universities were quite positive in their approach and only when universities' views were formally sought by the UGC had they come down substantially in favour of the Robbins proposals. The crucial element in the policy decision then became the advice to ministers from the UGC. If this had been positive the Government's decision to turn down the recommendations would have been much more difficult. Wolfenden's willingness to be influenced by the Ministry and his overwhelming concern to avoid subordination to the Comptroller and Auditor General was the turning point in the decision.

In principle the Robbins case was perfectly plausible: the colleges could have grown up alongside universities, the Ministry, through the UGC could have continued to control numbers and the LEAs could have continued to have had a significant 'social' input at the college governing body level. However, within the Ministry the argument for the preservation of university autonomy had for some time been conflated with an underlying criticism of the universities' sense of privileged independence, an argument undoubtedly reinforced by the universities' vocal resistance to departmental responsibility for them being transferred to the Ministry. The replacement of Part by Weaver, however, provided the critical drive to crystallize a rejection of the Robbins proposals. In spite of the overwhelming enthusiasm voiced for the Report as a whole the case for a transfer of the colleges into the university sector lacked champions where it mattered, in Whitehall.

Almost immediately after the decision Alexander wrote as follows in *Education*:

> The alternatives are clear: the steady movement towards one system of higher education under the general control of the universities, or on the other hand, the recognition of the need for two alternative systems. That is the universities on the one hand, and the colleges, under the general administrative control of local education authorities on the other, providing courses in higher education of degree standard over a much wider range of subjects of study. The decision now makes available the alternative system of higher education which clearly not only includes colleges of education, as they will be called, concerned with training teachers, it also includes the wide range of technical, commercial, art and other colleges which are offering opportunitities of higher education over a very wide range of subjects.
>
> (Alexander 1964)

This reprises both the NACTST local authority position and Weaver's views quoted above and laid down a key marker for the Woolwich speech.

One last postscript to the decision lay in the Study Group on college governance set up, under the chairmanship of Weaver, to honour the Secretary of State's commitment to the House of Commons. Sharp provides an authoritative account of the troubled and fractious proceedings of the committee which got off to a rough start with the refusal to admit either the CVCP or the Conference of Institute Directors to membership, though they were later invited to be in attendance (Sharp 1987; Stewart 1989). The Report itself was an inconclusive document (DES 1966b) but did establish that colleges should have their own governing bodies, separate from local authority committee structures, that they must have academic boards which, in consultation with their university institutes and subject to the governing body should be responsible for the academic work of the college and that the college as a whole should be subject to articles of government approved by the Secretary of State. These changes were implemented and the James Report six years later was able to say that 'very little evidence was found that principals or members of their staffs felt their freedom to innovate or to develop within present resources threatened either by local education authorities or by the DES' (DES 1972b para 519). The colleges had therefore progressed but the more relaxed approach to organizational structures evident in the Ministry's flexible options in regard to mergers with universities, submitted in evidence to Robbins, was replaced by a much more rigid application of the binary principle especially when the question of the sharp reduction in teacher manpower needs led to a demolition of the college sector in the later 1970s, where the local authority option in the NACTST report was rigorously enforced. Whether if the Robbins recommendations had been accepted the colleges might have been better protected from closure or forced mergers is doubtful, but a continuation of the *status quo* offered them no long term security.

The founding of the 1960s New Universities

Between 1950 and 1963 the UGC was at the zenith of its powers. It is no coincidence that for 10 of these years Keith (later Lord) Murray (of Newhaven) was its Chairman (1953–63). Once the initial post-War surge of student numbers had subsided numbers fell before beginning to rise again. It was the UGC that assumed the planning of the system, the forecasting of demand and the securing of funding to provide sufficient places to meet it. The establishment of the New Universities was a by-product of this. Robbins did not discover the expansion of the 1960s and 1970s; it refined and articulated forecasts already made by the UGC. Murray, interviewed by Walsh in the late 1970s, said that nothing Robbins said was a surprise: it 'confirmed UGC thinking'.[47] Butler, on his appointment as Chancellor of the Exchequer, had said that his job was to confirm the autonomy of the universities, and the UGC was given exceptional freedom to develop and steer the system.

Perhaps the most obvious manifestation of this freedom lay in the establishment of new universities. In the past universities had been founded by local communities or groups of city fathers, industrialists and interested citizens but in the case of these institutions, although expressions of interest going as far as formal bids were received from communities, it was the UGC that drove the process and shaped the institutions. This was a unique operation in British higher education history, where the state intervened to create wholly new universities, which had no back history of predecessor institutions, on green field sites. In all previous cases, except Keele and in all subsequent cases (except the Open University) new universities either served an apprenticeship as a college or grew out of previous institutions undertaking lower level work. These universities sprung into existence fully funded on virgin sites and with unchallenged degree awarding powers. In one sense they represented the ultimate realization of the concept of autonomy, the integration of disciplines and the high degree of academic participation in governance which had been the ideal prerequisites of university status articulated by the universities in the post-War settlement, and before; in another they reflected a tacit rejection of the restrictions imposed on local colleges pursuing higher education programmes aimed at local markets, from which the CATs were now being released.

The issue of the foundation of new universities went back to 1945 when two members, Tawney, the social historian, and Tizard proposed that if universities were unable to meet the required post-War expansion targets it might be necessary to found some new residential universities.[48] The idea made little progress on financial grounds but it prompted a UGC circular to universities which produced bids for expanded numbers which rendered the Tawney/Tizard proposal unnecessary. One result, however, was that the UGC accepted the claims of the University Colleges of Hull and Leicester, held over from the 1930s, to come onto the grant list. Tawney was himself an interested party in one project to found a new university college in Stoke and a meeting of its sponsors with Moberly was held in March 1946. The publication in May of the Barlow Report with its explicit call for the foundation of a wholly new university (albeit the Barlow Committee's thinking had been for a new technological university) sparked wider interest and the UGC received delegations from Bradford, Brighton and Norwich as well as from Stoke in that year and expressions of interest from elsewhere. Unlike Brighton and Norwich, the Stoke proposal had eminent academic backing from Lord Lindsay, the Master of Balliol and others as well as very strong local community support. (The Bradford proposal which might have won support on the precedent of the Manchester College, imploded when Bradford turned down Faculty of Technology status with Leeds.) In its *Note on University Policy* (1946) the CVCP had firmly rejected proposals for the creation of any new universities:

> If there were enough money, constructional material and equipment, and constructional manpower to spare for making a new University, in the national interest these had much better be spent in expanding the existing institutions properly. After the decade, if by then production from the present foundations proves to have reached what is hoped, and if there are still man-power, materials and money, the founding of a new University outside some suitable city or town would become reasonable, and would then receive the warm support from informed opinion which, the Vice-Chancellors venture to say, would not support it any earlier.[49]

This statement was, of course, primarily aimed at the Barlow proposed new technological university but the Stoke proposal was by then already in play. In January 1947 Moberly met the CVCP to seek its view on 'how a new type of university would affect the present and prospective development of existing universities and university colleges'[50] and in March the CVCP minuted 'that there was no case for the establishment at the present time of a new university institution at Stoke or elsewhere'.[51] In April the CVCP issued a *Note on the Stoke Proposal* which reiterated its financial arguments about establishing new institutions making the additional point that national student number targets were already being met but attacking the proposal from two other points of view. The first was that Stoke was seeking degree granting powers from its foundation instead of submitting to a period of probation under an external examination system as the existing university colleges had done, and the second was to object to what Moberly had called a new type of university in the following terms: 'The suggested basis [of academic studies] seems to provide not a new type of University institution but a new type of Technical College and in the view of the Vice-Chancellors such an institution could not be given even limited degree-granting powers without serious detriment to the whole university system' (CVCP *Note on the Stoke Proposal* 1947, quoted in Mountford 1972). This preposterous statement was quickly undermined by the decisions of the Birmingham and Manchester senates and Oxford's council to agree to give academic sponsorship to the new institution but it does lend credence to Anthony Part's view, quoted above, that the CVCP did not understand technical colleges since it was presumably equating the proposed 'Keele' curriculum with the general studies programmes to be found in college curricula. The *Note* bears all the marks of academic conservatism. The group in Oxford led by Lindsay which had championed the Stoke proposal were academic (as well as social) reformers who had pioneered the introduction of PPE in Oxford before the War. But resistance to an institution avoiding a probationary stage, neatly side stepped by the arrangements for university sponsorship, also smacked of self interest: the files contain a letter from Sir Hector Hetherington suggesting that granting limited degree awarding powers would open the door to the technical colleges, '(even Glasgow)'.[52] It is clear that the UGC reached its decision to support the Stoke proposal against powerful financial arguments primarily because it was attracted by the quality of the support for the plan, both academic and community and because 'it is in the interests of university education for an experiment on these lines to be carried out'.[53]

The University College of North Staffordshire, later Keele University, was a forerunner of the New Universities of the 1960s, and like many forerunners suffered difficulties which its successors did not have to face. First, it was founded on the same principles as other pre-War university colleges that the UGC was responsible only for deficiency funding, in other words making up the shortfall from income generated from fees and local support. By contrast the New Universities, while they were expected to generate some capital funds, were granted comprehensive recurrent funding from the outset. (Keele compounded this by mismanaging its financial affairs which were eventually sorted out by its Professor of Physics, Arthur (later Sir Arthur) Vick, who found himself appointed to membership of the UGC as a result.) Keele always saw itself as small and collegiate in scale, and therefore liable to issues of financial viability. At Sussex, however, John (later Lord) Fulton, the founding vice-chancellor, one of the key backers of the Stoke project and the intended founding Principal until he withdrew and went to be Principal at Swansea, saw viability in the much larger terms of 350 to 400 members of academic staff which demanded a student body of 3,000 calculated on the basis of a 1:8 staff student ratio (Fulton in Daiches 1964). Essex and Warwick were soon contemplating plans to grow to 20,000 students. Keele, while endowed with an attractive campus and a stately home, suffered from its initial unambitious title and from its location in an impoverished area while its successors, characterized as 'the Baedeker universities' by Harold Wilson or by others as 'the Shakespearean universities' were sited in and around historic towns and cities in comparatively affluent environments. Finally, Keele had the misfortune to have had rapid changes in leadership with four Principals in its first decade (Kolbert 2000). Although the foundation of Keele was of another age and undertaken on quite different principles, to the later New Universities it influenced them, and particularly Sussex, intellectually. Like Sussex it attracted an outstanding academic community, its Foundation Year foreshadowed the 'New Maps of Learning' at Sussex and its *raison d'être* was the reform of undergraduate education like Sussex, although Sussex because of its larger size and the more favourable economic climate when it began, was to develop much more rapidly in research. Keele remained a small but bold 'educational experiment' (Gallie 1960) whose impact was deferred for a decade or more until a new generation of universities came to be founded. The fact that it was created at all in an intensely unfavourable economic climate and without the formal support of the university establishment, represents a testimony, however, to the UGC's willingness to back a proposal simply on its academic merits.

A decade later conditions had changed considerably and were more favourable to institutional innovation. Murray, when asked by Perkin what was the driver for the New Universities' programme replied: 'It was one third numbers and two thirds new ideas' (Perkin 1970). Sloman, Vice-Chancellor of Essex, reported to Walsh that Murray had emphasized to him the importance he placed on the impact that their experimentation and innovation would have on the university system.[54] Perkin, however, concluded that the new universities 'owed their origins more to the need for the expansion of student numbers than to the demand for educational experiment' (Perkin 1970: 61) and the evidence of the UGC files, which were not open for reference at the time Perkin was writing, bears him out. This is not to say that there was not a widespread concern about over specialization in university courses; the UGC committed itself to a dubious piece of sociological analysis that when, some 50 years previously recruitment to university was largely from the upper classes and leisure was freely available to students 'the general education of the university student could be left to take care of itself . . . the university could concentrate on turning him into an expert without risk to the whole man'. But the widening social background of students and premature specialization in sixth forms had meant that it had become 'the first duty of the university . . . to teach him how to think. For this purpose he must be given not only competence in one field of knowledge but access to related fields and a general appreciation of the art of learning. He must be helped to acquire interests outside his special subject' (UGC 1958 para 39). The argument for greater interdisciplinarity was clearly part of the UGC's thinking in launching the idea of new universities even though the rationale was flawed.

However, student numbers remained the key policy driver. In the absence of any machinery for data collection in the Ministry of Education the UGC took on the task of forecasting student demand. The initiative must be accredited to Edward (later Sir Edward) Hale, the Secretary to the UGC from 1950 to 1957. The post-War expansion reached its peak in 1949 with 85,000 students in universities and fell to 80,000 in 1953 before beginning to rise again in 1954. Hale was the first to identify the 'trend, the increased numbers of children born in the 1930s staying on at school after the age of 17'. In a letter to Walsh,[55] he described how he wrote a paper on the implications which startled the Treasury but which was treated sceptically by the Ministry which thought that the explanation of the statistics was that sixth formers were taking more A levels. The identification of 'the trend', he said, led the UGC to 'exhume' approaches made by Brighton and Norwich in 1946. In the meantime Murray took soundings from vice-chancellors and having added up their expansion plans found that they fell 25 per cent below what UGC forecasts showed was needed. A discussion on 'The age bulge and its possible effects on university policy' at the Home Universities Conference (an annual official conference representative of all the universities) in 1955 showed little university appetite for rapid growth. Although the arguments for expansion were put persuasively by Lord Simon and by the Vice Chancellor of Liverpool, James Mountford, the response was muted, two speakers even arguing that 'the bulge', that is the short term birthrate increase deriving from demobilization, could be accommodated by a temporary rise in numbers in 1964–67 and a rearrangement of entry to National Service (Universities' Bureau of the British Empire 1955). Indeed in 1954 and 1955 there was some evidence that university entry levels were falling somewhat, and this is confirmed in the Robbins tables (Committee on Higher Education 1963, Tables 2 and 4). In 1955 the UGC sent a confidential memorandum for consideration by the CVCP showing that the number of passes at GCE A level had increased by 16 per cent between 1951 and 1954 and that there was an average 5 per cent per annum increase in qualified applicants to universities. The CVCP's response indicated that it was not resistant to expansion but that it had to be adequately resourced: less than half of the capital required for the immediate post-War expansion had so far been received.[56] These two reactions to the question of expansion represent a fair indication of university attitudes: the academic reaction, as at the Home Universities Conference, was largely conservative and reluctant to see their institutions grow; the CVCP's was to accept that growth was inevitable but to resist it without receiving guarantees of adequate recurrent and capital support. It is noticeable that as Richard Griffiths, a former UGC official, told Walsh, when in 1963 the UGC wrote to the universities saying that funding for expansion was available there was an immediate positive response.[57]

In 1956, almost coinciding with the publication of the White Paper on Technical Education which had noted the universities' success in meeting the Barlow target, the UGC received a memorandum from W.G. Stone, the Director of Education for Brighton who had been responsible for the approach to the UGC about a new university in 1946. The UGC was to pay tribute to Stone's paper as a turning point in the formation of its policy towards expansion (UGC 1964). Stone's argument for a new university was based on student demand – the demographic case, 'the bulge', and the enhanced staying on rate, 'the trend'. In 1956 the Treasury was forecasting the need for 106,000 student places in universities by the mid-1960s but in the following year, adopting Stone's analysis, the UGC was advising the Chancellor of a need for 124,000 with the possibility that the number would need to be increased by 10 per cent. In 1958 the Treasury accepted the 124,000 figure but later in the same year the AUT forecast the need for 145,000 (AUT 1958). Meantime the Home Universities Conference in 1958 had a session devoted to 'The size of universities and university departments and the need for new universities' which was opened by the Rector of Imperial College, Linstead, who discussed the 'right size' of universities and the dangers of a 'loss of cohesion and corporate feeling' suggesting that a maximum of 4,500 students might be appropriate for a four faculty university, that no university should be expected to double itself in a decade and that no new university should be expected to grow to more than 1,000 students in two quinquennia. (The founding of Sussex had been announced in February.) Other speakers echoed his views: the message from the rank and file in universities, from lay governors to elected senate representatives, was clear (Association of Universities of the British Commonwealth 1958).

In October of the following year Murray, armed with the conclusions of a UGC New Universities Sub-Committee, addressed the CVCP on the subject of New Universities. His address, fully minuted in the CVCP archive, was based on numbers and never mentioned experimentation, although perhaps that was omitted for tactical reasons. In the UGC's quinquennial report on University Development 1957–62 published in 1964, it claims that:

> In the rapidly changing world of today, when the growth of scientific knowledge creates ever more difficult problems for the educator, there is a need for constant experiment in the organisation of university teaching and the design of university curricula. New institutions starting without traditions with which the innovator must come to terms might well be more favourably situated for such experimentation than established universities.
>
> (UGC 1964 para 74)

This looks like a *post hoc* justification. Murray reported that 'the trend' assumption of growth rates of 5 per cent p.a. had now to be raised to 7½ per cent from 1955, although the Ministry of Education and the Scottish Education Department continued to hold to the more conservative 5 per cent. Although the Chancellor had already committed the Government to a target of 124,000 by the mid-1960s, this figure needed to be raised to 136,000 if the principle was to be maintained that the percentage of qualified candidates to be admitted should not fall; and a figure of 225,000–250,000 might be realized by the late 1970s. The UGC wanted to know from universities now, what their priorities were for 1964–65 in order to formulate a building programme for 1964–68 and where they thought they wanted to be by the 1970s. In the meantime the state of play in responding to approaches received since the Sussex announcement was as follows:

Active	Potential	Dormant
Coventry	Hereford	Bradford
Gloucester/Cheltenham	Lancaster	Bury St Edmunds
Norwich	Stevenage	Carlisle
Kent/Thanet	Whitby	Cleveland
York	Essex	Salisbury
	Bournemouth	

The Ministry of Education's view was that the students going to the CATs 'would come from the balance of those who did not go to the universities'.[58] Replies to Murray's subsequent letter to universities showed that many of the larger civic universities were reluctant to expand beyond 5,000–7,000 students. The UGC itself did not think that the smaller universities, some of which were keen to expand, should be permitted to expand too quickly and it accepted the Linstead dictum that no university should double its student numbers in less than a decade (Briggs 1991).

In March 1960 Murray put a paper to the UGC reporting on the progress of discussion with the various bodies making approaches and recommended to the Chancellor that some new universities in addition to Sussex should be founded and that formal discussions should be opened with Norwich and York. According to Briggs, who had joined the UGC in late 1959, the conclusion was greeted with acclamation (Briggs 1991). The decision on Sussex was not planned as opening the door to a stream of new foundations. The original decision was to establish a University College but Fulton, its first Principal, remembering the difficulties at North Staffs persuaded Murray of the advantages of conceding full university status *ab initio* and the automatic power to award its own degrees subject to safeguards that the Committee was due to build in. This was agreed by the Committee in June 1960, and for Norwich and York; the University College of North Staffordshire was at last given permission to become Keele University.

1960 was the key year for the designation of the New Universities. At the beginning of the year the Chancellor had authorized an additional 35,000–40,000 university places but the UGC had moved to adopting a target of 170,000–175,000 places by the early 1970s (although it was already thinking of a longer term figure of 200,000). At the June meeting the shortfall of institutional expansion offers led the Committee to minute that it might have to consider three more new university bids.[59] But decisions on new foundations were ultimately dependent on Government acceptance of student number targets in the early 1970s. Persuading the Treasury to accept these targets and the financial implications was, however, another matter, especially when the building allocations for 1962 and 1963 had yet to be agreed. At a meeting with the full Committee, the Financial Secretary to the Treasury, Henry Brooke, and Otto Clarke, the head of the public sector side of the Treasury, argued that any announcement about numbers in the early 1970s could await Robbins (Lord Simon had successfully moved the motion for the Inquiry on 11 May, and the name of Lord Robbins was already attached to it) but the UGC responded that 170,000 represented 'an absolute minimum' and had to be agreed now with any higher figure left to Robbins. The universities as a whole could not be asked to undertake further expansion without assurances of capital support. Clarke responded that the Committee was seeking 'preferential treatment' and that the schools building programme was not settled more than two years in advance: it was a 'very real problem for the Government to commit itself so far ahead as 1964–65 on one particular segment of the total national investment' when it had to compete with demands for capital allocations for hospitals and roads. Once the Financial Secretary and Clarke had withdrawn the Committee agreed that while its overall position must be preserved it might not need to commit for 1964–65 if a reasonable formula for later agreement could be arrived at.[60]

The situation was complicated by the continuing escalation of the cost of the Imperial College development. Although the funding was originally 'off ration', the Treasury now tried to make the remaining £8m of the Jubilee Scheme count against the UGC's allocation. The UGC resisted. By the December meeting of the Committee Murray could report that further negotiations and two meetings with the Chancellor had brought agreement on the building programme 1962–65 and on the 170,000 target, although this had had to be slowed down by one year. The Chancellor, Selwyn Lloyd confirmed the 170,000 target in the House of Commons on 25 January 1961.[61] This news released decisions on Essex, Kent and Warwick (Coventry) Universities. Lancaster, which the UGC was sympathetic to because it wanted to locate one new university in the North West, followed with an announcement by the Chancellor in November. In reality these were the only serious bids: Gloucester put up a poor case and were confused about their site; Thanet gave way to Colchester (Essex); Hereford and Stevenage dropped out and, at Bournemouth, the town council had voted the proposal down. There was never a pre-determined number: had the Chancellor not accepted the 170,000 student number target for the early 1970s or, if existing university bids for numbers had been higher, the number selected after Sussex, East Anglia and York would have been either smaller or none at all. Subsequent new foundations at Stirling and Coleraine came later in the 1960s and were driven by concerns about regional balance rather than the pressure of demand which formed the pre-Robbins list.

The creation of seven New Universities did not re-shape the university system – the full impact had to await the translation of the CATs to university status when, with Stirling, some 17 new institutions were added to the university list – but the 'seven sisters' as they were sometimes called, certainly provided a new dynamic to the system, in a way that the CATs did not. How was it that the UGC could pull off such a coup? The first reason was the good relations and trust that existed between the UGC and the Treasury. Murray and Bridges, the Permanent Secretary of the Treasury, dined together once a month.[62] Otto Clarke, who was in charge of public sector finance at the Treasury was pro-university expansion and pushed the Financial Secretary in that direction,[63] while Henry Brooke, as we have seen from the quotation above, was certainly sympathetic to university interests. Charles (later Lord) Morris, Vice-Chancellor of Leeds, told Walsh that the civil service 'regarded the universities as a power in the land, perhaps more powerful than the church, and they treated them, almost addressed them, as a power in the land'.[64]

It was also a time of financial optimism in British politics. Lord Thorneycroft, Chancellor of the Exchequer, together with Enoch Powell and Nigel Birch, had resigned in December 1957 because he was not able to secure approval for a reduction in public expenditure of £48m in order to ensure that the 1958–59 estimates did not exceed those of 1957–58. The Prime Minister was not prepared to cut back public expenditure on higher education any more than on defence and campaigned in the 1957 General Election with the famous words: 'most of our people have never had it so good. Go round the country, go to the industrial towns, go to the farms and you will see a state of prosperity such as we have never had in my lifetime – nor indeed ever in the history of the country' (Macmillan 20 July 1957, quoted in Hennessey 2006). Perhaps a clinching argument was that the Treasury thought that creating new universities was cheaper than expanding existing institutions. Boyle suggests that the Treasury actually encouraged the programme using the 'ingenious argument' that in terms of capital it was cheaper to start a new university of 2,000 students than expand a 3,000 student university to 5,000 because the latter would put in a case for a new library. This is such a financially illiterate argument that it is clear that financial concerns were a secondary consideration. Boyle, who was Financial Secretary in the Treasury at the time said: 'It seemed the right moment to launch a number of brand new universities, not simply to correct injustice, but also in order to seize the opportunities of an hour that seemed uniquely full of hope' (Boyle 1979).

In late 1959 however, according to Hennessey, the Prime Minister commissioned a report entitled *Future Policy Study* which contained, when completed in February 1960, a section on resources prepared by Otto Clarke. It said:

> In the next five years . . . there are no declining public programmes to make room for the expanding ones. The defence and overseas claims are expanding; public investment is expanding, education and health and public services generally are expanding. These are all good claims, and recently there have been a succession of new ones, such as a greatly expanded road programme.

If there was not moderation the impact would fall on the balance of payments and on sterling: 'This is invariably the consequence of overloading the economy with large and inflexible commitments'.[65] This did not constrain Macmillan or the successor Government that responded to Robbins.

Murray, therefore, benefited from a favourable public expenditure climate, and also from his own standing and experience as Chairman of the UGC for some seven years. Without this he could not have put such a personal mark on the programme. Not only did he chair the New Universities Sub-Committee which drew up the criteria for decisions and interviewed the bidders for new institutions but it was he who laid down the requirement that each bidder should offer at least 200 acres of land, and took pleasure in reporting later that the UGC had not had to pay out a penny for the sites. He visited all the sites offered himself, accompanied by the Secretary and appropriate colleagues. Having devised the Academic Planning Board idea to avoid embarking again on the Keele sponsorship route he took immense care in selecting the chairman and members of each committee and took a close interest in the academic shape of each institution and in the appointment of the first vice-chancellor. Although local interests clearly played a part it can truly be said that the initial academic thrust of the New Universities was laid down by the UGC and its Planning Boards.

The New Universities were not, of course, automatically popular within the university world. James Dundonald (later unveiled as John Lawlor, a professor of English at Keele) referred sourly to 'Trend-setting, indeed, became the mark of the new universities, and trumpet blowing has been its inevitable accompaniment', criticized the creation of schools of studies as obscuring the fact that 'there is little . . . that is genuinely original' and claimed that 'where the innovatory course-timid or adventurous, it makes no matter – is placed as an equal competitor with the orthodox offering, then orthodoxy will win every time' (Lawler, writing as James Dundonald 1968: 105). Civic universities however, took fright at their apparent popularity and began closing down their old general degree structures and creating joint degrees which looked more fashionable. Sir Maurice Dean, Second Permanent Secretary at the new Department of Education and Science, referred to them as 'the Universities of Noddyland' (Carswell 1980: 62) and it is true that, apart from in the media, they did not become real academic competitors of the older universities until the early 1980s.

More serious criticism, however, has come from the idea that while they were academically radical in creating programmes that broke down departmentalism and resisted specialization, they were socially conservative in concentrating on full time degrees aimed for the most part at traditional student markets. Halsey argues that 'As an idea they were essentially stationary' and sees them 'simply . . . [as] an alternative to the expansion of the ancient and modern institutions inherited from the nineteenth century' (Halsey 1992: 16). Other critics have seen them as too Oxbridge in their orientation. (Sussex was after all called 'Balliol by the sea' in its early years and three of the universities adopted collegiate structures.) A further complaint was that they were structurally isolated from other, local authority developed higher education institutions. Anthony Part, for example, in his interview with Walsh regretted that Sussex did not take the Brighton College of Technology and the Brighton Teacher Training College under its wing.[66] In fact Sussex had been keen to take over the Teacher Training College in 1965 but was prevented from doing so by the DES's insistence that institutions should not be allowed to cross the binary line. A similar interdict was applied to the proposed merger of Warwick and the Lanchester College of Technology in Coventry (Shattock 1994).

Lying behind these issues were deeply entrenched demarcations of spheres of influence between the Ministry of Education and the UGC. Thus when the decision was taken in January 1961 to support the case for three more new universities, the strong wish of the local promotion committee in Coventry was that the proposed university should major in applied science, to reflect the needs of the area and that this might be achieved by an 'organic association' with the College of Technology but the UGC minuted 'that this was not considered appropriate or consistent with the policy which the Committee had adopted in other comparable cases'[67] and refused to offer support for the development of engineering in the new university's academic plan, a decision it was later forced to reverse. At Norwich decisions taken by the UGC and the Academic Planning Board not to support engineering or other vocational studies at the University of East Anglia meant that no real relationship could be established between the University and the Norwich Technical College, on the upgrading of which the original Norwich case to the UGC had been based. As at Brighton, the local sponsors did not press the university/technical college linkage and the opportunity was lost. This was not a new policy. The Ministry had made its wish to maintain a clear separation between the university sector and the local authority sector in its condemnation of 'The comprehensive university' and its resistance to universities throwing their 'cloaks' over other institutions in their areas in its evidence to Robbins in 1962. The UGC may have shared this view. According to Sharp, Wolfenden, whose support for the DES's line on teacher training has been described above, was persuaded by the CVCP not to publish a memorandum expressing support for the separation of sectors described in the Woolwich speech and he deliberately stalled on the Warwick/Lanchester proposal at the Department's request until the speech had been delivered (Sharp 1987). The more liberal ideas about associations and mergers that had been encouraged in Part's oral evidence to Robbins were replaced by a hard line resistance to fraternization across the binary line. The failure of the New Universities to reach across this line was imposed by the state not by the institutions themselves.

Halsey's argument that the New Universities were more an addition to the existing stock of universities than a step towards any kind of realignment of higher education is clearly correct. But this, of course, is precisely what the UGC was seeking to achieve by linking the establishment of new institutions to the demand from appropriately qualified candidates, a principle which was to become fundamental to the later Robbins recommendations. The UGC's New Universities Sub-Committee sought written evidence from a considerable range of institutions, the research councils, the engineering professional bodies, the Royal Society and British Academy, the Federation of British Industries (FBI now the CBI) and from head teachers' organizations (Shattock 1994). But the striking aspect of their evidence was its consistency in being concerned with conventional university applicants; the CAT recruitment was for students 'who were just below the minimum intellectual standards at present enforced' by the universities.[68] There is no evidence from any of these bodies, which might be seen as representative of education as a whole, arguing for an investment in part time education, widening access through technical qualifications or emphasizing local industrial links. The FBI, for example, behaving as if the Barlow Report had not existed, believed that the new institutions should be small, around 2,000 students, and should not be sited in industrial centres but somewhere away from them. They wanted graduates who were rounded and balanced men; this they argued was particularly important because the CATs 'turned out men with the necessary technical knowledge'.[69] However critical we may be about such attitudes, they were representative of their time, and the UGC's programme for the New Universities reflected them. But within this framework the New Universities went on to become successful institutions: they performed much better than the ex CATs in the quality driven 1981 cuts and all but one have appeared throughout in the top half of the Research Assessment tables. On the other hand the most original, non-stationary, institution of the period, the Open University, was founded outside the UGC on a political initiative which owed nothing to the local authorities or to the views of officials in the DES. The UGC, for all its strengths, could never have contemplated such a radical departure from the norms of university structures and purposes.

The creation of the polytechnics and the establishment of the binary line

The most far reaching policy decision to affect the shape of British higher education was the creation of the polytechnics and the establishment of the binary line. Of course, as Venables was to say there had always been a binary line, long before Crosland announced it, but until the Woolwich speech it had not been the iron curtain that it was to become. Many universities had progressed from college to university college status: the Manchester College of Technology had changed from a municipal college to an Institute of Science and Technology on the UGC grant list and the CATs, only designated in 1956, had been recommended to transfer to university status by the Robbins Committee. The prospect of institutional changes in status had been held out in the Percy Report (1944), the NACEIC Report (1950), the NACTST Report (1962) and in the Ministry of Education's evidence to Robbins. The Labour Party's higher education blue print the Taylor Report *The Years of Crisis* (1962) reinforced the point, wanting to see a large expansion in the numbers of universities primarily through the upgrading of technical and teacher training colleges to university status. Robbins, in recommending a structure in which colleges could mature into universities and be upgraded accordingly, was doing no more than reinforcing and providing a validation of ideas that had been current ever since 1944.

There was, of course, an alternative view which had been nurtured in the local authorities, which championed recognition of the claims of institutions they had mentored and which had felt affronted by the decision to remove the CATs from their control. This was perhaps best articulated later in Eric Robinson's *The New Polytechnics* (1968) but according to Boyle it was also one strand of what Weaver used to describe as the 'dialectic within the office', between those whose broad views emphasized social justice and widening opportunities and those who gave greater priority to education as investment and its contribution to efficiency (Boyle in Kogan 1971: 123). Advocacy of the former did not, of course, predispose one to be in principle opposed to Robbins – the Robbins recommendations on student number expansion were, after all, based on liberal principles concerned with social justice and widening participation – but their proponents saw these objectives being more effectively realized in local authority controlled higher education than in a system dominated by the universities. There were therefore strong political and ideological alliances between Alexander, Education Officers like Clegg from the West Riding and Russell from Birmingham and officers of the Association of Teachers in Technical Institutions (ATTI) the leading further education trades union (of which Robinson was the President and Britton, the General Secretary) and Weaver in the Department. The AUT, on the other hand, was much more aligned to the CVCP and the ATCDE with the Directors of Institutes of Education and were, with slightly different emphases, strongly in support of the Robbins proposals. However, in more than any other major issue of higher education policy, the key decisions were driven by particular personalities. Boyle in his Joseph Payne Memorial Lecture given in 1979 summarized the post-Robbins decision making in the following terms:

> Education history is not only about the interplay of interest groups, or about the way educational systems display a tension between continuity and change. It is also the story of struggles for influence within the Department, of the ability of individual Ministers to impress their colleagues in Cabinet, and of the readiness or otherwise of experienced advisers to show themselves adaptable in the light of altered circumstances.
>
> (Boyle 1979: 17)

Certainly there were competing philosophies but what makes this case unusual was that a civil servant could have exercised such influence as to overturn so unceremoniously a report that appeared to command such public support: none of those interviewed by Walsh, or others close to the decision-making process had any doubt that Weaver was the architect of the binary line as presented in the Woolwich speech.

Boyle's interviews with Kogan (Kogan 1971) and his Joseph Payne lecture (Boyle 1979) make it clear that the Conservative Government, while committed to the Robbins recommendations on expansion, had not been fully convinced by the Robbins arguments about organization, and had been persuaded to support policies which maintained a binary rather than a unitary structure. The Labour Party, on the other hand, at least prior to the 1964 General Election, appeared to take a different view. As we have seen the Party's higher education study group, of which Crosland had been a member, argued strongly for a university based system of higher education. Its shadow spokesman, Dick Crossman, MP for Coventry, was strongly in favour and persuaded the Party leader, Harold Wilson to speak in Coventry in September 1964 specifically in favour of a unitary approach although he knew 'that officials in the Ministry were firmly committed against it' (Crossman 1975: 326). Indeed *Education,* quoted in Sharp, describes Wilson as condemning 'futile and senseless divisions between the various branches of higher education' and supporting the integration of colleges, such as Lanchester and Brighton with their newly founded local universities (Sharp 1987: 38). Had Crossman become Secretary of State, as he told McConnell,[70] he would have reversed the Department's policy. But he had offended the NUT in not supporting a pay claim for part time teachers and Wilson decided that he might be too controversial on the schools front and made him Minister for Housing.[71] As a result the post went to Michael Stewart, who had given evidence to Robbins on behalf of the Fabian Society in support of the Taylor Report. But after three months he was moved to the Foreign Office in place of Patrick Gordon Walker and Tony Crosland was appointed, the post first having been offered to Roy Jenkins, who refused it. Crosland was primarily interested in an economic Ministry and was distinctly under briefed but accepted the post because it carried membership of the Cabinet.

By the time Stewart took office, Weaver had firmly embedded a set of policy drivers, which, as we have seen had been approved at Cabinet level by the previous Government. Within two months of taking office Stewart was persuaded to adopt them and to reject the Robbins recommendations on teacher training. Godwin recounts how Weaver sent Stewart a paper on 'The future of non-university higher education' in late October in which he argued that it was doubtful whether a greatly expanded university sector would be capable of achieving a 'planned and coordinated system of higher education' and that 'a unitary system would lead to lower status for the senior technical colleges and would accentuate the distinction between "U" and "non-U" institutions'.[72] This paper Godwin argues formed the basis of Stewart's statement on teacher training to the House of Commons on 11 December 1964 (Godwin 1998: 182).

Weaver was unusual amongst career civil servants in coming from a blue blooded old Labour background. On his father's death when he was 19 he was offered a home by Sir Stafford Cripps and had married the daughter of Sir Charles Trevelyan, the former Labour President of the Board of Education. He inherited what Campbell describes as 'an austerely high minded strain of paternal socialism' (Campbell 2000: 219). He had been to a public school and Cambridge and had taught at Eton, as well as at an East End school in Barking, before entering local government as an assistant director of education, from which he progressed into the civil service. His belief in the social class characteristics of the higher education system is apparent in his reference to 'U' and 'non-U' institutions above and in his view, in a paper to Crosland, which was reflected in the Woolwich speech that Robbins implied 'that a university provides the only pukka form of higher education . . . that any self-respecting higher education institution should try either to get under the umbrella of a university or to merge with one or become one by promotion'.[73] He would have been at one with Robinson who argued that: 'The Robbins Report . . . assumed that higher education was only for an elite minority and that we should merely increase the size of this elite' (Robinson 1968: 10), that the functions of the public schools and the universities were linked and that the establishment of the 1960s New Universities reaffirmed 'the boarding school principle' (Robinson 1968: 39). In later writings Weaver reinterpreted this as

> a prejudice against the dominance of academic criteria throughout the whole of education . . . There must be a way of making higher education more accessible and more helpful to the great run of intelligent young men and women who did not primarily want to become scholars, whose virtues were not primarily to be measured by their capacity to get first class honours degrees.
>
> (Weaver 1994: 7)

He could not resist adding '(not withstanding that I achieved that goal)'.[74] Or on another occasion:

> To assess the value of quality of a person's education by reference to the level of scholarship he achieves is, however, to substitute an academic for an educational criteria. The undoubted skills needed for the successful pursuit of an academic life seem to have very limited transfer value in developing the capacities I outlined', which were 'to bring within our grasp in the hope of deriving from it sufficient wisdom to cope with our environment . . . to get from our education . . . the power . . . to learn from experience.[75]

In holding these views Weaver was, of course, part of a long intellectual tradition in British educational thinking – his father Sir Laurence Weaver, who designed the 1924–5 Wembley exhibition, was the first to use the design phrase 'fitness for purpose' (Burgess 2001) – but in seeking to realize them organizationally he was clearly exercising a political, with a small 'p' role. (The fact that he persuaded Boyle of the importance of a binary line absolves him from any accusation of seeking to take a party political role.) But the strength of his criticism of what he saw as the characteristics of the university sector was apparent in his regret in his briefing paper to Crosland that 'we took [the CATs] out of the hands of the LEAs, raised their sights, gave them large capital programmes, inflamed them with ambition and groomed them for entry to the university club' (quoted in Godwin 1998).

These sentiments translate easily into Crosland's criticism of the unitary approach as being 'hierarchically arranged on the ladder principle with the universities at the top and the other institutions down below' (Crosland, Woolwich speech, quoted in Godwin 1998) or his statement, again in the Woolwich speech: 'Let us now move away from our snobbish caste ridden obsession with university status' (Crosland, Susan 1982: 159). Weaver's preference for an alternative public non-autonomous sector and his conviction of the value of the local government contribution to higher education can be seen in his address to education officers in the wake of the Woolwich speech:

> But is it certain that under a so called unitary system of this kind, the universities as autonomous corporations would continue to enjoy, as they rightly do now, their privileged position and freedom from control under the aegis of the University Grants Committee. And would it strengthen the higher education system, and enhance its contribution to national needs, if the great resources of public initiative and concern, local patriotism and administrative and educational experience represented by local government were to be withdrawn from the provision of higher education institutions? I leave you to supply the answers.
>
> (Weaver 1965)

In his Joseph Payne Lecture he argued that: 'the needs of the community, and of those who study, teach and learn in our institutions are too richly complex and diverse to be accommodated holus bolus within the crude barriers of a single monolithic type of institution' (Weaver 1973: 16).

Weaver should not be seen as the only pressure on Crosland. Alexander had continued to campaign for the local authority role in the pages of *Education* but an equally important voice was that of the ATTI. The ATTI established a higher education advisory panel chaired by Robinson then a vice-principal at Enfield College, later part of the North East London Polytechnic. In November 1964 the Panel received a paper drafted by its General Secretary Edward (later Sir Edward) Britton entitled *The Future of the Regional Colleges* in which he argued that Robbins, other than recommending that some ten Regional Colleges, Central Institutions and Colleges of Education should be upgraded to be universities in the next decade (Robbins Report, recommendation 91), had no clear idea about the future of AFE and that any college undertaking 'only this kind of work will inevitably be looked upon as the place where students go if they fail to obtain a place at a university . . . at best they can only achieve fourth division status in the university league' (WUMRC, ATTI Higher Education Advisory Panel, 1964 quoted in Sharp 1987: 42). Britton argued that by utilizing the new machinery of the Council for National Academic Awards (CNAA) an 'alternative and distinctive, but still equal, type of course "could be developed" which is the only real guarantee of a vigorous future for the colleges'.[76] This paper re-drafted was published in March 1965 as *The Future of Higher Education within the Further*

Education System and was complimented by both Boyle and Crosland during the House of Commons higher education debate at the end of March.

The essence of the Robbins recommendations on the future pattern of higher education was that it must provide for organic growth and that the number of university places should be expanded to match the proportion of school leavers qualified to enter them (Committee on Higher Education 1963 paras 460 and 465). Although the Report did envisage the creation of some wholly new universities, one in Scotland and some new specialist scientific and technology institutions, the majority of the expansion would be catered for in existing universities, the transferred CATs and up to 10 upgraded colleges. Crosland was therefore presented with a choice, to follow the path outlined by Robbins or to accept the alternative views put forward by the Department, the local authorities led by Alexander, and the major trades union, the ATTI. These views, needless to say, were in conflict with those of the CVCP, the AUT, and, though by this time it was too late because the decision on the teacher training colleges had already been taken by Stewart, the ATCDE and the training college principals. Crosland's opinion of the CVCP can be gauged from his wife's biography of him when she alleges he said to her:

> The Vice-Chancellors this evening went on and on and on as if their precious universities weren't already rich and successful. I can understand micro economics. I can understand about sex. What I *cannot* understand is the desire of human beings to hear their own voices. Also, if one is to be truthful, I'm not frightfully interested in the universities.

And later in the evening: 'Tomorrow I shall tell the Vice-Chancellors they can stuff themselves. "Enough of this niggling and nagging" I shall say "I have other things on my mind than your petty preoccupations"' (Crosland, Susan 1982: 147).

According to his other biographer, quoting his then Parliamentary Private Secretary, Christopher Price, Crosland 'would put on a "supercilious drawl" when he felt university heads were trying to patronize him and gave the impression that he regarded all universities as being "effete" and remote as Oxford and Trinity [his College]' (Jeffries 1999). It was no wonder, as Susan Crosland says, that when Toby Weaver 'proposed the binary policy to Tony, Tony seized it' (Crosland, Susan 1982: 159). Halsey, an Adviser to the Department and a regular attender at his evening discussions about education said that Crosland because of his public school background did not understand secondary education or FE: 'I sometimes thought Tony's educational policies were a complicated internal battle between his love/hate for Oxford and his wish to identify with his Grimsby constituents' (Halsey 1996: 130). He was not much interested in higher education; his real interests were in comprehensive schools, a passion he shared with Weaver who also argued that the essential character of polytechnics was 'comprehensive' (Weaver 1973), and the establishment of the Public Schools Commission, a project that fell when he left Education and moved to the Board of Trade.

The truth of the matter is that Crosland was, in the eyes of one interviewee who knew him well, 'a big picture man' who was not interested in detail and relied too much on his officials.[77] In conversation with Kogan he said that he had intended to make no major policy statements for six months from becoming Secretary of State but ended up by making one in three: 'Officials should not have advised me to make a major speech at that time . . . I then had an only superficial knowledge of the subject'. He began, he said, 'by making an appalling blunder'; the speech 'came out in a manner calculated to infuriate almost everyone you can think of' (Kogan 1971: 193). His civil servants had wanted to get the policy on the record as soon as possible – this was largely because the Lanchester College/Warwick University merger which Wolfenden had agreed to slow down in the previous October to allow a long term policy for the local authority sector to be prepared, was now demanding a decision. The speech itself, though reflecting Weaver's paper, referred to above, was not in fact drafted by him according to Sir Herbert Andrew, the Permanent Secretary but by John Penmark in the Private Office ('Toby was always tending to claim credit or discredit whichever it was or no') but the 'final wording of the thing was very much Tony Crosland's'.[78] Crosland agreed in conversation with Kogan that he added to the draft 'which made it much more unpalatable' including, probably, the remarks about the universities' lack of social responsiveness (Kogan 1971: 194). According to one senior civil servant there was a great deal of ignorance in the DES as well as Crosland about what the universities were actually like in 1966. They had not assimilated the impact of the investment in technological education in the late 1950s and over estimated the possible contribution of vocational education in the colleges: an early draft of the Woolwich speech referred to MIT as an example of a non-university institution of higher techno-logical education on which polytechnics could be modelled.[79] The speech laid down five reasons for accepting a dual system of higher education:

1   The need for an increase in vocational education, which could not be fully met by the universities – 'it therefore requires a separate sector with a separate tradition and outlook'.
2   'If the universities have a "class" monopoly as degree giving bodies and if every college which achieves high standards moves automatically into the University Club then the residual public sector becomes a permanent poor relation . . . productive only of an unhealthy rat-race mentality'.
3   The unitary system would be characterized by 'a continuous rat-race to reach the First or University Division . . . [where] there would be a constant pressure on those below to ape the universities above, and a certain inevi-table failure to achieve the diversity in higher education which contempo-rary society needs'.
4   It was desirable that a substantial part of the higher education system 'should be under social control, directly responsive to social needs'.
5   Non-university sector should be degree awarding, develop postgraduate work and a 'healthy rivalry where their work overlaps'.

(DES 1965)

These five points are, of course, readily identifiable in the arguments that had been put to him.

Another example of Crosland's over reliance on his officials occurs in respect to his decision to raise the tuition fees payable by overseas students to a level higher than home students announced on 21 December 1966, the last day of Parliament. The policy was widely regarded as discriminatory within higher education but was also promulgated without consultation with either the UGC or the CVCP. The CVCP protested vigorously and publicly, while the Chairman of the UGC, consulted late at night on Preston station by the Secretary of State on the day of the announcement, after attending a speaking function with him, rang the Permanent Secretary the next day to say 'Well, if you are going to do this, you must make it clear as to why I haven't been consulted at all'.[80] No preparations had been made for the storm of protest that was to follow. Crosland told Kogan 'The officials had either misjudged or else failed to warn me of the likely reaction in universities and the whole announcement and presentation were totally mishandled' (Kogan 1971: 178). It is inconceivable that a Secretary of State, reading his briefs carefully, could not have recognized the dangers implicit in making such an announcement without proper preparation beforehand.

However, Crosland learned from his mistakes. He accepted that he had been too hasty in committing himself to the Woolwich speech but 'The more I thought about [the policy] subsequently the more I became convinced the policy was right' (Kogan 1971: 193). He established an advisory group under Reg Prentice, his Minister of State, to come up with an organizational framework for the non-university sector. The membership represents a significant pointer to the solutions proposed: Alexander from the AEC, Clegg from the West Riding and Russell from Birmingham representing the local authorities, Britton and Robinson from the ATTI and Hornby from the NACEIC. This met between June and November 1965. According to Burgess, Britton wrote the key paper for this group defining what was meant by the binary line (Burgess 2005). The group had to wrestle with a number of issues. Weaver supported by Alexander was concerned to ensure that there should be a concentration of advanced courses in 30 selected institutions while the ATTI representatives were opposed to such a restriction. Sharp suggests that one of the grounds for their objections may have been related to an inter-union rivalry for membership: the ATTI had lost members to the AUT when the CATs became universities and this situation might recur with the new selected institutions (Sharp 1987). The DES paper to the Prentice group argued that concentration was necessary if the colleges were to be 'an alternative to the universities which is attractive to teachers and students and is capable of enjoying the public esteem that is essential to the success of the dual system', (quoted in Sharp 1987: 48) and it was the DES view which carried the day.

A second issue was what the selected institutions should be called, and a DES paper, the fifth in a series to the group, said with a certain lack of conviction: 'No entirely satisfactory suggestion has been made but the best is perhaps simply "polytechnic" '.[81] This became translated into the title of the subsequent White Paper, *A Plan for Polytechnics and Other Colleges* (DES 1966a). A third issue was even more testing – which institutions were to be designated. The White Paper suggested that 28 polytechnics were to be established (the figure later rose to 30) and that the following criteria should be used to select them: the record of the demand for places, the needs of industry, the availability of lodgings, a balanced provision of courses and a minimum of 2,000 advanced students, a figure which could be achieved through mergers. The DES had provided a paper which suggested some mergers which would have been violently opposed by LEAs or where one college would have strongly resisted being subordinated to another.

It was typical of Crosland's lack of interest in detail that he left it to Robinson and Burgess to advise on which mergers might be feasible,[82] and the White Paper listed 50 institutions from which the 28 might be drawn. It was then left to local authorities to make proposals. The Prentice group's report was circulated to LEAs and although the ATTI deputation met the DES to try to secure changes, the White Paper publication served to settle the argument, though it did not satisfy two particular categories of interested groups. Crosland was famous in educational circles for his informal evening gatherings to which individuals who had sympathetic contributions to make to educational policy were floating invitees. On the university side Sir Eric (later Lord) Ashby, Sir Frederick (later Lord) Dainton and Chelle Halsey were frequent attendees, all critical of the binary line proposition. (Ashby told Walsh that Crosland said 'look, I seem to have made a mess of it; can you help me get over the Woolwich speech?'[83] On the other side invitees included Alexander, Russell, Clegg, who was a very regular attendee, Robinson, Burgess and Britton. Robinson and Burgess were key members but Crosland always turned to Clegg for final approval of an idea.[84]

In fact Robinson and Burgess, whose views were in a sense outriders of Weaver's, felt that their ideas had not been fully realized. Pratt and Burgess in *Polytechnics: A Report* (1974) argued that between the Woolwich speech and the White Paper the nature of the binary policy had changed. The concentration of advanced courses in a few institutions was damaging to part time programmes and the designation of 30 selected institutions represented an example of academic drift and would act as a disincentive on the rest of further education (Pratt and Burgess 1974). They argued strongly for the binary line as a matter of critical educational policy characterizing the autonomous sector as 'aloof, academic, conservative and exclusive' and the public sector as representing a service tradition 'responsive, vocational, innovative and open' (Pratt 1997: 9). They echoed an ATTI claim that the essential differences between the two systems lay in the control of syllabuses: in universities syllabus content was driven by academic concerns, in Pratt and Burgess's words 'the presentation, extension and dissemination of knowledge "for its own sake"' (Pratt and Burgess 1974: 9), while, in the non-university sector, community, that is 'public', involvement was regarded as essential: human knowledge 'may advance as much through the solution of practical problems as through pure thought' (Pratt and Burgess 1974: 10). But the difference lay in the fact that Weaver was sufficiently a civil servant to recognize that unless some selection among the colleges took place and some subsequent concentration of advanced work the sector would become dangerously unwieldy and the claim that the sector could offer competition to the universities could not be fulfilled. The ideological relationship with Weaver's ideas outlined above is easy to identify.

There is no evidence that Crosland shared such ideas. Though he appears to have been at one with Weaver in their personal prejudices about the university system (both ingenuously claimed at various times that the binary system provided a protection for the universities) where they particularly came together was in the political and organizational aspects of the policy. Both believed that the Robbins recommendation that up to 10 non-university institutions might need to be upgraded to full university status to contain the expansion opened up a 'rat-race' which would have a distorting effect on the sector. In his address to education officers in August 1965 quoted above Weaver said that the Report had resulted in 'leading technical colleges that could be counted in tens rather than units urging their claim to be promoted' (Weaver 1965). The White Paper laid down that there was to be no increase in the number of polytechnics for 10 years. But Crosland seems to have been much more influenced by political and to some extent social pressures exercised by the local authorities and the trades unions than the educational philosophies of some of his key advisers.

The binary line and the creation of the polytechnics was in part an administrative device to resist pressure, and it was successful in that, as Pratt points out, no addition to the number of polytechnics was in fact to occur for 20 years (Pratt 1997), but in another it was not because it in no way dampened institutional ambition. In its first year of meeting the new Committee of Polytechnic Directors resolved 'That each polytechnic should have as its legitimate and realistic aim the granting to it of a Charter confirming the right to award degrees and other academic qualifications'.[85]

In a final wrapping up of the binary line debate Crosland held a formal meeting with the CVCP on 11 November 1966 devoted to a discussion of the issues where he argued that 'there was no political possibility of establishing a unitary system composed wholly of autonomous universities'. He saw the establishment of the binary line 'as relatively advantageous to universities' and that the polytechnics would be 'primarily to provide teaching' though research was not ruled out. He did not now like the word 'binary' and would prefer 'pluralist' and, while the Woolwich speech implied a rigid division, he would now wish to see it interpreted more flexibly, although he did not enlarge on what the structural implications, if any, this might be.[86] In January 1967 he reprised the Woolwich speech in an address at Lancaster where he sought to undo some of the impressions caused by that earlier event. This was an altogether more balanced presentation, constructed on the basis of the work of the Prentice group in putting flesh on the bones of the initial ideas and in the light of the White Paper's planned process for the designation of the institutions. It acknowledged the achievements and strengths of the university sector but went on to claim that:

> The plain fact is that we did not start off *tabula rasa*; we started off with a given historical situation. A plural system already existed; and whatever anyone's views as to how they might have liked to start from scratch, we could not two years ago have done a major surgical operation and converted the existing system into an entirely different one.
>
> (Crosland, Lancaster speech 27 January 1967 printed in Pratt and Burgess 1974)

In any assessment of the judgements which went into constructing the binary policy this represents a crucial statement. Over the previous 20 years two sectors of higher education had grown up with a demarcation of status, which was reinforced by a demarcation of state responsibility between the Treasury and the Ministry of Education which served to keep the development of the two sectors entirely separate. To the local authorities, members of the ATTI and to key members of the Ministry the Robbins recommendations appeared as a confirmation of the dominance of the status of the university sector; to the university side they appeared to be a natural extension of the pattern of institutional development reaching back to the pre-War years. The 'ladder' concept was not new. There were arguments for either approach. The criticisms of university aloofness and unwillingness to act disinterestedly in the national interest had some force, as has been shown above, particularly in relation to teacher training, but the universities' concern to retain degree awarding powers in institutions which were self governing and autonomous was based on principle as well as on expediency. That it was unwise to permit the autonomous sector to absorb 88 per cent of higher education is refuted by the decision in 1992 to extend precisely the rights of autonomy to all those institutions which then comprised the public sector of higher education. It is true that by this time the UGC had given way to the HEFCE, by way of the UFC, and the state had assumed much greater steering powers but the principle of institutional autonomy was retained. The UGC under Wolfenden showed itself to be pliable in relation to the binary line and there is no reason why it would not have shown a similar flexibility had national need been demonstrated in respect of particular elements of a unitary system. Crosland, however, was captured by what Caston described to Walsh as 'the old Ministry lobby'[87] and backed the local authority interest in higher education.

There was no formal response to the rejection of its recommendations by the Robbins Committee itself which had long since been disbanded before the Woolwich speech. The chairman on the other hand responded vigorously. Three themes run through his various speeches and writings: the first that the Committee was very much seized as to what the expanded numbers of students would be seeking, the second that he saw the Committee's policy as evolutionary rather than involving dramatic breaks with the past and third that he saw the Report as 'seeking to dissolve artificial hierarchy' (Robbins 1966: 49) rather than creating new layers. On the first, responding in March

1964 to issues about whether the Committee had considered creating new types of institutions (presumably liberal arts colleges since the speech was given at Harvard):

> The first question which arose in this connection was whether to meet the expansion here mainly by an expansion of universities or whether to create new types of institutions to take some of the burden. On this from the beginning there was no doubt of the desires of the probable applicants – with us the prestige of a university career and a university degree is such as to render most alternatives a second best.
>
> (Robbins 1966: 23)

He reserved his most considered criticisms for the House of Lords debate held on 1 December 1965 in response to the Woolwich speech. The Secretary of State:

> may paint the most splendid picture about the future of the so-called 'public' sector of his Binary system. But he will not convince either the teachers or the students that the picture is a true one. He will not prevent most students, with the necessary qualifications, from first seeking entrance to the universities, traditional or technological.
>
> (Robbins 1966: 150)

and he concluded:

> I do not believe that the Binary system will be a success. I do not think that the 'public sector' as the Secretary of State conceives it, can be built up to match the status or efficiency of the autonomous sector. I do not believe that this will be so, either as regards research or as regards training. Nor do I believe that the respective students can be brought to regard them in this light. I am confident that the system, as presently conceived, is not ultimately viable.
>
> (Robbins 1966: 156)

In an interview with Boris Ford in the *Universities Quarterly* also in December 1965 he continued the argument:

> Here you have a Labour Government which is attempting, for good or bad, to introduce the comprehensive principle into schools, which I think is the right thing to do providing it is done with sense and prudence. At the same time they are deepening the existence of lines of division in higher education and actually announcing as a matter of policy, that the decisions are to be permanent. They are making the system more hierarchical than ever . . . what we had in mind . . . was an evolving system in which as the demand expanded and as standards were raised in further education and the teacher training colleges, institutions could be upgraded and in which a common spirit informed the whole. Higher education in our conception was indeed a continuous spectrum.
>
> (Robbins and Ford 1965)

Doubts were also beginning to emerge on the local authority side. An editorial in *Education*, normally strongly attuned to public sector views, commenting on the commonality of views expressed by Boyle and Crosland in the recent House of Commons debate said:

> The trouble is that the more the rationale is expounded the less convincing it seems to sound . . . True as these statements undoubtedly are, the echo of past speeches about the secondary modern schools is uncomfortably loud . . . There can be little doubt that bilateralism is the right policy. The problem is how to make it credible.
>
> (*Education* 1965)

Robbins in his interview with Ford quoted above cited as an example of 'our perfectly practicable evolutionary possibilities . . . [which were being] stifled,' the rejection of the Lanchester College/University of Warwick merger, describing it 'as pedantic myopia of the most backward-looking kind' (Robbins and Ford 1965). The reaction of the two local authorities, Coventry and Warwickshire, to the decision in a statement by the leader of their delegation to a meeting at the DES with Crosland and Weaver makes it clear that not all local authorities agreed with DES policy:

> His authority believed that the whole of education should form a unitary system under State control. They opposed the binary policy principally on the grounds that it would perpetuate what they regard as artificial divisions between the maintained and the so-called autonomous sector. Advances in the school system had grown out of local experiments.
>
> His Authority believed that similar experiments should be allowed in a unitary comprehensive system of higher education. Coventry appreciated that there were outside pressures being exerted to contain Lanchester within the Government's binary system. However they believed that an experiment in Coventry would not weaken the Government's hand elsewhere as the situation in Coventry was, in their opinion, unique. The integration proposals . . . were the natural development of Coventry's desire for a technologically based system of higher education which had been their objective for the last five years and was supported by local industry.[88]

When the universities came under the Treasury, the Treasury officials regarded the UGC as the policy driver, except in regard to the provision of finance. This was much less the case when the transfer to the DES took place. Initially the intention was that the Department should have two joint Permanent Secretaries one responsible for the universities and science and technology and the other for the traditional concerns of the old Ministry. When Labour came to power much of the science and technology moved to the new Ministry of Technology and Anthony Part was promoted to be Permanent Secretary in that Department, to be succeeded by Weaver who brought together the local authority higher education, over which he had already had charge, with the universities office transferred from the Treasury.

This was then a period of flux. The new unifying Permanent Secretary, Sir Herbert Andrew, who had come from the Board of Trade in 1963 had been in the UK negotiating team for entry to the Common Market, to which Britain had just been denied entry, and was not, one assumes, knowledgeable about higher education. His natural tendency, according to Carswell 'accorded with the traditions of the Department in which he had till then spent his career, which were to intervene as little as possible and stand in readiness to manage crisis' (Carswell 1980: 69). Weaver, then, had a remarkably free hand to exercise influence. He was encouraged in this by the tradition of policy making in the Department. Boyle, interviewed by Kogan said 'this is the difference between education and some other subjects. I would say overwhelmingly the biggest number [of policies] originated from . . . the "education world", if, you like, from the logic of the education service as it developed' (Kogan 1971: 46). In discussing the role of officials as against Ministers Boyle quoted one, who must have been Weaver, as saying 'I can honestly say that there is not one new policy in my sector of responsibility that I have not started or substantially contributed to over the last twenty years' (Kogan 1971: 41).

No official exercised as much influence as Weaver in the next 50 years, and only one John (later Sir John) Vereker, Deputy Secretary 1988–93, is remembered as actively seeking to exert influence in this way. It was Weaver's good fortune that his period of Deputy Secretary 1962–73, coincided with a period when a vacuum existed in the ability of the Government to respond to Robbins on organizational issues, which he was able to step into. Crosland himself did not take the binary line issue or the creation of the polytechnics to Cabinet where there might have been some opposition and the Prime Minister, who in opposition had given signs of having a different view about the future pattern of higher education, was fully occupied with the economy and devolution and chose not to get involved. One interviewee, who was in the Government at the time, suggested that Crosland would probably have told him, after the event. Crossman contemplated writing to him but recalled how irritated he himself had been when Stewart, who had held the Housing brief in opposition, sought to intervene on a policy matter when Crossman was Secretary of State, and thought better of it (Crossman 1975).

Colleagues wondered how Weaver would respond to the arrival of Mrs Thatcher to the post of Secretary of State. Campbell in his biography of Thatcher gives an unforgettable account. Thatcher, like Crosland, arriving in office signally unprepared to tackle educational issues, and like him much more interested in economic policy, 'clicked' with Weaver:

> He would stay late to have a word in her ear at the end of the day; he always seemed to be a step behind her, whispering what she needed to know about people she was about to meet. He was particularly good at letting her think she was winning – his own recollection – even as he persuaded her to implement his, or the Department's policies.
>
> (Campbell 2000: 220)

According to Campbell, when she left office she wrote him a profuse letter of thanks and nominated him for a knighthood. Later she believed that he and the Department had pulled the wool over her eyes, and he was deeply upset to receive no mention of himself in her memoirs. Nevertheless he played a key role in the work leading up to her White Paper, *Education, A Framework for Expansion* and, according to Burgess played a part in the James Committee's creation of the two year Diploma in Higher Education (Dip HE), the predecessor of the Foundation Degree (Burgess 2001). Indeed paragraph 4.19 of the James Report describing the purposes of the Diploma where it contemplates modifying entirely the idea of a university reads like pure Weaver, and not a bit like Lord James (DES 1972 para 4.19). He remained consistent in his beliefs. On retirement he went on to chair the board of Burgess's School of Independent Study which pioneered a radical form of the Dip.HE, became deeply involved in the RSA's Capability for Education movement and was a member of the Board, again with Burgess, of the Department of Trade and Industry's Enterprise in Education project.

From a binary to a unitary structure

It took a quarter of a century between 1967 when Crosland presented his list of proposed polytechnic sites to Parliament to the passage of the Further and Higher Education Act of 1992 which gave both university status to the polytechnics and established a new governing structure for the whole of the British higher education, for the structural effects of the speech to be reversed. One can interpret this period in a number of different ways: the rise to maturity of the polytechnics, the elimination of the local authority interest in higher education, the impact of the transformation from so-called elite to mass higher education, the development in state machinery to control and exercise direction over the higher education system or the transition from a post-Robbins social to a 1980s economic view of higher education. In practice these themes are interwoven as policies evolved. It is tempting as Salter and Tapper do to see a long term strategy in the elimination of intermediary bodies and the creation of structures which entrenched DES control over higher education (Salter and Tapper 1994) but while this may have been a distant gleam in the eyes of some officials the evidence suggests that the Department stumbled towards that solution in a series of often faltering steps, each step being the product of spasmodic pressures. Even when achieved in 1992, the decision to devolve responsibility for higher education to Scotland and Wales, and the subsequent decision in England to split off higher education from the Department to what had been the Department of Trade and Industry, suggests that within Government, at least, no consistent policy existed.

Although in his Lancaster speech Crosland had restricted himself to presenting the polytechnics as simply 'fulfilling a distinctive role from the universities' (Crosland, Lancaster speech 1967 quoted in Robinson 1968) the presumption had always been that the policy had been to create a 'separate but equal' sector. Sir William Pile, by now Permanent Secretary, but previously a committed opponent of a unitary system when head of Teacher Supply within the old Ministry, told the polytechnic directors in 1974 that the long term aim was to achieve a unified structure of higher education yet with diversity, and with the public sector ultimately standing side by side with the universities, matching them in student numbers, in resources and in standing.[89] Such a policy, however, proved slow to realize. The Committee of Polytechnic Directors, which was to become a key driver for institutional autonomy, degree awarding powers and university status, was only prompted to come into existence by Shirley Williams, then Minister of State at the DES in a conference speech in 1969 (Sharp 1987) and was not formed until 1970 but even then it had no independent standing. It was only finally agreed by the local authorities that a secretariat of three could be funded in 1972, after protracted negotiations, and, at a meeting with the Council of Local Education Authorities (CLEA) in 1975, the CDP minutes record that CLEA, having seen the CDP's evidence to the Layfield Committee on Local Government Finance, which was critical of local authorities' controls, 'was not disposed to concede that the CDP case [for a larger secretariat] could be discussed in principle. The tenfold increase in the CVCP office was brushed aside as an irrelevant abstraction'.[90]

The polytechnics had not achieved national status in the eyes of schools: 75 per cent of applicants for places applied to only one polytechnic and only 39 per cent of polytechnic applicants also applied for a university place.[91] Although the 1972 White Paper had predicted that the polytechnics would have 180,000 students by 1981 the CDP was more concerned that the polytechnic identity might be lost in a wider AFE environment and spent much of its emotional energy questioning the DES's commitment to the polytechnic idea. In practice the decision to roll up the colleges of education into the polytechnics, the strategy for which was devised by Weaver, tended to reinforce their position but any comparison between the CDP and the CVCP illustrates the difference of standing of the two sectors: the CVCP was addressed annually at its conference by the Secretary of State, while the CDP had to be satisfied with a more junior Minister and, even as late as 1988, sometimes with only a civil servant; the CVCP communicated on an almost weekly basis with the UGC with whom it shared the running of the sector, while the CDP was generally embattled in its relationship with its local authority masters and had little or no executive control over its sector, not least because AFE extended to competing colleges that had not been given polytechnic status; the CVCP minutes illustrate the extent to which universities were drawn into national issues while the CDP concentrated on narrow mostly self referenced concerns. In 1979, 12 years after they were designated, one polytechnic director summed up the position as 'whereas universities have a role based on tradition, polytechnics have not yet convinced the public that they provide a comparable but alternative kind of higher education'.[92] On the other hand, on any reading of its minutes, the CVCP seems always to be on the back foot with the Government, trying to defend the university system and preserve its position and funding, while the CDP was on the attack, seeking to enhance and exploit its position, pushing at an open door with DES officials and emphasizing the need for an ambitious change agenda.

The most significant issue for the public sector was how power and resources could be distributed to develop the sector effectively. From the beginning AFE funding was 'pooled', in other words LEAs drew on a pool to fund student numbers in AFE level courses wherever they were approved by HMIs and the DES. This favoured institutions which were based in large centres of population and led to differential rates of growth and to a concern in smaller LEAs that larger authorities were exploiting their catchment and benefiting disproportionately. The system was also open ended and therefore inflationary in that it encouraged expansion. This accorded well with DES policy to build up the public sector to match the universities in student numbers but, from a Treasury point of view, it lacked accountability except at the level of each local authority although accountability on quality was controlled by the CNAA. The UGC system, on the other hand, offered tight controls on student numbers, and therefore on sectoral funding. Moreover the university system was subject to public accountability through the Permanent Secretary, as its Accounting Officer.

The local authorities opened the argument in 1970 with a proposal by the Association of Municipal Authorities (AMA) for a Polytechnic Grants Committee (PGC), which would be made up of representation from local government associations, teacher unions and industry. It was suggested that it might operate in a way similar to the UGC. Not surprisingly this attracted support from Weaver because it was not unlike ideas floated by the old Ministry of Education to Robbins. However the other local authority associations did not wish to deal separately with polytechnic funding and the AMC proposal was transmuted to the establishment of a Local Authorities Higher Education Committee (LAHEC) which would cover the whole of AFE. This came into being in shadow form in 1972 and was officially welcomed in Margaret Thatcher's 1972 White Paper. This, however, was to be entirely local authority run and was intended to have a significant Regional Advisory Committee input. In the course of discussion its remit was widened to cover all of FE. A significant secretariat was envisaged. While ostensibly a way of controlling the FE and AFE pool it also represented a claim to assume exclusive control over FE and AFE. Having originally welcomed LAHEC the DES changed its mind. It argued, first, that a remit which extended over all the colleges was too broad and that there should be a concentration on those institutions which had a majority of AFE courses and that, second, it was too heavily weighted towards local as distinct from national interests.

Meantime the CDP had come out publicly in its evidence to the House of Commons Expenditure Committee and to the Layfield Committee in favour of a Polytechnic Board or Commission which would concern itself only with polytechnic funding. Its minutes are critical, over many meetings with DES officials, where it believed that the Department was indecisive in its planning of higher education. The DES might have replied, as in fact Edward Simpson, the Deputy Secretary for higher education, did that the problem of national planning was 'the presence of so many constraints' by which he meant the LEAs wish to retain a comprehensive control over education in order to ensure that decisions were made locally.[93] It was the need to reconcile these constraints that in 1977 prompted the Labour Secretary of State, Fred Mulley, to set up the Oakes Committee (named after the Minister who was to chair it) to produce a system of management and control of higher education in the maintained sector which would also address issues of coordination with the universities. The Oakes Committee recommended the creation of a national body but had great difficulty in reaching agreement on its membership except to recognize that it would be representative in nature; but legislation was overtaken by the 1979 General Election and the return of the Conservatives to power.

Initially the Conservative Government was no more decisive than Labour in resolving the problems of managing the public sector but its hand was forced by three related events. The first was that partly as a stalling mechanism the Secretary of State, Mark Carlisle, had invited the new Select Committee for Education, Science and the Arts to undertake an inquiry into higher education. This had the advantage of subjecting the views of all the interested parties to the Oakes Committee to public scrutiny and cross examination and the Select Committee duly came up with a recommendation that a national Committee for Colleges and Polytechnics should be created to advise on the planning and finance of AFE (Select Committee on Education, Science and Arts 1980b). A second factor was that as a consequence of the reductions in public expenditure imposed in the new Government's first budget the LEA pool was 'capped', that is cash limited. (On the universities' side the UGC had administered the cuts differentially between universities and had imposed a 3 per cent reduction in student numbers to preserve the unit of resource.) The capping of the pool, a measure entirely directed from the Treasury, meant that the open ended funding of expansion in the public sector was brought to an end and machinery had to be created to distribute resources in a way that reflected central policy considerations. The UGC decisions, which became public on 1 July 1981, raised even greater concerns within the DES because of the public storm of protest they aroused, particularly in relation to the reduction in student numbers which seemed to contradict government policy since Robbins. In the House of Commons the Secretary of State found himself answerable for a policy which he had had no hand in creating.

But the most compelling policy driver was a leak of a draft paper in the *Times Higher Education Supplement*[94] intended as a response to the Select Committee's report, which Carlisle had circulated to Cabinet colleagues for comment. Drafted by Stephen Jones, an official, probably at the behest of Dr Rhodes Boyson, the strongly Thatcherite Minister of State in the Department, it proposed a grants committee which distributed funds directly from the DES to 98 public sector institutions, cutting out the LEAs altogether, and a transfer of ownership of these institutions to the state. Legislation was promised in 1982–3. The *THES* editorial called it 'Dr. Boyson's Trojan Horse'.[95] The leaked document was immediately welcomed by the CDP but attacked by the LEAs. More seriously the Conservative dominated Association of County Councils (ACC) was almost as hostile as the Labour led AMA and when Cabinet Committee H failed to agree on it Carlisle was instructed to produce a consultative paper for wider public discussion (Sharp 1987).

Meantime CLEA had been in the process of drafting its own proposals following the collapse of Oakes. It argued for a local authority body to manage and coordinate maintained higher education which would, like LAHEC, cover all FE and AFE on the grounds that when institutions were removed from local authority control (like the CATs) they progressively ceased to be responsive to local needs and as a consequence FE colleges had to grow a new top level of study. This new body would distribute funds through formulae through the existing FE pool. In an angry response to the DES, at a meeting with Richard Bird, the new Deputy Secretary for higher and further education the CDP pointed out that the polytechnics were no longer local institutions and that 75 per cent of their budgets were not attributable to their own controlling authorities; their catchment was now national.[96] However the DES was in conciliatory mood. Its Consultative Paper *Higher Education in England outside the Universities: Policy, Funding and Management* (DES 1981) offered two models, the one effectively the CLEA proposal and the other a direct take over by the DES, and at a Chartered Institute of Public Finance and Accountancy (CIPFA) conference in October, *Education* reported John Thompson, an official at the DES, as saying 'I recognise the resentment of the local authorities when 70 of their polytechnics and colleges were going to be taken away. We ought belatedly but in due humility to recognise this effect and having served our penance try to find an equal solution'.[97]

It was out of such sentiments that NAB was born, a compromise devised by a new team of Ministers, Sir Keith Joseph and William Waldegrave replacing Carlisle and Rhodes Boyson, with the help, according to Sharp (1987) of a working party of the Conservative National Advisory Committee on Education. But the leak of the DES intention to direct fund a substantial slice of AFE had the effect of making the local authorities more amenable to a compromise solution. The NAB constitution, while cumbersome, represented an ingenious representation of national, that is DES, and local authority interests with a Board, chaired by a Minister (initially Waldegrave) and a Committee, which reported to the Board, chaired by a chief executive, an externally appointed academic, Christopher (later Sir Christopher) Ball. An unusual feature was that the Board contained six representatives from the DES, all civil servants, and three each from the AMA and ACC with additional representation from CDP, the National Association of Teachers in Further and Higher Education (NATFHE), the successor to the ATTI, and a number of other bodies. The appointment of Christopher Ball, as Chairman of the Committee and chief executive was balanced with the appointment of John Bevan, from the Inner London Education Committee, as the Secretary. From the start, in the eyes of some DES officials, NAB was seen as an interim solution. This was made more likely by a decision, encouraged by Bevan, to permit votes being taken at Board meetings. The local authority culture saw no difficulty in this but the prospect of the Minister and his officials being outvoted led to distrust in the whole process in the DES. Waldegrave was said to be relaxed about votes being taken; his successor Peter Brooke was extremely effective in handling the local authorities and the matter did not arise; but George Walden hated the local authority atmosphere.[98] According to one DES official the main reason why NAB, which had been appointed initially for three years and was renewed without dissent, was replaced was the conflictual attitude of the local authorities and of Bevan, the powerful and abrasive Secretary.[99] Another reason may simply have been that the Thatcher Government's increasing hostility to local government, as demonstrated in the decision to abolish the Metropolitan Authorities and its urge to centralize decision making put a natural end to an occasionally uncomfortable partnership in the control and management of AFE.

Nevertheless the six years of NAB (1982–86) had had some important benefits. Although as a planning body the NAB Committee undertook remarkably few rationalization exercises either within the public sector or in conjunction with the UGC, which was one of its *raison d'êtres*, it had established a student led funding system which provided a more rational planning basis than had gone before. With the pool capped the new funding system drove institutions to expand recruitment even at the price of lowering unit costs. As one influential player put it, the NAB model was essentially inflationary: those institutions that took more students got more money. A second benefit was the encouragement it gave to institutional self-management and a growing separation of their affairs from their controlling authorities. The polytechnics, in particular, had outgrown their local authorities, and in some cases had budgets larger than the local authority that was required to control them. A third benefit was to raise the profile of the polytechnics themselves. Although the CDP had complained of its modest representation on NAB in fact the standing and effectiveness of the CDP had risen particularly in the eyes of the DES and in stark contrast to that of the local authorities. The reputation of Ray Ricketts, the Chairman of the CDP was particularly high in the DES. (It was strongly rumoured that his contacts, along with Durrand's from Huddersfield Polytechnic, stretched up all the way to No.10.)[100] Finally, although the results of collaboration with the UGC were in the main restricted to warm expressions of mutual support for widening access and lifelong learning, the exchange of observers on one another's committees and the establishment of dialogue across the binary line raised issues about the need for an 'overarching body' which foreshadowed the eventual reversion to a unitary system.

There can be no doubt that, although from the time of the leaked DES document in 1981 DES civil servants had wanted to obtain more direct control over the management and direction of the public sector and had had the support of the Treasury for doing so, the key trigger was the behaviour of the local authorities. From their earliest days there had been complaints from polytechnics about the burdens of local authority control which ranged from low level bureaucratic restrictions particularly in relation to junior staff posts to wider questions of independent decision making over site development. One former polytechnic director reported that one of the prime reasons he had had for seeking independence was that he wanted, against the wishes of his local authority, to dispose of some off main campus assets in order to finance developments on his city centre site.[101] One issue on which almost all members of the CDP could agree in their dialogues with DES officials was their dissatisfaction with local authority control. By 1981 this had become fully recognized in the DES which included a telling sentence in its leaked document in the *THES*: 'I have also become convinced that the extent of mutual disenchantment between many major institutions in PSHE [Public sector higher education] and their maintaining LEA's is such as seriously to undermine the effectiveness of the system'.[102]

Peter Knight in a persuasive article in the *Guardian* argues that a crucial stage was reached at a meeting of the CDP in 1986 to be addressed by Sir Keith Joseph, when CDP members decided rather than challenge the Secretary of State on policy issues to describe the reality of trying to work with the LEAs: meetings of governors that were preceded by meetings of the Labour group meant 'you had to "fix" the Labour group or nothing happened', the banning of *The Times* in some polytechnic libraries because of the Wapping dispute, the removal of institutional budget surpluses at the end of the year offering no inducement to income generation. 'As these stories progressed, the change in the demeanour of the Secretary of State was astonishing. It was clear he was horrified. By the time the meeting closed, Joseph was a different man' (Knight 2007). At a meeting in October of the same year with Kenneth (later Lord) Baker, Joseph's successor, the CDP argued that the management framework and systems of control were now the key issues when considering how to improve their efficiency, effectiveness and standing. They listed the following:

- bureaucratic controls;
- constraints on capital spending;
- political pressures;
- unspecific central administrative charges;
- articles of government inappropriate for major institutions of higher education;
- inflexibility and inability to respond to entrepreneurial needs;
- ill defined legal identity;
- restrictions on virement.

Baker responded sympathetically: 'The relationships defined when the polytechnics were set up reflected conditions which no longer obtained'.[103] A DES official interviewed by Kogan and Hanney, confirmed the officials' response to CDP evidence: 'Our motivation as officials was that operation within local government stood in the way of the management of polytechnics as effective educational institutions' (Kogan and Hanney 2000: 136). This view was reflected in the Baker White Paper in the phrase 'the good management of polytechnics and colleges is inhibited by the excessive engagement in their affairs of local authorities exploiting their role as employer of staff and overseer of budgeting and purchasing matters' (DES 1987 para 3.29) and the dismissal of the idea that the polytechnics could be given corporate status but remain under the LEAs (as the Inner London Education Authority (ILEA) had given to the London polytechnics) because LEAs could still impose restraints by imposing conditions on funding. A polytechnic director interviewee simply saw NAB as local government control writ large: 'institutionally it effectively reinforced a local authority grip – a collection of local authorities . . . brought to the forum all the local authority perceptions and misconceptions and perhaps multiplied them up' (Kogan and Hanney 2000: 130). The local authority role in higher education was dead in the water. Baker, a new Secretary of State anxious to restore a sense of optimism and change in higher education after the pessimism of Keith Joseph's Green Paper, would have had no difficulty whatever in obtaining the support of the Prime Minister for their removal.

In March 1987 the CDP issued a report on polytechnic government which reiterated the case for direct funding. In a telling reversal of roles CLEA sought a meeting with CDP to express its concern that Government might be influenced by this report rather than by the Report of the Good Management Practice Group *Management for a Purpose* which had been set up and led by NAB and which, unsurprisingly, assumed the continuation of NAB (NAB 1987). But the die had already been cast and the White Paper (DES 1987) was about to be published. The CDP's hopes had been realized. There was only one dissenting voice, that of Eric Robinson, now Director of Preston Polytechnic, who disassociated himself from the CDP report and, remaining consistent with the principles of the Woolwich speech, saying that: 'It demonstrated that directors were in fact set on achieving university status for polytechnics and were no longer concerned with fulfilling the educational role for which polytechnics were established'.[104] The model of how the new higher education sector was to be separated from the wider further education, published in the White Paper goes some way to illustrating his argument. Using the criteria of more than 350 FTEs studying at higher education levels, and more than 55 per cent of the total student body being categorized as higher education, produced a very clear dividing line between higher and further education, and a consequential rejection of the idea of the 'comprehensive' institution which incorporated advanced and non advanced further education within one institution (see Figure 2.1).

The White Paper did not limit itself, however, to changing the control arrangements for the public sector but addressed issues in relation to the 'autonomous sector' as well. In his evidence to the Education, Science and Arts Select Committee, Alan Thompson, Deputy Secretary for further and higher education, argued that in 1980 higher education had reached a point

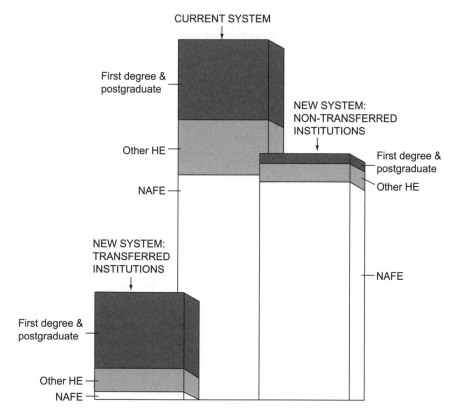

Figure 2.1 Distribution of polytechnic and college students* – present [1987] and proposed systems

Note: *Full-time equivalents.

Source: DES (1987), Figure Q, p. 35.

of change. For the previous 30 years higher education had been expanding both in student numbers and in state resources 'but it does seem to us that we have to take seriously the scenario that higher education may not be resourced for the future at any higher level than it is for this year and next . . . this is a new situation' (Select Committee on Education, Science and Arts 1980, para 35). The question he then asked was whether steering the system, and preventing stagnation and creating room for new developments was best left to the institutions themselves or 'that however difficult it is, it is the responsibility of government to take some sort of view about the shape, the profile, of the system as it is now and as it is going to develop in the future' (para 35). This was reinforced by a statement by the Secretary of State to the UGC that

it might be appropriate for Ministers to take more responsibility than they have hitherto for determining priorities affecting the broad character of the allocation of resources to universities ... the main thrust of policy for the universities must take due account of policy for higher education as a whole and of national social and economic policies ... at this level there will be some strategic decisions for which it would be appropriate for Ministers to take explicit responsibility and to answer to Parliament.

(Joseph 1982)

The creation of NAB represented a compromise towards establishing machinery to enable the Secretary of State to provide a broad steer across universities and the public sector. The NAB, however, was found increasingly unfit for purpose. But the UGC was also showing signs of no longer offering appropriate machinery. It was all very well acting as a 'collective Minister' when there was no Minister but continuing to do so when in 1981 it took what Ministers regarded as a 'political' decision to reduce student numbers in the university to preserve the unit of resource was another matter. There was also the question of the UGC's legal standing: as a committee originally established by the Treasury it was simply transferred with no change in legal status to the DES in 1964. Just as the Chancellor of the Exchequer had been formally responsible for its decisions so the Secretary of State for Education and Science took on the responsibility. When the Secretary of State found himself answering questions in the House about why he had cut student numbers in 1981 or why the cuts had been administered without regard to regional needs he was defending decisions from which he had been specifically excluded. The 1981 leaked DES document made it clear that the Department proposed to come back to the UGC's legal status.

However accountability for policy decisions paled into insignificance in the Whitehall context as compared to financial accountability. The Permanent Secretary was the Accounting Officer for the university system and had access as an observer to UGC meetings but was required by convention to leave the meeting when discussions about individual universities' finances took place. Even if the convention had not existed the Permanent Secretary's position would have been anomalous since he had no control over the financial decisions the UGC made. The Jarratt Committee had recommended a review of the UGC's legal status but added impetus was given to the review that was eventually set up through a committee under the chairmanship of Lord Croham, a former Permanent Secretary to the Treasury, by the Cardiff financial breakdown. This was a case where the UGC had failed to take action to prevent University College Cardiff from reaching the verge of bankruptcy, where the College auditors had refused the UGC access to their reports and where the Principal had permitted an accumulated deficit to arise as a 'political' protest against the budget reductions generated by the 1981 cuts (Shattock 1988, 1994). The Public Accounts Committee (PAC) was severely critical of the UGC for taking too passive a role in failing to challenge the College's own view of its financial position (PAC 1990). The DES evidence to the PAC was that the UGC would be replaced by a Universities

Funding Council a principal objective of which was 'to reorder and clarify responsibilities for propriety and value for money in relation to public funding made available to universities . . . it will be an executive body which determines and makes payments to individual universities' (PAC 1990). This suggests that the reform of accountability responsibilities was the prime reason for the change but, in fact, the White Paper went much further using the opportunity to redraw the respective distribution of powers of the main policy-making bodies in higher education in favour of the Secretary of State.

From the creation of NAB and the nurturing of a relationship between NAB and the UGC the need for a trans-binary 'over arching' body had been much discussed. The Croham Report highlighted this with its proposal for a National Education Commission. In rejecting it the White Paper made it clear that this was a role to be exercised by the Secretary of State, that he had powers to direct the Universities Funding Council, the successor to the UGC, as much as he had for the new PCFC and that the UGC's privileged policy-making role was brought to an end as effectively in its way as the local authorities' role in the development of the public sector. That this was a watershed in the policy-making machinery was emphasized by the introduction of the notion of higher education institutions contracting for funding against meeting defined objectives, the appointment of the two funding council chief executives (the chief officer of the UGC was no longer to be its chairman) as accounting officers for their sectors and the establishment of financial memoranda which imposed service conditions on institutions receiving funding; tenure was to be abolished. This went beyond a tidying up exercise, though it was presented as such, but represented a significant change in the special position which universities had occupied within the Whitehall community. In its *Strategy for Higher Education in the 1990s* the UGC had said:

> that an intermediary body is essential. We are not the servants either of Government or of the universities. As one half of our task we shall continue to assert to Government the needs of the universities for resources which will enable them to provide teaching and research of the highest quality as they must always aim to do. As the other half of our task we shall guide and encourage universities towards the changes we are convinced they must make . . .
>
> (UGC 1984 para 11.22)

The White Paper and subsequent legislation made it abundantly clear that the UFC was to be a 'servant of Government' and that its role of independent adviser was to be conducted behind closed doors. (According to a senior official interviewed by Hanney it was the Treasury not the DES which vetoed the UFC's advice to the secretary of state being tendered publically.)[105] By the same token the removal of local authority control and the granting of degree awarding powers brought the polytechnics into a position of legal parity with the university sector which offered, from the perspective of the state, a much more fruitful basis for the coordination of a much larger higher education system than had existed before.

The Baker White Paper and the subsequent Education Reform Act marked, in some senses, a bigger turning point in relations between higher education and the state than the 1992 Act which translated the polytechnics into universities, abolished PCFC and UFC and devolved funding to Scotland and Wales. Hindsight might suggest that the 1986 White Paper provisions might have made the 1992 merging of the sectors inevitable but that is not how contemporary actors saw it. Evidence obtained from civil servants conducted by Kogan and Hanney, and later myself, certainly point in the direction that they saw the 1986 decisions as being likely to last for some time. McGregor, who succeeded Baker as Secretary of State, seemed only too happy to follow in Baker's footsteps and as late as the CVCP's 1990 September Residential Conference, McGregor in his speech raised no issues of great substance and certainly no mention of any immediate change in polytechnic status.[106] Both CDP and CVCP were extremely exercised about funding issues. The 1989–94 spurt in the growth in student numbers was in full swing and questions about expansion at marginal costs dominated the discourse. But changes were afoot in both camps. The CDP as a body had come a long way from the rather ragged committee which had to beg for funds from CLEA to form a secretariat. Representation on NAB had given it a part in the policy process and relations with DES officials were always much better than the CVCP's. Within CDP there had been a tendency for southern directors to dominate and Ray Ricketts from Middlesex had a long reign as chairman both because his proximity to the Department meant that consultation was easy and because his politics gave him an entrée to Government. In 1986, however, a *coup d'état* was organized and a northern director, John Stoddart, from Sheffield Hallam, with a much more radical political background, was elected. Stoddart was a formidably shrewd political operator and, taking on the representation of CDP just at the point when polytechnics became free of the local authorities, gave him a powerful base.

Two other issues, however, tell us something about CDP attitudes post the 1986 White Paper. The first was a concern about title. In 1987 Leonard Barden, the Director of Northumbria Polytechnic circulated a paper to the CDP suggesting that the forthcoming 1988 legislation should change the polytechnics name to Polytechnic University. This was primarily a recruitment device: there was, he argued, a status gap in relation to home students but the case was even stronger in relation to students from overseas where the polytechnic title was 'either a source of suspicion or [was] simply confusing'. He wanted, he said, parity of status, but he thought it would take 20 to 30 years more to achieve.[107] The second was a concern about mission. Barden argued that he did not want polytechnics to become traditional universities but to 'preserve the distinctive role laid down in 1966'. This was a view shared by many polytechnic directors, including Stoddart. Difficult to define, this was to remain a muted theme in the further development of higher education.

In January 1991, the CDP commissioned John Pratt and Michael Locke of the North East London Polytechnic to prepare four papers on CDP strategy, a PR campaign, negotiating machinery for a unitary higher education system and to identify further issues. Even at this late stage, when it was apparent that consideration within the DES was already being given to the abolition of the binary line and only three months before the publication of the decisive White Paper there remained indecision about whether the discussion three years previously should be resurrected to seek the title polytechnic university rather than expect the full university title to be granted. Such a decision certainly did not seem inevitable to the CDP. Although Stoddart showed foresight in commissioning the briefing of these papers their timing makes it clear that the speed of the change of heart within the DES took the CDP by surprise.

Meantime the CVCP had commissioned an internal report on its operations conducted by Lord Flowers, its chairman. The Report prompted an extensive internal debate about the CVCP's role. Parkes (now Vice-Chancellor of Leeds), Flowers' successor as chairman had produced an outline of the CVCP's view of its mission which Sir Eric Ash, Rector of Imperial College, was asked to present as a full document for discussion at the October 1990 residential conference. The fate of his response marks an important change in CVCP policy. His paper roundly rejected the basis of Ball's argument in *More Means Different* (Ball 1990) which restated the Barden view about mission, in the following terms:

> There is little benefit to be derived from disguising with soft focus, egalitarian language, the fact that the special responsibility of the university system is the education of the most able of our youth, the pursuit of research – pure and applied – at the highest levels of endeavour, and the role of the guardian, interpreter and critic of our cultural heritage . . . the accumulation and concentration of talent is not a symptom of contrived elitism. It should be seen for what it is – a natural phenomenon.[108]

This was a robust defence of traditional university aspirations. However it was not adopted as the CVCP's view of its mission and Ash was encouraged to publish the document under his own name rather than under the CVCP's as was originally intended. The reason it was not adopted was that although perhaps a majority of vice-chancellors supported the vision that it articulated, it was no longer deemed politic to express university objectives in these terms. The CDP's mission was seen to have gained traction with Ministers.

Earlier that year the CVCP and the CDP had set up a joint working group – five members from each side chaired by John (later Sir John) Ashworth, vice-chancellor of Salford – to look at long term funding mechanisms for what, in the rapid expansion of student numbers, had now become a mass higher education system. McGregor had argued in a speech at Portsmouth that in the 1990s higher education could be paid for out of efficiency gains and raising non-government income.[109] The group's report, which was agreed by both bodies, rejected this and canvassed for the first time top-up fees and repayable loan schemes. It concluded that: 'Simply to continue with present policies will lead to a demoralised, poor quality system, which will be incapable of meeting the real needs of society. Wait and see is not a viable option'.[110] Stoddart, in his speech taking over as chairman of CDP, echoed the report's conclusions: 'There is a balance to be struck between quality and price and, although some further modest efficiency gains may be obtainable and any further significant increase in numbers without an increase in resources must mean that the quality of education provided will fall'.[111] The significance of the working group's findings and of Stoddart's speech was not so much the solution proposed but the shared concern: the CDP and the CVCP had reached a common view. At a dinner between CVCP and CDP in January 1991 both sides agreed: 'that the binary system had largely had its day. A single funding council would, the CDP felt, increase the diversity between institutions'.[112] The adoption of a common cause on how to respond to the funding crisis had brought the two sides together: DES/Treasury parsimony had created a common enemy. It was not at all what DES officials expected when they removed local authority control over the public sector.

Three factors combined to bring about the 1991 White Paper: the first was that with the arrival of Stoddart as chairman of the CDP the CDP adopted a much more effective political style. It is evident from both CVCP and CDP files that the joint working group on funding increased the personal respect on both sides; it also proved they could work together. These messages were picked up in the DES where there had been a change in Secretary of State from the competent but conventional McGregor, himself a former university administrator, to the much more robust Kenneth Clarke fresh from confrontations with the NHS. The officials thought that a review was necessary and asked Clarke whether he wanted to give them a steer. He declined preferring to see what the review concluded. Papers were commissioned and recommendations made; Clarke concurred without external consultation, except for one late night session with vice-chancellor cronies at the bar after a conference; a paper went to the Cabinet committee on education and was nodded through. Indeed there was so little reaction at the meeting that Clarke wrote afterwards to members to ask them to confirm their support.[113]

The actual initiative lay with the DES officials, but politically there was a following wind. Clarke could be assured of the Prime Minister's support. Major, in his autobiography writes of his dislike of 'inverted snobbery' in education and of the need 'to abolish the false divide between polytechnics and universities' (Major 1999: 212). Major was not in any sense an initiator of the decision; more persuasive was that the proximity of the 1992 General Election gave the Conservatives an opportunity to spike Labour's guns. Perhaps only an iconoclast like Clarke would have seized the moment with such vigour. Apparently he had no doubts about the conferment of the full university title unlike some members of the CDP. Kogan and Hanney quote a conversation with a polytechnic director about granting degree awarding powers without a full university title. 'Clarke seemed to think this was just messing about "let's take the plunge and make them all universities, let's get rid of all the arguments"' (Kogan and Hanney 2000: 138). Officials suggest that his successor, John Patten, would certainly not have reacted in the same way; George Walden, a previous Minister for higher education, was opposed to it and argued that polytechnics were made universities because of 'class consciousness'. On voicing his misgivings to ministers he was 'In effect . . . told that the pressure for change had become irresistible, and that it was one of those ideas whose time had come'. He thought that the Government 'had lost the will to resist' (Walden 1996: 184).

There was, however, an overriding economic argument for ending the binary line. As one civil servant put it: 'the government wanted to create competition for expansion . . . inevitably if you've got two distinct sectors then that competition is somewhat weakened and by drawing the two together into a single unified sector, everyone competing with one another on equal terms you can gain more from competition'.[114] The sudden acceleration in student demand from 1988–89 had encouraged a resort to market approaches by the PCFC and the UFC. The former had successfully sought to stimulate growth at marginal costs only, while the latter had embarked on an ill thought out bidding exercise based on so-called price levels. This had proved to be an embarrassing failure with the universities all bidding at a more or less common price level. The unit costs of the two sectors had accordingly diverged. Bringing them together and rationalizing the band price per discipline was to produce significant economies at the pre-1992 universities' expense. In a situation where the Department had to solicit repeated supplementary allocations from the Treasury to contain the alarming expansion in student numbers any move to a more economical funding system was much to be welcomed.

The abolition of the binary line provoked two further important changes to the shape of higher education: devolution of decision making to Scotland and Wales, and the replacement of the PCFC and the UFC with new Higher Education Funding Councils for England, Wales and Scotland. The dominant mode of thinking behind the White Paper was the need to coordinate better a rapidly growing and increasingly expensive higher education system. To have sought to do this on a unitary basis would have immediately run up against the technical issue that FE and AFE in Scotland were the responsibility of the Scottish Education Department. The writ of the Woolwich speech had only run in England and Wales, and the 1988 Act had no purchase north of the border. Indeed the 1987 White Paper had had to pay special regard to the widely respected recommendations of the Scottish Tertiary Education Advisory Council's (STEAC) report *Future Strategy for Higher Education in Scotland* (1985) which had urged the establishment of a single funding body for universities and non-universities in Scotland. The 1987 White Paper response was a special Scottish committee of the new UFC with a reporting relationship to the Secretary of State for Scotland. This, in Scots eyes, was an inadequate half way house. Abolishing the binary line outside Scotland thus raised an immediate political question. The mood amongst politicians was that more concessions needed to be made to Scotland and political decisions overrode any belief in the efficacy of maintaining a unified university system especially if it involved confrontation with the Scottish Education Department.

Similar considerations did not, however, apply in Wales and many Whitehall officials were concerned that Welsh higher education was too small a system to warrant devolution especially when about half the places in Welsh universities were recruited from England. The devolution of Welsh higher education was a political consequence of decisions in respect to Scotland. One argument for the devolution could have been to introduce greater diversity into higher education decision making but interview evidence suggests that it was solely a political decision.[115] Subsequent events, apart from the decision by the Scottish Parliament not to follow the English decision to charge tuition fees, have not suggested wide divergences in policy. The retention of a unified Research Assessment Exercise (RAE)/Research Excellence Framework (REF) and quality assurance, though the latter has a Scottish variant, has ensured that the main drivers of the British higher education system remain in place although the greater proximity of the Scottish Government and the Welsh Assembly to their institutions has undoubtedly encouraged greater localism in the policy process. The HEFCE remains the dominant Funding Council if only because it is responsible for a much larger system with 131 higher education institutions in 2009–10 against 19 in Scotland, 11 in Wales and four in Northern Ireland.

The replacement of the PCFC and the UFC by HEFCs followed naturally from the decision to abolish the binary line. The UFC had not been a success. The appointment of Lord Chilver as Chairman of the UFC with a clear political intent to marketize the university system did not sit comfortably with the model of a post-Croham UGC, especially when the former outstandingly effective UGC Chairman, Sir Peter Swinnerton Dyer, remained as chief executive. The divisions within the UFC rendered it ineffective and paved the way for its replacement by a very different sort of body. By comparison the PCFC a bureaucratically rationale and transparent alternative to NAB was popular with its constituents. The new HEFCE not only acquired Sir Ron (later Lord) Dearing, the chairman of the PCFC, as its chairman but took over many of the procedural characteristics of the PCFC. It was a funding not a planning body, 'unjustified differences in funding methodologies' were to be eliminated (DES 1991 para 24), subject committees were to be abolished and research rewarded competitively through selectivity, determined objectively, by RAEs. This was a body set up to monitor and encourage institutional competition to promote the most cost effective use of resources within an imperative to contain public spending; policy was to be pushed 'upstairs' to the Department to be delivered through annual letters of guidance from the Secretary of State. As Scott described them 'The new funding councils are agents of government not buffer bodies . . . The job of HEFCE and other councils is to implement governments predetermined objectives through second order policies' (Scott 1995: 27). This may be too bleak an assessment because as Tapper argues, it tends to underrate both the private interplay between the Funding Council and officials in the Department and the policy choices implicit in implementation (Tapper 2007: 41). Taggart, however, also describes the fundamental shift in the relationship with the state in the following terms: 'it was once the role of the state to provide for the purposes of universities; it is now the role of universities to provide for the purposes of the state' (Taggart 2004: 113).

The passage of the 1992 Act marked the end of a process initiated by the Woolwich speech where an alternative sector to the universities was consciously created by government. On the one hand, one might argue that the Robbins wheel had come full circle. Robbins argued that by 1980 some 10 non-university institutions of higher education might have qualified for upgrading to university status and by 1992 the expansion in student numbers might realistically have justified, on Robbins criteria, the upgrading of the 29 English and Welsh institutions and eight Scottish institutions which changed their status as a result of the Act. However, numbers do not tell the whole story. Viewed from the perspective of 1992 none of the arguments for a dual system of higher education quoted in the Woolwich speech proved to have been realized. On the first, that there was a need for a separate sector with a separate tradition to take forward the required increase in vocational education, Booth shows that by 1987 the percentage of students following engineering and technology in polytechnics had fallen from 44 per cent to 18 per cent, and that the numbers in science only amounted to 17 per cent; part time numbers had grown more slowly than full time and sub degree programmes even more slowly (Booth 1999). Indeed, in 1983, in response to Sir Keith Joseph's consultation exercise NAB had said: 'A policy which identifies one side of the binary line as more vocational than the other is neither accurate nor helpful' (NAB 1983). Growth had primarily taken place in the social sciences and the humanities (partly driven by the mergers with colleges of education), and in full time degrees. With university numbers held back the polytechnics, in particular, acted as a second choice for university applicants. The binary policy did not halt academic drift and it certainly did not 'reverse a hundred years of educational history', a claim made by the senior civil servant who advised the government (presumably Weaver) quoted by Pratt (1999), rather it exemplified it.

The creation of an alternative category of institutions did not eliminate 'a continuous rat race to reach the First or University Division' (DES 1965) rather it accelerated it. From its second meeting the CDP set as one of its targets the achievement of university status and much of its lobbying of Ministers was directed to this end. But the title of polytechnic never achieved the cachet which it had on the continent of Europe. In a paper entitled 'Institutional Title: What's in a Name' written in 1988, Lewis the CDP Secretary argued that the lack of the university title was a decisive disadvantage in recruitment, and particularly of international students. The marketing image was the determinant. Although ministers talked, he said of a separate mission 'It is difficult to see how their respective missions are so very different, but the claim that there is a difference provides a convenient pretext for the Government's retaining the disparity levels between the universities and the polytechnics'.[116] In practice 'healthy rivalry where their work overlaps' (DES 1965) did not really occur. Booth concurs that parity of esteem was never achieved (Booth 1999).

But the greatest failure lay in the argument for the need for a sector subject to social control. There were, as we have seen from their reaction in the 1950s to the extension of degree awarding powers for technological studies and for teacher education, grounds for regarding the universities as aloof and conservative but the argument that they lacked a sense of social engagement was almost certainly rooted in a metropolitan view of Oxbridge and the University of London. To anyone familiar with the civic universities, particularly the 'JMB' universities in the north of England or the ancient Scottish universities, it produced no resonance whatsoever. The criticism was even less true of the newly upgraded CATs which were strongly local in character. Booth in his account of the rise of the 'new' universities states (and he was himself a DES official for part of this period) that DES officials of the 1960s and 70s subscribed to the maximum extent to the idea of devolution to local authorities and quotes Mulley, a Labour Secretary of State, as saying that if one stopped a civil servant in the corridor and asked him the time he would answer 'Sorry Minister but that is a matter for the local authorities' (Booth 1999). However for Weaver, as for Robinson and Burgess, it was also an ideological issue which again, based on a metropolitan (ILEA orientated) view of local authorities, failed to take account of the dynamics of provincial local authority control. The dominant characteristic of LEA oversight was not pressure for social relevance in the curriculum but for political and financial control. Even Pratt, an apologist for the binary line and the leading authority on the polytechnics, accepted that ultimately the polytechnic policy had proved to be unsuccessful 'particularly the key issues of social control' (Pratt 1999).

The failure of the binary policy, however, had deeper consequences. Robbins, in an address at Harvard in 1964 before the Woolwich speech, argued that one rationale for a unitary policy was simply that the prestige of a university career and degree was such as to render most alternatives a decidedly second best (Robbins 1966). The binary policy, as Robbins prophesied, increased the sense of hierarchy in British higher education rather than lessened it. Crosland's intention was to avoid a 'ladder' principle where there was 'constant pressure from below to ape the universities above' (DES 1965). At a meeting with the CVCP in November 1966 he suggested that 'there was no political possibility of establishing a unitary system composed wholly of autonomous institutions' and that therefore a binary line was 'relatively advantageous to universities'. The polytechnics were 'primarily to provide teaching' although research would 'not be ruled out', and would have lower costs.[117] Such a policy constituted a contradiction of any idea of parity of esteem and, when the Advisory Board of the Research Councils (ABRC) produced its *A Strategy for the Science Base* 20 years later identifying three institutional types, R, T and X defined by research capacity, the polytechnics fell naturally into Type T as 'Institutions highly competent in undergraduate and MSc teaching with staff engaged in scholarship and research necessary to support and develop that teaching, but without provision of advanced research facilities' (ABRC 1987). The definition was confirmed by the 1992 RAE.

Rather than providing a sector to compete with the universities the 1966 *Plan for Polytechnics* condemned public sector institutions to an alternative and much less favourable regime for around a quarter of a century from which it has proved hard to recover. Whereas ex CATs like Loughborough, Bath and Surrey pulled out of the pack to be CATs only in 1956, less than a decade before the Woolwich speech, flourished both academically and in the media league tables, none of the ex polytechnics have as yet been able to overcome the disadvantage of entering the RAE on such unfavourable terms. Looked at from the perspective of 2012, 20 years after the abolition of the binary line, although it is evident that many post-1992 universities have developed into strong institutions and some performed effectively in the 2008 RAE the disadvantages inherent in the regime of their previous 25 years continued to prejudice their reputation and ability to compete with the majority of pre-1992 institutions in terms of recruitment and research income. It is, of course, arguable that the Robbins evolutionary approach might have foundered in the economic stringencies of the 1980s but the processes of system management since 1992, even tailored as they were to mass higher education student numbers, do not suggest that steering an enhanced body of autonomous universities would have been any more difficult, or less liable to produce institutional diversity than managing two sectors with allegedly differing missions. The 1992 Act and the subsequent upgrading of higher education colleges has to some extent redressed the decisions of 1965–66 but has not removed the effect of the binary line. The creation of reputational groupings of the Russell Group, the 94 Group and Million Plus serve to emphasize that the hierarchical divisions imposed by historical forces, while not immutable, are hard to eradicate.

Since 1992 the institutional shape of higher education has remained unchanged except for the upgrading of some 13 further institutions to university status. One question, however, that remains is whether the abolition of the binary line produced any fundamental change in what constituted a university. The CDP and particularly Stoddart was concerned that in merging with the university sector the distinctive features of the polytechnics would be lost and that the polytechnic tradition should not be 'overwhelmed or derailed'.[118] These distinctive features were not defined with any clarity but may be deduced as a commitment to widening access, to part time education and to local engagement, as well as a more business like style of management than in the pre-92 universities. Stoddart put an optimistic gloss on the implication of the 1992 Act in a final message in the CDP Newsletter *Direct*:

> The abolition of the binary line was not a belated ticket of admission to the university 'club' but a recognition, and indeed affirmation of the educational, social and economic importance of the type of higher

education the polytechnics offered. In abolishing the binary line the Government was redefining the notion of what higher education actually is.

(Stoddart 1992)

The publication of the first *Times Good University Guide* in October 1992 prompted early recognition of the public reaction with Stoddart's own university, Sheffield Hallam, ranked at 68th. Only Ulster, which was created as a result of a merger between Belfast Polytechnic and the New University of Ulster at Coleraine, appeared below the break point of pre- and post-1992 universities. The chairs of the CVCP and CDP wrote a joint letter of protest to which *The Times* replied quoting Adam Smith: 'the discipline of colleges and universities is in general contrived, not for the benefit of the students but for the interest, or more, properly speaking, the case of the masters' (*The Times* 14 October 1992). When the post-92 universities were invited to enter the 1992 RAE only the University of Central England chose not to do so. In some ways the absorption of the polytechnics into the CVCP organization was a symbol of the whole issue of distinctiveness although this would ignore the much greater commitment to widening access in most post-92 universities.

In the late 1950s many of the civic universities were in the process of dropping non-degree vocational courses, for example in textiles at Leeds, because of the pressure of applicants for full time degree programmes. It was still the case that, prior to the creation of the Universities Central Council on Admissions (UCCA), most of their recruitment was local. At the same time many of the university colleges on the UGC grant list like the University College of the South West (Exeter) or that of Hull were only beginning to build up research. In that sense the merger of the two sectors could be said to have aligned the character of the new merged system with the university sector of the early 1960s, but it could not be said that it brought fundamental change. The two sectors had already grown significantly by 1992 and it was the impact of the RAEs and the reputational benefits which universities derived from them which served two decades later to re-define the unitary system. What had changed was the relationship between the universities and the state. The greater coordination required by the merger of the two sectors, the increasing concern in Whitehall over the costs of the system and the bureaucratic machinery implicit in the operation of HEFCE, and the other Funding Councils, imposed a much more regulated approach to the management of higher education.

The governance of the system: changes in the policy-making machinery

We have seen in the preceding sections how changes in the shape of British higher education were driven by the expansion of student numbers, the expedients which different governments employed to steer and/or manage the system and the impact of politics and personalities on the process. Throughout the period the key bodies comprised the responsible government department, the intermediary funding bodies and the representative bodies of the heads of institutions. After 1964 the Treasury ceased to be the responsible department and assumed a new and constant role which is described in Chapter 3. On relatively rare occasions Parliament itself became involved through the House of Commons, the House of Lords or the PAC or a select committee but these were episodic interventions which may have been game changing but which did not issue from any consistent commitment to steering and/or merging the system. The three major governance components varied in their policy weight over the period within the general trend of an increasing dominance by the government department as public expenditure on higher education grew and as the conduct of government business became increasingly centralized. Between 1946 and 1981 it is clear that the effective organs of policy making, except in respect to the overall financing of the system, lay for the universities in the hands of the UGC, working in close partnership with the CVCP, and for institutions in the public sector, the local authorities. (The DES had created the polytechnics but adopted a hands off approach to management of the public sector until the creation of NAB in 1982.) But from 1981, and the UGC's implementation of the Thatcher cuts in public expenditure, until 2011, what we see is a cumulative transfer of policy-making weight to the responsible government department through the 1988 and 1992 legislation and the 2003 and 2011 White Papers at the expense of the intermediary and representative bodies. In addition, between 1997 and 2011 we see an increasing attempt to integrate higher education policy with wider government policies through the operation of New Public Management (NPM) approaches.

In the period up to Robbins, the policy-making machinery rested essentially with a troika of authorities, the Treasury in respect to funding, but not in what would now be regarded as higher education policy, the UGC in respect to resource allocation and university policy, the latter, however, being developed in close consultation with the third leg of the troika, the CVCP. Somewhere off to the side one found the Board, then Ministry, of Education mostly concerned with primary and secondary school education but with control over teacher education, which was functionally linked to the universities' own interests in education through the PGCE and in respect to links with the colleges. Again, as we have seen, both Butler and Wilkinson cast aggrandizing eyes on the university sector when in charge of education, although Butler did not pursue the issue as Chancellor. The UGC, particularly under Murray's chairmanship from 1953 to 1963, pursued a symbiotic relationship with the Treasury. In areas of contention between the Ministry and the universities, the universities had powerful allies: their monopoly of degree awarding powers was protected and the decision by the Treasury to invest in the expansion of science and technology in the universities blew a hole in the arguments put forward by the Ministry and the local authorities for a move towards parity. The 1956 Technical Education Act, while influential for the future, represented a second best, symbolized by the restriction placed on the CATs to award a Dip.Tech. instead of a degree. The Ministry was a low status department in Whitehall. Even as late as the mid-1970s Donoughue could write:

> The problem for all of them [Secretaries of State for Education] was that their department had little power. Education was conducted by the local authorities and the teachers' unions, with the Department of Education, as Harold Wilson once commented to me, being little more than a post box between them.
>
> (Donoughue 1986: 110)

On the other hand the Ministry had one considerable strength, the concept of the 'seamless robe', the belief that educational policy from primary to university levels was linked and ought to be brought together under one roof. This argument was thought to have merit even by those in the Treasury who had little respect for the Ministry's capabilities. Nowhere was this more evident than in respect to teacher education where the argument that the Ministry was responsible for teacher supply, held sway over the case made by Robbins for strengthening the colleges by linking them administratively to the universities. The Ministry, therefore, might appear not to be a significant force but actually its position was quite strong and could easily be underestimated.

Paradoxically the CVCP's position was the opposite – it seemed to be a powerful force, and certainly included some powerful advocates, but in the end it suffered from three chronic weaknesses. The first was that it represented a spectrum of institutions of varying size, history and national standing so that to reach a common view and to be able to act quickly and decisively was always difficult, and was to become more so when the 1960s new universities and the ex CATs joined it. Vice-chancellors also represented only themselves and could not always rely on their home institutions to support them. Peter (later Sir Peter) Venables, the Vice-Chancellor of Aston, commented that when he joined in 1964: 'The Committee could not speak for universities in any constitutional sense of acting collectively on their behalf without prior approval from each and every institution in membership. Great caution amounting to distinguished inertia was always inherently possible' (Venables 1978: 53).

A second chronic weakness was that its members tended, perhaps because they were so effectively buffered from outside pressures by the UGC and the Treasury, to cling to unrealistic views of their status. In 1954, for example, the Committee loftily agreed that all four university colleges on the UGC grant list (Exeter, Hull, Leicester and Nottingham) should be permitted to become members instead of only two representatives on the grounds that it was 'Unlikely that any further university colleges will be set up in the next 20–30 years'.[119] They took what can only be described as a dismissive view of the Ministry and showed little interest in engaging in dialogue with officials there. One can only speculate what effect cultivating Weaver might have had but the gulf of understanding in the Ministry about the universities outside London was only equalled by the gulf in the CVCP's understanding in how the Ministry worked. The divorce from the Treasury would not have seemed so sharp if it had been appreciated how respectful the Department would be towards the UGC's position right up to 1981. In an interview with McConnell in 1970, Weaver explained that if it was necessary for him to write officially to Berrill, then Chairman of the UGC, he would list the points and invite Berrill to draft the letter. If a Minister had said anything significant publicly about the universities he would have lunch with Berrill to pass any messages on. In a second interview in 1973 he claimed that he and Berrill had devised together most of the DES/UGC policies of the period.[120] The CVCP made a grave error in judgement in being so publicly resistant to the idea of responsibility for the universities being transferred to the Ministry.

The third chronic weakness was that the CVCP could only achieve real influence through the UGC. When Murray was in charge it could expect a sympathetic, if not a uniformally collegial response. But with the arrival of Wolfendon relations became more formal, and as we have seen Wolfendon showed himself to be much less supportive of university interests in respect to the teacher training colleges as compared to those of the DES.

As with much else in the development of higher education the discussions and conclusions around the Robbins Report proved to be a watershed in determining the future structure of the policy-making machinery. It was already becoming apparent within the Treasury that it could no longer be the department responsible for financing the university system. Public expenditure on higher education as a whole had more than doubled between 1954 and 1955 and 1960 and 1961 (of which the universities' share was almost 60 per cent) and internal drafts of the Treasury's evidence to Robbins suggested a fourfold increase might be necessary by 1980 and that the proportion of GDP might rise by two- or threefold.[121]

Otto Clarke, who was in charge of public expenditure, had already set in motion the Plowden Review, which was to make radical changes in the Treasury's role in the allocation of public expenditure (and was to precipitate the crisis in relations with the UGC in 1962 – see below) and it was clear to officials that the Treasury's position in relation to the control of, and the accountability for, university finance had become increasingly anomalous. It was also clear to most officials that the Treasury's support of the universities' objection to being accountable to the Comptroller and Auditor General and the Public Accounts Committee also had to go, not least because the Treasury's guilty secret about the over expenditure on the development of the Imperial College site might, if it ever became public, expose it to serious questioning as to the moral high ground it adopted in relation to financial control in other departments.

It is evident from the files that Treasury officials while accepting that they must divest themselves of responsibility for university affairs were also anxious to preserve the autonomy implicit in the UGC's role and were prepared to cast around for solutions other than the obvious one of a transfer to the Ministry of Education. The Treasury was careful not to make a recommendation in its public evidence as to the precise location of Ministerial responsibility. However a letter from Burke Trend, the Permanent Secretary, to Robbins himself, asking to give evidence on this question in private, commented on an early draft of the Report that 'I doubt whether the chapter as it stands gives quite a fair run to the proposal to entrust the whole of education to the Ministry of Education. Although I have always had – and still have – doubts about this proposition. I think both you and I felt that, the more we considered it the less unattractive it became'.[122] This was hardly a resounding endorsement of the Ministry but as the letter went on to argue such a transfer would at least ensure that a single Minister would command a seat in Cabinet while, if responsibility was divided across two Ministries, as Robbins eventually proposed, one part of higher education, probably the universities, would not be so represented.

The Ministry of Education's evidence represents a curious split in opinion. The written evidence was fairly obviously prepared by Weaver and was critical of the involvement of the universities in wider areas of higher education policy but the oral evidence which was led on the first occasion by Anthony Part, who had been responsible for creating the CATs, and on the second by Dame Mary Smieton, the Permanent Secretary, who attended UGC meetings and was clearly influenced by this, presented a very different picture. While they made a strong case for a single Minister of Education taking responsibility for the universities they were also ready to conceive of a single Minister responsible for the whole of higher education. At the first session Part offered two alternatives both of which involved setting up a new department. One was for a department which was to be responsible for a number of grants committees, modelled on the UGC, one catering for the universities, one for the College of Aeronautics (later Cranfield), the Royal College of Arts, the CATs and the Scottish central institutions, and a third for most or perhaps all of the regional technical colleges and all the teacher training colleges (some 220 institutions outside the universities). The second alternative was more modest: to restrict the grants committees to two, one for the universities and one for university colleges (a category of institution not defined but to include the CATs). This would exclude the regional technical colleges and most of the teacher training colleges; inclusion would be restricted to those institutions which had full academic autonomy. The university colleges would be designated by the grants committee in consultation with the relevant Ministry or Department. He argued that this alternative was evolutionary and allowed the local authorities 'to assist the further development of these colleges up to the point where a college is ready to become a university college or part of a university'.[123] The problem over the second alternative was that it would involve a selection within the teacher training colleges 'between those "promoted" within the grants committees' ambit and those who would regard themselves as "left behind" especially if they were to remain under the local education authorities' (Committee on Higher Education 1963: 180).

There is little here of the subservience to local authority views which was to characterize the views of the DES when Weaver took over responsibility for higher education. A Higher Education Council would coordinate the two grants committees. This is the first appearance of the idea of an overarching body which would coordinate university and public sector higher education and safeguard 'the essential liberties of institutions at a time when public interest in higher education may be expected to grow rapidly' (Committee on Higher Education 1963: 109), that is to protect institutions from meddling by ministers or civil servants of whatever Ministry to which responsibility for higher education was to be transferred. The idea of an overarching body was to be much canvassed after the creation of NAB and had a late flowering in the 1989 Croham Report but in practice it would have been surprising if any government department would have abrogated its power to coordinate higher education policy to an external body of the great and the good either in the 1960s or in the 1980s.

At the end of the second session Lord Robbins summed up the fears expressed by university witnesses about universities being put under a 'schools Ministry' but Part replied robustly that such fears were unnecessary. The spearhead of the opposition to transferring to the Ministry of Education, though it was voiced by many others giving evidence, was the CVCP on the grounds that it would be a step towards coordination and that it would lead to the kind of detailed controls over universities that vice-chancellors believed the Ministry exercised over schools.[124] Neither argument could be said to be justified by the Department's actions at least until 1981. In practice the CVCP was divided between those who clung to the partnership with the UGC and wanted the UGC to remain under the Treasury and those like its Chairman, Sir William Mansfield Cooper, who recognized that the Treasury could not continue in its previous role and therefore favoured the establishment of a separate department.[125] This was, in fact, what the Robbins Committee came to recommend, though it widened the proposed department's brief by the inclusion of the research councils and the Arts Council's museums and galleries, which were also located under the Treasury. The recommendation provoked the Note of Reservation by H.C. Shearman who opposed a Ministry of Arts and Science, on the seamless robe argument particularly quoting the issue of teacher training.

This argument was subsequently to triumph in that a new Department of Education and Science was created which incorporated the old Ministry of Education. Lord Hailsham, who as Lord Privy Seal had been given responsibility for implementing Robbins, became Secretary of State for Education and Science and Sir Edward Boyle, who had been Minister for Education, stepped down to become Minister of State for Education, responsible for higher education, but retaining his seat in the Cabinet. Boyle told Kogan that there was 'considerable interest in whether there should be one Minister or two with the Treasury very much supporting the former but the issue could not be discussed in Cabinet because it offended the principle of the Prime Minister's right to appoint Ministers' (Kogan 1971: 106). According to

Carswell the eventual decision was brokered by Sir Lawrence (later Lord) Helsby the Head of the Civil Service (Carswell 1985) but Boyle told Kogan that the decisive moment was the speech by Lord James of Rusholme, Vice-Chancellor of York, in the House of Lords debate on Robbins, where as a former headmaster he argued for unity within the decision-making machinery for education. James's stance illustrates only too clearly the divisions within the CVCP; James was of course too 'junior' a vice-chancellor to have been included in the group which gave oral guidance to Robbins. There was, however, more than a nod in the CVCP direction in the decision to give a second Permanent Secretary post to the new Department solely for higher education, the holder to be Accounting Officer for the universities. This apparently was intended by Helsby as an ingenious insulation of the universities from being answerable to the Comptroller and Auditor General, which Robbins had recommended firmly against. Part was appointed to the post but the arrangement collapsed when the Labour Government took office in 1964. Part was transferred to become Permanent Secretary of the new Department of Technology and was not replaced; Weaver was promoted from being Under Secretary in charge of schools to be Deputy Secretary responsible for higher and further education.

The dispute about Departmental responsibility and financial control was, however, entirely separable from any change in the status and autonomy of the UGC. Indeed, the upgrading of the Chairman's post to Permanent Secretary equivalent grade, could be seen, through civil servants' eyes at least, as an increased recognition of its standing. The UGC's estimates had to be incorporated into the DES submission to the Public Expenditure Survey Committee (PESC) instead of going direct to the Treasury and suffered sharp rebuffs under the pressures of the oil crisis but, on questions of policy, it remained unchallenged until 1981 when the incoming Secretary of State, Sir Keith Joseph, made it plain that the days of a policy vacuum in the DES in respect to universities were over.

In spite of the Ministry's apparent upgrading to DES and the dramatic rejection of the Robbins structure and the reinforcement of the binary line, the Department was much more responsive than directive in its relations with higher education. It exercised no control over the expansion of the polytechnics away from the vocationalism promised by Crosland. Summing this up in 1987, Annan wrote:

> The LEAs exercised little control over the polytechnics and the CNAA saw its job as validating courses put up to them by the polys. They asked whether courses were academically respectable rather than asking whether they are appropriate to the institutions. Large numbers of arts courses and degrees were established that had no relationship to business and industry.
>
> (Annan 1987: 171)

Although the DES ruthlessly cut back the colleges of education in the 1970s, it was doctrinaire in its subservience to the concept of the binary line in ensuring that all but two of the consequent college mergers occurred within the public sector instead of being cross-binary.

Margaret Thatcher, who became Secretary of State in 1971, soon discovered how closely linked her officials were to the teachers' trade union leaders and local authority politicians. She condemned the Department's ethos as 'self righteously socialist' (Thatcher 1995: 166) and warned Keith Joseph when she appointed him Secretary of State: 'You have an awful Department' (Baker 1993: 161). Her biographer says that Heath sent her to Education simply because he had to send her somewhere and describes the Department in the 1970s as having:

> an entrenched culture and a settled agenda of its own which it pursued with little reference to Ministers or the rest of Whitehall. The conviction was that education was above politics: government's job was to provide the money but otherwise leave the running of the education system to the professionals. Political control, such as it was, was exercised not by the DES but by educational authorities up and down the country . . . Political interference in the conduct of education was absolutely taboo. The Secretary of State, in fact, had very few executive powers at all.
>
> (Campbell 2000: 212)

These are, of course, Tory voices but they would have received tacit support from a Labour Minister for Higher Education, Lord Crowther Hunt, an academic from Oxford who found himself drafted into the DES by Harold Wilson in 1974 having distinguished himself in civil service reform. He described how, on appointment, he sought advice first from the Prime Minister and then from the Secretary of State, Prentice, as to what the Government's policy was on higher education and received no satisfactory answer. He supported fully an OECD Review's criticism of policy making in the Department that it was secretive in that it was not subject to outside comment, that its planning function was limited to identifying existing trends and that its thinking was too purely educationally orientated (Crowther Hunt 1983; OECD 1975). He proceeded, in a series of speeches and articles, with the notable absence of support from officials, to define some policies relating higher education outputs more closely to the economy but the initiative died as soon as the Wilson Government left office. While Maurice (later Lord) Peston who was head of policy in No.10 congratulated the Minister on 'stirring up these issues' officials and higher education as a whole believed that in articulating ideas about policy he was trespassing in a secret garden that was in the care of the UGC and the CVCP (Peston 1976).

It was perhaps inevitable that with Thatcher as Prime Minister, Government would choose to exercise greater influence over higher education. The economic crisis and mounting inflation, post the oil crisis of 1973–4, had been a policy neutral period punctuated, as far as the university sector was concerned, by alarming discrepancies in pay settlements as compared to the public sector. Her first Secretary of State, Mark Carlisle, was a dim figure, for the most part heavily dependent on his civil servants but one of these, the

Department's Deputy Secretary for Further and Higher Education, Alan Thompson, gave evidence to the new Select Committee advocating the need for the Department to 'steer' higher education rather than let it find its own way. In the context of the absence of any central direction for the public sector and the dominance of the UGC in respect to the university sector, this was regarded by most policy watchers in higher education as threatening and an infringement of institutions' right to steer themselves. The absence of steering became abundantly clear when in July 1981 the UGC imposed a reduction of student numbers in the university sector to protect the unit of resource. The subsequent Parliamentary debate emphasized the political risks of a wholly hands off policy; if the Secretary of State was to be answerable in Parliament for such activities then policy decisions, such as a reduction in student numbers on financial grounds, had to be taken at a political level.

It was precisely at this point that Sir Keith Joseph, then Secretary of State at the Department of Trade and Industry, replaced Carlisle. His standing in the first Thatcher Cabinet and his role as her intellectual mentor, together with his genuine interest in education, served to cement the change. There is no doubt that Joseph's period of office represented the watershed when the power (and wish) to steer policy passed to the DES. It was under Joseph that the NAB was created, a significant first stage in the removal of the public sector of higher education from local authority control, and it was on Joseph's initiative that the UGC and NAB produced public documents advising him on their proposals for the future of their sectors. Finally, Joseph was the first Minister to attempt to define a higher education policy in his Green Paper (DES 1985). This was much criticized at the time. Robert Rhodes James, an MP (and a historian), resigned from the somewhat nebulous post of Higher Education Advisor to the Prime Minister saying that he considered the document 'not only illiterate but innumerate' (Denham and Garnett 2001: 402) while the UGC in its response described it more temperately as 'a disappointment' (UGC 1985 para 2). The Secretary of the UGC described it as 'more prep and less pocket money' at a THES/SRHE Conference.[126]

Much of the criticism was based on the Green Paper's gloomy financial forecasts deriving from what were to emerge as over pessimistic scenarios of student demand but in fact much of the philosophy that underlay the document was to influence Government policy throughout the Conservative Party's tenure of office and arguably beyond. The Green Paper's main concern was that it was 'vital for our higher education to contribute more effectively to the improvement of the performance of the economy . . . the reason [being] simply that, unless the country's economic performance improves, we shall be even less able than now to afford many of the things which we value most' (DES 1985 para 1.2). This did not mean, it argued, being anti the arts and the humanities but it did mean being beware of anti business snobbery. Institutions, it said, should consciously seek to develop links with industry and commerce but also with their local communities including collaborating in the provision of artistic, cultural and recreational facilities. Reflecting the UGC's advocacy of the universities' research role the document sought to provide a balanced assessment of the role of higher education as a whole: 'the universities are the principal guardians of pure academic excellence and the main source of creative research [but] they are not the paradigm of higher education as a whole' and it went on to spell out the public sector's contribution in vocational and part-time education (DES 1985 para 1.8). It is easy to see how such statements might inflame contemporary opinion especially in a period of financial stringency but they represented the first attempts by a Secretary of State to articulate a policy framework since Crosland 20 years before.

Joseph was undoubtedly a controversial figure. Warned by his Prime Minister about the Department he set his civil servants reading lists; Rhodes Boyson, one of his Ministers, said that 'ministerial meetings became rather like postgraduate seminars' (Boyson 1995: 159) and anecdotes abound of civil servants and the Chairman of the UGC with busy diaries being trapped for hours in philosophical dissections of policy options. Joseph was disarmingly intellectually honest. He believed in reducing public expenditure and both his biographers and his civil servants testify that rather than fight his corner in a PESC round he was more likely to offer up budget cuts of his own volition (Denham and Garnett 2001: 387). This intellectual honesty and occasionally prejudice often got him into trouble, and rightly so: his commissioned inquiry by Lord Rothschild into the Social Science Research Council backfired badly; his attachment to the works of Martin Wiener and Corelli Barnett (*English Culture and the Decline of the Industrial Spirit* (1981) and *The Audit of War* (1986)) was misplaced, subsequent historians having cast doubt on their arguments about Britain's alleged betrayal of technological development; and his politically ill-conceived ideas about tuition fees needed to be bailed out by the Chancellor in the face of violent backbench opposition from his own party (see below). Nevertheless, unlike almost any other Secretary of State Joseph came to the job with enthusiasm, and led a shift in the policy-making machinery that his successors in both main political parties have built on. Whatever colleagues might say about his agonizing before taking a decision it could not be said after his departure as his predecessor Lord Hailsham apparently did some 20 years previously: 'In the Admiralty you are a person of authority. You say to one person "come" and he cometh and another "go" and he goeth. It's not so in the Ministry of Education, you suggest rather than direct. You say to one man "come" and he cometh not and to another "go" and he stays where he is' (Kogan 1971: 31).

Joseph left office under the cloud of mounting criticism of the Green Paper and a sense that he had been less than successful in carrying through the kind of reforms in the schools that he and the Prime Minister had hoped for. His successor, Kenneth Baker, was a very different character, proactive rather than reflective, and anxious to capture and retain the political limelight. Taking his cue from his leader who wrote in retirement of her officials in the DES that 'these were people who retained an almost reflex belief in the ability of central planners and social theorists to create a better world' (Thatcher 1995: 166), Baker claimed in his autobiography that his

DES officials were 'rooted in progressive orthodoxies in egalitarianism . . . It was devoutly anti excellence, anti selection and anti market' (Baker 1993: 168). Much of this reflects relations with officials over schools policy but Baker was robust in pushing through change. His 1987 White Paper, a glossy brochure with pictures which contrasted sharply with Joseph's drab Green Paper, promised expansion where Joseph had envisaged contraction; he took the public sector institutions out of local authority control and abolished the UGC and replaced it with the UFC subsequently appointing Lord Chilver, a known market enthusiast, as its chairman. Perhaps equally significant was the 'deal' which Baker achieved to secure policy objectives with the CVCP and the UGC. The issues involved had all been pressed by Joseph but it is hard to imagine Joseph settling them in this way. After a series of meetings with Sir Peter Swinnerton Dyer, Chairman of the UGC and Maurice Shock, Chair of CVCP, each was required to address a formal letter to him (4 November 1986, 5 November 1986) committing themselves to real progress in selectivity to produce a greater concentration of research, the rationalization of small departments, better financial management in universities, improved standards of teaching and assurances on academic standards, the implementation of the Jarratt recommendations, acceptance that something had to be done about tenure, and the introduction of staff appraisal. In return Baker released funds to enable a stalled salary settlement for university staff to go ahead and promised an increase in funded student numbers. Variously called the Action Plan (UGC) or the Shock Concordat (CVCP) it was the kind of deal a Secretary of State might have made with a recalcitrant nationalized industry that was thought to need modernization. It represented a step change from the independence of the UGC in 1981.

Baker was succeeded by John McGregor and then in 1991 by Kenneth Clarke, fresh from a robust performance in the reorganization of the health service. Clarke was much more a public sector modernizer than having any particular interest in higher education and his ready acceptance of the idea of abolishing the binary line almost immediately on appointment should be seen in this light. It is tempting to see the period 1981–92 as one where the steps towards the 'nationalization' of higher education have a certain inevitability. Richard Bird, senior DES official in charge of higher education, in an unsparingly frank account of the period wrote that 'to most of us with a stake in all this it did seem that the 1988 set-up must be unstable . . . there was inevitability about the evolution of a single higher education sector. The surprise for many was that this point was reached in 1992 rather than perhaps 1997' (Bird 1994). Bird identified six issues which he saw as the most dominant through the period:

- Should policy be directed to raising the numbers of higher education students?
- Should resourcing be tightened?
- Could better value for money be achieved?
- Is research funding sufficiently disciplined?

- Are students making enough contribution to the costs of their education?
- Should institutions become more accountable for the service they give and for quality within that service?

(Bird 1994)

We shall meet all these themes in later chapters. He described the process of policy making as often inherently 'disorderly' with most of the significant developments of the decade happening 'in a piecemeal and pragmatic fashion . . . the creation of an embracing strategy was always beyond reach' (Bird 1994). In the immediately previous period, the mid-1970s to early 1980s a Permanent Secretary commented that while the DES was activist in relation to a schools policy it essentially 'let it happen' in higher education.[127] This was not the case in the next decade but in a telling passage Bird discounted any consistent policy objectives either by civil servants or Ministers: officials' views were not 'monolithic' and alternatives would be presented; different secretaries of state had different priorities and were in any case influenced by their junior ministers and by their political advisers; on many issues the views of other Government departments had to be taken into account. If there was a 'guiding philosophy' at all it was the 'promotion of some sort of "market" whose functioning compels greater attention to the customer' but even this was pursued unevenly and was resisted at least on the university side of the binary line (Bird 1994).

The passage of the 1992 legislation completed the process begun under Joseph of a transfer of policy-making initiative to the Department. However, the 1987 White Paper and the 1988 legislation were also a catalyst for change in the main policy groups outside Government, the CDP and CVCP. The CDP, as we have seen above, transformed itself as a lobbying organization, and equipped itself with a small but effective secretariat. In particular it showed an acute appreciation of the value of public relations and appointed an ex journalist, John Izbicki, who was given considerable freedom, to enhance its visibility. The CVCP asked its Chairman, Lord Flowers, Rector of Imperial College, to undertake a review of its activities. Flower's report, presented in January 1988, was predicated on the need for the CVCP's organization to change to reflect the changing political climate. 'It is clear that a shift in power and control is in progress with the elimination of the "buffer state" and a polarisation of interests . . . it will fall to [the CVCP] to take on the historic and necessary role previously played by the UGC in "speaking up" for universities and ensuring that their needs are appreciated by government'.[128] The Report proposed that the CVCP should become proactive, rather than reactive, that it should reinforce its information unit and that it should either have a full time chairman or a new director general with, by implication, the freedom to act, rather than a secretary who was dependent on committee decisions. An alternative would be a vice-chancellor seconded for two years working with a chief officer. A new executive committee should replace the current unwieldy divisional structure where committees were linked to particular themes. Predictably the Committee opted for a director general and a vice-chancellor as an active chairman, but then compromised by retitling the director general's post as secretary general with all the restraints that had been envisaged on the previous secretary so that the net effect was as before. As a vice-chancellor was to write a decade or so later after the merger of the CVCP and CDP had taken place: 'Politically the university sector's problem is that it is far too articulate and elitist to evince much sympathy, yet far too incoherent and undisciplined to constitute an organised force to which governments must pay heed – a political weakness to which the conversion of the polytechnics to universities has much contributed' (Williams 1997).

A more significant development after 1988 was the common ground developed by CVCP and CDP joint working party on funding policies. This was not something anticipated by the DES and the effectiveness of the working party was clearly a factor in the DES recognizing that the binary line was melting before its eyes. However, when merger came the CVCP held the whip hand over the CDP and the vulnerability of the CDP institutions was exposed. One option could have been to have abolished both organizations and create a new body representative of the whole of higher education, along the lines of the American Council for Education. The CVCP had no intention of this happening, which in its eyes would have risked losing the research distinctiveness of the pre-1992 universities, and so proceeded to invite the new universities individually to join the CVCP. This left the CDP with an agonizing choice because many directors were anxious that the distinctive features of the polytechnics should not be lost. The CDP found itself facing three options; going it alone as an organization and risking losing members, joining the CVCP without negotiation or 'making a pretence of fighting prior to capitulation';[129] it recommended that its members accept the CVCP offer.

The new CVCP organization came together with surprising efficiency but very quickly the strain of representing the interests of such a diverse set of institutions, present as we have seen even when only the pre-1992 universities were members, became apparent and in 1994 a group of pre-1992 universities set up a new organization, the Russell Group, which claimed to represent the interests of the research intensive universities. This was not, however, a rigorously selective group, at least in origin, but the merger of two groups of universities: the universities with medical schools (and therefore substantial research income) and the members of a so-called group of five, Oxford, Cambridge, Imperial, UCL and Warwick, which had just extended its membership to LSE. Of the medical group Leicester did not join because its vice-chancellor believed that, as the current chairman of the CVCP, his loyalty should be given to that body while Warwick, as the only 1960s new university did by virtue of its membership of the group of five. The Russell Group has subsequently been joined by Cardiff University and Queens, Belfast, and, in 2012, Durham, Exeter, Queen Mary University of London and York. Membership of the Group created a formidable brand for its members. Close on the heels of the Russell Group, another group of pre-1992 universities created the 1994 Group. Initially known as 'the small but beautiful' group this group has emphasized its research intensity and indeed if a competition on RAE scores rather than total research income was to be the criteria some of its members would be eligible to join the Russell Group.

The creation of these two groups, although their members retained membership of the CVCP, clearly undermined the CVCP's authority. They were followed into existence by the Group of Modern Universities, later re-named the Million Plus universities made up of many of the post-1992 universities and by a yet further group of Non-Aligned universities. Although the Chairman of CVCP retained a coordinating role and acted as spokesman on major issues such as on 'top up' fees, prior to the formation of the Dearing Committee, the establishment of so many separate groups, all of whom lobbied for their own interests, further dissipated articulation of a single university message. The re-naming of the CVCP as Universities UK, and the transformation of the Scottish committee to Universities Scotland based in Edinburgh and the creation of Universities Wales, which have direct negoti-ating links with the Scottish Education Department and the Welsh Assembly, have further fragmented the universities' voice on key issues.

By contrast, the new Funding Councils proved to be much more business-like bodies, with constitutions and internal structures owing far more to the PCFC than to the old UGC. All of them have been strongly officer led, HEFCE, for example, being driven by an executive group made up of the chief executive and his three Directors responsible for Finance and Corporate Resources, Education and Participation and Research, Innovation and Skills. This officer team with their Associate Directors interface with government departments on the one hand and the institutions they fund on the other although in HEFCE's case the latter is very much more at an arms' length relationship than the much more intimate relationships enjoyed by universi-ties with the UGC. In Scotland and Wales political authorities have had a close, and often directive, relationship with their funding councils; Letters of Guidance have tended to emphasize the contribution of higher education to the economy at the expense of wider issues. In England, the Secretary of State addressed similar Letters of Guidance to HEFCE varying between the mina-tory (David Blunkett 1997 and 1998), the reiterative (Morris 2001 – in which the Secretary of State emphasized that she would judge HEFCE's perform-ance by the extent to which the targets were met) and the instructional (Clarke 2003 following up the 2003 White Paper on the *Future of Higher Education*).

It is clear that when Labour took power in 1997 HEFCE was seen as an agency with none of the aura of UGC autonomy which had clung to it in the last years of the Conservative Government. While it retained the important role of acting as an intermediary in the funding process to prevent the Secretary of State having a direct relationship with individual universities, HEFCE was essentially an instrument of government and its allocation processes, particu-larly in relation to research, were subject to strong Departmental influence. On one occasion a Minister summoned HEFCE to say that too many 5 star departments had been identified in an RAE. HEFCE's initial stalling response was that the material on which judgements had been based had been destroyed and when that did not convince convened the Chairs of the RAE panels who unanimously voted to confirm the ratings on the grounds that the criteria for them had been published.[130] On another occasion, HEFCE was forced to record being overruled by the Department in respect to a directive to reward academic departments which had had 5 star rankings in two successive RAEs (Taggart 2004). This is not to say that HEFCE officers did not also play a valuable mediating role in presenting their views of desirable and undesirable policies to officials in the Department. Thus, HEFCE consistently opposed and did not implement instructions to explore reflecting teaching quality assessments in funding allocations and Taggart suggests that HEFCE's strategic plan published in 2002 exercised a considerable influence on the 2003 White Paper (Taggart 2004).

Nevertheless the attitudes of successive Labour Secretaries of State was that HEFCE was an instrument programmed to deliver policy rather to assist in its creation. When Government wanted to reform the RAE the Chancellor of the Exchequer announced it in a budget statement and HEFCE complied; when Government was persuaded to impose a tuition fee/loan regime in 2003 the impetus came from the Prime Minister privately urged by Lord Jenkins, the Chancellor of Oxford, and Andrew Adonis, Blair's senior policy adviser in the Cabinet Office, and HEFCE was, in effect, side lined. The decisions to charge or not to charge tuition fees in Wales and Scotland were political decisions in which the respective funding councils appear to have played no part. HEFCE's role became, therefore, more that of a delivery agent and a regulator of the system; and the policy issues had moved upstairs. The implementation of the Browne Report (2010) confirmed the trend. In 2010 HEFCE abandoned the pretence it was a 'buffer' and redefined itself as a 'broker' (HEFCE 2010).

The foregoing might tempt one to the conclusion that the DES created to oversee Shearman's 'seamless robe' was set to become one of the most powerful departments of state. This was not, however, to be the case. As we have seen, until 1981, the Department had largely left the UGC to manage the university system with the local authorities managing public sector higher education. The appointment of Keith Joseph and the creation of NAB followed by the 'nationalization' of the polytechnics, the abolition of the UGC and the creation of the PCFC and the UFC were stages in what might have been the consolidation of DES power in the 1992 Act, except that the Act devolved responsibility for higher education in Scotland and Wales to the devolved governments. In the following year the Department lost responsibility for the research councils which were transferred to the Department of Trade and Industry, and the DES became the Department for Education (DfE). It was then reinforced by a transfer of training responsibilities from the Department of Employment becoming the Department for Education and Skills (DfES) until in 2006 higher education was removed from it altogether with the creation of a new Department for Innovation, Universities and Skills (DIUS) which reunited higher education and the research councils. This latter move was widely welcomed in higher education, many seeing it as a reversion to the Robbins solution of a separate Ministry dealing with universities and research. The decision constituted one of the grounds for the initial swell of approval for Brown's assumption of the premiership and was interpreted as the realization of a policy, which he had fostered as Chancellor, to favour investment in the knowledge economy. (Another interpretation is that the prime motive was to create a Department to give wider government experience to Ed Balls who, however, turned it down and insisted on a major post as Secretary of State for Education.)[131] Whatever the interpretation, DIUS had a short life and was swept into an enlarged Department of Business, Innovation and Skills (BIS) calculated in size and range to match the title of First Secretary which was accorded to Lord Mandelson.

The argument for the changes might be that the policy issues around skills and research had become too enmeshed in the future of the British economy to sit easily in a department that was primarily concerned with education up to the age of 18. The extensive failure of the Learning and Skills Council, a Blunkett creation which replaced the Further Education Funding Council, might also suggest a lack of confidence in the Department. But the unwinding of the DES with such ease, also casts light on the fragility of the seamless robe argument. Margaret Thatcher, with Weaver's help, was the only Minister to attempt to produce an integrated education and higher education policy in her 1972 White Paper (DES 1972a). One of the problems was always the brevity of a Secretary of State's tenure: after 1981 only Joseph, Baker and Blunkett held office for more than two years and left a significant personal mark on policy. Of these the least successful was Blunkett, who as the first Labour Secretary of State in 1997, after a long line of Conservatives, had a unique opportunity to make a creative impact on policy making. Blunkett failed to grasp the chance offered him by the Dearing Report to make effective reforms to the existing funding regime and, aping Crosland, went to the University of Greenwich, the site of the Woolwich speech, to deliver a tendentious oration which launched a revamped Dip.HE as a Foundation degree and the E-University, perhaps the biggest financial white elephant in British higher education's history. Blunkett's failure to implement the Dearing Report's proposals on finance provoked the need to review the system again in 2003 leading to the introduction of the increased tuition fee and income contingent loan arrangements which narrowly won Parliamentary approval in 2004.

When the next round of reform of the funding of higher education was introduced in 2010 it was not from a Department for Education but from a Department of Business, Innovation and Skills. Within Whitehall, at least, policy making in higher education was once again located within a department with a predominantly economic role and was wholly detached from a Department for Education which in its remit and concentration looked remarkably like the former Ministry of Education, albeit with a more highly charged proactive role. However, as the Comprehensive Spending Review demonstrated BIS did not offer the protection to the university system that the Treasury had provided.

3

The financial drivers of higher education policy

Higher education policy has been peculiarly susceptible to being driven by financial decision making not just because of its dependence on public funding but also because throughout the period 1946–2011 its growth in terms of student numbers far exceeded the growth of the national economy. To maintain a constant level of support for higher education would have involved Government in making compensating reductions in other deserving areas of public expenditure, raising taxation or embarking on cost sharing devices of one kind or another. At various times and often simultaneously all these policy options have been drawn on. People working at the coal face in higher education might like to hope that higher education policy would be driven by issues and events arising out of higher education itself but this is to ignore the fact that the underlying policy context has always been the availability of resources to finance the system. As is self evident a constant level of support has by no means been maintained. What Figure 3.1 demonstrates is the fluctuations in public expenditure of which higher education expenditure was a part.

This chapter seeks to demonstrate how the twists and turns of public financial policy have driven policy in higher education, how public financial strategies for resource allocation have sometimes had unintended consequences and how the architecture of Government financial decision making has shaped the higher education system and its institutions.

The economy, the Treasury and the funding process

It would have been easy to forget in the 1920s and 1930s that higher education, which in effect meant the universities, represented an element in public expenditure. Between 1900 and 1980 Glennester shows that the share of the nation's income, taxed or borrowed, to finance education, housing, health, income maintenance and social services rose from about 2.6 per cent to 25 per cent (Glennester 1990). Throughout the 1920s and 1930s the state

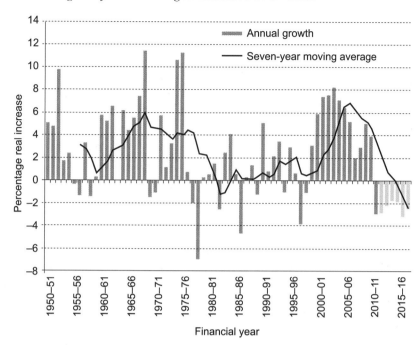

Figure 3.1 Public expenditure actual and forecast 1950–51 and 2015–16

Note: Spending on public services defined as total public spending less both gross interest payments and net social benefits spending.

Source: http://www.ifs.org.uk/ff/lr_spending.xls

met only about one third of university expenditure, with funding calculated on a deficiency basis, the remainder being generated from tuition fees, about 30 per cent (paid usually by the student but sometimes also in part by local authorities), and the rest from a range of sources including endowment income and local authority grants. By 1979–80 the state's contribution, comprising recurrent grant plus fees, now paid by the state via the local authorities, had risen to about 80 per cent. The inter-War years had been characterized by slow economic growth but had also been a gestation period for the ideas which later came to characterize the Welfare State, and the Labour Party's 1945 manifesto *Let us Face the Future* promised that planning would supersede the price mechanism in financing state enterprise. The expansion of higher education fitted naturally into that agenda; there was never any doubt that governments of either political hue accepted that university education should be made available to all those qualified to enter it and the Robbins recommendation to this effect, the so-called 'Robbins principle,' merely confirmed the effective *status quo*. The major economic policies of the 1950s, nationalization and full employment, were again entirely coincident with policies adopted towards higher education where the proportion of state funding in university budgets had continued to rise. They were fully endorsed in the two 1963 reports from the National Economic Development Committee (NEDC) *Growth of the United Kingdom Economy* and *Conditions Favourable to Foster Growth* which envisaged a 4 per cent annual growth in the economy from 1961 to 1966 and served to legitimate the Robbins forecasts.

By the late 1970s, however, this consensus had broken down under the pressure of inflation and low economic growth. Callaghan in a speech at the 1976 Labour Party conference represented the changing mood:

> For too long, perhaps ever since the War, we postponed facing up to fundamental changes in our society and in our economy. That is what I mean when I say we have been living on borrowed time. The cosy world we were told would go on for ever where full employment would be guaranteed at the stroke of a Chancellor's pen, cutting taxes, deficit spending, that cosy world is gone.
>
> (Callaghan quoted in Jenkins 2006: 36)

The arrival of the Thatcher Government in 1979 foreshadowed an immediate change: the Public Expenditure White Paper in 1980 spelled out that public expenditure was 'at the heart of Britain's present economic difficulties'. 'Public spending' it said 'has been increased on assumptions about economic growth which have not been achieved. The inevitable result has been a growing burden of taxes and borrowing' (HM Treasury 1980). Education spending, which had risen from 3.2 per cent of GDP in 1951 to 5.3 per cent in 1979, a faster rate of growth than expenditure on housing, health or social services, but not as fast as social security which had grown to 9.8 per cent, was bound to suffer, and by 1992 was almost back to 1960 levels. One manifestation of this was the imposition of the 1981 cuts on universities and the cap on the pool funding of public sector higher education and the continued pressure on higher education budgets thereafter. Another result was a marked change of tone in the Government's attitude to higher education. Crowther Hunt signalled this even before Callaghan's Ruskin speech in 1975 where he argued that 'The economic difficulties of the country require an education system producing people the country really needs' (quoted in Glennester and Low 1990).

But the evidence of a permanent change of policy was to await Keith Joseph's Green Paper where the statement: 'The Government believes that it is vital for our higher education to contribute more effectively to the improvement of the performance of the economy' marked a sharp shift of emphasis (DES 1985 para 1.2). The consequences for higher education were that staff student ratios would be tightened (the universities had moved from 9.4:1 in 1980–81 to 10.1:1 in 1985–86 and the polytechnics from 8.1:1 to 10.1:1 over the same period), institutions were urged to seek greater financial independence from state support and a review of student finance was to be launched which was clearly intended as a first step to cost sharing. The prime message was directly economic: public expenditure could not sustain the rising costs of higher education; industry and commerce were not delivering the improvement in the economy that was expected. The Green Paper was, as we have seen, widely criticized but in practice its underlying messages were to be reiterated by every one of Joseph's successors. The pressure to reduce public expenditure introduced another theme, the search for greater, that is more cost effective, efficiency. The Rayner efficiency studies across Government departments (the Financial Management Initiative) were the inspiration for the Jarratt Committee's review of efficiency in universities and the process which culminated in the concordat between Baker and the CVCP and the UGC, referred to above. The effect was to impose unwelcome internal changes in the management of universities (though not particularly in the polytechnics) including the largely symbolic loss of tenure which reinforced the sense of a radical rebalancing of relations between the state and higher education.

The continuing pressure on public expenditure had two other important consequences stretching right across government but which had significant impacts on higher education. The first lay in the extent to which higher education could be regarded as a priority for public expenditure. Vice-chancellors or directors of polytechnics, facing expanding student numbers and internal pressures for resources, had few doubts about such priority but the situation looked rather different from a central government perspective. Baker, in his address to an unresponsive CVCP residential conference, tried to spell out some of the policy dilemmas for the Government. He was, he said, under pressure from employers (see below) to increase the volume of qualified manpower but spending on the health service had to increase by 1 per cent p.a. simply to keep pace with demography. The cost of health care for those between 65 and 75 had increased by four times, and for the over 75s, by nine times. Against this the cost to the tax payer of a three year Arts degree was £14,100 (grant plus student support) and for a medical degree £46,000, and these subsidies were devoted to only one in seven of the 18–21 age group. If he was to win his case, by implication, with the Treasury he had to have the 'outward and visible signs of your commitment' to selectivity in research funding, the rationalization of small departments, better management, arrangements for monitoring teaching quality and the removal of tenure.[1] The second consequence was the gradual abandonment of Keynesian demand management to supply side policies. High inflation in the 1970s had led to the introduction of cash limits to control public expenditure but the issues of the 1980s increasingly prompted the employment of market approaches. Thus the sudden acceleration in demand for higher education in the late 1980s led to a rise in tuition fees and to an encouragement to institutions to expand on the basis of fee income alone. The polytechnics took the bait and expanded vigorously; the universities resisted the UFC's guide price strategy and expanded much more slowly. The recession of the early 1990s and the alarming level of supplementary allocations which the Treasury had to provide brought the burst of expansion to an end in 1994 with tight controls re-imposed on higher education numbers. The impact on funding is well set out in the Dearing Report (see Figure 3.3, page 131).

With an expanding economy the Blair and Brown Governments were able to increase funding through HEFCE (see Figure 3.2).

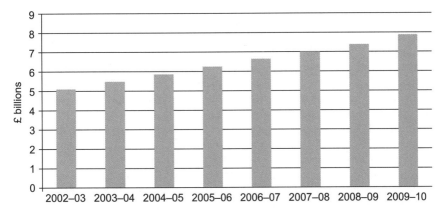

Figure 3.2 Higher education funding through HEFCE 2002–03 to 2009–10

Source: HEFCE.

But these increases, modest by comparison with those granted to the NHS or to defence, were insufficient either to match the demand for investment in research, now seen as a crucial economic driver, or to meet the Blair ambition to maintain the position of British higher education in the global league tables, let alone to fund a growth in the participation rate from 30 per cent to 50 per cent. Cost sharing – that is requiring students to contribute to the cost of their education, which had been resisted by the Major Government conscious of the furore amongst Conservative MPs when Joseph dipped his toe into that water in 1985 – became, in the eyes of the Government, the only practicable possibility of rescuing a mass higher education system whose demands the state was unable to meet in the face of equally fierce pressure from the health services, the care of the elderly, the administration of justice, social security and defence. The main policy issue in the decade to 2006 was how to devise and make politically acceptable a new system of funding universities which would reverse the commitment to full state funding adopted and implemented in the period from 1946 up to Robbins.

The economy was a key driver of policy partly because the funding system that had been created demanded resources at a faster rate than the economy was expanding, and partly because the Government adopted a bidding process for state funds, through PESC which put higher education into a competitive position with other sectors within education and ultimately between education and other state resourced items of national expenditure. This meant that policy changes were far more often driven extrinsically as by-products of a budgeting process rather than intrinsically, that is, out of the evolution or needs of higher education itself. The architecture of the budgetary process and, necessarily, because of the consistently constrained nature of the British budget, the main stimulus for policy change was the Treasury, operating through the PESC process. Higher education policy issues were rarely taken to Cabinet: the creation of the polytechnics and the establishment of the binary line, taken together one of the most fundamental structural decisions ever taken in British higher education, was decided without reference to the cabinet or a cabinet committee, while the decision to reverse the process in 1992 went as far as a cabinet committee which, as we have seen above, acted as a rubber stamp to the Secretary of State's decision. According to Kogan, Crosland took only two educational issues to Cabinet, his circular announcing the comprehensive school policy and the appointment of a Public Schools Commission. Kogan goes on to say that when appointing Crosland to be President of the Board of Trade, Wilson complained that they had not had a single conversation about education (Kogan 1971).

In practice policies in higher education originated with officials and were not initiated by Ministers. Boyle in conversation with Kogan said: 'I would say overwhelmingly the biggest number were originated from . . . the "education world", if you like, from the logic of the education service as it developed' (Kogan 1971: 46) but for Boyle that 'world' was dominated by Weaver rather than by the CVCP. Weaver's claim to McConnell that he and Ken (later Sir Ken) Berrill, the chairman of the UGC, devised most of the policies emanating from the DES or the UGC during the period when they overlapped in office is referred to above. Interviews with civil servants recalling policy changes in the 1990s and 2000s confirm that this continued to be the case. There were, of course, exceptions: Wilson's advocacy of the University of the Air, Shirley Williams 13 Points, Crowther Hunt's much resented (by DES officials) incursions into policy, Keith Joseph's Green Paper and Blair's championing of 'top up' fees, but perhaps we should not find this surprising. As Watson and Bowden noted in their assessment of higher education policy under the 18 years of Conservative Government, Conservative Education Ministers apart from Joseph, were in post for at most only three years and were inevitably dependent on policies maturing within their Department rather than bringing new ideas to the table (Watson and Bowden 1999). More significant, however, is the extent to which these policies were influenced on a short term or a long term basis by Treasury thinking and by the dialogues between the Department and the Treasury which were part of the PESC process. Higher education policy had to be aligned with the Treasury's long term view of the economy as well as with short term budgetary considerations.

As we have seen between 1946 and 1962 the universities occupied a special position in respect to their funding because of the UGC's location under the Treasury. Recurrent finance was negotiated on a quinquennial basis on principles originally adopted in the 1920s when the state was only a minority funder. In the fourth year of the quinquennium universities drew up their financial demands for the next five years usually simply on the basis of a summary of the combined plans of their various academic departments. Central intervention by the university authorities, except on capital issues, was rare although some rationalization of demand so as to present a coherent case to the UGC was always necessary. This system had worked well in the 1920s and 30s when the UGC's role was only to fund the deficiency in university budgets but was much less satisfactory from a public finance point of view when, in an expanding situation, the state was called on to assume the primary funding responsibility. Historically, the UGC's task was to total up the universities' bids and submit them to the Treasury with whatever commentary it thought fit. From 1946, however, the total student number target for which funding was to be provided became a key element in the UGC's case. The whole process was complemented by a formal meeting (in morning dress) between the full CVCP and the Chancellor of the Exchequer when the universities set out their priorities for the next quinquennium. (The meeting was continued with Crosland, following the transfer of responsibility for the universities from the Treasury, but abandoned for the 1972–77 quinquennium.) There is no doubt that the universities occupied a privileged position in respect to their claims for resources from the state.

This privileged position was sharply reversed by a decisive change in the Government's financial procedures. The Plowden Committee, which had been proposed by Sir Richard (Otto) Clarke, had been set up in 1959 and its Report *Control of Public Expenditure* was published in June 1961. The Report's central recommendation 'that arrangements should be introduced for making surveys of public expenditure for a period of years ahead and that all major decisions involving future expenditure should be taken against the background of such a survey and in relation to prospective resources' might have seemed to fit with a quinquennial funding system but the essence of the new system was that a decision had first to be taken at Cabinet level which put a ceiling on public expenditure against which government departments competed. If departments wanted to incur expenditure above the limit agreed they had to obtain approval from the Cabinet both on the principle of the new activity but also on the implications for total public expenditure. To reinforce and give political weight to the process a new post of Chief Secretary was created which had Cabinet membership. In 1962 when the PESC process was first used, Henry Brooke, the Chief Secretary provoked a political crisis by turning down the UGC's quinquennial estimate for 1962–67 (see below).

The creation of PESC, and the subsequent transfer of the UGC's budget to the DES, where it became part of, though separately identified, in the total Education budget, marked a turning point for the universities. Budget requests could no longer be settled, if they ever were, over a monthly dinner but were part of a formal process of discussion between a Treasury officer responsible for pre-determined areas of public expenditure and a designated Principal Finance Officer of the DES. It was not just that the UGC's case might not be put so persuasively but that the Department's negotiator might concede a UGC priority in favour of a priority in another area of the Department's budget. A good example of this, although the concession was made at a much higher level than by an official, occurred in 1967 when Crosland committed himself to a trade-off of increased tuition fees for overseas students to fend off a Treasury proposal to charge for school meals (Lee 1998). In a situation where concern about the economy and the level of public expenditure was often paramount in government the Treasury, through the PESC round, became a powerful influence on higher education policy, especially when the continued expansion of higher education made legitimate demands for greatly increased funding.

The Treasury's interest was the economy although its public expenditure division prided itself on its background knowledge of policy issues in the various sectors. Heclo and Wildavsky writing about the Treasury at the end of the 1970s described it as follows:

> The Treasury as an institution has never believed in the philosophy of economic growth. Its officials may not be against growth as such but they are vehemently against committing resources on the basis of what one deputy secretary called 'a hoped for, phoney paper growth rate, which only leads to false expectations, disappointments, cuts and further disillusionment' . . . It is not growth but the limit on national resources that is the staple of Treasury doctrine.
>
> (Heclo and Wildavsky 1981: 48)

This was not a climate which was conducive to seeing the growth of higher education as an investment.

Initially, however, PESC was essentially Keynesian in its concept, emphasizing the planning and control of resources measured in volume terms. Higher education benefited from this because 'the Robbins principle' of places needing to be provided for all those qualified for entry and the forecasts of numbers up to 1980–81 was easily translatable into the PESC expenditure forecasts and, since there was strong political support for the numbers both from Conservative and Labour Governments, into expenditure commitments. Booth calls it 'the prime example of a "policy-led" expansion programme' (Booth 1983). On the whole the new PESC system worked well in its early years although Booth suggests that simply rolling forward programmes allowed a certain amount of surreptitious expansion beyond agreed targets and that there was some evidence of the Treasury being willing to fiddle the figures under pressure from some ministers. There was also concern over the inability to control local authority expenditure.

Where the machinery was weak, however, was that it was not well constructed to cope with inflation. In the past, when salary awards had had to be made in the university sector the cost of supplementary awards was added to the quinquennial grant. Salary inflation was not new before the oil crisis of 1973–74 – university salaries had been caught by the Selwyn Lloyd 3 per cent limit in 1962 and had been referred to the new National Prices and Incomes Board in 1966 – but became chronic after it. PESC was in crisis; in 1975–6 the Government sought assistance from the International Monetary Fund, and in April 1976 a new approach which replaced volume planning with cash limits was introduced. As described by Sir Leo Pliatzky who, as second Permanent Secretary in the Treasury, took over responsibility for public expenditure in 1975: 'Instead of waiting to see what the rate of inflation turned out to be and providing cash to cover it when the time came, the government would, in some terms, be calling its shots on inflation and declaring in advance what cost increases it would finance.' It meant the end of 'funny money at constant prices' (Pliatzky, quoted in Hennessey 1990: 133–4). The new policy was announced in the White Paper *Cash Limits on Expenditure* HMSO Cmnd. 6440.

For universities the oil crisis meant the abrogation of the quinquennial system, never to be revived, serious cuts in student number plans and capital programmes, and a dependence for some years on annual allocations. In the public sector the concern over local authority expenditure led to the establishment of a Consultative Committee on Local Government Finance which created a number of sub groups including the Education Expenditure Steering Group chaired by a Deputy Secretary from the DES, which had control over the quantum of local spending in this area but not over the decisions of individual authorities with the result that polytechnic growth was largely protected. This, however, was very much in line with DES thinking which was to build up the public sector of higher education in line with the original ambitions of the 1966 Polytechnic White Paper (Booth 1983). On the other side of the binary line the UGC cut student numbers in 1981 to protect the unit of resource. In 1980, the new Conservative Government tightened Treasury controls yet further. Under Cash Limits, once a volume programme had been settled, an allowance for inflation was also cash limited but some 'wriggle room' was provided for further supplementation in special circumstances. The new policy, Cash Planning, allowed no such flexibility and a succession of public expenditure white papers set absolute cash limits for each year from 1981–82 to 1984–85. Cash Planning was an essential element in the Thatcher Government's policy of controlling inflation but it imposed severe restrictions on universities in particular because the index of university costs showed that the cost of consumables, equipment and libraries rose independently of salary inflation, the main object of the Government's counter inflationary policy.

Table 3.1 devised by Booth illustrates very clearly the extent to which higher education but particularly the university sector was buffeted by the financial turbulence of the decade. From a position in the 1960s when a quinquennial approach seemed to guarantee continued expansion at a steady rate of funding and when universities had been encouraged in 1972 to submit ambitious plans up to 1977, on course to match the Robbins 1980 forecast, they were thrust into cut backs in numbers, disrupted building programmes, year by year uncertainties in funding and mounting salary inflation. From the high point of the Robbins predicted expansion they were

Table 3.1 The impact of public expenditure decisions on higher education 1972–82

Publication date and Cmnd number (in brackets)	Target for full-time and sandwich places in GB by 1981/82: thousands	Notes based on White Paper texts
Dec 72 (5178)	750	Reflected policy of *Education: A Framework for Expansion*. Large capital programme for buildings and student residences.
Dec 73 (5519)	750	Reductions in universities' recurrent grant and equipment grant could be 'accommodated without detriment to planned growth'.
Jan 75 (5879)	640	'. . . revised figures maintain the Robbins principle . . .'. General 'slowing of demand for education' because of lower than expected trends in staying-on at 16 and number qualifying for higher education.
Feb 76 (6393)	600	'. . . implies some increase in competition for entry in some subjects compared with recent years'. Age participation rate expected to grow from 14% to 15%, . . . little if any scope for increasing staff numbers after 1976–77 . . . capital expenditure . . . severely restricted . . .'.
Feb 77 (6721)	560	Tuition fees for home and overseas students to be increased sharply in 1977–78. Limitation on numbers of overseas students proposed. No increase in total number of academic staff. Continuing severe restrictions on capital expenditure.
Jan 78 (7049)	560	Assumed division between universities and public sector: universities 310,000 by 1981/82, public sector 25,000 by 1981/82. Intended that in 1978–79 the number of overseas students be reduced to about the level of 1975–76, an implied reduction of about 12% or 11,000 places.
Jan 79 (7439)	544	Downward adjustment because enrolments in 1977/78 lower than expected. APR of 13.8% by 1982–83.
Nov 79 (7746)	No forecast	'. . . resources available for home students in higher education will be about the same as in 1979/80'. New overseas students expected to meet the full cost of the their tuition. Capital expenditure halved.

Mar 80 (7841)	[500 implied]	Home student numbers to remain broadly constant, implying fall in admissions. Small reduction in expenditure on institutions and student support, especially in the non-university sector.
Mar 81 (8175)	No forecast	Fall in planned expenditure owing to (a) removal of subsidy to overseas students, (b) reduction in expenditure on home students, so that 'by 1983/84 institutional expenditure (net of tuition fee income) will be rather more than 8% below the level planned in Cmnd 7841' . . . 'This is likely to lead to some reduction in the number of students admitted to higher education with increased competition for places; but the Government expects institutions to admit, as they have done this year, as many students as they can consistent with their academic judgement . . . the plans assume a significant tightening of standards'.
Mar 82 (8494)	[1981/82 target not applicable]	Total spending by institutions in 1984–85 expected to fall by at least 10% in real terms below 1980–81 level. Loss of 10,000 teaching posts, fall of 10% in student numbers and 13% in undergraduate admissions over the same period.

Note: The actual numbers of full-time and sandwich students in higher education in GB in 1981/82 was about 500,000 as compared to the Robbins forecast of 558,000 for 1980–81.

Source: Quoted from Booth, C., DES and Treasury, Table 2.1, in Morris and Sizer (1983).

plunged, only eight years later, into the 1981 UGC cuts. From seeming to be a priority for government their dependence on state funding put them at the mercy of downturns in the state's financial fortunes. Long term planning was replaced by short term expediency. The UGC, which had seemed under Murray's decade of chairmanship to be a powerful advocate of university interests, became increasingly little more than an uncomfortable conduit between PESC decision making and the universities themselves.

As higher education moved beyond the protection of the 1980 limit of the Robbins forecasts, which had in fact not been realized, and as decisions between the two sectors took on greater importance the PESC process became more significant. PESC concentrated on the macro issues of the total student number commitment for public expenditure but Booth makes clear that the DES in preparing its forecasts made policy assumptions about the division between the university and the public sector. The PESC time-table required all new policy proposals to be developed by the spring in each

year (although prior negotiation with the Treasury was an essential preliminary). By the summer, PESC would produce a report on the expected financial projection based on the forecast costs of existing policies and any new
ones. Once Cabinet approval was obtained for an overall spending target the
Chief Secretary would conduct bilateral meetings with Ministers to adjust
financial plans to the agreed total spend. Booth emphasizes that, from a
departmental point of view, success was 'determined by negotiating skill, the
quality of briefing provided by the department, the political standing of
the ministers and the political importance, as seen by the Cabinet and the
parliamentary party of the spending programme under attack' (Booth 1983:
27). On rare occasions the so-called 'Star Chamber' of senior ministers might
be brought into being to decide high priority competing departmental bids.
(Mrs Thatcher used her deputy, Whitelaw, to chair such meetings.) On other
occasions a minister might exercise a right to take an issue which could not
be settled through the normal process to the Cabinet itself. Gillian Shephard,
Secretary of State for Education (1994 to 1997) chose to do this on behalf of
the education budget, but not specifically for higher education, but lost.
Keith Joseph, on the other hand, was so convinced of the need to cut public
expenditure, that to the despair of his officials, he would readily concede
reductions on policies which the Department gave priority to.

The PESC process changed in some of its details over the years but the
essential principle of a powerful Treasury, bargaining with government
departments whose bids added up to more than the Government as a whole
in Cabinet believed could legitimately be afforded, remained the core determinant of policy. PESC itself became simply PES (Public Expenditure
Survey) because the Committee, which was made up of the principal finance
officers of the various departments, never met. After the mid-1980s the
process provided a firm decision on resourcing for the immediate year and
provisional agreements for the next two years but this could vary with
Treasury demands that, after the first year, the provisional budget for the
next two years was fixed and could not therefore be reopened. In 1997, when
Labour returned to office, Gordon Brown wanted to take a longer view
and, from 1998, the PES process was extended to a fixed first year and three
provisional years but with a Spending Review after every two years.

Discussions were conducted initially at officer level, the department's
officials having cleared the bid with their ministers and, when concluded, the
Chief Secretary sent a Settlement Letter to the Secretary of State. If the
Secretary of State was not satisfied with the settlement then a bilateral discussion took place with the Chief Secretary. The process became elongated in
that it was no longer a single 'shoot out', except in the extraordinary circumstances of 2010, but a dialogue that extended throughout the year. In
Education both a HEFCE and a CVCP/Universities UK (UUK) submission
to PES was permitted, although the HEFCE submission was also part of the
overall DES/DfE submission; the CVCP/UUK submission was generally
ignored. Bargaining remained an essential part of the process. While the
HEFCE bid was always realistic officials interviewed admitted that the overall

Education bid was padded for negotiating purposes and that a final decision would often depend on giving up some item to win approval for another. External factors, such as the demands of other departments could play a part in the final settlement as could, within education, the political priorities of the various schools programmes *vis-à-vis* higher education. Policy changes based only on balancing a budget could have unintended consequences. In 1989 the doubling of tuition fees was only undertaken to balance up a deficit on the local authority side. This, however, nourished a 'fees only' expansion in the public sector which was largely ignored on the university side. The result was to fuel a rapid expansion in the public sector, already encouraged by the PCFC market driven funding model. Ultimately this required the Treasury to step in, in 1994, to demand that fees be halved and that institutions exercise strict control on numbers in order to contain student support costs but this was not before the Treasury had had to concede two years of supplementary grants to the DES budget. In the longer term the Treasury benefited because, after the 1992 merger of the two sectors, this low cost expansion reduced the unit of resource across the whole of higher education and not just in the public sector.[2]

Inevitably, the fact that there was a bargaining process affected the bidding exercise in that bids were more likely to be successful if they fitted Treasury requirements. In February 1984, for example, the Chairman of the UGC suggested that the proposed efficiency review (which Jarratt would later be invited to chair) should be a CVCP initiative because this would be 'particularly relevant' to the PESC exercise coming up in April. At the same meeting an Office note described a meeting on the removal of tenure with the DES officials who said that they were required to report back to ministers no later than mid March. This was almost certainly in the hope that a positive decision would meet a Treasury demand and sweeten the pill for the PES round.[3] The Treasury officials engaged in the process were well informed but looked at higher education from a different perspective than the DES/DFE officers, normally the Principal Finance Officer and the head of policy, by whom the departmental bid was being negotiated. They were themselves likely to have a rather different perspective from UGC/UFC/HEFCE officers who were necessarily much closer to the issues in the sector.

The Treasury perspective was primarily geared to delivering a set of figures which fitted in to a national budget, although confusingly, the team conducting the departmental negotiations were not always informed as to the target they were to aim at because the Public Spending Group in the Treasury kept the figures confidential. This could potentially create a further layer in the decision-making process. But within this framework it is evident that some broad policy themes could be observed though there was never a long term plan for higher education. Thus between 1981 and 1986 the dominant theme was efficiency, one aspect of which across all departments were the Raynor scrutiny studies, of which the university and the public sector variants were the Jarratt Report and the public sector Good Management Practice Group. (The latter, which assumed a continuance of local authority control of the polytechnics, became immediately redundant with the decisions contained in the 1987 White Paper.) On the university side the efficiency theme can be readily identified in the pressures to achieve the removal of tenure, the rationalization of small departments and so forth which provided the agenda for the concordat signed with Baker by the UGC and the CVCP.

A second and later theme was the encouragement, on qualified manpower grounds, to bring the age participation rate to up to 33 per cent but after that to seek cost sharing, that is tuition fee income paid by students, to defray the additional costs.[4] In other words the Treasury would only support further expansion if alternative funding could be found. This was frustrated by the inability of politicians, until Blair did so in 2004, to generate support in the House of Commons, for such a move. When a target of 50 per cent age participation rate by 2010 was announced by the Prime Minister in a party conference speech – the target itself was attributed to a middle ranking political staff member at No.10 – the Treasury and the Department agreed a toning down of the statement to progress 'towards' rather than 'to' the target. In the words of a senior civil servant interviewed: 'In Treasury speak "towards" is different from "to" '.[5]

A third and consistent theme after the publication of the 1987 White Paper on Civil Research and Development was the support for funding research in science and technology and for a concentration of research into fewer centres. The Treasury gave strong support to the RAE and it was Brown, as Chancellor, who provided the impetus to push it towards giving weight to research impact in order to maximize its links with the economy. It was the Department's lack of interest in supporting this theme adequately which led to the transfer of higher education to a new department.

The conclusions of the PESC/PES process for higher education was the issue of a Letter of Guidance from the Secretary of State to the funding council. Up until 1962 the universities would feel confident that the position of the UGC *vis-à-vis* the Treasury was such that the quinquennial planning process ensured that university generated priorities were likely to be matched by funding decisions. For the next decade (quinquennial 1962–67 and 1967–72), even after the universities transferred from the Treasury to the DES, the aura of Robbins was such that university priorities remained dominant. But this changed with the oil crisis and the extreme turbulence in the nation's finances. Cash Limits, Cash Planning and Government thinking about the reduction of public expenditure meant that the PESC process became a great deal more challenging and competitive. By the 1990s what higher education wanted in terms of priorities, even as transmitted through the prism of the HEFCE bid, bore only an almost fortuitous relationship with what it asked for. Not only had major policy decision making passed to the Department but the Department's priorities were diluted and often driven by Treasury priorities. The Secretary of State's letter may have seemed like a clear statement of policy but was in fact an amalgam of funding policy exchanges that were the product of a hierarchy of processes connected only remotely with the day to day issues being addressed by the institutions themselves. Institutions tended to become reactive rather than pro-active in policy making, finding themselves at the end of an extensive decision-making chain.

Financial crises in higher education

Financial crises in civil society like wars in the wider society can be forcing houses of major policy change. For contemporary commentators higher education has been continuously wracked by financial crises but in fact four stand out: the rejection of the UGC's quinquennial estimates in 1962, the impact of the oil crisis in 1973–74, the university cuts in 1981 and the continued fall in the unit of resource which led to the CVCP campaign for 'top up' fees in 1996–97. Each of these acted as a significant spur to policy change and in each case it is possible to argue that they generated a turning point when the policy framework was decisively altered.

1962: a crisis of trust between universities and the state

As we have seen above, the 1962 crisis marked a jarring breakdown in relations between the Treasury and the UGC and the first sign that the growing demands of the university system were becoming difficult to reconcile with the wider concerns of government policy relating to the public sector of the economy. Berdahl rightly identified the 1962 crisis as fundamentally about university-state relations (Berdahl 1962) but argued that this was probably a temporary hiatus in what he had portrayed in his earlier book as a generally warm and harmonious relationship. The subsequent availability of archive evidence, however, shows that the crisis both foreshadowed the problems that arose in the implementation of the Robbins Report, which Berdahl could not have anticipated, but also influenced the Government's reaction to the Report's student number forecasts.

The crisis was precipitated by the introduction of the PESC machinery. Otto Clarke addressed the UGC in January 1962 and congratulated the Committee on the scope and thoroughness of its Quinquennial Report but said that: 'The scale of university finance was now such that decisions could no longer be taken by Treasury Ministers on their own but had become the responsibility of the Government as a whole'.[6] However, the crisis of trust was also about university salaries and the Chief Secretary's statement to the House of Commons on 14 March 1962 dealt with both issues. The context was important: in late 1960 the CVCP took its decision to set up what was to become UCCA to deal with the rapid increase in applications for university admission; the Anderson Committee's Report had been accepted so that from 1961–62 candidates admitted to a place in higher education would automatically receive support for tuition fees and, subject to a means test, for maintenance support, through their local authorities; the Robbins Committee had been established to recommend a new pattern for higher education. Expansion looked to be set fair.

In November 1960 the UGC had met Edward Boyle, the Financial Secretary to the Treasury and Otto Clarke and had argued that while it believed that 200,000 places would be needed by the early 1970s it would accept a provisional figure of 170,0000 at a cost of £175m, 50 per cent of which was represented by arrears and obsolescence. Timing was important because new money was urgently required for building starts in 1962 and 1963. Decisions on capital grants for 1964 and 1965 were required at the same time so that universities could develop coherent plans. Boyle temporized by asking whether decisions on numbers could not wait for Robbins but the Committee replied that 170,000 was 'an absolute minimum' but that the higher figure could wait for Robbins. It went on to say that universities could not be asked to undertake further expansion unless capital support was provided because it was on this basis that universities had agreed to expand. Clarke accused the universities of seeking 'preferential treatment'; even the school building programme, he said, was only settled two years in advance. There was a 'very real problem for the Government to commit themselves so far ahead as 1964–65 on one particular segment of the national investment'.[7] By January 1961 the UGC had secured some improvement in the capital provision 1962–65, resisting an attempt by the Treasury to include in the figures the remaining £8m required to complete the Imperial College redevelopment, and had obtained acceptance of expansion to 170,000 by the early 1970s.

But at the January 1962 meeting, with the new PESC process under way, Clarke sought to bring to the attention of the Committee the new economic realities: the Treasury's view was that GDP would not rise above 2.5 per cent; unless public expenditure could be constrained to between 40 per cent and 45 per cent of national expenditure tax increases would be necessary; the Government was facing enormous demands from the health services and the roads programme. 'The problem for the Government was to see whether and how increases of this order [in the UGC budget] could be fitted in to a reasonable allocation of national resources over the next five years'.[8] On 14 March, Henry Brooke, the new Chief Secretary, reported to the House of Commons that 'considerations of economic policy, which are of course, right outside the scope of the [UGC's] responsibility have made it necessary to depart from the Committee's recommendations' (Berdahl 1962). The actual settlement was not far short of the UGC's quinquennial bid: it did not provide recurrent resource to bring the staff/student ratio back to 1:9.6 from 1:10.7 (the universities had actually overshot their student number targets) and capital provision (which included for residences) was not guaranteed at the level requested to meet the 1966–67 target of 150,000. But the crucial issue was the deferment of acceptance of the 170,000 figure till 1973–74 a year later than the end of the following quinquennium and of the UGC's own projection of the need for places. The CVCP immediately issued a statement which said that the Government had not accepted the advice of the

UGC and that the target of 150,000 by 1966–67 could not be achieved with the limited provision made available.[9]

The reaction in the House of Commons was also immediate and in special debates in both Houses on 5 April and 16 May the Government faced severe criticism. Gaitskell, leading for the Labour Party in the Commons, described the Government's action as 'discreditable in substance, dishonourable in presentation and deplorable in its consequences', Lord Longford in the Lords argued that the action made it clear that the universities could not be left under the sponsorship of the Treasury (Berdahl 1962). Perhaps more significant was that the decision was criticized by Conservative speakers in the Commons, and not just by the Opposition.

But running alongside this issue lay another, the question of salary comparability, where once again the increasingly anomalous special position of the universities was in question. The UGC had taken over responsibility for deciding academic salary scales in 1947 at the request of the CVCP. This made obvious good sense because any increase in salary scales, unless anticipated in the quinquennial settlement, required Treasury approval for supplementation of the settlement for an increase to be implemented. Thenceforth decisions on salary scales involved a so-called 'stately minuet' of discussions between the CVCP, the AUT and the UGC followed by formal submissions by the UGC to the Chancellor, a process which offered ample opportunities for informal sounding outs prior to each stage of the process. This machinery had delivered a salary increase effective from 1 January 1960 which had taken into account a rise in civil service pay (and particularly the starting salary of the grade of principal against which university lecturer salaries were notionally aligned in the eyes of the universities), effective from the autumn of 1959. In the summer of 1960, however, the Treasury conceded a further increase of 21 per cent to the scientific civil service and 24 per cent to principals in the administrative civil service. In its Quinquennial Report for 1957–62 the UGC said bitterly that it had been 'unaware of the changes contemplated' and that the CVCP had advised it that if it had known of the intended civil service increase it was extremely unlikely that a maximum of £1,850 for the lecturers' grade would have been either proposed or agreed to' (UGC 1964 para 102). The UGC understandably felt that its close relationship with Treasury officials would have ensured that it would have been alerted to such an intended increase. To make matters worse, academic salaries in the CATs and teacher training colleges, which were part of the Burnham (state teachers) pay machinery were later increased by 17 per cent. The civil service pay award led to an immediate claim for rectification by the AUT and discussions were initiated between the CVCP, the UGC and the AUT which led to an informal understanding by early 1961, between the UGC and the Treasury, of an 8 per cent increase backdated to 1960, subject to a recommendation by the UGC about the distribution of the award amongst academic grades. In its later Quinquennial Report the UGC stated explicitly that discussions with CVCP and AUT were, at the suggestion of the Treasury, kept in step with the review of salaries by the Burnham Committee which was being undertaken in the spring and early summer 1961, and which resulted in the CAT teacher training rises quoted above (UGC 1964 para104).

Meantime public sector pay was escalating and the Chancellor, Selwyn Lloyd, declared a pay pause of 3 per cent wage and salary increases from July 1961. The UGC thought that its claim had been accepted by the Treasury and had rushed over a set of proposals on the distribution of the 8 per cent to the Treasury by the due date. The Treasury, however, ruled that because there had been no formal commitment by the Government to provide the necessary supplementation before 25 July, the due date, the universities' case fell within the terms of the pay pause. Once again the Treasury appeared to reject its relationship with the UGC especially because the Burnham settlement was waved through. For the one and only time in its existence the UGC members considered resignation. The Chief Secretary told Murray that Treasury Ministers had been prepared to support a salary award of between 8 per cent and 9 per cent but that other ministers were very reluctant to permit any breaking of the pay pause. According to Murray, UGC members were split 50:50 on the issue of resignation (one member unable to be present had already sent in her conditional letter of resignation) but he broke the tie on behalf of the Treasury.[10] At a meeting with a new Chief Secretary, Boyd Carpenter, in September the UGC minutes quote Murray as saying:

> In recent months relations between the Treasury and the Committee had not been very happy . . . The Committee had been rather proud of the fact that for some 70 years or more they had been regarded as part of the Treasury and as confidential advisers on academic matters to Treasury Ministers. Recently, however, they had felt that they were not being regarded as part of the Treasury and their advice on academic matters had been questioned.[11]

The last sentence reflected a decision to override a Treasury view as to the distribution of the 3 per cent pay award which, with the warm concurrence of the CVCP, was entirely devoted to the improvement of the position of assistant lecturers in order to assist the recruitment of staff to meet the growth in student numbers. A less worthy reason may also have been to provide competition with teacher training and civil service starting salaries which were now considerably higher than applied in universities.

The strength of the public concern and its potential effect on the coming General Election ensured that this breakdown between the UGC and the Government was quickly repaired in financial terms: in May 1963, five months before Robbins reported, the Chief Secretary announced an additional grant for the last four years of the quinquennium, and the salary question was referred to the new National Incomes Commission (NIC) which in April 1964 agreed a 10 per cent award. But its wider impact was considerable and drove decisive policy changes. These may be summarized as follows:

- The constitutional implications of the application of PESC procedures to the consideration of the UGC's quinquennial estimate and the salary issue made it absolutely clear to senior officials in the Treasury that it could no longer be the department responsible for the universities. Until this point the universities could be funded through the Treasury under what could be seen as private, 'back pocket', arrangements. Once wider scrutiny was applied, whether through PESC or on pay, a more sceptical view of the priority of university funding, as compared with other areas of government spending, emerged. The need to transfer the university vote out of the Treasury was a clear theme in the Treasury's evidence to Robbins and the distrust of the Treasury aroused by the events of 1962 within universities made the transfer ultimately easier politically.

• The political impact of Brooke's confession to Parliament that he had not been able to meet the UGC's financial recommendations was very considerable on a Government that was already unpopular and facing criticism of its economic management. The electoral implications of cutting back on the opportunity of going to university were all too obvious. Within 24 hours of the publication of the Robbins Report the Government issued a statement accepting its projection of 197,000 students in universities, including the CATs, by 1967–68, instead of the previous target of 150,000, and 217,000 by 1973–74 instead of the previous 170,000. This was a remarkable reversal of the position adopted only 18 months before when Brooke turned down the UGC's much more modest figures. Carswell makes it clear that the damage caused by the 1962 rejection of the UGC's estimate was responsible for the *volte face*. Edward Heath, a senior Cabinet Minister at the time, said bluntly 'We had no choice'.[12]

• The two serious rebuffs, on the 1962–67 estimates and particularly on salaries, demonstrated that the UGC's 'insider' role was inevitably, bearing in mind the changes in the machinery of government and the pressures of managing public sector inflation, doomed to be replaced by a more arms length relationship with the centre of government. When the NIC hearings on university pay took place in 1963–64 the UGC, for the first time, publicly disagreed with Treasury evidence, and, one result of the Commission's findings was that the Committee lost its role in university salary determination. The CVCP, in its evidence to Robbins, made great play of the importance of the informal relationship between its own senior officers and the UGC's but in practice once the UGC lost its intimate links with the Treasury it had to exercise a more independent role *vis-à-vis* the CVCP unless it was to appear to be simply a spokesman for university interests. The appointment of Wolfendon and his head masterly style in dealing with university matters contributed to distancing the CVCP from the UGC and weakening its influence. At a dinner for him in 1968 the absence of applause for his retirement speech was said to sum up vice-chancellors' resentment of his admonitory style.[13]

The events of 1962 represent, therefore, a watershed between the universities' privileged existence under the Treasury and the less protected position as a small cog in the much larger machinery of government. This new status was emphasized by the decision by Crosland to support the Public Accounts Committee's demand that the universities' accounts should be subject to public accountability (see below).

The impact of the oil crisis 1973–74

The decade, that is the two quinquennia between 1962 (once the Chief Secretary's decisions had been reversed) and 1972, represent what later commentators described as 'the Golden Age' of university funding and development. It was easy to forget the rejection of the Robbins proposals on structure and Crosland's decisions on the binary line when universities were expanding, capital programmes were changing the faces of university campuses and recurrent grant levels were closely linked to student number growth. However, beneath the outward signs of untroubled progress there were issues which were to surface when the financial waters grew choppy. Reputationally universities suffered severely with the public and with Government from the student revolts of 1968 to 1973, a loss of sympathy and respect which had serious consequences for funding in later years. The media headlines arising out of the troubles at LSE, Warwick and Essex as well as other universities significantly weakened the respect in which universities were held in Whitehall. In the CVCP there was concern about the longer term implications of the growth of the polytechnics and the effects it might have on decisions on the universities' share of the growth in student numbers. (In the 1962 crisis the universities had been, in Parliament's and the public's mind at least, a monopoly provider). But more important, the Treasury and therefore the DES were becoming concerned at the cost implications of the Robbins expansion and discussions were initiated between the UGC, now under the chairmanship of Ken (later Sir Ken) Berrill, an economist, the DES and the Treasury. The indications were sufficiently serious that the CVCP abandoned previous practice of a meeting of the full Committee with the Secretary of State (now Margaret Thatcher) to set the scene for planning the new quinquennium, and substituted a more informal meeting with members of its General Purposes Committee. It was already clear to the DES that the pressures on public expenditure generally were such that further expansion would have to be at lower cost.

At a meeting in September 1969 between the DES, UGC and CVCP the expectation that the staff:student ratio would worsen by 10 per cent had been canvassed openly.[14] Discussion of Shirley Williams' 13 Points (see below) had also alerted universities to future funding difficulties though the Points were of such a character that each individual university could see grounds for thinking that they did not really apply to them. However the general economic position was weakening all the time. When the Heath Government came to power in 1970 the new Secretary of State, Margaret Thatcher, was in a difficult position in having been committed to higher education expansion without having the standing either with the Prime Minister or with the Cabinet to demand the necessary resources. At the CVCP's first meeting with her in September 1970 she stonewalled on future student numbers, on capital grants and on the next quinquennium. As inflation rose to 10 per cent in 1973 so the quinquennial system came under threat and a provisional year was declared for 1972–73 with longer term decisions being deferred to a Public Expenditure White Paper, eventually published in December 1973, itself a reaction to the oil crisis. The financial downturn was sufficiently grave for GDP to become negative in 1974 (–1.3 per cent) and 1975 (–0.6 per cent).

The impact of the White Paper was immediate: a moratorium on new buildings starts until June 1974 was declared. (To give an example of the impact of this on a 1960s New University, Warwick, which had a social studies building caught in the moratorium, had to locate its social history centre in a nearby farmhouse, its sociology department in the chemistry building and its new psychology department in engineering.) The impact was also on recurrent grant: a planned supplementary grant to cover inflation was cut by half, minor works money was cut by nearly half, together with a reduction in student number expansion. The White Paper aimed to cut 20 per cent of capital expenditure and 10 per cent of procurement costs across the public sector. The CVCP estimated that 'most if not all universities will have to plan for and incur deficits in 1974–75 and these are bound to be substantial in some cases'.[15] In addition, wage freezes, in place since November 1972, were replaced when Labour regained power in March 1974 with wage control through the Social Contract ultimately leading to new controls on public expenditure imposed under pressure from the International Monetary Fund (IMF). The previous PESC system, operating on the basis of allocation on the basis of volume planning, had broken down. The Treasury had lost control of public expenditure with the public sector ratio of government expenditure rising from 51.1 per cent in 1973–74 to 57.3 per cent in 1974–75 to 58.5 per cent in 1975–76 with the threat of exceeding 60 per cent in 1976–77 when the new cash limits policy was introduced in April 1976 (Middleton 1996).

These developments constituted a remarkable shock to a university system which, although it did not at the time recognize it, had been enjoying the most secure planning and funding framework at any time in its history. The Letters of Guidance from the UGC which had been begun under Wolfendon's chairmanship dried up under Fred (later Lord) Dainton's chairmanship because the quinquennial system once interrupted in 1973 could never be reintroduced. Universities, still substantially funded from Government sources, were increasingly dependent on the twists and turns of the public expenditure process. This was reflected in the following policy changes:

- The ending of the quinquennial funding system became inevitable when rising inflation led to repeated demands for supplementation, driven for the most part by the absence of control over public sector pay. This removed a process which provided a framework within which university development over an extended five year period could be discussed on a broadly concensual basis between the DES, the UGC and the CVCP. The impact of the oil crisis and the downturn was to make bidding for resources, especially when reduced to a year by year process, a much more frantic and political exercise.

- The introduction of a cash limits policy meant that institutional planning became no longer simply a question of student number planning, to which resources would be attached, but began the process of an internal integration of financial with other planning elements which is now the norm in university strategic planning. But it also emphasized, as the cash limits policy was intended to do generally, that institutions dependent on public money could no longer expect protection from the state if things went wrong. The public expenditure sector of the Treasury was inclined to treat education like any other public service and the UGC, now one stage removed from a relationship with the Treasury, was dependent on a DES and a secretary of state that were inevitably concerned as much with the political priorities within expenditure in education as with the less immediate demands of a system which saw funding for expansion as an entitlement. Student activism had dimmed the respect in which universities and their vice-chancellors had previously been held and the universities represented just another claimant on an increasingly contested budget.

The 1981 cuts

By 1980–81 student numbers in the public sector had grown to 146,000 full time and 46,000 part time as against the university sector, 269,000 and 18,000. During the 1970s overall expenditure in local authorities had mushroomed from some 25 per cent to some 33 per cent of total public expenditure as a result of an increase in their responsibilities in education, health, social services, housing and the environment. The increase in expenditure on public sector higher education was very much part of this. The need to assert control through PESC was urgent (Thain and Wright 1995).

The local authorities had established a national pooling machinery for FE and AFE in 1958 under which LEAs recouped resources according to their AFE provision estimated on the basis of time devoted to advanced teaching. This was primarily a technical exercise and had no DES involvement. It was also open ended in that individual LEAs could build up large institutions at no direct cost to themselves. It was open ended in another way in that although all new course programmes had to be approved by the DES Inspectorate with degree programmes requiring approval by the CNAA, there was no national mechanism to prevent programme duplication or Letters of Guidance to institutions issued by the UGC as in the university sector. The Oakes Committee Report in 1978 expressed concern at the lack of sector wide planning and of machinery to control expenditure. As we have seen above the Report was overtaken by the 1979 change of Government and one immediate result was a decision to cap the pool from 1980–81. The creation of NAB in 1982 was an obvious response to the need to allocate a fixed resource base and was fully in line with Treasury thinking. NAB proved to be effective in controlling total expenditure but exercised little planning function at the institutional or programmatic levels. Student number growth proceeded unaffected.

The university sector provided a complete contrast. Ted (later Sir Edward) Parkes, who had succeeded Dainton as Chairman of the UGC in 1979, had been Vice-Chancellor of City University and had experienced the difficulties of the 1970s at first hand, including the consequential decline in the unit of resource. With no quinquennial planning structure to guide it the university sector seemed rudderless. Reflecting the uncertainty of a change of government and ignorance of the new Government's financial policies, Parkes embarked on a planning exercise in which each university was invited to prepare scenario plans against a 2 per cent increase, level funding or a 5 per cent reduction (most universities believed the last figure was completely implausible). This was followed up by 'Dialogue' meetings between each institution and the Committee at which it was made clear that the UGC intended to make value judgements in its allocation of recurrent and capital resources between universities. The exercise was almost immediately undercut by the new Government's decision to end the funding of international students producing savings of £100m beginning in 1980–81. The new Secretary of State promised that these were sufficient to provide for level funding for the rest of the sector. However this guarantee only lasted until December 1980 when a further 3.5 per cent was cut from the UGC budget for 1981–82. The Government's intention, coupled with the introduction of cash planning, was to reduce public expenditure significantly, and a further round of cuts of 5 per cent for 1982–83 and 1983–84 was announced in May 1981.

The UGC was faced with a commitment to make 'dirigiste' decisions on university development in a situation where the university system was facing a reduction of recurrent grant, plus the removal of the cost of international students, of around 17 per cent. It chose to undertake the exercise by following three principles: the first was to seek to improve the unit of resource by reducing overall student numbers by 5 per cent, the second was to reverse the trend towards arts-based disciplines, turning a 50:50 arts/social studies:science split in 1978–80 to 48:52 in 1984–85, and the third was to assess the quality of academic departments through its existing subject sub-committees. It had considered and rejected options to close some institutions, to move to a tiered system which divided universities into research intensive and teaching intensive institutions or to simply apply the cuts *pro rata*. The key to its approach, Parkes said, was that 'we made no value judgements about institutions at all. We have worked on a subject basis' (Parkes 1982). Even the weakest universities had parts that were worth preserving either in terms of student choice for particular courses or for research in particular areas. The application of the three principles outlined above led to a very varied distribution of the cuts ranging from Salford 44 per cent to York 6 per cent. The UGC's approach in its attempt to re-structure the sector on the basis of academic merit, and the need to sacrifice student numbers to regain what it regarded as an appropriate unit of resource in order to maintain 'a healthy, flexible and innovative university system',[16] could not have been more different to what happened in the public sector where the pool was capped but where institutions continued to expand, albeit from a lower resource base.

The UGC's decisions provoked an enormous public outcry both in the universities and in Parliament. Within the universities, the UGC was regarded as being an agent of Government and there were calls for its resignation. The CVCP did not join this chorus but was very critical of the decision to reduce student numbers thus, in a sense, reversing a position which its discussion in 1966 (see below) might have taken it to, where maintaining the unit of resource with the corollary that the overflow of candidates should be accommodated in the public sector, might have had a greater priority than expansion. Strategically it was right to do so but the much lower and more flexible unit costs of expansion in the public sector was welcome to the Treasury and the DES showed no willingness to try to ameliorate the UGC's decision. The UGC's position of *de facto* autonomy in decision making had insulated it from the need to seek approval from or even to brief Ministers so the Secretary of State, now Joseph, was forced, in the House of Commons, to defend the denial of opportunity to enter university, the ground on which much of the public criticism was made, on the basis of the UGC's independence from Government. This was a highly political issue for the Government, especially at a time when the imposition of public expenditure cuts was reflected in increased unemployment.

However, inside the university system, questions of institutional balance were equally important arising from the decision to change the subject balance more towards science and technology, a decision which Parkes said was taken in 'the national economic interest' (Select Committee on Education, Science and Arts 1981). Thus eight universities found themselves shorn of more than 10 per cent of their students, with three former CATs, Salford, Aston and Bradford losing 30 per cent, 22 per cent and 19 per cent respectively because their technological courses were seen to be attracting students of insufficient calibre (although they satisfied the Robbins 'A' level criteria). A further issue arose in Medicine where an ongoing expansion, agreed with the Department of Health and Social Security was brought to a halt, because its costs were six times an arts and twice a science and engineering place, and because even holding student numbers at 1979–80 entry levels would produce a 5 per cent rate of growth. One result of the UGC's decision on student numbers was to change the balance between the two sectors: a paper prepared by the DES for the NAB board and the UGC in 1983 spelled out the planned figures (see Table 3.2). By 1985–86 the public

Table 3.2 Planned numbers in higher education 1980–81 to 1985–86

		1980–81 000	1981–82 000	1982–83 000	1983–84 000	1984–85 000	1985–86 000
AFE	**Ft**	146	162	177	184/193	185/194	179/191
	Pt	46	48	47	47	47	47
Universities (excluding OU)							
	Ft	269	272	268	259	251	251
	Pt	18	18	19	19	19	19

Source: DES Higher Education: comparison of Funding and Costs across Sectors. Note for the NAB Board and UGC 6 July 1983, CVCP Archive, October 1983.

sector might be expected to have nearly caught up the universities in terms of 'heads' if not in full time equivalents.

At this distance in time it is hard to realize the shock to the university system that the 1981 cuts delivered. Apart from the 1962 event, described above, and this after all involved only a potential reduction in future expansion (which was reversed within months) not a reduction in actual income, the universities had since 1946 enjoyed a continuous expansion in student numbers and in matching recurrent grant. The events of 1973–74 had blown the system off course but the arrival of a Conservative Government, which had traditionally had close links with the university system, seemed to many in universities likely to offer a period of welcome stability. The drama of the UGC's letter of 1 July and the realization that cuts of this magnitude had inevitable consequences for individuals, a prospect which had not been contemplated even in the recession of the 1930s, completed a process of breakdown of trust in the state which had begun to take root in the early 1970s.

The CVCP was able to negotiate two ameliorations of the 1981 cuts. The first was the financing of a generous early retirement scheme. However, the cost of the scheme had to be found outside the DES budget. This was a card that the universities would never be permitted to play again. The second was the financing of a new injection of young talent into the universities. This was the outcome of a dinner in May 1982 attended by the Prime Minister, Joseph, William Waldegrave, the Minister for Higher Education, representatives of the CVCP and the Presidents of the Royal Society and the British Academy, and the Chairman of the UGC. The object of the dinner was to be to discuss the universities' role in preparing young people for work in a market economy and the question of university management. (The Rayner led Financial Management Initiative had been launched in Whitehall and was in due course to be applied in the universities by the Jarratt Committee and by the Good Management Practice Group in the public sector.) However, discussion turned to the impact the cuts were having on the career prospects of young scientists whose recruitment to academic posts was prohibited while universities were reducing their staffs. The result was that the Government found funds for 750 'New Blood' posts and 140 Information Technology posts, spread over three years, to be awarded on research criteria by the UGC and the Research Councils. This certainly acted as a fillip to the science community but the award of posts tended inevitably to replicate the UGC's academic judgements in 1981 so offered little succour to universities which had been hit the hardest.

The effect of the UGC's actions in 1981 was to begin the process of differentiating the university system which was to be reinforced by the introduction of the RAE in 1985–6 and thereafter. Hitherto, the UGC's resource allocation process had essentially funded universities on a broadly comparable basis taking account of student numbers and different subject weightings but otherwise exercising judgement in the allocation of additional resources only at the margins and on the advice of subject committees. A comparison of the upper and lower ends of the table of reduced resources reflecting the 1981 cuts and the subsequent investment in New Blood and Information Technology posts shows how over the period 1980–81 – when UGC recurrent grant plus tuition fees represented 80 per cent of universities' budgets – to 1986–87 the balance of the university system was changed. Not only was the myth of its homogeneity destroyed but the differentiation placed some institutions firmly on a route of travel from which they found it hard to escape once the research assessment process took hold. Clearly, too much weight should not be placed on single percentage differences but what Table 3.3 illustrates is the way the budget reductions began to create a new ranking inside the university system. What it also shows is how the university system was essentially re-shaped over the

Table 3.3 Reductions in Government income to universities 1980–81 to 1986–87

	1981 cuts to 1983–84		*Comparison with 1980–81 income in 1986–87 after New Blood and IT post investment*
Largest reduction	%		%
Salford	−44	Salford	−43.2
Keele	−34	Keele	−35
Bradford	−33	Hull	−35
Aston	−31	Bradford	−33
UMIST	−30	Aston	−31.7
Stirling	−27	UMIST	−28.1
Surrey	−26	Surrey	−24.6

Aberdeen	−23	Aberdeen	−24.4
Kent	−21	UWIST	−24.4
Sussex	−21	Stirling	−22.7

Lowest reduction	%		%
Southampton	12	Oxford	−12.4
Edinburgh	11	Cambridge	−12.3
Glasgow	11	Heriot Watt	−10.1
Durham	10	Southampton	−9.4
Cambridge	10	Glasgow	−7.8
East Anglia	9	Warwick	−7.3
Leicester	9	Leeds	−8.1
Loughborough	8	Loughborough	−6.3
Bath	7	Bath	−4.6
York	6	York	+1.5

Sources: 1981–84: Sizer (1987), Table 2; 1986–7 comparison: Answer to Parliamentary Question 9 June 1986 quoted in CVCP Archive, CVCP papers June 1986.

period 1981–86 even before the effects of the 1985–86 RAE were felt. Those universities most severely affected in 1981 had to adjust to the loss of funds and the internal restructuring which as a consequence became a permanent institutional realignment. Not all universities that had suffered least necessarily held 'top ten' positions in later media league tables. The 1981 cuts and their aftermath represented a watershed in the development of the university system.

The implementation of the 1981 cuts and the period that followed marked a policy divide in the history of higher education:

- The reductions in public expenditure were not aimed specifically at higher education, although the universities certainly assumed that they were, but were one element in a wider economic policy being pursued by the Thatcher Government. The contrast between the way the two sectors approached the reductions was bound to raise questions of coordination in the minds of ministers and civil servants, and the absence of accountability and control on the public sector side, together with the different attitude which the Conservative Government displayed towards the local authorities as compared to their Labour predecessors, were the policy drivers which resulted in the creation of NAB and the attempts to stimulate collaboration between NAB and the UGC as a way of developing more effective coordination across the binary line.

- The UGC's decision to cut student numbers in order to preserve the unit of resource would have been seen as a challenge by any Government and was a political mistake of the first magnitude. It reinforced a sense, which was already present in the Department, that the Secretary of State had to assume a steering function over higher education and Joseph made his intentions plain in that respect as soon as he was appointed. In some senses the UGC action represented a last hurrah for a university system independent of government, publicly funded but self regulatory and internally directed. Giving the maintenance (or in this case an improvement) of the unit of resource as a priority over student demand for places might well have accorded with the views of some sections of the CVCP in its discussions in 1966 (see below) but it condemned the UGC to be seen as out of step with public opinion and as a tool of Government (which, as we have seen, it certainly was not). Its decision on student numbers was taken with the best of intentions but its description as a 'buffer' between the university system and the Government of the day was no longer convincing to university opinion. This was the major reason why its dissolution in 1989 caused so little outcry within the university system.

- Neither the DES nor the UGC (whose members should have done) recognized the legal obstacle to removing academic staff from the payroll to bring down costs. Tenure had not been tested in any situation since 1945 and it was short sighted of the UGC to assume that it would not be a problem. The effect of the need to provide an early retirement fund was to ensure that the Treasury and later the Public Accounts Committee would insist on steps being taken for its removal, as indeed happened following the 1988 legislation (see below).

- The implementation of the cuts on the university system imposed for the first time a differentiation based on academic performance. Although the details of the methodology and of the data on which it was based were widely challenged, it could not be said that the results did not reflect the unspoken assumptions of informed people within the sector. There is no doubt that this changed the sector and prepared the ground for the more rigorous differentiation introduced by the RAE.

The 1995–96 funding crisis

The decade between 1985–86 and 1995–96 can be defined as the period of the search for an alternative to public funding to finance the rapid growth in the system. A figure presented in the Dearing Report (NCIHE 1997) described the issue with great clarity (see Figure 3.3). This disastrous funding profile, from an institutional point of view, though not from the Treasury's, created 'a real sense of crisis in UK higher education' and was accompanied by 'a sense of paralysis within the major political parties in terms of what to do about it'. (Watson and Amoah 2007: 7–8.) For perhaps the first time since the 1940s it was the CVCP, stiffened by its new CDP membership, which forced a way forward.

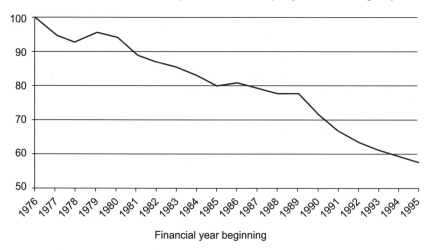

Financial year beginning

Figure 3.3 Index of public funding per student for higher education 1976–77 to 1995–96

Source: NCIHE (1997), chart 3.16.

The CVCP's first attempt was hardly auspicious. The Committee established a working party on alternative funding under Professor Burnett, Principal of Edinburgh, in 1983 prompted by a letter from Joseph to the UGC in which he argued: 'The higher the proportion of university income that comes from non-government sources the greater their freedom of action and their capacity to survive the fluctuations in the level of recurrent grant'.[17] The Burnett working party reported back in July 1984. It began by quoting the proportionate elements of university income over a period of 30 years (see Table 3.4).

Table 3.4 Components of University income 1951–52 to 1980–81

	1951–2	*1960–61*	*1970–71*	*1980–81*
	%	%	%	%
1 Exchequer grants	66.5	75.2	71.2	62.6
2 Fees & supplementary grants	14.8	9.2	6.3	17.2
(Total recurrent funding)	81.3	84.4	77.5	79.8
3 Endowment, donations	7.1	3.6	1.5	0.9
4 Research grants & contracts	–	9.1	12.7	12.9
5 Income from other sources	11.6	1.9	2.9	2.9
6 Other	–	4.0	5.3	3.5

Source: Report on The Feasibility of Alternative Funding for Universities (the Burnett Report) CVCP.[18]

The Report saw little prospect of generating any additional income from lines 3, 5 and 6, having decided that most of the activities added costs rather than useable income, and accepted as given that Exchequer grants plus state paid tuition fees must continue. Astonishingly, it made no allowance for an increase in income from tuition fees from international students. It concluded that: 'It seems inevitable, therefore, if distortion is to be avoided, if the broad sweep of studies is to continue and if academic standards are to be maintained, that universities must inevitably restrict the acceptance of alternative income'.[19] This was an ostrich-like reaction especially when some universities had already demonstrated that alternative income was available if the right steps were taken to generate it, although none of them would have suggested that it could offer any serious alternative to state income.

The Burnett working party was replaced four years later by the Brundin Group on Alternative Funding which reported in 1988. Once again the Group could see little prospect in generating any significant new income from fund raising, the scale of services or other activities but it did recommend that tuition fees should be doubled as this would give universities the incentive to increase their student numbers. The Group did not, however, suggest any change in the source of the finance for fees, so in effect, it was merely suggesting a transfer of government funding from one head to another.[20] In September, Baker gave his response at the CVCP Residential Conference when he said 'No foreseeable British Government – whatever its political complexion – is likely to increase taxation and public spending substantially'. Public expenditure still accounted for more than 40 per cent of GDP and, with an ageing population, would be difficult to hold at this level. Since GDP was rising universities should try to get a share of it.[21]

The result was a further working party but this time, jointly with the CDP now released from local authority control, with five members from each side and chaired by John Ashworth. This time it avoided the limitation of addressing alternative funding but took as its title the Working Group on Funding Mechanisms. This altogether more robust body reported in August 1990. It offered four models for funding the system: full cost tuition fees plus scholarships; 'top up' fees paid by students supplementary to government paid fees with fee levels varying according to subject; a repayable loan scheme operated either through the tax system or national insurance; a graduate tax. These ideas were to frame the search for a new model for the next decade. The Report concluded: 'The continuation of the present funding policies for higher education will not achieve the expansion of student numbers that the Government wishes to see at the quality which society demands.' Increased funding was therefore necessary and the source had to be the students themselves unless the Government were to step in. 'Simply to continue with present policies will lead to a demoralised, poor quality system which will be incapable of meeting the real needs of society. Wait and see is not a viable option'.[22] 'Wait and see', however, was precisely the option which the Government chose to follow. The Government's immediate response was a call for greater productivity and both the Minister, Alan Howarth and the

Chief Executive of the UFC, Graeme Davies, urged the adoption of modu-larization and semesterization as a way of reducing costs. In April 1991, Kenneth Clarke formally rejected top up fees opting for a market-led approach where institutions were invited to expand on the basis of fee income alone. This was confirmed as Government policy at a CVCP meeting with the Prime Minister, John Major, in December when the CVCP minutes record him as saying that he was 'not in favour of the proposals such as top up fees. He did not want to get in a fight with the university sector but it was not sensible to force the Government into a corner on this issue'.[23]

It was the Government's turn to put its head in the sand. The CVCP did not, however, let up on its pressure for a solution. A new group, now called significantly, on Additional Funding, chaired by Clive (later Sir Clive) Booth commissioned a report from the consultants, London Economics and produced a progress report which offered four options, refining the models proposed by the Ashworth Group: a graduate tax; a fee income-contingent loan scheme based on the Australian Higher Education Contribution Scheme (HECS); a maintenance income-contingent loan scheme, for student maintenance only; and 'top up' fees paid for by income-contingent loans with universities independently setting the level of fees.[24] It was recog-nized that only top up fees would guarantee additional funding. At its meeting on 8 December 1995 the Committee reacted strongly against the Chancellor's budget statement for 1996 which imposed further recurrent grant reductions. The Committee agreed that this 'could have only one outcome' and formally endorsed the top up fee proposal. The meeting was due to be addressed by a Minister who withdrew at the last moment and sent a civil servant to read his speech; the Committee refused to hear the speech. In February the Executive Committee agreed that unless there had been movement on the Government side by the September Residential Conference it would recommend that a 'special levy' of £300 be charged to the 1997–98 student entry.[25] The pace had been forced by a group of politically experi-enced post-1992 vice-chancellors, hardened in the battles over the 1988 and 1992 legislation, and it was entirely characteristic that the motion was proposed by a post-1992 vice-chancellor, Lesley Wagner. In March, the Secretary of State, Gillian Shephard, announced the Dearing Inquiry with the support of the Labour Party. Neither political party was willing to commit itself to top up or any other form of tuition fees payable by students before the General Election and it was left to Lord Dearing, who had already demonstrated his skill as a 'fixer' in education, to find an answer acceptable to a new Government.

At one level the creation of the National Committee of inquiry into Higher Education (NCIHE), better known as the Dearing Committee, represented a triumph for the CVCP's effectiveness in forcing the Government to consider the long term issue of how an expanded higher education sector (it had already reached an age participation rate of 28 per cent and was expected to reach 33 per cent by 2000) was to be funded. Without CVCP pressure it is hard to see either political party grasping the nettle. Chapters 19, 20 and 21 of the

NCIHE Report which recommended new funding arrangements (including the introduction of cost sharing) represented an endorsement of the broad direction of the CVCP's argument. The CVCP threat to impose top up fees if the Government failed to take action had more than an element of bluff about it. The plan was to reach a final decision at the September Residential Conference and then to recommend them to university governing bodies. With mounting student-led opposition there could be no guarantee that all, or even a majority of universities, would have implemented them. And in fact NUS pressure on Blunkett, the shadow Education Secretary of State exacted a promise not to introduce top up fees immediately after the Election. When an amended version of the Dearing proposals was eventually introduced the Treasury took account of the income due to be raised by reducing the recurrent grant thus nullifying the effect of the new income stream. Nevertheless, although at the deeper level of actually providing additional funding for the universities within an immediate timescale, the CVCP may be said not to have succeeded, its pressure forced a recognition that new mechanisms had to be found to fund higher education which eventually bore fruit in 2004.

Student numbers and funding policies

The post-War expansion of demand for higher education was the fundamental driver of funding policies throughout the period 1946 to 2011, although the ways it influenced policy and the pressure it exerted varied over the period. The growth in demand from 1962, when UCCA first began to centralize application statistics, is well illustrated in Figure 3.4. Applications to public institutions were not recorded systematically until the creation of the Polytechnics and Colleges Application System (PCAS) in 1986 but there was a considerable overlap between applications through UCCA and those made direct to public sector institutions (Whitburn *et al.* calculated this to be 67 per cent in the mid-70s; Whitburn *et al.* 1976). Prior to 1961–62 applicants applied direct to institutions and overall demand statistics were estimates only, although Kelsall's major study in 1957 (Kelsall 1957) along with the increasingly administrative burden on universities facing multiple applications, provided the CVCP with the rationale to plan and bring into existence a centralized application system.

The rate of demand for places in higher education has, since the War, exercised a potent political pressure on government which did not occur in the same way in many other countries. The historian, Gardner, argues that during the Blitz an informed social contract was forged: 'People who "took it" should be entitled to "get it" – if "it" meant better housing, a fairer education system, more job opportunities' (Gardner 2011: 366). Any denial of opportunities to enter higher education has historically been regarded as a political issue and lay at the heart of the outcry in 1962 and the opposition to the UGC in 1981 (see above). Thereafter, and until 1992, the flexibility of the public sector ensured that, even with severe reductions in the unit of

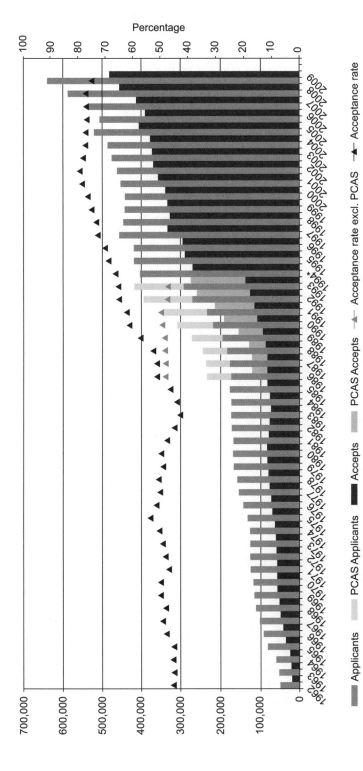

Figure 3.4 Full-time undergraduates (all domiciles) 1962–2009 applicants and accepts through UCCA, PCAS and UCAS

Note: *UCCA and PCAS merged in 1994 to form UCAS.

Source: UCAS (2010).

■ Applicants ■ PCAS Applicants ■ Accepts ■ PCAS Accepts ▲ Acceptance rate excl. PCAS ▲ Acceptance rate resource, arguments about the denial of opportunity could not be sustained. However, they were to resurface in 1994 when the Treasury imposed a halt to the post-1989 burst of expansion and in 2010 when the Comprehensive Spending Review imposed a limit on student numbers.

The Robbins expansion

The argument that demand must be met was particularly influential in respect to funding policies in the period up to and including Robbins to the extent that the Report was mostly celebrated for its so-called 'Robbins principle' which was effectively no more than a codification of a policy which governments of either party had followed since the War. The more important contribution of the Report was the forecast of the growth of student numbers for which financial provision would be necessary, from 216,000 in 1962–63 to 558,000 in 1980–81 (Committee on Higher Education 1963, Table 30). These numbers took on an added significance because they were immediately accepted up to 1973–74 by the Conservative Government, acting under the pressure of the backlash from the 1962 crisis. Under the volume planning regime adopted by PESC, they were then written into the Treasury's budgeting and provided a secure backdrop for quinquennial planning. One result was that the UGC embarked on planning for the 1972–77 quinquennium by inviting universities to consider substantial expansion targets.

Another reason for optimism, at the time, was that Margaret Thatcher, the newly appointed Secretary of State, perhaps to gain a march on her Cabinet colleagues, decided to adopt the new Government management fad Programme Analysis Review (PAR), one outcome of which was the 1972 White Paper, an ambitious attempt, and the only one of its kind, to pull together a programme for the whole of education in one document, a project in which she had the strong support of Toby Weaver. The inspiration for the exercise was the Government's White Paper *Reorganisation of Central Government*, which took a systems management approach to dealing with policy issues stating that the objective was: 'To improve the quality of policy formulation and decision taking by presenting ministers, collectively in cabinet and individually within their departments, with well defined options, costed where possible, and relating the choice between the options to the contribution they can make to meeting national needs' (HM Treasury 1970). Thatcher was later to describe the approach as 'all too typical of those over ambitious, high spending years . . . [and] the high point of the attempts by Government to overcome the problems inherent in Britain's education system by throwing money at it' (Thatcher 1995: 191).

As Booth says, PAR as a budgeting system ran out of steam because it was too complex (Booth 1983), but at the time the numbers it forecast for both the universities and the polytechnics provided a reassurance (but not for colleges of education) of a secure funding regime. In fact, the White Paper's forecasts, particularly in relation to the school population, proved to be inaccurate but the assumptions of the White Paper were also fatally undermined by the financial crisis shortly to be faced by the Government. Many of the academic departments recommended for closure in 1981 by the UGC were founded in this period against buoyant student number targets which were then to be sharply reduced and the departments left vulnerable. The persistent demand for the rationalization of small departments in the 1980s can be traced back to the optimism generated by the White Paper forecasts.

However, even if the oil crisis had not occurred, the higher education system would have faced serious financial pressure because the Robbins recommendations were based on a false economic prospectus. An examination of the various drafts of the Treasury's evidence to the Committee reveals that there was a serious and sophisticated debate amongst officials as to how the prospective growth of student numbers was to be paid for. From the outset there was full agreement as to the economic and social gains of expansion but the question was 'how to justify the loss of national income'.[26] Three memoranda were to be prepared: A, The economic and financial aspects of expansion; B, The future pattern of higher education in Britain: the implications of a unified administration; and C, Parliament and the Control of University Expenditure. Each were discussed not just with the Chief Secretary, Boyd Carpenter, but also with the Chairman of the UGC, Murray. Memorandum A required by far the largest number of drafts. The Treasury was not in any doubt about the desirability of the expansion – an early draft quoted Macaulay's speech on the Charter Act 1833 to the effect that any learning makes someone to 'be a superior man to him who lacked the accomplishments' and the final submission extended the reference to a full quotation:

> Whatever be the languages, whatever be the sciences, which it is in any age or country the custom to teach, those who become most proficient in those languages or sciences will generally be the flower of youth, the most acute, the most industrious, the most ambitious of honourable distinctions. If the Ptolemaic system were taught in Cambridge instead of the Newtonian, the Senior Wrangler would in general be a superior man to the Wooden Spoon.
>
> If instead of learning Greek we learnt Cherokee, the men who understood Cherokee best, who made the best and most melodious Cherokee verses, who comprehended most accurately the effect of the Cherokee participles would in general be a superior man to him who lacked these accomplishments.
>
> (Committee on Higher Education 1963,
> Evidence Pt 1 Vol F para 43: 1963)

It concluded that 'the scarcest of all resources is people of high ability and the contribution that higher education expansion makes to their discovery and most effective use is an important economic consideration' (p. 1964).

But it found it difficult to quantify the return on investment of a male participation rate rising to 20 per cent. (It did not even consider female participation rates.) It was also concerned that, with the growth of the public service, an undue element might be diverted away from the private sector. It received a range of options for reducing the state contribution by injecting private income into the system using what were later to become very familiar arguments. Tuition fees, it noted, had in the 1930s comprised 30 per cent of university income but had fallen to only 12 per cent now and, following the Anderson Report, were paid by the state. Did not higher education, it argued, bring private as well as public benefit and was it not inequitable, unless fees were covered by loans, for the state to be subventing the 20 per cent of the male age group at the rate £6,000 (the anticipated equivalent of the cost of a university education in 1962) 'which the remaining 80 per cent, including many whose abilities may not be significantly different from those of the 20 per cent do not receive'? (para 60). What was the justification for paying the fees of international students? The Treasury was at pains to make clear that it was not arguing against the international student interest in particular but for the economic costs of higher education to be recognized or 'the expansion itself will in the end be imperilled' (para 61).

The Treasury offered two possible models, what it called the Alpha and the Beta scenarios. The Alpha envisaged 500,000 students in 1980 of whom 250,000 would be in universities, two thirds of whom would be in residence; the universities would receive a 10 per cent improvement in staffing. Beta, on the other hand, assumed present levels of funding and no further increase on the figure of 170,000 already agreed for universities in 1973–74 with any increase beyond this to take place outside the universities. It assumed a constant rise in GNP of 2.5 per cent per annum pa which was higher than the previous decade and thought to be about double the average for the past 100 years and on this basis projected the costs of its two alternatives as a proportion of GNP as in Table 3.5.

It pointed out that even Beta represented nearly a doubling of the proportion of GNP and that the case for higher education had to compete against three other nationally identified priorities in education: improving primary

Table 3.5 Treasury cost models of the growth of higher education 1962

	Recurrent cost %	Capital cost %	Total cost %
1959–60	0.79	0.13	0.92
1980 Alpha	1.70	0.20	1.90
1980 Beta	1.57	0.15	1.72

Source: Treasury evidence to the Robbins Committee.

education and abolishing class sizes of over 40; improving secondary schools and extending the leaving age to 16; extending part time technical education. In addition there were wider public demands for the physical rebuilding of industrial communities, in the NHS and help for the increasing numbers of the elderly. If expenditure in 1959–60 had been at Alpha levels it would have required an additional six pence on the standard rate of income tax; if at Beta levels five pence. The Treasury's view may be summed up as follows:

> There is likely to be a large expansion of public expenditure in the next decade and it can reasonably forecast that governments will continue to limit the rate of growth of each service in order to keep the aggregate within tolerable limits. The development of all publicly financed services is therefore bound to depend upon the Government's choice of priorities between a large number of objectives, all desirable in themselves, but not simultaneously practicable.
>
> (para 58)

Robbins' response to the Treasury's submission was surprising considering Lord Robbins' own professional background as an economist with long term experience of working in and with the Treasury. It was contained in Chapter XIV of the Report, 'The financial and economic aspects of our proposals' comprising no more than 17 out of 296 pages of the Report and in Appendix Four, Part IV 'The Cost of Higher Education'. It is impossible not to conclude that the Committee regarded the funding question as a second or even third order problem. The Report tacitly rejected the Treasury's Alpha and Beta scenarios because its 1980 forecast was for 558,000, broken down as shown in Table 3.6 and made the valid point that the predicted costs must take account of the different costs per student obtaining in the three sectors: universities £777, teacher training £576 and advanced further education £606. (The main difference apart from subject spread, between the universities and rest was, it said, the research element.) Like the Treasury it was unable to construct a plausible rate of return analysis for graduates and it contented itself with reliance on a generalized human capital argument that 'communities that have paid the most attention to higher studies have in general been the most obviously progressive in respect of income and wealth' (para 626) as a justification for the continued investment required. The Report responded positively to the point about tuition fees and recommended that

Table 3.6 Robbins' forecast of student numbers in higher education in 1980–81

Universities (including the CATs)	346,000
Teacher training colleges	146,000
Advanced further education	66,000
Total	558,000

they be raised to the equivalent of 20 per cent of institutional total income (though not that they be paid out of UK students' pockets) and that this would meet the Treasury's wish to increase the contribution for international students without introducing any discriminatory element. The Report recommended against loans in the immediate future but conceded that there might be a case for introducing them in the future. (Robbins, writing in 1980, regretted that the Report did not advocate the introduction of loans (Palfreyman 2012).)

The most striking departure from Treasury calculations, however, related to the anticipated growth in GNP. In February 1963 the National Economic Development Committee (NEDC), a body set up by Macmillan, published its Reports on economic growth to 1966 (NEDC 1963) which forecast an annual increase in GNP of 4 per cent based on a growth of output per head of the working population of 3.25 per cent with an addition of 0.75 per cent for demographic growth. This was the target figure adopted by the then Chancellor, Maudling, midway through his 'dash for growth'. The actual average growth in GDP between 1964 and 1980 was 2.5 per cent, precisely the figure the Treasury had included in its evidence. The 1963 and 1964 growth figures represented a blip in the figures. Robbins calculated the increased cost of the Committee's recommendations at constant prices to be as shown in Table 3.7

In addition the Report estimated that the capital requirement over 18 years would be £1,420m, that is £79m per annum. Robbins chose to rely on the much more optimistic NEDC predictions of the rise of GNP than the Treasury's approach. The result was that the increase in cost to GNP rose from 0.80 per cent in 1962–63 to 1.90 per cent in 1980–81, a figure remarkably like the Alpha prediction but with a considerably larger university sector contained within a larger student number figure. The implication of the decision to adopt the NEDC GNP forecast was to disguise the financial impact of the student number projections. The Report asked the question: 'Is this extra proportionate call on the national income likely to cause an undue strain on the resources of the future?' (para 634) and answered it in what might be described as an ingenuous manner: 'In the last resort, public money is spent

Table 3.7 The Robbins Committee's calculations of the cost of expansion at constant prices

	Teaching and research	Student maintenance	Loan charges	Capital expenditure	Total
	000	000	000	000	000
1962–63 (estimated)	£98.1	£46.2*	£4.8	£57.0	£206.1
1980–81	£392.2	£221.0*	£16.1	£113.0	£742.3

Note: These figures represented merely a projection of current costs and did not include the 10 per cent uplift factor for universities in the Treasury's Alpha model.

on what people want; and if they want more higher education then, on the estimates we have made it should be possible to finance it without imposing intolerable strains on the budget or the economy' (para 636).

The Report had generated enormous popular momentum and the Conservative Government was all too conscious of the need to expunge from the national memory the events of 1962. How else is one to explain the paper which the Chief Secretary addressed to Cabinet on 1 October 1963? The paper set out the anticipated costs as described in the Report but argued that: 'This would achieve remarkable social change in one decade. At present 13 per cent (men) and 6 per cent (women) of each age group successfully complete a course of higher education. By the mid-1970s it would be about 22 per cent (men) and 12 per cent (women) – as big a proportion of men as now gets three or more "O" levels or better'.[27] Technically the paper was recommending agreement to the figures up to 1973–74, the 10 year programme, and it did so by spelling out that it represented a growth from 0.80 per cent to 1.3 per cent of GNP and could be achieved within a growth rate of 5.9 per cent already agreed by the Cabinet within Education up to 1967–68. The growth rate of GNP was assumed to be 4 per cent per annum: 'this additional charge can be accepted if it is regarded as having priority both within the educational field and indeed over other proposals for increased expenditure'.[28] It is obvious from the Treasury evidence to Robbins and the way this paper was couched in terms of social/cultural arguments that the idea of university expansion (almost certainly more than higher education expansion) ignited a latent idealism even in those charged with managing the nations' finances. Whether Treasury officials were overridden by the political necessity of giving a positive response to Robbins, or whether in order to get a desirable development through they were prepared to swallow their professional instincts, they must have recognized that the financial arrangements were a fudge which were bound to be unpicked and cause trouble at some future date. The Government had accepted something that looked rather like the Alpha model, but by 1980–81 the Beta model looked much closer to reality on the ground.

Shirley Williams' 13 Points

By the beginning of the 1967–72 quinquennium it was already clear that Robbins' financial projections were beginning to unravel. Not only had the Woolwich speech destroyed the post-Robbins consensus but the devaluation of the pound and the poor overall economic situation had replaced the 'dash for growth' that had characterized the Conservative Government's and Maudling's two years in office as Chancellor, 1962–64. Demands were being made for greater university efficiency.

The CVCP was not insensitive to concerns about costs and had itself, in 1967, launched inquiries aimed at improving universities' efficiency and had sponsored studies on space utilization and university cost analysis and had encouraged the Vice-Chancellor of Lancaster to embark on the experiment of financing the building of new student residences through a mortgage rather than from capital grant. These exercises were prompted partly by its wish to convince Crosland that it took the question of the need for greater efficiency seriously but also because in 1966 it had engaged in a fundamental debate about the universities' future in a post-binary situation as a preliminary to reorganizing its internal machinery into a divisional structure to match what it saw as new demands. To start the debate, it commissioned two papers: one from the Vice-Chancellor of Birmingham, Sir Robert Aitken, and the other from the Vice-Chancellor of Warwick, Jack (later Lord) Butterworth. The former concluded that there were two alternative ways forward: if a staff:student ratio of somewhere between 1:8 and 1:7.5 was not sustainable or a change in the balance of commitment to research and teaching had to take place, universities must be open about the alteration to university standards that would follow; the alternative was an 'elitist' solution whereby the staff:student ratios and the research and teaching balance were maintained against a pre-determined number of students in the university sector leaving the public sector to take the remainder at lower costs. Butterworth's paper was concerned to analyse the student number situation and the need to emphasize the universities' social responsiveness in order to dispute Crosland's accusation in his Woolwich speech.[29]

These papers were responded to at the CVCP's first summer retreat conference in September 1966 in which two of the papers took radical and prescient views on Aitken's paper. The first, by the Director of the LSE, Sir Sydney Caine, offered a third alternative (what might be called the UGC 1981 solution):

> to accept some university standards amongst universities, so that while meeting the demand for a high level of expansion at the expense of some sacrifice in some parts of the university system, standards could be fully maintained elsewhere ... if there is a shortage of jam may it be better to discriminate in its distribution rather than spread it so thinly that nobody is satisfied?

The second, by the Principal of Edinburgh, Michael (later Lord) Swann, was concerned about the distribution of research support (and proposed what might be described as leaning towards the RAE solution): 'At this moment [research support] is spread almost completely uniformly by the UGC and more uniformly than might be expected by the research councils. Britain, in short, is very egalitarian when it comes to the support for science and her 50 odd universities.' He went on to compare the centres of excellence in the US and argued that the research councils should make 'a concerted attempt to concentrate support in a limited number of centres'.[30] He did not go so far, however, to suggest that the UGC should adopt this policy, although this was the logical implication of the paper. But the discussion as a whole shows that there were elements in the CVCP which were willing to at least contemplate radical change.

Treasury and DES concern about the costs of expansion in the 1972–77 quinquennium and beyond led to a significant all day meeting, held at UCL, between the Minister for higher education, Shirley Williams (Crosland having been succeeded by Ted Short as Secretary of State), the UGC and the CVCP in September 1969. The subject of the meeting was the future shape of higher education and the relationship between the university and the public sector. The CDP had yet to emerge but the CVCP committed itself to consult with it when it did. However the meeting offered the first opportunity for the unveiling of what became known as Shirley Williams' 13 Points, a list of 12 (or, if you believe the DES minute, 10) suggestions for cost reduction.[31] These 13 Points subsequently acquired totemic status when Waldegrave suggested in 1982 that their rejection by the universities marked a lost opportunity to respond flexibly to the ideas for cost reduction advanced by a notably sympathetic Minister: 'All of Shirley Williams' points gave warning of the need for reform which higher education ought to have foreseen'.[32] Later it has been widely quoted as evidence of the universities' intransigence in the face of change. The facts, however, do not support these claims. Neither the CVCP nor the DES accounts suggest that the ideas ventilated at the UCL meeting were any more than ideas and were discussed in this spirit. One addition, in the final list of 13, was the restriction of international numbers which would certainly have excited some argument and was commented on in the formal CVCP response.

A final version of the 13 Points was delivered to the CVCP in October 1969 and was first considered there in November. They arrived in the form of a letter from the Minister and were never endorsed by the UGC. It was clear from the outset that this was intended as one element in an ongoing discussion following the UCL meeting on the development of higher education up to 1980, the limit of the Robbins' forecasts. This process, which might have enabled some of the mistakes of the next decade to have been avoided, was, however, brought to an abrupt halt by the fall of the Labour Government, and the arrival of a new Secretary of State, Margaret Thatcher, and a new Minister for higher education, William Van Straubenzee, who approached such issues in a much more confrontational way. The CVCP sought comments from universities on the Williams document and provided a formal response in the spring of 1970 (CVCP 1970).

The 13 Points was couched as a personal document. In an interview Williams made it clear that DES officials, presumably Weaver, did not want her to embark on the exercise.[33] Nevertheless it represented an amalgam of ideas, some of which can be traced back to Treasury discussions when it was preparing its evidence to Robbins (see above). Some of the ideas, like two year degrees, have become a recurrent proposition whenever economies have been sought right up to 2011 (BIS 2011b). They are, therefore, intrinsically interesting because they represent a kind of agenda, posted in 1969 as ideas for discussion, which recurred in various forms over future years. The CVCP response, rather than a brusque rejection, comprised a reasoned answer, point by point, which was not intended to close off further discussion. The 13 Points and the responses were as follows:

1 A reduction or removal of student maintenance grants coupled with a system of loans. *Response*: CVCP was opposed to a full replacement of grants by loans, although some element of loan contribution could be considered; a move over to loans would not, however, produce any savings in the short term.

2 Replacement of grants by loans at the postgraduate level only. *Response*: loans could usefully supplement grants but postgraduate study needed encouragement and any diminution of postgraduate numbers would damage research.

3 A more restrictive policy for the admission of international students. *Response*: the numbers were only small; there was some sympathy in the sector for restricting further growth but there would need to be support for developing countries; the admission of international students represented an investment in goodwill, future commercial relationships and political dividends.

4 A requirement that grant aided students should enter specified kinds of employment for a period after graduation. *Response*: rejected as harmful and unworkable.

5 Greater use of part time and correspondence courses. *Response*: some support in the sector for more part time courses but not in replacement for present full time programmes; the contribution in numbers would be limited; part time programmes were not appropriate for science and engineering; there was no wish to seek to duplicate the Open University correspondence course programme.

6 Introduction of two year degrees for the most able students. *Response*: universal opposition – British degree programmes were already the shortest in Europe.

7 Introduction of two year courses for the less able. *Response*: well worth considering but best developed in the polytechnics rather than the universities although 2+2 programmes with flexible transfer arrangements might be possible.

8 The insertion of a gap year between school and university. *Response*: widely supported though not as a compulsory provision.

9 More intensive use of buildings. *Response*: the sector was aware of the problem but the spare capacity was mostly in science buildings where there was a shortfall in student numbers.

10 More sharing of facilities. *Response*: willing to explore but there were obvious difficulties.

11 More home based students. *Response*: opposed on the grounds of freedom of choice; universities in small towns would suffer at the expense of large urban areas.

12 Student housing associations or other forms of loan financed residences needed to be developed. *Response*: the problem of loan financed schemes was the high cost of interest rates and a national scheme was required.

13 A worsening of the staff:student ratio. *Response*: this might be possible with economies of scale including selective increases in those departments

where the ratio was favourable. There were suggestions that 1:10, 1:11 or 1:12 were variously the lowest points that could be contemplated but it should be noted that staff:student ratios were better than this in polytechnics and colleges of education and that a good staff:student ratio was the key to low wastage and graduation in three years – 'any major change . . . would totally alter the character of British universities and would not be in the best interests of the country in the long run'.[34]

The view that the CVCP minuted privately on the exercise was that 'almost all the thirteen ways of reducing unit costs suggested by the then Minister of State are open to objection on either academic or practical grounds and that while some of them may be worth exploring further, none of them is likely to result in significant economies in relation to the overall cost of higher education as a whole'.[35]

The new regime of Thatcher and Van Straubenzee did not respond to the CVCP document and the dialogue died. Whether it would have continued if Labour had won the election is not clear. When Williams became Secretary of State in the next Labour Government to take office she showed no inclination to revive it. Failure to follow up the 13 Points could be thought of as a missed opportunity but with Labour's departure from office there was little prospect of the dialogue being continued.

The 1980s and the emergence of the idea of a market

The 1980s were in many ways the crucible in which the pressures for change from a planned to a more institution based system of higher education took place. Richard Bird, quoted above, argued that if there was a 'guiding philosophy' it was the 'promotion of some sort of market' although it did not go so far as to be described as a 'market approach' (Bird 1994). Indeed, Ministers like Kenneth Baker might talk about a market but progress in that direction was slow and localized. One area in which it did develop was in capital programmes. As we have seen above, the provision of Government funded programmes was crucial to the expansion up to Robbins and delays in provision and doubts about the future availability of capital programmes lay at the heart of the reluctance of universities to expand to the level the UGC would have liked. Outside Oxbridge, with the two Universities' capacity for fund raising, universities were entirely dependent on public funding for new buildings. The very expensive development of the Imperial College site, for example, was financed entirely out of the Treasury's back pocket. William Pyle, the DES Permanent Secretary, told McConnell in 1971 that the DES controlled growth in higher education via the capital programme and chose to influence its shape by releasing capital resources for specific uses, such as to encourage the development of science and technology.[36]

The availability of capital grants was also affected by the Treasury's use of the release of capital for road, hospital and educational building as a measure to stimulate the economy so higher education's case could be strengthened or weakened by fluctuations generally in the labour market. The greater commitment of public sector institutions to part time study gave them more flexibility than the universities enjoyed in this respect.

Two events were to introduce market-led flexibility into a situation where institutional development was in effect determined by the central decisions on capital grants. The first was the realization that, following the experiment at Lancaster, student residences could be funded through mortgages or other borrowing which could be repayable through student rents. The proportion of students in the university sector living at home had fallen from 42 per cent in 1938 to 16 per cent in 1975 and the provision of student residences had represented a substantial element in the Robbins' capital estimates for the expansion. Transferring this element of capital financing to the private sector thus offered a significant relief to the Treasury which had been urging an experiment along these lines. It also offered an opportunity to universities, which had been constrained by the rigid restrictions on space, bathroom provision and layout imposed by UGC capital grants, to proceed to build residences appropriate to the development of a vacation conference trade. (There was no incentive for a polytechnic to do this because any surpluses from earned income activities were claimed back by the local authority.)

The second event, towards the end of the decade, was the release of the public sector institutions from local authority ownership. The NAB funding methodology through the AFE pool had encouraged expansion and the momentum thus developed was fuelled further by the aggressive funding policies adopted by the PCFC together with the increase in tuition fee levels which encouraged a 'fees only' expansion. Utilizing their new legal freedom many polytechnics embarked on ambitious commercial borrowing schemes, essentially guaranteed against rising student numbers, both to refurbish their estate and to provide new facilities. The universities, whose numbers had been cut in 1981 and were restrained throughout the 1980s, were not able to follow suit until the 1990s but in the competitive climate engendered by the ending of the binary line, were quick then to exploit an active lending market. The overall effect was to detach capital planning from government decision making except in so far as the new Financial Memorandum imposed overall restrictions on the proportion of institutional expenditure which could be devoted to interest and capital repayments. A second effect was to modernize university financial management by integrating capital and recurrent financial planning.

If the 1980s saw a freeing up on the capital side recurrent funding remained closely linked to government student number forecasts. These were initially tied to the Robbins' projections but, even by the late 1960s it became clear that these projections required revision. A number of such revisions were undertaken in the 1970s beginning with a euphoric forecast in 1970 by the DES in a booklet entitled *Student Numbers in Higher Education in England and Wales Education, Planning Paper No.2* (DES 1970). The DES 1970 forecast was carried over into Margaret Thatcher's 1972 White Paper but had to be repeatedly scaled back over the 1970s as set out in Table 3.8.

Table 3.8 Revisions in planned numbers of full time students in higher education, 1971–72 to 1981–82 (000s)

Month and year of 'plan'	October 1963(1)	December 1972(2)	November 1974(3)	February 1976(4)	February 1977(5)	February 1978(6)
1976–77	453			516	515	
1977–78	475			523	519	518
1978–79	499			533	519	517
1979–80	528			550	522	525
1980–81	558				541	541
1981–82	596	740	640	600	560	560

Sources: Committee on Higher Education 1963, Table 30; DES (1972); DES Press Notice 25 November 1974; *Public Expenditure* H.M. Treasury Cmnd 6393; *The Government's Expenditure Plans* H.M. Treasury Cmnd 6721-II; *The Government's Expenditure Plans* H.M. Treasury Cmnd 7049-II.

From a policy perspective what stands out is the very high planning figure for 1980, arrived at in the 1972 White Paper, and the gradual scaling back from it the more closely the forecast could be related to the actual numbers. The variations arose from two factors: the first was the impact of demography and the second the age participation rate. Although the birth rate had been in decline since 1960 both the Office of Population and Census and Surveys (OPCS) 1965 and 1970 forecasts had assumed that the fall would be short lived and growth would return. In fact the decline continued until 1975 and doomed the 1972 White Paper to monumental inaccuracy in its forecast. This in turn affected teacher supply estimates and was the driver for the drastic reduction in teacher training places and the radical restructuring of the colleges of education sector. The second variant related to the age participation rate which peaked at 14.2 per cent in 1972–73 and declined to 13.4 per cent by 1974–75. As wage levels rose for younger workers higher education became less attractive to qualified school leavers, and the proportion of school leavers with two or more 'A' levels entering permanent employment rose from 17.6 per cent in 1966 to 22.2 per cent a decade later. The impact of this slowing down of the growth rate in student numbers had a depressant effect on funding regimes and made it easier to impose reductions in numbers in the aftermath of the oil crisis.

However, the longer term prospect for higher education was considerably worsened by a wide ranging report by the Central Policy Review Staff (CPRS), now chaired by Berrill, the former Chairman of the UGC, entitled *Population and the Social Services*. This concluded that:

> In the mid 1980s the number of young people participating in Higher and Further Education will reach a peak. Present policy is to make staff/ student ratios less generous in this period. In the 1990s numbers will fall substantially. The options are:

(i)   To allow staffing ratios to improve in the 1990s and accept that buildings and facilities will to some extent be under-used.
(ii) To encourage participation rates in the 1990s to rise higher than is currently expected.
(iii) To limit provision for the 1980s peak demand e.g. by a temporary restraint on participation rates in higher education or tougher staff ratios and accommodation standards.

Option (i) may be unattractive and wasteful. Option (ii) may be more plausible for further than for higher education.

Option (iii) would influence decisions in the new few years on provisions for the 1980s.

(CPRS 1977)

One can exaggerate the impact within government of a CPRS publication, although the phrase 'tunnelling through the hump' to describe the implementation of option (iii) suggests a strong Treasury involvement. However, it prompted a response from the Secretary of State, Shirley Williams, in the form of a Discussion Document (DES/SED 1978) which offered a wide variety of possible alternative future projections. Unfortunately the incorporation of any of these ideas into public policy making was vitiated by a change in government.

The arrival of the Thatcher Government and the substitution of financial targets for volume planning pushed immediate further consideration of student demand into the background although the rise in unemployment, particularly amongst the young, brought an increase in the age participation rate. The UGC's decision to cut numbers in the universities meant that this pressure was transferred to the public sector. Joseph, however, was anxious to return to longer range planning and having commissioned public advice from the UGC and the NAB laid out his views in the Green Paper (DES 1985). The Green Paper made it clear that public expenditure plans implied a tightening of staff:student ratios but went on to offer future scenarios for the projection of student numbers (see Figure 3.5 (a)–(d)).

The pessimism as to the projected decline in student numbers accounted directly for the unpopularity of the Green Paper as a whole, and was drawn essentially from the thinking that lay behind the CPRS report and took little account of the more optimistic alternatives put forward in the Williams' Discussion Document. It was not improbable, the Green Paper said, that some institutions might have to be closed or merged over the next ten years. Having managed their way through the cuts on the university side and the capping of the pool on the public sector side what the Green Paper was offering was a continuation of shrinking resources for another decade. The outcry was immediate. Perhaps the most serious criticism came from the UGC, a body, which after all, had been widely thought to be doing the Government's bidding. 'Like other bodies, its response said "the Committee found much of the Green Paper a disappointment"' (UGC 1985 para 2) but it went on specifically to criticize the number projections as representing 'an inadequate and defeatist approach' (para 9). '"We wonder", the response asked, "why the Government should . . . be so pessimistic about the chances of its own policies in relation to schools"' (para 11). The response bore the heavy imprint of its Chairman, Swinnerton Dyer, and goes some way to explain why, in the 1988 legislation, the Treasury was insistent that the UFC's advice should be made confidential to the Government.

The resignation of Keith Joseph led to a reversal of policies under his successor Kenneth Baker. Baker, effervescent, optimistic and capable of waging a charm offensive on his Prime Minister (Major said that 'he handled the Prime Minister on the subject [of education] better than anyone else I ever saw' (Major 1999: 103)), represented a significant contrast to the intellectual but indecisive Joseph. It was inevitable that Baker would have wanted to change the legacy of negative attitudes which Joseph had created but fortuitously an argument was offered him shortly after he took office. In 1986 a new body, the CIHE, had been formed at the suggestion of Sir John Cassells, the Director General of the National Economic Development Office. It persuaded Lord Prior, a former 'wet' in Thatcher's first Cabinet but now Chairman of GEC to take the chair and Patrick Coldstream, a financial journalist, to be its Director. This body had a first meeting with Baker in 1986 and expressed its concern that the prospective downturn in student numbers described in the Green Paper was not congruent with the manpower needs of industry. In the following year it set out its ideas in a document, *Towards a Partnership, Higher Education – Government – Industry*, which argued:

> At present the UK's plans for the development of highly educated people are at odds with its ambitions for national renewal and growth. After forty years in which the annual output of graduates has multiplied almost six fold (from 20,000 to 115,000 per annum) the *highest* of four recent government statistical projections now suggests that the student population by the end of the century could be little over 4% higher than it is today. In that case (which we do not accept) industry, in order to grow at 2% per annum would have to expand about eight times faster than its supply of highly qualified manpower.
>
> (CIHE 1987 para 3.1, original emphasis)

By September 1986, at the CVCP Residential Conference, Baker had reversed the policy of his predecessor. Facing a fall of 33 per cent in the number of 18–19-year-olds over the next decade Baker argued that priority should be given to demand: 'the contraction of the system and the closure of institutions simply does not square with the country's need for qualified manpower . . . I have read articles about the possible closure of a university. I want to make it clear that I will not even consider such a proposal'.[37] In January 1989 in his Lancaster speech 'Higher Education: the next 35 years' he said that he wanted to see the participation rate of 18.5 per cent pushed up to one in three by 2000, a much higher figure even than the 20 per cent envisaged in his 1987 White Paper. His civil servants confirm that these ideas did not come from the Department (Kogan and Hanney 2000). They represented a rare

Figure 3.5 The projections of higher education entrants in the Green Paper 1985

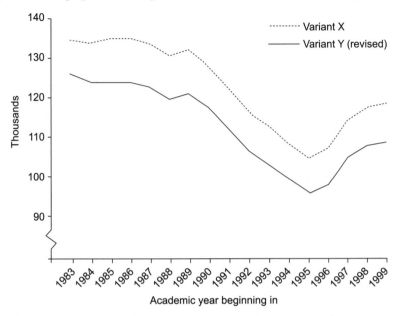

(a) Projected home young entrants (full time and sandwich)

Source: DES (1985).

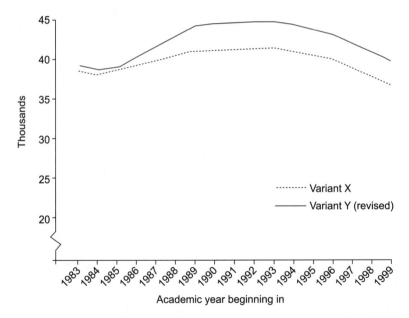

(b) Projected home mature (i.e. over 21) initial entrants (full time and sandwich)

Source: DES (1985).

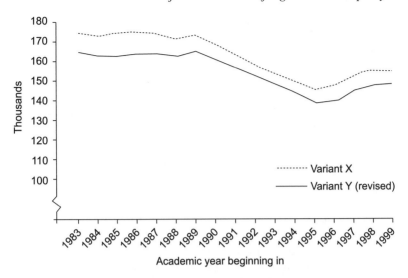

(c) Projected total home initial entrants (full time and sandwich)

Source: DES (1985).

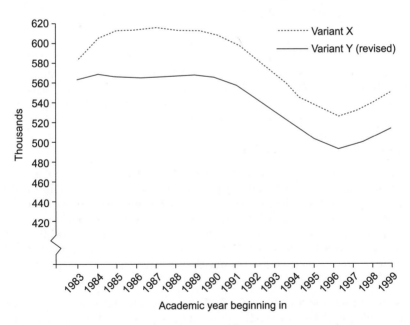

(d) Projected total student numbers (home and overseas, full time and sandwich)

Source: DES (1985).

example of a politician's direct contribution to policy, prompted by the CIHE.

Although in one sense this was good news for higher education what was not clear initially was that there was a financial price to be paid. The Treasury had been informed about the Lancaster speech but told that it did not need to worry because the growth in numbers extended over 25 years (Kogan and Hanney 2000). However, what Baker did not say in his Lancaster speech was that he was uncoupling student numbers from the provision of finance; what he actually said was that he was putting a 'time bomb under the Treasury'.[38] As we have seen above, the rationale of the UGC's 1981 cuts in university sector numbers was to maintain the unit of resource. When NAB, which had used a unit of resource methodology in its first 1982–83 planning exercise, sought to follow suit in 1986–87 and considered reducing student targets by 17 per cent to protect the unit of resource, Baker was so concerned that he increased its budget by 8 per cent (Pratt 1997). In his autobiography, however, published only four years after the Lancaster speech Baker claimed to have abolished the unit of resource as an argument for resources. 'The UGC', he wrote, 'had developed an ingenious system where a unit of resource was established which represented the amount needed to teach one student. This formula became sacrosanct and meant that if student numbers were to be increased then the amount paid through the unit of resource had to be increased *pro rata*'. This meant, he claimed, that the rate of expansion was determined by the Treasury whereas what he wanted to see was 'a system where expansion would be determined by demand'. According to the UGC, expansion could not be undertaken at marginal costs, although, he claimed, this was just what was happening in the polytechnics (Baker 1993: 233).

As it happens we have a view on Baker's approach to funding from the other side of the Treasury table. John Major was Chief Secretary from 1987 to 1989 and scrupulously followed PESC procedure by securing Cabinet approval for an overall spending limit, writing to departments challenging their assumptions and costings and holding one to one bilaterals with the ministers concerned. Baker, he wrote:

> [W]ould bound in full of enthusiasm and with lots of ideas all of which, he assured me, would be hugely popular with the electorate and would guarantee another election victory . . . When detailed questioning on cost were put to Ken, he was often poorly briefed. His spending plans were grossly inflated and it never took long to reduce the padding. At the end of our negotiations, Ken bounded out as cheerfully as he had come in, but with much less money than he had sought.
>
> (Major 1999: 103)

This could not exactly be described as a time bomb. Baker faced the conundrum, which he himself set out to the CVCP in 1988, of how the state could afford the demands placed upon it by the growth in student numbers, by simply rejecting arguments based on staff:student ratios and by promoting expansion at marginal costs. A senior civil servant told Hanney that it was quite clear to anyone with a civil service background that the unit of resource argument would have to go.[39] The PCFC funding methodology, under which polytechnics retained funding only if they expanded year by year to higher targets, the UFC's guide price exercise and the 'fees only' expansion were the natural result. The key government watchwords were greater efficiency and the introduction of market mechanisms. Across Whitehall producer-led financing was being replaced by customer-led policies; the ideas embodied in public choice economics had taken root. The change of policy in higher education coincided, however, with the resumption of rapid expansion in demand between 1989 and 1994 which was to change the higher education landscape.

The critic might argue that Baker's interest was to drive expansion largely for presentational reasons, irrespective of finance. It was good politics to change the mood and his White Paper (DES 1987), glossy and full of pictures and diagrams, struck an immediate contrast to Joseph's Green Paper. One way to secure greater efficiency was to encourage growth in numbers by utilizing market competition between institutions to drive down costs. Baker was not entirely insensitive to the impact on institutions and was keen to explore loan options for student maintenance which might have released more funding for the system but it was not his first concern, and with cost sharing, in the sense of students contributing by paying their own fees, being politically too toxic to contemplate after Joseph's failure to win Parliamentary support, he was severely boxed in. Perhaps a true measure of his success could be seen in the student number projections issued by his successor but one, Ken Clarke in his 1991 White Paper (see Figure 3.6). Six years after the pessimistic forecasts in Keith Joseph's Green Paper the policy had been reversed and the expected age participation rate by 2000 had risen officially to 33 per cent, the target announced in Baker's Lancaster speech.

But the policy had consequences. The cutting of the link between resources and student numbers, the maintenance of the unit of resource, once conceded, as Baker certainly did, left future DES negotiations with the Treasury on very shaky ground and Figure 3.3, above, was the natural result. The strength of the Treasury's position can be judged by its insistence that the 1989 burst of expansion be closed down in 1994, by implication, at least, until a new loans and fees policy could be introduced. A further consequence was that the main burden of the expansion fell on the polytechnics. The CVCP was wholly hostile to the UFC's invitation to universities to bid for funding against a 'floor' guide price and a second (lower) price for additional numbers, and, at its Council meeting in January 1990, agreed that universities should be encouraged to align their bids at or close to the 'floor' guide price.[40] In October, Parkes, by now Chairman of the CVCP, issued an uncompromising press statement: 'The UFC is in complete disarray. It has belatedly realised what the most junior lecturer could have told it months ago that available resources would be unlikely to permit funding at or near guide prices and expansion. The UFC seems to be torn between lower quality and a larger intake; and a properly funded but less rapidly expanding system'.[41] The result was the creation of a virtual cartel to bid for a 19 per cent

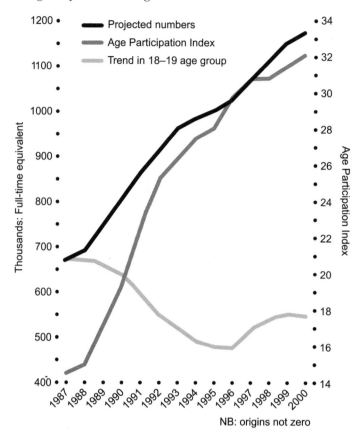

Figure 3.6 White Paper (1991) projections of home students in higher education (GB)

Notes:
a. The Age Participation Index (API) – plotted to the right hand scale – is the number of young home initial entrants to full-time higher education expressed as a proportion of the averaged 18-19 year old population.
b. The line marked "trend in 18-19 age group" – plotted to the left hand scale – is the movement in the 18-19 year old population multiplied by 1987 home full-time equivalent student numbers.This gives some indication of what would have happened to numbers in higher education if participation had remained at 1987 levels. As it is, the fall in the age group to the mid-1990s is more than offset by increases in the API.
c. The numbers of students in higher education – plotted to the left hand scale – and the API are projections from 1990 onwards. Before then, they are actual figures.

Source: DES (1991).

increase in numbers but only at the higher price, in effect to maintain the unit of resource argument. The coherence of the universities' rejection of the Chilver designed market meant the collapse of the bidding exercise.

On the polytechnic side, however, there was much less unity. The sector had been geared by NAB towards expansion and, from an institutional point of view, increased student numbers had represented the only source of additional funds to upgrade local authority provided buildings, rationalize a multiplicity of sites and compete with one another and with neighbouring universities. The PCFC went much further by holding back 10 per cent of the funding available and inviting institutions to recruit extra students and rewarding the lowest financial bids from the funds held back. In the following year the average allocation per student was reduced to the actual average calculated after the bidding exercise was completed thus reducing the standard income per student for all institutions whether or not they participated in the bidding (Williams 2004). This was certainly marketization. In November 1987, the CDP had agonized over the unit of resource issue and whether the argument could be maintained but it was clearly apparent that, with some polytechnics aggressively exceeding their targets, the sector could not sustain a common position and that institutions must be left to bid for numbers at marginal costs.[42] Three years later the situation had not changed and the CDP Secretary was writing a paper saying that this was the third bidding exercise and that once again polytechnics had put in low price bids for large numbers of students. 'Institutions run the risk (again)', he warned, 'of undermining the case being made to the Government about the level of resource in the sector. Responsibility for the continued deterioration in unit funding from the centre will be laid, with some justification, at the door of institutions'.[43]

The universities' resistance to the bidding exercise ensured that the polytechnics took up the overflow of places and grew at a much faster rate than the universities. Although, after the unification of the two sectors, the funding councils rationalized costs by undergraduate discipline so that resources for teaching were equitably provided on a *pro rata*, but lower basis, for the pre-1992 universities, across the system the impact of the very rapid expansion in the polytechnics over the period was to contribute significantly to fulfilling the R,T and X prediction made by the ABRC five years before. A final consequence was that as demand showed every indication of continuing to rise after 1994, if at a slower rate, the political consequences of not acceding to it had always to be balanced against the political costs of finding ways to defray the costs of doing so. The Dearing Committee was established to provide the solution.

Tuition fees and the creation of a real market in higher education

The contribution of tuition fees to the funding of higher education and the source of the fee payments were a continuing underlying thread in the evolution of policy, and changes in fee policy have marked some of the sharpest controversies in the whole period covered by this study. One interpretation of events would be to see them as simply an example of the development of fiscal policy as to how higher education was to be paid for, while another would be to see them as representing a slow reversal, except in Scotland, of the view, strongly held in 1945–46, that the provision of opportunities for higher education was a public rather than a private good for which the state must, therefore, be responsible. A third alternative might be to regard the development of a tuition fee policy as part of a wider question of whether the efficiency of public services could most effectively be achieved by the application of market-led policies, while a fourth has been to see it as an opportunity to rectify the injustice, perceived by some, in imposing a tax burden on elements of the public, mostly the least advantaged, to pay for a service that they would enjoy only tangentially but which would be of lifetime personal financial benefit to the direct recipients. At various points in the period each of these interpretations has been given prominence but in the day to day development of policy it seems clear that the fiscal issue has been dominant and the issues of principle have been drawn on largely to provide retrospective justification for decisions that arose out of the mundane need to balance the books.

The issue of fees was largely dormant until the publication of the Anderson and Robbins Reports. At the end of the War universities did not think that it was timely to raise fees from their pre-War levels; these had been set on an individual institutional and not on a national basis although apart from Oxbridge's the fee levels were not dissimilar. There was little incentive to raise fees because the UGC was operating on a deficiency grant basis so a rise in fees would merely lead to a deduction from grant. In 1953, the Vice-Chancellor of Bristol circulated a note to the CVCP about fee levels. He found there were wide variations of between 7.7 per cent and 21.6 per cent in the proportion of total income which undergraduate fees and fees, paid by the Ministry of Education for teacher training places, represented. Four sources of fee income were cited: Ministry of Education awards, scholarships awarded by the university, LEA local awards, and parents, but 68 per cent of students were covered by public funds either through the Ministry or the LEA.[44] The Committee agreed that it would be unwise to upset LEAs who were paying fees from locally raised income, by raising fee levels, so the question was not proceeded with. This situation was overtaken in 1961 by the Anderson Report and the adoption of a common fee structure, apart from Oxbridge, across universities and local authority institutions. The Report also established student maintenance allowance arrangements to be paid by local authorities. Both fees and maintenance grants became items to be charged against the central rate support grant.

We have seen above that the question of fees to home and to international students exercised both the Treasury in its evidence and the Robbins Committee itself. The Robbins recommendation that fees should be raised to 20 per cent of institutional income was founded on the safeguard it offered to institutions that 'all their income does not come immediately from one administrative source' (Committee on Higher Education 1963: 274). The CVCP was quick to note its implications: to raise fees to only 11 per cent of income by 1967–68 would mean an increase in fee levels of 70 per cent but to raise their contribution to 20 per cent would require a 208 per cent increase. This would require financial assurances being given to the LEAs and the question of fee levels in the public sector would have to be addressed. Great concern was expressed on the impact this would have on international students.[45] The Committee referred the matter to the UGC for resolution. Meantime the Robbins recommendation was endorsed by the Parliamentary Committee on Estimates, 1964–65. For the DES the salient position was not the level of home fees or the principle of the need to maintain a multiplicity of sources of income but an unsubstantiated belief that rich American and European students were benefiting from a heavily subsidized British higher education (Lee 1998).

Discussions between the UGC and the DES on the fee issue proceeded slowly with DES officials canvassing with the UGC a proposal that the funding system should include a capitation element (a sensible suggestion since at that time an institution's recurrent grant was determined by the UGC on the basis of its historic level with a further judgemental element added on). According to Lee, Wolfendon, on behalf of the UGC, turned down both the capitation idea and the proposal to charge a differential fee for international students (Lee 1998). However, within the PESC process the DES was being pressed for economies and in November Crosland on his own initiative conceded an increase in fees for international students from £70 to £250 in order to forestall a Treasury proposal to introduce charges for school meals. DES officials immediately recognized the damaging publicity that would inevitably be generated and delayed the announcement to a written reply to a Parliamentary Question published on 21 December on the day the House rose for Christmas. The Permanent Secretary, Sir Herbert Andrew, interviewed by Walsh, however, saw no problem at all in raising fees for international students.[46] There was no consultation with the CVCP, UGC or with representatives of Commonwealth Governments. Wolfendon's response is quoted above.

Predictably, reaction within higher education was intense. At the first national conference on overseas student welfare held at Roehampton in January, Lord Murray abandoned the chair to speak critically on the issue and in the House of Lords, Lord Longford the Lord Privy Seal, found himself defending the decision against hostile ranks of ennobled academics, including Lord Fulton, making his maiden speech (Lee 1998). Across universities student protest was vociferous and 'sit ins' were provoked; senates passed critical resolutions and two universities, Oxford and Bradford, refused to implement the proposal (both universities decided some two years later that the cost implications were not sustainable). The CVCP issued a clear statement of its opposition to the discriminating effect of the decision and the damage it did to the international character of universities. Crosland was forced to have two meetings to attempt to placate vice-chancellors. At the first, he claimed that the delay in coming up with a proposal for a general fee rise was due to opposition from the local authorities and at the second, that he did not consult vice-chancellors before the decision because he knew they would oppose it but that he wished 'to make clear that this decision did not betoken any new pattern of relationships between the Government, the UGC and the Committee'.[47] Interviewed by Kogan in 1971 he said: 'The officials had either misjudged or else failed to warn me of the likely reaction in the universities and the whole announcement and presentation were totally mishandled' (Kogan 1971: 178). These facile comments did him little credit.

As Lee makes clear, in a closely researched article, there was a genuine division of view outside the confines of the universities and Whitehall about the question of the subsidy for a growing number of international students and the protests against the decision were as much about the way it was done as against the content. In part it precipitated a range of disappointed hopes and guilt arising from Britain's decolonization policy and the apparent absence of adequate support being given to the educational needs of former colonial dependencies. Within the strictly British context it gave a fillip to the foundation of the UK Council for Overseas Students Affairs (UKCOSA) and, as an example of increasing Government interference, was one of the main spurs to the establishment of a planning board for the breakaway foundation of the University College (now University) of Buckingham (Lee 1998).

The question of international student fees did not, however, go away. On the one hand, the CVCP adopted the principled policy of pressing for an increase in home student fees to end the discrimination between home and overseas fee payers, while on the other the DES (see Shirley Williams' 13 points above) argued for a voluntary restriction on international students' entry in order to contain the level of the subsidy. In 1970 the DES turned down the CVCP proposal that home fees should be raised to £250 on the excuse that this might incentivize universities to exceed their student number targets by taking 'fees only' students but in fact, according to the UGC, it was because the proposal was resisted by the local authorities primarily on these grounds and on the effect it might have in further education.[48] Rather surprisingly there was no action on the fees front while Mrs Thatcher was Secretary of State but on Labour being returned to office there was evidence of some sympathy for the CVCP position with a doubling of home fees from £70 to £140 but a much more modest increase in international fees from £250 to £320 with effect from 1975–76. The CVCP set up a working party with support from the UGC to look again at the fees problem. Having interviewed the AUT, the NUS, the British Council and the DES it produced an Interim Report in November 1975. By now the mood had changed somewhat. In a period when demography might reduce demand, universities were more cautious about a high fee regime which might penalize universities that undershot their targets but to abolish fees altogether would have adverse effects in further education; international student numbers had not been constrained by the 1966 fee rise and had risen by 10 per cent. The subsidy was now at £50m. This pointed simply to a question of limiting or reducing the level of the subsidy. It therefore sought to consult universities on the following propositions:

(a) opt for higher fees but invest more heavily in overseas aid arrangements;
(b) limit international numbers by quota;
(c) either establish a tariff quota by which so many were admitted at current fee levels, and after, the remainder at higher levels, or raise home fees to equal international student fees.

The Report raised a wide spectrum of comment from universities with only three voting for moving to something like the Robbins position, 13 voting for something like 10 per cent and eight for between 5 per cent and 9 per cent. Several vice-chancellors reported that they had not been able to achieve consensus within their institutions for any one of the alternatives. However 33, a very substantial majority, wanted to see parity between home and overseas students. The Final Report recommended this latter position and the principle of maintaining fees at a 10 per cent proportion of university income. But it also concluded that there should be a voluntary agreement on the part of universities to limit the international numbers they admitted.[49] This was a significant concession of principle (and probably administratively unworkable) but was undoubtedly influenced by the expectation that unless some limit on numbers was introduced the costs of any additional subsidy would be levied on the system as a whole. The Report had the full support of the UGC. Submitted in June 1976 it was instantly kicked into touch by the Government which in July announced a new fee structure altogether of £650 for home and £750 for postgraduates (previously the fees had been undifferentiated), and £650 for international undergraduates and £550 for postgraduates effective from 1977–78. The explanation given for what was, in effect, a brutal rejection of a combined CVCP/UGC set of proposals was based on public expenditure considerations. The Treasury saw a rise in fees as a contribution to saving in public expenditure. The Government's expenditure plans envisaged a fall in international numbers to 1975–76 levels of 48,000 and a continued fall to 44,000 in 1981–82. However, the fee rise also dealt a blow to the vulnerable home postgraduate market. The Government's decision represented a real rebuff to both CVCP and UGC. When Shirley Williams took over from Fred Mulley as Secretary of State the home undergraduate fee was reduced to £500 but the overseas fees were not changed so that the differential was restored. Williams engaged in lengthy discussions with the UGC to try to introduce a voluntary limitation on overseas numbers but to little effect. What the history of fees since Robbins shows is the extent to which, in the absence of any worked out policy towards tuition fees, decisions were constantly taken on short term basis with priority being given to the maintenance of year on year public expenditure targets. It also illustrates clearly the gap which had developed between the CVCP and the UGC on the one hand and the DES and the Treasury on the other. But the history can also be seen as a long and stumbling march towards the final decision to remove the subsidy for international students altogether in 1979–80.

The 1979–80 decision on overseas student fees was in many ways a re-run of the 1966 decision in terms of the absence of prior consultation with appropriate authorities which included the UGC, the CVCP, the CDP and the Foreign Office. The decision was, in fact, taken by the new Secretary of State, Mark Carlisle, within two or three days of the Thatcher Government taking power. Legend has it that a Treasury official pointed out to him that the requirement imposed immediately on him by the Government's initial cuts in public expenditure of £100m, over the first three years of the new Government, could simply be met by removing the subsidy which would enable the rest of higher education to go unscathed. Carlisle, of whom one very senior civil servant said that he 'did more or less what he was told by the Treasury and by civil servants to a worrying degree',[50] jumped at the idea and felt able to promise level funding to higher education thereafter (a promise he had to renege on within six months).[51] Rhodes Boyson, the Parliamentary Secretary for higher education told the Overseas Development Sub-Committee: 'It was a financial decision. That is why it was made and made quickly' (Select Committee on Education, Science and Arts 1980a para 22).

As in 1966, the decision was met with widespread protest, this time as much from Commonwealth sources as from British higher education, and the Education Select Committee's Report generated a full scale debate in the House of Commons. The Committee and the higher education community saw the decision as a serious reduction in income. They would have been astonished to learn that international student fee income contributed nearly £6bn to British higher education income by 2011. If there was one decision which may be said to have contributed to the marketization of British higher education, it was this. In the next 30 years British universities opened recruiting offices overseas, campuses overseas, hired professional agents, engaged in franchising courses overseas and established international offices charged with international student recruitment competing fiercely with higher education systems in America, Australia and increasingly continental European countries. None of this was anticipated in 1979–80 either by the ideological marketeers in the Conservative Party or by the Treasury, the DES or, to begin with, by universities and polytechnics. International student fees became the income source which compensated for the continuing decline in the unit of resource provided for home students and British universities became utterly dependent on it.

The 1979–80 decision on international student fees brought to an abrupt end the CVCP's attempts to equalize home and international student fee levels but home fee levels remained a live issue. A Public Accounts Committee Report, published in June 1981, noted that although UGC funding was subject to cash limits, cash limits had not been imposed on tuition fees and student maintenance support. The costs of fees and the open ended budget for student support became known as 'the bag of gold' issue. One result was that tuition fees for home undergraduate students were reduced from £900 in 1981–82 to £480 in 1982–83 on the argument that this reduced the incentive for institutions to recruit students over their targets and thus raise the cost of student support above the Treasury estimate. Institutions were compensated for the loss of fee income by a corresponding increase in grant. The PAC report had the effect of directing attention to the sums spent on student support. Ever since the Anderson Report means tested maintenance grants had been available to all students securing a place in higher education at levels which were annually uprated for inflation. From 1981, however, Joseph raised the support levels at less than the rate of inflation arguing, according to Lawson, who was Chancellor of the Exchequer at the time, that this reduced the injustice of taxing parents whose children were not going into higher education to pay for the maintenance grants of those who did, and using the savings for other purposes within the higher education budget (Lawson 1992).

In 1984 he sought to extend this strategy. He obtained approval from the Treasury for a scheme whereby he could invest £20m into the science budget by abolishing the minimum level of maintenance grant altogether and extending means testing to tuition fees, so that students from the wealthiest homes would have to pay the full £520. The Treasury was happy to support the idea because it was self financing. The overall saving would in fact have been £40m. When Joseph reported it to the House of Commons, however, he met an immediate adverse reaction. One hundred and eighty Conservative MPs, half of the Parliamentary party, signed an early day motion opposing it because they could immediately see how unpopular it would be with middle class voters. When he addressed the weekly meeting of the 1922 Committee a proposal by William Benyon MP that the whole idea should be scrapped was greeted with cheers and banging of desks (Denham and Garnett 2001). George Walden, a former Conservative Minister for Higher Education commented in his book *We Should Know Better: Solving the Education Crisis* 'That, in effect, was the extent of the debate on the financial future of our higher education system in the Parliamentary Conservative Party' (Walden 1996: 173).

Labour offered nothing better: when its shadow Minister for Higher Education, Jeff (later Lord) Rooker, issued a paper proposing a graduate tax he was sacked by John Smith, the Labour Leader. Lawson describes a tense meeting between Thatcher, Joseph and himself where the idea was formally withdrawn and a contribution of £10m for the science budget was found from the Government's contingency fund (Lawson 1992). Joseph agreed to carry out a review of loans but when in 1985, with Lawson's help, he had produced what he considered to be a viable scheme, Margaret Thatcher opposed it (Denham and Garnett 2001). The backbench revolt against the Joseph proposals killed off any prospect of new ideas about cost sharing being produced while the Conservatives were in power. As we have seen above, Major took a similar line over the 'top up' fees proposal in 1991. While it was recognized that some form of cost sharing was the only way of breaking the log jam on financing higher education the topic was deemed to be too political to be taken forward. The result was a decade of under-funded expansion, imposed 'efficiency gains' and a growing dependence on international student fee income. Eventually, as we have seen above, the CVCP pressure for 'top up' fees led to the establishment of the Dearing Committee which had the task of producing a solution.

The Dearing Committee reported shortly after the new Labour Government had taken office. It proposed a complex but carefully thought out set of measures that included the introduction of tuition fees of about 25 per cent of the cost of a first degree (about £1,000) to be paid direct by students on an income contingent basis balanced by the retention of maintenance grants. This would have meant raising fees to more or less the level recommended by Robbins but treating the income it produced as additional to recurrent grant, so that some rectification of the fall in the unit of resource portrayed in Figure 3.3 could be achieved. These proposals were frustrated for two reasons. The first was because Blunkett had given a private commitment to the NUS in the run up to the General Election in respect to low income students that maintenance grants would be means tested but that fees would be remitted in the new arrangements post Dearing.[52] The second was that the new Chancellor had decided to maintain the previous Government estimates for the following two years (the next Comprehensive Spending Review was due in 1998) and these had included further 'efficiency gains' which absorbed the increase in income that the £1,000 tuition fees produced when they were introduced in 1999. From the CVCP's perspective this was a disastrous outcome. It was also very unpopular with students because no attempt had been made to restore maintenance grants. In Taggart's words, it was 'a short term financial fix' (Taggart 2004: 95).

The results of the Comprehensive Spending Review were little better. Taggart says that Blunkett believed that he had secured a favourable settlement for higher education because he was able to point to an additional £280m in 1999–2000 and £496m in 2000–01 to provide another 36,000 and 61,000 student places (Taggart 2004: 96) but the Labour Party manifesto had promised a target of an additional 500,000 student places in further and higher education and HEFCE had shown that the unit of resource had fallen by 35 per cent in real terms in higher education in England between 1989–90 and 1998–99. Although the next Comprehensive Spending Review produced the first increase in funding per student for a decade, the additional resources were geared to the Secretary of State's own priorities, research, widening participation, the disastrous E-university, foundation degrees and academic salaries, and did little to address the fundamental problem. Moreover, the recurrent grant letter in 2000 confirmed the Government's commitment 'that 50 per cent of those between 18 and 30 should have the opportunity to benefit from higher education by the end of the decade' (DfES 2000 para 17). Some sort of train crash seemed to be in the offing.

At this point a wholly new argument entered the frame. Hitherto the issues over fees had been how to balance the books, how some change in fee levels might act as some sort of financial make-weight to satisfy the requirements of PES or the Comprehensive Spending Review. The Dearing proposal that students should make a direct contribution to their education represented a new approach but the additional resource involved, even discounting the efficiency gains, was not commensurate with the further growth in numbers which the Government was contemplating. As late as 1998 Blunkett was firm in ruling out 'top up' fees. The new argument related to the competitive standing internationally of Britain's 'top' universities. It was first articulated to Blair by Lord Jenkins in his role as Chancellor of Oxford and had the support of Andrew (later Lord) Adonis, Blair's senior political adviser and Jenkins' official biographer. It was later reinforced by the publication of the Shanghai Jaio Tong league tables which were dominated by American universities but which accorded high placings to Oxford, Cambridge, Imperial College and UCL. What was significant was the extent to which tuition fees, which had been seen as a technical fiscal issue between the Treasury and the Department and whose importance was largely restricted to the world of higher education, became a major political issue on which a Prime Minister was prepared to stake his political future: 'The closest I came to losing my job, ironically was not over Iraq but over tuition fees' (Blair 2010: 480). According to Rawnsley, Blair urged on by Jenkins, saw better arrangements for financing universities as a legacy project (Rawnsley 2010) which he was prepared to lead on personally against the opposition of his Secretary of State, Estelle Morris (succeeding Blunkett), a large element of the Parliamentary Labour Party and, until a very late stage, the Chancellor of the Exchequer, Gordon Brown.

The disagreement between Blair and Brown led to the resignation of Morris. Rawnsley quotes Morris as saying: 'It froze, nothing happened. During those long months when I had on my desk lots of options as to the way forward and I had my own views, I thought I can't resolve this until they resolve it between them' (Rawnsley 2010: 231). The debate was restricted to a narrow group of Ministers and civil servants and, according to Darling, 'was never discussed properly (in Cabinet) so the result was no collective ownership' (Darling 2010).

Blair says in his autobiography that by 1999 he realized that a reform of universities was necessary but it is clear that his interest lay not in the system of higher education but in a restricted range of institutions. The Tories had converted 'so called polytechnics into universities . . . which was fine except that it fuelled a myth that all universities were of the same academic standing'. This produced 'a typical egalitarian muddle' (Blair 2010: 482). The Labour Party manifesto in 2001, influenced by Blunkett, had declared its opposition to 'top up' fees but during 2001–02 detailed work was done under Adonis's direction in relation to the introduction of a graduate tax (Baker 2010). However the turning point appears to have been a visit of key members of the Russell Group to Downing Street in late 2001 urging the case for more funding. 'Once the university chiefs laid out the problem I knew we had to act' (Blair 2010: 483). They were supported by the President of UUK, Ivor (now Sir Ivor) Crewe: 'Ivor got the politics completely, and he was unequivocal that there had to be change' (Blair 2010: 483). The Prime Minister saw the problem of higher education finance in a broader picture of New Public Management reform:

By the beginning of the second term, we had fashioned a template of the reform: changing the monolithic nature of the service; introducing competition; blurring distinctions between public and private sector; taking on traditional professional and union demarcations of work and vested interests; and in general trying to force the system up, letting it innovate, differentiate, breathe and stretch its limbs.

(Blair 2010: 480–1)

The introduction of tuition fees was part of this process, a 'troubled process' he says, 'but it is the structure upon which future reforms will be built' (Blair 2010: 481). In his book Blair offers a specific justification for taking up the higher education funding issue:

I looked at the top fifty universities in the world [presumably through the eyes of the Shanghai Jaio Tong league table] and saw only a handful in the UK, and barely any in mainland Europe. America was winning this particular race with China and India coming up fast behind. The point about the US was especially telling. Their domination of the top fifty – and top hundred for that matter – was not by chance or by dint of size; it was plainly and inescapably due to their system of fees. They were more entrepreneurial; they went after their alumni and built up big endowments; their bursary system allowed them to attract poorer students; and their financial flexibility meant that they could attract the best academics. Those who paid top dollar got the best. Simple as that.

(Blair 2010: 482)

Simplistic as this view of American higher education undoubtedly is, this was not an argument arrived at in hindsight. Mullin in his diaries reports Blair, criticized by the Executive Committee of the Parliamentary Labour Party in 2002 about the activities of Adonis who 'was urging politically disastrous university top up fees', giving him a very similar argument (Mullin 2009: 321). Mullin told him, as the Conservative backbenchers had told Joseph, that the middle classes would not like it. Two years were to elapse between the discussion with the Russell Group vice-chancellors and the publication of the 2003 White Paper. This was almost entirely occupied by highly fraught arguments between the Chancellor and the Prime Minister, and between Ed Balls, on behalf of Brown, and Andrew Adonis over the issue. The Chancellor was opposed because, expecting to succeed to the premiership before the next General Election, he did not want to have a campaign dogged by the fees question but philosophically he would probably have subscribed to the arguments ascribed by Blair to Balls that moving to variable fees represented a trade-off between equity and markets and that this took marketization too far. Against that Adonis/Blair argued that it made higher education more accountable to consumers and that this was where public services were heading in other advanced industrial nations.

On the resignation of Estelle Morris who 'felt caught between the two of us' (Blair 2010: 483), Blair appointed Charles Clarke (coincidentally son of

Otto Clarke) as Secretary of State who, with the assistance of a working party that included the chief executive of HEFCE, brought forward recommendations which abolished up front fees and replaced them with an income contingent Graduate Contribution Scheme from 2006 under which institutions were free to charge up to £3,000 p.a. to be initially funded by the Government as a student loan but to be repaid after graduation. It restored maintenance grants to disadvantaged students and required institutions to draw up Access Agreements which would have to be approved by an independent Regulator before the level for institutional tuition fee proposal could be agreed (DfES 2003).

Brown was bitterly opposed to the proposals. In discussion he had repeatedly called for further investigation and had suggested an external review like the Wanless Review of the NHS. He had, according to Rawnsley, been defeated in a Cabinet committee chaired by the Deputy Prime Minister, John Prescott, while the Clarke proposals had been commended because he did not have an alternative scheme to put forward. He sent a 25 page fax opposing the proposals to Clarke on the day Clarke was making his statement in the House of Commons. When the proposals were published, 160 Labour MPs signed a motion opposing them. In November 2003, Prescott hosted a dinner with Blair and Brown to produce a reconciliation of views on tuition fees and on foundation hospitals, another bone of dispute, and when Blair agreed not to run for a third term, Brown agreed to support the proposals and stand down the opposition of his two prime lobbyists in the Commons, Nick Brown and George Mudie (Blair 2010; Mandelson 2010; Rawnsley 2010). The Parliamentary majority was five, with the Conservatives recapitulating their opposition to Joseph's proposals, voting against. Blair described the tuition fee decision as an essential example of the New Labour philosophy and the 'supreme fulfilment of my mission to show how progressive politics . . . could modernise the nation' (Blair 2010: 495). Blair remained in office and fought and won a third term.

This decision on tuition fees represented a culmination of a campaign by the CVCP for a better structure, except in Scotland, which continued to resist fee charging to its own students, and a clear break from the past. Although Dearing had begun the process, the 2004 decision was a much more complete overturning of the Robbins funding framework where higher education was regarded as sufficiently a public good to require a full financial subsidy for all students engaged in it. The House of Commons debate, moreover, represented the most serious political discussion of higher education since the Parliamentary reaction to the 1962 rejection of the UGC's quinquennial bid. (The main Robbins and Woolwich speech debates took place in the House of Lords.) Higher education was pulled irrevocably into the political arena and the decision was essentially political. The Prime Minister had persuaded a reluctant Party to vote for his vision. However, his vision compounded two ideas – the creation of a market in which institutions would charge differential fees to match their different quality or reputation and the enhancement of the 'best' universities so as to be more competitive internationally and to prevent them being overtaken by universities in China and India. (It also, of course, espoused further expansion and widening access.)

The White Paper made specific recommendations about the differentiation of research intensive and teaching universities which were largely realized but was much less successful in the creation of a market because, when invited to establish their tuition fee levels, universities in the post-1992 much enlarged university sector behaved precisely like the pre-1992 universities had in relation to the UFC guide price exercise – all but two universities opted to charge the full £3,000. This time there was no injunction from the CVCP (now Universities UK) and many Russell Group universities might have expected some differentiation to have emerged. Institutional self-esteem had frustrated the Blair free market in fees. The scheme now looked almost exactly like the HECS in Australia on which it had been partially modelled. On the other hand it represented a further considerable step away from the dominant continental European model where higher education, with some notable exceptions, remained free (Johnstone and Marlucci 2010).

Much of the criticism of the new tuition fees policy was based on the deterrent effect it might have on applicants reluctant to commit themselves to such substantial debt, and one of the several concessions made to secure a majority in Parliament was that an independent commission would be established three years after the introduction of the new fee structure in 2006–07 to review the outcomes. As Figure 3.4 above indicates, and in common with the Australian experience with HECS, demand remained unaffected, apart from an acceleration in the year immediately prior to the new scheme; evidence also emerged that some improvement was evident in the participation of students from disadvantaged backgrounds. Except for the continued opposition of critics opposed in principle to cost sharing the new scheme seemed to be a success and the additional resources flowing into universities, even if moderated by the requirement to provide bursary schemes, together with increased capital support for infrastructure, particularly on the science and technology side, offered the prospect of a considerably more favourable economic climate for higher education. It had always to be recognized, however, that, since the up-front costs of the income contingent loan system fell on the Government, the Treasury would remain in control of student numbers and the rate of expansion to meet demand.

Meantime the Brown Government, honouring the commitment entered into in 2004, established the independent commission appointing as its chairman Lord Browne, former chief executive of BP and a Blair confidante.[53] A reasonable expectation of the Browne Committee's Report would have been that it would have confirmed the Blair model but would have raised the fee maximum to encourage a greater differentiation in the fee level market. Instead the Report, entitled seductively *Securing a Sustainable Future for Higher Education* (Browne Report 2010) opted for an almost totally marketized solution where institutions would be free to charge market priced fees, student choice would allegedly drive up quality and no limit would be placed on expansion except that access to student loan facilities, which would be provided by the government, would be limited only by achievement of a minimum tariff entry standard to be set by the Government each year. HEFCE, the Quality Assurance Agency, OFFA and the Office of the Independent Adjucator for Higher Education (OIA) would be replaced by a single Higher Education Council. It would have been interesting to see how a Blairite government would have dealt with this Report in a period of relative prosperity but both Blair and Brown had gone to be replaced by a Coalition Government of Conservatives and Liberal Democrats which was facing the most severe economic recession since the 1930s. Moreover higher education was no longer the responsibility of a Department of Education but was now part of the Department of Business, Innovation and Skills headed by a Liberal Democrat Secretary of State but with a Conservative Higher Education Minister, David Willetts, who had strong market credentials and had once been a Treasury official.

In a situation where the 2010 Comprehensive Spending Review was based on a reduction of 25 per cent in public expenditure it was clear that an open ended commitment to support Government borrowing costs against an uncontrolled fee charging backcloth, and with a Liberal Democrat interest in protecting widening participation and therefore easing loan repayment conditions, was not sustainable: controls over fee levels and student numbers were inevitable. More interesting was the change of dynamic between sorting out budgeting priorities with a Department with responsibilities for higher education and also for industry and skills. For whatever reason higher education took a 40 per cent cut which had the effect of replacing state support altogether with fee income alone in respect to first degree programmes except in the case of science and technology programmes and some other programmes of economic importance. This represented a very radical development from the 2003 White Paper proposals. Tuition fee levels were capped at £9,000 but left open to institutional decision making subject to moderation by OFFA, through enforceable Access Agreements. The result, while not quite on the scale of the guide price 'cartel' or the response to the £3,000 fee maximum, was to push fees inexorably to a much higher level than initial BIS estimates, which led to severe criticism from the Higher Education Policy Institute as to the Treasury estimates of borrowing levels which the new scheme would require (HEPI 2011). The eventual White Paper (BIS 2011b) sought to retain the spirit, if not the substance of the Browne Report. Having rejected the tariff standard idea as unworkable, it tried to reintroduce some market flexibility into the control of student numbers by adopting a 'core and margin' approach, by which a subsidiary market of student numbers was created by withdrawing some 85,000 student places from the currently allocated student numbers in 2012–13, to be competed for against the achievement of AAB grades at A level or against the recruitment of widening participation students. The competition for the 20,000 places in the latter category led to the transfer of 10,000 places to FE colleges offering

Foundation Degree places at much lower fees. HEFCE (now more a regulating than a funding body) QAA and OFFA remained with their constitutions and powers unchanged pending legislation. The new provisions promised more, rather than less, bureaucracy and an intensification of regulation to manage the market now created.

The history of tuition fees tells us a great deal about the involvement of the state in British higher education. From the 1930s when fees represented a little over 30 per cent of university income and were to a large extent paid direct by the student, we moved to a period when the arguments about fee levels for home students were to some extent academic because they were about which state budget, the local authorities' or the DES's from which the funds would be drawn, to a reversion to fees paid by students with the repayment and interest carried as part of the Public Sector Borrowing Requirement. Through one lens, home and international students were once again treated equitably with each paying full cost fees (with the partial exception of home students in 'strategic and vulnerable' subjects; BIS 2011b para 1.10). Through another, home students would be subject to a graduate tax which was expected to repay 70 per cent of the exchequer costs and loans over a 30 year period. The fact that the 2010 Comprehensive Spending Review decision would generate £3bn savings in grant annually by 2014–15 (BIS 2011b para 1.6) reminds us that this decision, like almost all decisions on fees described above, could be said to be covered by the description by Rhodes Boyson of the 1979–80 decision on international student fees: 'It was a financial decision. That is why it was made and made quickly'. Without exception, decisions on system wide fee levels deemed to be likely to be unpopular were taken behind closed doors and without consultation with the universities, polytechnics and colleges required to implement them. On the one occasion when the CVCP sought to engage in a policy orientated discussion on future tuition fee policy in 1976 it was crudely rebuffed by the announcement of an alternative set of figures. British universities have historically claimed considerable legal institutional independence and the pre-1992 universities have written into their charters and statutes the right of their governing bodies, after consultation with their senates, to determine fee levels (a leftover from the pre-War years) but between 1945 and 2004 fees were controlled and manipulated for policy purposes, by the state and, since 2004, when the costs of the higher education system in effect outweighed the ability of the state to cover them, they were hedged around with maxima and moderating provisions which severely limited managerial autonomy. In no area of policy has the state more consistently abrogated to itself key decision-making powers.

4

Research and policy

The development of policy towards research, distinctive from policy on higher education, took a long time to take root in Britain. When it did it was driven by two considerations: the need to concentrate research in larger academic groupings, which presupposed greater selectivity in research grant policy and the need to seek value for money across government expenditure on research which implied resources being directed where they might be used the most effectively. The first began to be ventilated in the 1960s in the research councils, the second only in the 1980s with the introduction of Cabinet Office Annual Reviews of Government Funded Research and Development. Their impact on higher education was, in a sense, secondary in that they affected the policy environment but were not an intrinsic component of higher education policy. This was to change with the UGC's decision to embark on the Research Selectivity Exercise in 1985–86, the first of a series of RAEs, and the issue of the Advisory Board of the Research Councils' *A Strategy for the Science Base* in 1987 (ABRC 1987), which suggested a reordering of higher education institutions according to the quality of their research. From that point till the culmination of the policy in the 2003 White Paper *The Future of Higher Education* (DfES 2003) the measurement of research excellence became a critical restructuring agent within higher education and a central element of both the Government's higher education policy and of the policy of the institutions. This chapter will seek to identify the stages in the development of the policy and who were the main drivers.

Research and teaching undifferentiated

Between 1945 and 1985 research was an assumed function of all universities. As late as 1982 the Chairman of the UGC could tell the PAC: 'We give block grants to universities . . . so it is for the university itself to decide on a disposition of resource between departments' teaching and research and so on. That is what is meant by university autonomy' (PAC 1982 para 567). The traditional view was best summed up in Robbins: 'There is no borderline between teaching and research, they are complementary and overlapping activities. A teacher who is advancing his general knowledge of his subject is both improving himself and laying foundations for his research. The researcher often finds that his personal work provides him with fresh and apt illustration which helps him to set a subject in a new light when he turns to prepare a lecture' (Committee on Higher Education 1963 para 557).

This was the pure Humboldtian view of a university. Scientific research might be financed through recurrent grant or direct by the Department of Scientific and Industrial Research (DSIR) the Agricultural Research Council (ARC) or through the Medical Research Council (MRC) which were the main contributors to research funding in science and technology but in each case the independence of the researcher was protected by 'the Haldane principle' that gave the three bodies freedom to determine their own research priorities without intrusion from government. This was reinforced by the existence of alternative sources of research support. The CVCP in its evidence to the Trend Committee, which was to recommend the reorganization of the research council system after Robbins, emphasized the point in what might be regarded as a classic statement of the importance of avoiding the dominance of a single source of funding for research:

> It is essential to university research that financial support be available to it from multiple and alternative sources. Ideas are born in the minds of people in the laboratories. They compete for money, of which there is never enough. If it all comes by one channel it is the controllers of that channel, whether in the university or in a higher authority, who must choose and reject. They cannot in this unpredictable field be always right. The individual research worker or group of workers should therefore have the chance of persuading independent controllers of money that his idea is 'one of timeliness and promise'. Only if the organisation of science makes this possible will a too heavy mortality of ideas be prevented.[1]

This statement was intended to reinforce the dual funding system and the principle of the UGC's recurrent grant supporting the 'well found laboratory' while the research councils funded project grants, an approach to research funding that dated back to the 1920s. This did not mean that research capability was spread evenly across the university system. Research was recognized in the UGC's calculation of recurrent grant to institutions; one of the important roles of the UGC subject committees was to advise on individual universities' research capability in their field. Some categories of universities were favoured above others: Oxbridge, of course, but also London (and, separately, Imperial College) and the older civic universities, while the new 1960s universities, because their foundation was geared to meeting student growth targets, were treated as much more orientated towards teaching. The UGC did not reveal the basis of its decisions on the grounds that this might jeopardize universities' autonomy of decision making in distributing resources so the differentiation was camouflaged or simply lost in quinquennial expansion targets. In 1970, Berrill, addressing the CVCP, explained that UGC resource allocation was based on 17 subject groups with the subject committees having the power to recommend variations from the standard figure, and asked whether universities would like fuller indications of how the figures were arrived at. The CVCP's response was 'that more detailed "indications" might result in greater UGC control' and that 'the discretion of universities would *de facto* be limited since those departments for which favourable treatment had been proposed would be unwilling to accept any adjustment which the university might think desirable'.[2]

It should not, however, be assumed that research was restricted to the universities. A circular from the Ministry of Education in 1946 laid down a definition of mission for technical colleges which in many ways foreshadowed the mission given to the polytechnics two decades later: 'The main function of technical colleges is the advancement and dissemination of knowledge, especially knowledge of value to industry and those engaged in industry. Here the importance and educational value of research work cannot be over emphasised'.[3] The circular went on to criticize the negative attitudes to research displayed by some local authorities and to emphasize that research, and particularly applied research undertaken at the request of industry, should be regarded as a normal function of a college. Two events in 1956 were to weaken the effect of this injunction. The first was the decision to invest heavily in science and technology facilities in the university sector and the second was the designation of the most research active colleges as CATs leading ultimately to their withdrawal from the college sector. In his address to the CVCP in the aftermath of the Woolwich speech Crosland chose deliberately to de-emphasize research in the polytechnics when he merely said he would not rule it out. This was not a ringing endorsement. But neither the regional colleges nor the later polytechnics had the benefit of the dual funding system; funding from the FE/AFE pool was geared entirely to student numbers and took no account of research. In 1987 ABRC calculated that the polytechnics spent about £100m on research of which £60m came from general income as compared with over £1.2bn in universities. Although NAB tried to carve out a research role for them, with their concentration on teaching and the very rapid expansion of numbers it was not surprising that the former polytechnics were ranked below the lowest ranked of the pre-1992 universities in the 1992 RAE.

The one opportunity to consider research in the context of higher education policy in this period was through the Robbins Committee but the Committee, as we have seen above, saw research and teaching in universities as indivisible with no requirement to consider research as a separate component. Thus, as far as Oxbridge was concerned, Robbins' concern was entirely directed to the undue attraction they exercised in respect to the best qualified undergraduate candidates and the Report was anxious to create conditions whereby such candidates were dispersed more equitably around the university system (Committee on Higher Education 1963 paras 211–23);

it did not concern itself at all about the two universities' research standing. In one respect only could Robbins be said to address research as a separate policy issue and this was in the recommendation to create five Special Institutions for Scientific and Technological Education and Research (SISTERs). The Committee had been impressed by its visits to the Zurich Technical High School (now ETH, Zurich), the Delft Technical University and MIT, and wanted to see such models more widespread in Britain. As a result of decisions taken a decade before special investment had been made in Imperial College to create one such institution but Robbins proposed that further investment be made in the Manchester College of Science and Technology (soon to be UMIST), the Royal College of Science and Technology, Glasgow (soon to be Strathclyde University, and one of the CATs, and that one wholly new institution be founded, to parallel the New Universities, to create a new category of institution devoted entirely to teaching and research in science and technology. In some ways this looked back as if to extend the decisions of 1956, which themselves drew on the Barlow Report of 1946 which saw investment expressly in science and technology, both in teaching and research, as the universities' prime contribution to the economy rather than as an investment in research in general. The SISTERs recommendation never got off the ground and was killed off by Crosland with the result that the undifferentiated investment in research across all universities was left undisturbed.

The Report generated, as we have seen, criticism on the left from Weaver, Burgess, Robinson and others, who favoured a more 'domestic' form of higher education based in existing local authority institutions, but there was one critic who adopted an altogether different argument. The Robbins Committee, in the course of its visit to the US had visited California, which in 1960 had adopted the California Master Plan which had established a layered higher education system with the University of California at the top and the state university and the community college sectors below, the three sectors being linked with well defined student crossover arrangements. It was perhaps natural, therefore, that the Robbins Report should have attracted criticism from a young Berkeley sociologist, Martin Trow, who argued that the pattern the Report projected 'is that of an inverted pyramid with the elite institutions, the universities, maintaining pre-eminence in numbers as well as prestige. As a result the special conditions attaching to the elite institutions . . . are therefore the characteristics of the bulk of British higher education'. One of these characteristics in the modern era, although Trow did not mention it explicitly, was the research function. But he went on to ask what was the price to be paid for this decision, and he concluded by asking whether Britain would not have been better served 'by a system of higher education that is shaped like a pyramid rather than an inverted pyramid' (Trow 1963). In one sense, the development of British higher education, in relation to research, represents a working out of this policy issue (Shattock 2012).

Meantime the issue of the need for greater selectivity in the research funding of science began to attract attention. The Trend Committee on the

Organisation of Civil Science was mainly concerned to tidy up the research council system by separating off industrial research into the new Ministry of Technology replacing DSIR with a Science Research Council (SRC), to become later the Science and Engineering Research Council (SERC), and creating the Natural Resources Research Council, later to become the Natural Environmental Research Council (NERC). Having noted the rising cost of civil science the Committee adopted the assumption that 50 per cent of the costs of university science departments were devoted to research; no one explored what the implications of this might be in the period of expansion which Robbins had forecast (Trend Committee 1963). Selectivity was, however, beginning to appear on the policy agenda. The DSIR in its final report took a forthright position recommending that universities should accept guidance on how they could make their most effective contribution to scientific research (DSIR 1965) and the SRC issued a report in 1970, *Selectivity and Concentration in the Support of Research* (SRC 1970), which stated that it intended to concentrate research support on departments which had recognized research track records. (SRC 1970). By the mid-1970s all the research councils including the Social Science Research Council (SSRC) (later re-titled the Economic and Social Research Council (ESRC) to placate Joseph's suspicion of the social sciences) were signed up to selectivity and to some degree of concentration of research funding through programme grants to favoured departments or centres. There was, however, little coordination with the UGC (Shattock 1994). Nevertheless selectivity policies delivered through the research councils began to prepare the ground for the introduction of selectivity in UGC funding. Meantime, under the pressure of potential budget cuts the UGC was itself beginning to change its ground. Although Parkes in an address to the CVCP in October 1980 was not speaking specifically about research, his call for a system in which all universities should seek 'to be good at *some* things but we want you to concentrate on your *strengths* and *not* support pallid growths which are now never likely to reach maturity'[4] pointed the UGC in that direction.

The beginnings of selectivity

Financial pressures proved to be the trigger which forced change. The Rothschild Review of 1970, which had dismissed the Haldane Principle as being inappropriate to the modern needs of government, had introduced the 'customer-contractor principle' to the commissioning of research and had transferred 25 per cent of research council funds to be administered directly by government departments. This had proved to be ineffective with hard pressed government departments re-directing research funding into other activities. Dissatisfaction with this and a growing recognition of the economic importance of the research base led to the Cabinet Office mounting an annual assessment of research expenditure across all government departments, including, of course, the DES and the universities. By

1984 the universities could claim to be doing half the nation's basic research (UGC 1984). The UGC recurrent grant to universities did not differentiate between teaching and research, and assumed, as we have seen, that all universities had a significant research function. This was challenged by the Treasury which argued that a 'Black Hole' existed in the £635m which it was estimated was spent on research in universities (UGC 1984) and that the process lacked accountability. Some universities were clearly more successful than others in research; this was recognized by the research councils in their responses to individual applications for support but not in UGC allocations (Bird 1994; Kogan and Hanney 2000). A critical point for the formulation of policy was the absence of any detailed assessment of universities' actual expenditure on research. In 1972 a CVCP diary exercise (CVCP 1972) had suggested that 30 per cent of academic time was spent on research, including postgraduate supervision and that this would rise to 42 per cent if unallocated and external time were taken into account. In 1983, in response to an enquiry from the Department of Trade and Industry, the UGC estimated the figure at 43 per cent. However, a DES calculation undertaken at the request of NAB, produced a figure of 25 per cent. All these calculations assumed that research activity was spread evenly across the university sector.

It was clear from the responses to the UGC's 28 questions in 1984 that there was no enthusiasm amongst universities for greater research selectivity: only two universities replied positively to the question. This mirrored the response of the CVCP which in opposing research selectivity said that the UGC 'should not be involved directly in making assessments'.[5] Nevertheless, driven by its Chairman who was both a scientist and a long time member of ABRC the UGC's reply to the Secretary of State made it clear that it intended to develop a 'more systematic and selective approach to our approach to our allocation of funds for research' (UGC 1984 para 5.2).

The question that then arose was how this should best be done. Both the CVCP and the UGC were agreed that research was a defining charteristic of a university. The CVCP said in its response to the 28 questions 'in our view a university which did not have *some* good research in *most* of the subjects taught would not be worthy of the name'[6] and the UGC said in its response to the Secretary of State: 'Only institutions with a substantial commitment to research as well as teaching should be on the UGC's grant list' (UGC 1984 para 1.9). One approach might have been to rely on universities themselves. The Merrison Report argued that universities should determine their own research priorities through institutional research committees (Merrison Report 1982) but a later UGC report indicated that only about half the universities had such bodies, Merrison's own university, Bristol, being one of those that had not. The UGC conceded that individual universities were not able to draw on a broad enough body of experts in each subject to give their decisions internal credibility. The Muir Wood Committee, a high level committee set up jointly by the business orientated Advisory Council for Applied Research and Development and ABRC even more unrealistically, recommended that each university should decide what level of research activity it should adopt and then it should fund it accordingly (Advisory Council for Applied Research and Development 1983).

The problem was twofold: how to decide how the concentration of funding required should be undertaken, and who should do it. On the first, Kogan and Hanney quote evidence from Sir Christopher Ball of a dinner party in 1983 organized by Swinnerton Dyer where the issue of whether selectivity should be judged on the basis of institutions, the view of the ABRC which was anxious to take control of the research element of the UGC finances, or on the basis of academic departments, was discussed. According to the Ball account each of the 12 persons present were invited to list the 12 leading research universities but their lists, when compared, included 20 names. This demonstrated for Swinnerton Dyer that an institutional approach would not work. Ball reports that Swinnerton Dyer believed that even 12 research intensive universities was more than could be afforded (Kogan and Hanney 2000). This may have been an opinion forming discussion but it was no more than that. The UGC's culture very much rested on its subject committees and it was much more natural, as with the 1981 cuts, for them to favour a discipline based approach. Moreover the UGC had a significant precedent in its Report on Russian Studies (UGC 1979) which had spelt out the advantages of the larger disciplinary groupings and had recommended a rigorous rationalization of the 40 teaching units in Russian across the university sector.

On the second, although the ABRC and the research councils would have been keen to take a leading role, it was the UGC which took up the challenge. There is no doubt that the originator of the RAE approach was its Chairman, Swinnerton Dyer, and that it was he who put the proposal to the UGC Main Committee which the Committee endorsed. Neither the DES nor the Secretary of State personally were at all involved in the decision and neither were consulted beforehand. This was a fundamental decision, perhaps more important in retrospect than at the time because of the cumulative effect of successive RAEs, but fundamental because it had systemic consequences and because, although it played to current thinking in Whitehall about selectivity for financial as well as scientific reasons, it was taken independently of Government.

The introduction of research selectivity and its strategic implications

One consequence of the decision was that the UGC found itself embarking on a very large exercise because a subject based methodology necessarily involved a much more detailed set of judgements than an institutional rating might have required. The process the UGC adopted for reaching these judgements determined much of institutional development over the next 20 years. Essentially, deciding on a research assessment by discipline meant the adoption of a departmental approach where disciplinary panels rated departments' research performance on a scale of 1–5. Translating these ratings, which were based on publication, research funding and research student number criteria (the precise criteria varied over the many RAEs that followed but these remained the key components), into funding allocations determined institutional futures. In 1985–86 the methodology that Swinnerton Dyer devised was to take the score given to each department for its research performance (assessed by the disciplinary panels), multiply it by a measure of the size of the department based on weighted student numbers, with research students being allocated a higher weighting than undergraduates. The research element for the funding of the subject field nationwide was then calculated on the basis of informed opinion of those close to the field within the UGC, rescaling the figure so that the figures as a whole added up to the total sum attributed to research. Funds were then distributed by subject between universities in proportion to the weightings of each department.

Of course the fundamental element of the methodology was the research ratings themselves, as much, if not more, because of the reputational effect rather than the funding involved: a top rating had an important effect on concentration because of the impact it had on staff recruitment, particularly at the senior levels. The financial figures were aggregated and while the block grant principle still applied the introduction of transparency in how the grant was calculated had a major impact on how the funds were distributed within institutions. From a position where the UGC grant was a black box, to be decoded by only a few experts within the institution, every head of department could now calculate an 'entitlement': at minimum a top rated department was offered a powerful card to play in any internal resource allocation exercise. It was not the case, however, that this first selectivity exercise, distributed all the funding attributable to research on this judgemental basis. The formula used for the distribution of the 1985–86 grant in respect to research continued to provide a research floor for all universities reinforcing the principle embodied in the 1984 response to the Secretary of State that all universities must have 'a substantial commitment to research'. This was much less extreme than Joseph would have liked to have seen. In a speech in July 1985 he called for the research selectivity exercise to be 'very rigorous indeed' and saw no contradiction in a university being 'primarily a teaching institution', thus foreshadowing the conclusion of the 2003 White Paper 18 years later.[7] The formula for the research element, 40 per cent of total grant to institutions, was as follows:

- SR (Student Resource) representing 14.8 per cent of aggregate block grant: intended to provide a basic 'floor' for research calculated on the basis of student numbers;
- DR (Dual funding Resource) representing 5.2 per cent of aggregate block grant: distributed on the basis of income obtained from research councils and charitable bodies at the rate of 40 per cent of such income;
- CR (Contract research Resource) representing 7.0 per cent of aggregate block grant: distributed between universities in proportion to their income from industry and government departments for contract research;

- JR (Judgemental Resource) representing 14.2 per cent of aggregate block grant: distributed between universities based on their research excellence as assessed by the UGC subject committees.[8]

Thus the actual research selectivity element (JR) comprised only a relatively small element of total grant although universities already successful in research might expect to benefit from the DR and CR elements. The significance of the 1985 resource allocation process was the way it established a direction of travel towards a more differential system. Although in 1985–86 the reiteration of RAEs in 1989, 1992, 1996, 2001 and 2008 was not at all envisaged, 1985–86 established an escalator, upwards or downwards, which very few institutions were ever able to escape except by tactical decisions about how selective to be in the numbers of staff whose research was to be submitted for assessment. The RAE system represented the operation of the 'Matthew Principle' in its purist form: success in one RAE bred success in the next; failure in one was extremely hard to recoup in later Exercises because the reputational impact of the process, together with the financial investment involved, exercised a powerful influence on institutional futures.

The higher education system was still digesting the effect of the 1985–86 Selectivity Exercise when the potential longer term consequences of selectivity were articulated in the ABRC Report, *A Strategy for the Science Base* (ABRC 1987). The Report described itself as a discussion document about the future of science funding and contained two sub texts, a bid for support for the creation of interdisciplinary research centres (IRCs) through which a large part of research council funding might be channelled and a rejection of the Morris Report which had recommended a merging of the research councils to better integrate research strategy across the science area. What the Report will be remembered for, and particularly in the light of its exceptionally heavyweight membership of research council heads and chairmen, the Chairman of the UGC, the Chief Scientific Adviser in the Cabinet Office, scientific advisers from government departments and senior industrialists, was its recommendation that:

> The future pattern of higher education provision appropriate to the needs of research would be differentiation between three types of institution:
>
> Type R: offering undergraduate and postgraduate teaching and substantial research activity across the range of fields;
> Type T: offering undergraduate and MSc teaching with associated scholarship and research but without advanced research facilities;
> Type X: offering teaching across a broad range of fields and substantial research activity in particular fields, in some cases in collaboration with others!
>
> (ABRC 1987 Recommendation 5)

It added that concerted action would be necessary to achieve the rapid evolution of this pattern of provision.

The R, T and X recommendation was never formally accepted as policy by Government and represented no more than a broad and simplistic statement of aspiration with no evidence of being based on a detailed study of the higher education system. Nevertheless, it articulated the conclusions of a group of highly influential people who included the most senior policy makers, outside Ministers, in the higher education system, and could therefore legitimately be regarded as authoritative. It must also be regarded as essentially a research council view and a view from big science; a view from the humanities and the less grant dependent social sciences would have been different and would have favoured a more dispersed approach. The Report was greeted, as one might have expected, with widespread alarm within higher education both because it was assumed that the Report would not have been issued unless it had Ministerial support and because no one knew (but there were many speculations) as to where the lines between R, X and T might be drawn. T it was assumed would mostly cover the polytechnics but perhaps might include some universities, but where would the line be drawn between R and X? The Board tried to argue that the categories were intended not as a recommendation but as a prediction, but the wording of the Report did not support this interpretation. In the event, whether as an over enthusiastic recommendation or simply a prediction, the differentiation underlay discussion about higher education for the next quarter of a century. The strength of the RAE subject based approach as originally introduced was that it supported outstanding research performance in universities outside an elite group of research intensive universities and offered encouragement to research groups to remain in less research active universities and prosper. In particular it accorded both esteem and resources to non-science based disciplines for whom the arguments for concentration on the same basis as science were much less clear cut. It also offered support to specialist institutions like the LSE on the non-science side or small research intensive science based institutions like the London School of Hygiene and Tropical Medicine which were implicitly ignored in the broad sweep of R, T and X. As we shall see below the Report proved to be a poor predictor of concentration, at least to the level that some advocates were seeking and even its attempt to create a new vehicle for research funding, the IRCs, proved to be short lived.

A further corrective to the Report was to be delivered by the Review of Earth Sciences, an exercise launched by the UGC under the leadership of Ron (later Lord) Oxburgh as the first step in an effort to rationalize subject provision and concentrate research into fewer centres. The Report, which covered the activities of 33 departments of geology, geophysics, geological science and earth sciences, two departments of environmental sciences and a department of geophysics and planetary physics, was published in May 1987 and recommended that support for earth sciences should be at three levels, the first to recognize substantial research, the second to identify primarily teaching departments with some research which did not demand expensive equipment and the third would be general centres providing first and possibly second year earth sciences courses intended as service courses for other departments. It concluded that there should be 10 or so large departments of between 25 and 30 academic staff and 30 PhD students in order to ensure that the discipline was pursued to a world class standard (UGC Oxburgh Report 1987). The Report was warmly endorsed by *A Strategy for the Science Base* as an example of the degree of concentration required in the experimental sciences (ABRC 1987). However, from the beginning, it had been intended that the review should have two stages, and a second 'national' committee was established to implement the Report taking into account the realities on the ground. This committee produced a more nuanced set of recommendations which divided departments into 'mainstream', 'interdisciplinary' and 'joint'. The 13 'mainstream' departments were divided into a first and second group for resourcing purposes but all were expected to run single subject undergraduate programmes and to undertake research. The five departments in the 'interdisciplinary' category were regarded as having the same status but to be less specialist and to be linked with adjacent scientific disciplines, while the three 'joint' departments were small and medium sized and preserved for teaching for joint degrees. Four departments were recommended for closure but a sum was set aside to cover staff transfers, mergers and redundancy. This second stage integrated teaching into the equation and produced a much less determinist solution. It was the intention to use the same review process for all the experimental science disciplines but the translation of the UGC into the much more market orientated UFC under Lord Chilvers' chairmanship brought sympathy for an academic planning solution to the issues of research concentration to an end. When they were re-addressed in the 2003 White Paper, *The Future of Higher Education*, it was to be in a very different way.

Meantime, the momentum for the abolition of the binary line and the re-designation of the polytechnics as universities was proceeding apace. The polytechnics were keen to enter the next RAE, due in 1992, the year of the merger of the two sectors, and almost certainly overestimated their research capabilities. Tactically, having operated without the dual funding support available to the universities, they might have been better advised to keep their powder dry for the next RAE period and enter when they were better prepared. The results when published seemed to confirm the R, T and X prediction. The original funding formula for the 1992 RAE was for the Research component to represent 33 per cent of grant, Teaching 66 per cent and a Seed Corn fund 4 per cent (the reduction of the Research component from 1985–86 reflected the exceptional growth in student numbers since 1989). The Research component itself was divided as follows:

- SR (Student related resource) 12 per cent;
- DR (Dual funding resources) 5.4 per cent;
- CR (Contract research resource) 0.7 per cent;
- JR (Judgemental resource) 14.9 per cent.

However, the merger was to cause the phasing out of SR, because it would have been too costly to spread across the enlarged sector and a new category

Dev R (Developmental Research) at 7 per cent comprising about £50m) was introduced to be available only to institutions not benefiting from the Research funding category. This was to be a one off attempt to encourage investment in promising research areas in the former polytechnics. But the overall effect of the merger of the two sectors, particularly with the phasing out of SR and the reliance on JR funding against the 1 to 5 criteria was to reinforce the selective funding of the system as a whole. The gap between the post-1992 universities and the research intensive element of the pre-1992 had widened.

Institutional differentiation and economic impact

Under a new Labour Government, higher education moved to centre stage politically in a way that it had not been since Robbins. In 1992 Alistair Darling recounts that John Smith the Labour Leader in Opposition offered him the opportunity to shadow higher education but he refused: 'Worthy though this was, I couldn't see it going anywhere. In politics you are judged by how you perform in the chamber and in the media' and higher education offered no such opportunities (Darling 2011: 242). He might have been less certain about his decision a decade later. Labour policy was dictated by the relationship it saw between higher education and the economy. The question of the contribution of research to national wealth had, of course, been around for a long time and the White Paper, *Civil Research and Development* (Cabinet Office 1987), the intellectual origin of which lay in Joseph's Green Paper made it clear that, in the Government's view, science and technology were central to economic performance, that selectivity and exploitability were to be central criteria for the allocation of resources and that public sector research should be directed towards areas of utility for industry. Gordon Brown, more than any other politician since Keith Joseph, wanted to harness the outputs of higher education to economic growth. In research this message was distilled most clearly in the White Paper *Investing in Innovation: A Strategy for Science, Engineering and Technology* (DTI, HM Treasury and DfES 2002) but it was reinforced in the 2003 White Paper:

> Research lays the long term foundations for innovation which is central to improved growth, productivity and quality of life. . . . The USA, Japan, Canada and other nations are significantly increasing their investment in research. To maintain our position and build on our generous Spending Review settlement we need to think carefully about how research is organised and funded.

> (DfES 2003: 23)

The result was a considerable increase in HEFCE funding for the research component of the recurrent grant, the creation of the Higher Education Innovation Fund (HEIF) and a parallel increase of funding for the research councils. But a second line of policy was that Britain needed a greater differentiation of function between research intensive and other universities so that it could compete internationally in innovation. Blair in his *The Journey* makes clear that by 2001 he had concluded 'that the future of developed nations, such as ours, . . . depends on having a vibrant, dynamic and world class higher education system', which he strongly associated with research excellence (Blair 2010: 482). He describes how this led to two years of disagreement with Brown and to the eventual publication of the 2003 White Paper which served as a vehicle for Blair's views. The White Paper noted that other countries concentrated their research in relatively few institutions and adopted as one of its 'key points': 'we will invest even more in our very best research institutions, enabling them to compete effectively with the world's best universities' (DfES 2003: 23). The point was reinforced in the Government's response to the Lambert Report where it stated explicitly the need for 'a significant number of research-based institutions that are able to compete with the rest of the world'.[9] This did not mean that research excellence outside the leading research intensive universities was not to be further incentivized – the White Paper noted that there were 52 institutions, outside the top 25 universities which had been awarded 75 per cent of the RAE funding, which had at least one department rated at 5 or 5* in the 2001 RAE – but it did mean that the RAE methodology would be amended to favour institutional concentration. This was manifested in an instruction to HEFCE to increase the differentiation in funding weighting between the top and the lower RAE ratings and to identify a '6*' of the very best of the 5* departments for immediate additional funding. The 2007–08 HEFCE funding model illustrated a very sharp upscaling of weightings. The research component comprised 22 per cent (as compared with 40 per cent in 1985–86 and 33 per cent in 1992) the lower percentage for research reflecting the continuing rise in student numbers. The research component (Quality Research – QR) was divided as follows:

Mainstream QR	65 per cent
Research degree programme supervision	14 per cent
Charity support element	12 per cent
Business research element	4 per cent
Best 5* allocation	2 per cent
Other	1 per cent

In addition a Research Capability Fund of £22m was established to support research in what were described as 'emerging areas' like nursing or art and design.

With the disappearance of SR funding the previous link between teaching and research funding was removed, a process finally completed by the implementation of the decisions of the 2010 Spending Review, which separated Teaching funding – to be entirely provided through tuition fees except for some support for science, technology and 'strategic areas' – from Research funding to be provided exclusively through the REF, the successor to the

RAE. The incorporation of a significant element of funding in the framework to support research degree supervision clearly rewarded universities with large graduate schools and the enhanced supplement to charitable funding favoured institutions with large medical schools. Finally the 'Best 5*' allocation reflected the instruction contained in the White Paper, which was reluctantly implemented by the Funding Council in a special allocation of £20m to departments achieving 5* rating in both 1996 and 2001 and to departments achieving 5* for the first time in 2001.

The methodology thus further reinforced the differentiation of universities successful in the RAE from the rest. But this was even further intensified by the allocation of resource weights to the RAE ratings where funding was only awarded to subjects achieving 4, 5 and 5* with the weightings for these calculated at 1, 3.175 and 4.036 respectively. This was later changed to a scoring of 4*, 3*, 2* and 1* for which the resource weightings were 4*–9, 3*–3 and 2* and 1* nil thus eliminating any financial support for research described as being in the category 'quality that is recognized nationally'. If an individual's research fell into the excellence category but less than two thirds of the unit of assessment's did the unit of assessment would receive no funding at all.[10] This exemplified the philosophy of concentrating funding on significant sized groups of researchers but penalized departments trying to develop research from a not very high base. From a higher education perspective one effect was to discourage fluidity in the system and to confirm historical division.

For the period from 1985 to 2001 the UGC/UFC/HEFCE were pursuing a policy of academic concentration which had the effect of reinforcing research excellence wherever it was identified, and which also, but almost incidentally, strengthened universities which had all round research strengths *vis-à-vis* the rest. From 2001 the selectivity process was deliberately used to reinforce institutional rather than subject differentiation. This was a policy driven by the Prime Minister and by senior members of the Government, not particularly by the science community. Indeed the Royal Society's evidence to the 2003 White Paper was concerned that the level of financial selectivity envisaged would ossify the system and would place in jeopardy high quality Research Council projects awarded to outstanding individuals in departments not themselves highly rated and it quoted examples of major scientific breakthroughs that had occurred in departments which would not, at the time, have justified a high rating.[11] The policy was implemented through the adjustment of technical instruments such as the RAE itself, the criteria for rating research performance and the financial weightings attached to them. The process was essentially bureaucratic and was not the subject of widespread public debate. This is not to say that the policy was controversial: there is no indication that the Conservative Party Opposition or the Department of Business Innovation and Skills in the new Coalition Government were other than entirely supportive of the general direction of policy.

At the same time, the Brownite economic impact ideas were beginning to take root. The Lambert Review of Business-University Collaboration,

commissioned by the Chancellor, argued that the level of industrial investment in R and D was declining and that increasingly the university system
would be the locus for fundamental discoveries. This was a compelling
argument with the Treasury. The proposal to incorporate 'Impact' as a new
criterion in the new REF was announced in a pre-Budget Statement by the
Chancellor and has had an increasing impact on the Research Councils.
Response mode funding has been replaced by Research Council driven
thematic agendas, and it is widely believed that the Research Council budgets
survived the Comprehensive Spending Review in 2010 much better than the
higher education system because of the way their bids were justified on 'Impact'
criteria. An interview with the chairman of the Biological Sciences Research
Council illustrated the ambiguity of the relationship between the Research
Councils and the Treasury. While recognizing that adopting strategic priorities helped research councils to gain a favourable hearing with the Treasury,
Professor Kells denied that this research concentration agenda was drawn up
with officials in mind. Bids to the Treasury made on the basis of response
mode funding would, he said, receive short shrift but targeted bids against
'really important problems that affect the world' would attract Treasury
support (Jump 2011: 22). International comparisons and citation indices
suggest that British research has flourished in this climate and under these
policies. On the one hand, universities can congratulate themselves on the
extent to which the importance of research, one of their two primary products,
is recognized by the nation but on the other, it should be noted that the
machinery is now in place for the Government to exercise much more
direction into the kind of research to be undertaken if it chooses to exercise it.

The impact of research related policy

The creation of a distinct and separate set of policies relating to research
which emphasized selectivity and concentration might have been expected
to impose over time a major restructuring of British higher education,
perhaps along the 1987 R, T and X lines. Twenty five years after the launch
of the first RAE, however, British higher education seems stubbornly to have
resisted being corralled into a tidy model. The conventional picture that is
drawn is that 25 per cent of RAE funding is claimed by only four institutions
and 75 per cent by 25 but this does not tell the whole story. In the 2008 RAE
49 universities and colleges had some research in the 'world leading' category in all of their subject based submissions and 53 per cent of the submissions from 118 institutions fell into the two highest grades ('world leading'
and 'internationally excellent in originality, significance and rigour') when
the commitment was given to recognize quality wherever it existed.[12] In other
words high quality research was much more widely disposed than might have
been expected from the winnowing process of five RAEs.

This is confirmed if one compares the top 25 universities in the *Times
Higher* RAE league tables in 2001 and 2008 with a ranking for those years

based on research grant and contract income. What this shows is that the rankings are by no means congruent: eight universities in 2001 and six in 2008 that appear in the top 25 for winning research grant and contract income do not appear in the top 25 in RAE performance and the individual rankings can be very different. While there is consistency in the top four of Oxford, Cambridge, Imperial and UCL, Glasgow and Liverpool score well in the research grants and contracts league table, based on Higher Education Statistics Agency (HESA) data, but do not appear in the RAE top 25 rankings, while Warwick and York which consistently appear in the top 10 for RAE performance, feature towards the bottom of a ranking of the top 25 in terms of research grant and contract income. The differences arise because of subject mix, which has been in part determined by the history of the institutions themselves. Oxford and Cambridge have maintained their historic hegemony but have been joined in the top four by Imperial and by UCL, both benefitting from the rationalization of the independent medical schools in London in the 1980s which transformed their research capacity in areas of major research potential. Indeed if one looks closely at the universities which appear in a top 25 research grants and contracts ranking, but which do not appear in one of the 2001 or 2008 RAE top 25 – Aberdeen, Belfast, Dundee, Glasgow, Leicester, Liverpool, Newcastle and Nottingham – it is the ability of their medical schools combined with powerful life sciences to generate research grant and contract income which represents the common factor in positioning them in the ranking. Subject balance is probably also the determining factor in the positioning of Warwick and York in this table since both began their growth in the 1970s when the swing away from science and technology was at its highest in schools so that they developed more strongly in arts based subjects which scored well in the RAE but generated much less external grant income. Both having now acquired medical schools might expect to change their positioning in a research grants and contract league table over time.

If one looks at research council policies one might again expect to see a mounting level of research concentration but in fact the contrary appears to be the case. Comparing the distribution of research grant income over the years of the RAEs in 1996, 2001 and 2008 one finds a considerable degree of stability of funding patterns with a tendency in 2007–08 to mirror the greater dispersal of research capacity illustrated by the 2008 RAE results (see Table 4.1). The safest conclusion that can be reached is that while four institutions seem dominant, with Manchester after its merger with UMIST close behind, the policy of concentration has been less effective than intended, with at least 35, rather than 25, universities having a reasonable claim to be regarded as research intensive. The various refinements in the RAE funding formulae may have had some effects at the margin but the research batting order appears to have changed very little since 1992. The R, T and X prediction has also not been realized. The 2008 RAE results, quoted above, show clearly the extent to which research capacity is dispersed amongst universities that would in 1987 automatically have been placed in

Table 4.1 The concentration of Research Council grant funding 1995–96 to 2007–08

	1995–96 %	*2000–2001* %	*2007–08* %
Top 4 institutions	26.9	28.1	27.4
Top 15 institutions	58.0	59.0	54.0
Top 25 institutions	72.1	70.0	68.0

Source: HESA tables.

the T category. The ABRC's 1987 Report made clear the extent to which it believed the Oxburgh Report on Earth Sciences laid down a marker for a wider restructuring of the higher education system. (The Oxburgh Report's recommendations were, as we have seen, amended by a subsequent national review.) But the findings of the 2008 RAE panel provides an interesting commentary on the Oxburgh recommendations of some 20 years earlier. They show that there were 41 submissions in Earth Sciences (11 of them from post-1992 universities) as compared with 33 main line departments reported on by Oxburgh. Of these 14, which covered 25 or more staff (the Oxburgh recommendation), had 70 per cent of them graded at 4* or 3*, while 28 with 10 or more staff (including 4 from pos-1992 universities) had over 40 per cent graded at 4* or 3*. The 14 departments included 10 from universities which fell into the top 25 RAE performers, but significantly four which did not while the 28 included Manchester Metropolitan, Plymouth, Portsmouth and Abertay Universities which would certainly have been categorized as T universities under the ABRC model. Thus the concentration recommended by Oxburgh but amended from 10 departments to 13 by the national committee has borne fruit but has been widened by an additional department. More remarkably there are 28 other departments with significant research some of which might, if suitably reinforced, aspire to join the leading group. Earth sciences was not a subject area which participated strongly in the very rapid expansion of student numbers in the 1989 to 1994 period but steady organic growth had taken place bringing with it new centres of research performance. One could conclude that, rather than simply concentrating research into fewer stronger centres, the RAE has had the effect of galvanizing the creation of new sites of research expertise and, because of the existence of research assessment exercises these new sites are stronger and more likely to survive and grow than would have been the case in the pre-RAE era. On the other hand, the 'pyramidization' of research has not taken place, in the sense that concentration in some universities meant a depletion of research in others; rather it has stimulated emulation and competition.

What the data seems to be pointing to is that the Government's aim to concentrate research into fewer universities has been frustrated by universities' own ambition to succeed in the RAE and by the reluctance of staff to allow themselves to be constrained by the institutional model of a teaching only university. In spite of all pressures to the contrary – and these have been very intense in many of the post-1992 universities which entered the RAE system extremely ill prepared in terms of past funding policies – British higher education clings to the Humboldtian concept of universities which incorporate research with teaching. The extent to which this can be realized varies considerably depending on the institutional context but the result is a much more variegated and diverse system than national policies would imply. The measurement of research excellence has had some success as an agent to re-structure the system but it has also been partly outflanked by institutions' sheer competitiveness and by a seemingly unstoppable individual, as well as a corporate drive, towards the research university model. The RAE/REF has been at the heart of the process but it has restructured upwards, not downwards; appeals to institutions to define themselves as teaching only seem likely to fall on deaf ears.

5

The politics of accountability

It is customary to think of policy in higher education as being delivered either bottom up via the institutions themselves or top down from the Secretary of State or indirectly through the interrelationship between Government, the funding body and the institutions. Occasionally Parliament itself made policy, as for example, when Conservative MPs rejected Keith Joseph's proposal about student loans, when it narrowly voted through the Blair tuition fee proposal in 2004, or when an energetic Select Committee put forward ideas, but such interventions have been the exception rather than the rule. Parliament has always had another route into policy making through accountability for public funds because the machinery of government through the PAC requires accountability to Parliament from those organizations, whether government departments or para governmental bodies, which government has funded. The PAC makes policy, not through direct action, but because its political independence and its power to recommend direct to the House of Commons generates respect, if not fear, across Whitehall. A PAC hearing can be a gruelling experience for those subject to examination and the threat of recall, if criticisms are not remedied, are as decisive, if not more so, than Ministerial guidance.

Pressure by the PAC on the grounds of financial accountability was decisive in determining the modern governance structure of the higher education system. The universities always saw themselves as a special case but the PAC, although accepting that the preservation of academic freedom and autonomy made them different from government departments and other publicly funded bodies, took the view that 'The successful combination of operational autonomy with the central oversight of financial performance has to be secured in many private and public sector activities; it is no less necessary in the university sector' (PAC 1990 para 25). The PAC, while respectful of its status, was never comfortable with the UGC's ambiguous constitutional position, and welcomed the UFC and its new powers following the Croham Report. These new powers, including those relating to accountability, were carried over to the HEFCs and it is noteworthy that, since then, active PAC interest in higher education has been largely restricted to exploring institutional governance scandals as at Huddersfield and Portsmouth Universities, and the Swansea and Southampton Institutes. Indeed in 2010, a National Audit Office Report gave a glowing account of HEFCE's procedures and controls.

Throughout, the PAC has firmly eschewed, as it had promised when it gained access to the universities' books, showing any interest in matters of academic policy. But in the 1980s a new dynamic was to emerge: academic accountability to the public. This was first raised in a speech in July 1985 by Keith Joseph when at a conference on the Green Paper he said that he was 'not convinced that the universities in particular . . . are conscious of the weight of responsibility that they bear for the monitoring and preservation of their own standards'. More needed to be done, he said, to provide 'public reassurance'.[1] This was followed up by Baker when, after the publication of the first Reynolds Committee's report on a code of practice for external examiners and internal procedures for monitoring the content of courses and the quality of teaching, he told the CVCP: 'We look to the universities to show still more clearly to the public how their standards are monitored and regulated'. Later, to the North of England Education Conference he asked, rhetorically, 'Do they [the academics] accept an obligation to give an account of their stewardship to their customers and the tax paying public?'[2]

These sentiments sprang from the Conservative Government's interest in public choice economics and for developing market approaches to the running of public services which led to the increasing adoption of New Public Management practice. For universities, however, they breached a firewall, maintained throughout the period since the War, that while reluctantly they could accept intervention in efficiency and value for money issues like better room utilization, centralized purchasing policies or financial planning, the business of teaching students, with all its manifold aspects, was a secret garden solely under the control of the universities themselves. The translation of this accountability, from the nebulous concept of 'the public' to the Government imposed QAA, represented, therefore, a fundamental step away from the concept of the university as a self regulating autonomous institution. As we shall see, although an academic superstructure of committees and peer review was established to provide a semblance of academic control of the quality machinery, the critical decisions which drove the process lay in the hands of government. Part of the motivation for the investment in a formal quality process, following the closure of the CNAA and the assumption of degree awarding powers by the former polytechnics, was that some Ministers and civil servants were left with the suspicion that the former public sector continued to need some form of academic monitoring. A deeper reason, however, was an ideological commitment to the reform of public services via greater public accountability. For universities, both pre- and post-1992, this was to create a massive bureaucratic burden and a significant change in their sense of academic integrity.

The decision to grant the Comptroller and Auditor General access to the universities' books

The establishment of the PAC was initiated by Gladstone when he was Chancellor of the Exchequer. Its function then, as now, was to scrutinize the appropriation accounts of government departments. Since the 1990s, with the growing complexity of government, rather than review every department, its Reports have been increasingly selective in concentrating on particular issues or actions brought to its attention by the National Audit Office via the Comptroller and Auditor General (C and AG) a post itself established in the Gladstonian era. The Committee was, and is, non-political in the sense that it represents Parliament, not the Government or the Opposition, and is part of the machinery which Parliament employs to monitor the executive. Initially primarily concerned with incidents of maladministration, from the early 1980s it widened its interests to efficiency and value for money. Its intrusion into higher education policy, therefore, sprang not from concerns about policy but from a public service perspective which treated expenditure in higher education on the same terms as public expenditure across all government departments.

During the 1920s and 1930s the universities' accounts were not open to scrutiny by the C and AG because only about a third of their income was attributable to UGC recurrent grant. When in the immediate post-War years the UGC grant rose to well above 50 per cent, the PAC's normal point of entry for scrutiny, the PAC began to show interest, and in the 1948–49 Parliamentary session it took evidence on the issue from the Treasury. The Treasury was strongly opposed to its informal but supportive relationship with the UGC being exposed to the kind of cross examination that the C and AG might provoke; it also had a principled view of the need to maintain the independence of universities from state interference and saw itself as a guardian of university autonomy. On this first occasion these arguments carried the day, although the PAC raised, for the first time, whether a solution might be found by giving the UGC statutory status under which it would be directly accountable for its expenditure. (This was also the issue addressed by the Croham Report some quarter of a century later.) The Treasury was not prepared to consider the option and the Committee concluded by regretting that a more effective way of securing Parliamentary control could not be found but urged the Treasury to consider what further steps, 'without impairing the independence of the universities,' could be found to inform Parliament more precisely how their funds were spent.[3] The Treasury was, however, confident in its own ability to control costs and maintain scrutiny over expenditure. Edward Playfair, who was in charge, within the Treasury, of the financing of the university sector, commented in evidence to the Parliamentary Select Committee on Estimates, on 'the Treasury mindedness of UGC officers' and emphasized the special position of the UGC in these terms: 'The situation is not quite the same with the UGC [as with the Ministry of Education] who are in our minds, part of the Treasury. Their job is to do our job . . . we regard them as being our agents and trustworthy agents'.[4]

The Committee returned to the issue in 1950–51, 1952–53 and in 1957. The chief point of entry for the PAC was the rapidly increasing capital expenditure in the university sector, and a series of reports on UGC procedures for making capital grants and universities spending them were prepared to keep the Committee at bay. In 1957 the Committee conceded that the Treasury had gone a long way to meet its concerns and suggested a three year trial of the new procedures. The scene was thus set for a further exploration of the general issue in 1961, when the Robbins Committee was established; this required a further deferral. An indication of how seriously the Treasury viewed the threat can be judged by the fact that its evidence to Robbins was divided into three parts, the third of which was devoted wholly to the question of the C and AG's access to the universities' books. As before, the Treasury was motivated by principle but one also suspects by a sense of self protection. On the first, the Permanent Secretary, Sir Edward (later Lord) Bridges, held especially strong views and had led the defence of the UGC and the universities in previous encounters with the PAC. His view may be summed up in the statement in Memorandum C, Parliament and the Control of Public Expenditure in the Treasury's evidence to Robbins:

> The Treasury has throughout taken the view that the relation between the Government and the universities is unique, justifying therefore exceptional arrangements in the field of financial control, notwithstanding the very large and growing subventions to the universities from public funds. They have been unable to agree that the imposition of Treasury control, or the granting of access to the books and accounts of the universities to the Comptroller and Auditor General would not threaten an infringement of the degree of independence in matters of academic policy or standards which they have thought vital to maintain in the public interest.
>
> (Committee on Higher Education 1963, Minutes of Evidence, Treasury para 7, 23 May 1962)

A significant element in this argument rested on the status of the UGC, described by the Robbins Report as a unique British 'administrative invention', a 'device of interposing between the Government and institutions a committee of persons selected for their knowledge and standing and not for their political affiliation . . . [which ensures] that the measures of coordination and allocation that are necessary are insulated from inappropriate political influences' (Committee on Higher Education 1963 para 727). Because the UGC's membership was 'independent of ministerial and departmental control and is composed chiefly of persons with intimate knowledge of university life and its conventions' (para 728) it could be trusted to operate scrupulously in the university interest and to exercise scrutiny over the universities individually. In practical terms, with the C and AG's concerns about capital expenditure met, with the UGC's annual returns to Parliament and the universities' own accounts available to the PAC, and in the knowledge that 50 per cent of university expenditure was devoted to academic salaries (closely monitored, it was said, by the UGC), the Robbins Committee could see no grounds for any change in arrangements. There is no doubt that there were voices in the Treasury that strongly agreed with this view. In addition the Treasury had its guilty secret, the substantial financial slippage in the capital programme to expand Imperial College, which it would have been anxious to conceal from public scrutiny. One can only speculate how this classic example of over expenditure on a capital programme was prevented from surfacing in the argument.

It was inevitable that the PAC would wish to return to the issue. Three changes in the environment had taken place. The first was that Bridges had retired and there is evidence from the Treasury files that if the universities were to be transferred away from Treasury responsibility to a single Minister, whether the Lord President of the Council or the Minister for Education, then immunity from scrutiny by the PAC would have to be conceded.[5] The introduction of the PESC process and the events of 1962 emphasized the extent to which the universities' vote had become part of public expenditure rather than a private fiefdom of the Treasury. Finally, the decision to accept the Robbins Committee's recommendation to upgrade the CATs to university status, which had since 1961 been subject to the C and AG, meant that the dangers to academic independence of scrutiny by the PAC could be tested by actual practice.

It was clear that this time the PAC meant business. It invited written and oral evidence not only from the Treasury, the DES and the UGC but from the CVCP and the AUT and from an impressive cast of academic representatives from the House of Lords. The inquiry and taking of evidence extended over three months between October and December 1966. To modern eyes the argument that the universities should be open to scrutiny by the PAC would seem to be incontrovertible. Between 1945–46 and 1965–66 university expenditure had increased from £3.7m to £134.5m, and 70 per cent of it came from the state. However, the nub of the issue for the universities was the role of the DES *vis-à-vis* the UGC. The UGC was a non-statutory body so that the Accounting Officer had to be the Permanent Secretary of the DES. Would that mean that the DES, whose responsibility for the universities the CVCP had fought hard against, would weaken the UGC's autonomy by exercising a scrutiny function over the UGC and its decisions about individual universities or academic development? The UGC was known to be worried about this and it was widely believed that one reason why the new Chairman, Wolfendon, had sided with the DES over retaining the teacher training colleges in the public sector was his fear that transferring them to the universities would tip the balance over C and AG access to the universities' accounts since they, like the CATs, were presently subject to C and AG scrutiny. Crosland, of course, was not sympathetic to the universities' position.

It is evident that a great deal of private discussion took place before the evidence gathering sessions. The Comptroller and Auditor General himself,

Sir Bruce Fraser, had previously been Permanent Secretary of the Ministry of Education and was well respected in education circles and it very much looks as if private understandings had been reached in advance of the formal meetings. Sir Herbert Andrew, the Permanent Secretary at the DES was notably restrained in his evidence and stated a clear reluctance, as the Accounting Officer of the university system, to become involved in any form of close scrutiny of the UGC or the universities. Fraser offered the standard guarantees of not questioning decisions on policy but went further by drawing a distinction between the examination of financial method and the examination of policy. When asked by Wolfendon whether if the policy decision pointed one way, but the arithmetic another, he would feel bound to pursue it, he answered in the negative. Wolfendon then asked two, what look like well rehearsed questions: the first was whether a higher level of capital expenditure for experimental purposes on a hall of residence would attract C and AG criticism, to which Fraser, equally well rehearsed, gave the reply that 'the freedom [to experiment] . . . was very precious and indeed necessary to any virile or energetic administration' (PAC 1967 para 1035); and the second was in respect to a university following an unorthodox investment policy (relevant because universities were still funded on a deficiency basis), to which Fraser replied that he would expect to leave it 'un-criticised on learning that these matters were under the control of persons who were skilled and understanding about them'.[6]

The PAC's final Report seemed to give all the safeguards the universities could have asked for. It confirmed the UGC's role as an essential 'buffer': 'From the Government's point of view it is the accepted source of expert advice on university affairs including the allocation of resources which the Government makes available; from the universities it is the accepted medium for representing their opinions and needs to the Government and for ensuring the allocation is equitable' (PAC 1967 para 10). It accepted that the most important issue was 'that the DES might be driven into taking closer control than they would otherwise wish to do over activities of the UGC and perhaps of the universities too' (PAC 1967 para 28) and recommended that conventions be established to define the relationship so that the PAC would go direct to the UGC so as to preserve 'the proper autonomy of the UGC and the universities' and to set at rest any fears that the C and AG would be a threat 'to proper academic freedom' (PAC 1967 para 29). Three years later four universities were interviewed by the Committee and all confirmed that visits from the C and AG had caused them no difficulty. (In fact they had been picked out as non-Oxbridge collegiate universities which charged additional college fees to their students, which the latter passed on to their LEAs. The vice-chancellors concerned received a roasting from the Committee as to how the costs were calculated; in two of the cases the fees had been introduced within the quinquennium and had not been reported to, and therefore taken into account in grant calculation, by the UGC.)

Nevertheless a rubicon had been crossed. The universities were never again to be regarded as 'unique'. Without the protection of the Treasury the university world was exposed to the various pressures of government expenditure planning and to the standardization of many operational aspects of university management with management practice employed in Whitehall. It may have been the product of a simpler view of life when Wolfendon was alleged to have said that he knew things were going to be all right when the C and AG staff who were based in the UGC chose to play for the UGC in the annual cricket match with the DES. He could not have been more wrong. As we shall see, the PAC's concerns about accountability were one of, if not the major driver, of the demise of the UGC and its replacement by the UFC.

Policy making and the Public Accounts Committee

By the 1990s the PAC's remit stretched over some 170 or so different heads of public expenditure and it is unsurprising that its impact on the universities was spasmodic. However, when the PAC took up an issue it was generally game changing. Its remit did not extend to local authority controlled expenditure so that public sector higher education, while it inherited the results of PAC interventions when the two sectors were merged in 1992, was not subject until then to C and AG interest. At one level the C and AG and his staff were concerned with operational and managerial issues, sometimes usefully, sometimes intrusively. A significant PAC report on Purchasing in 1994, for example, alerted universities to public sector best practice in this area but also raised centralizing bureaucratic issues in institutions about the existence of departmental stores, the role of central purchasing officers, and delegated ordering arrangements in laboratories. C and AG staff were keenly interested in space utilization and were critical of universities which did not adopt space charging, an off the shelf management tool which some, but by no means all, universities regarded as helpful. In the same Report (1995)[7] they criticized universities' approach to recovering overhead costs on commercially sponsored research, and the absence of machinery in institutions to determine the element of recurrent grant spent on each of teaching and research. (This ultimately led to the TRAC exercise.) C and AG staff visited universities on a regular basis inspecting internal audit arrangements and commenting on governance arrangements, following adverse national reports on scandals at Huddersfield and Portsmouth Universities and the Southampton and Swansea Institutes of Higher Education. These activities increased the bureaucratic demands made on universities but rarely raised issues of major principle.

This was not the case, however, in three other cases where major policy questions emerged. The first was in 1970 and concerned the old chestnut of capital expenditure and represented an immediate test of commitments made at the hearings in 1966. The C and AG had identified two universities, Keele and Essex, where, partly owing to the swing of student choice of subject away from science, partly to the slow down from the overall forecast expansion, and partly because both Universities' admission targets had been affected by bad publicity, considerable surplus capacity existed in science buildings. At Keele, the surplus extended further to dining and catering capacity. In each case the UGC had approved capital projects but had taken a realistic approach to the prospects of expansion so that the recurrent grant provision for student number targets did not match the building capacity. In Essex's case, for example, like all the 1960s New Universities it had been allocated a capital provision of £1m p.a. for six years to bring it up to 3,000 students but in 1967 it had only reached a population of 750 and an expansion to 1,700 by 1972 was considered to be a realistic target. The PAC expressed concern at what it saw as 'the large waste of resources represented by the surplus capacity at some universities' and identified two causes, inadequate information and inconsistency of decision making. It recommended that a decision on awarding a capital grant should signal an adjustment of student targets and recurrent grant and that the UGC should exercise much more management control over universities' use of the building capacity they already had.[8] The first of these recommendations would have cut right across the quinquennial system of university planning and would have severely inhibited the UGC's ability to match institutional growth with student demand. In practice, the sharp economic downturn of 1973–74 aborted new capital expenditure, and student number targets had inevitably to be cut back to the capacity of the buildings they had. But the UGC sought to resist the second recommendation on the grounds that its function was not to second guess the management of universities, which in any case, it said, it did not have the staff to do, and that it believed that the discipline of operating within a quinquennial grant permitted universities autonomously to decide their own management approaches. This was an argument that the PAC was perennially unwilling to accept; the whole basis of its response was that the UGC was an executive agency with conventional powers of enforcement.

The PAC was acting perfectly within its 1966 statement of intent in being critical in respect to the overprovision of science accommodation but it is arguable that it was going beyond it in recommending that student numbers should be adjusted to accommodation capacity because this trespassed on the UGC's policy-making powers in respect to the academic development of institutions and meeting student demand. Moreover the PAC's vision tended to be a limited short term balancing the books approach, unsympathetic to longer term institutional needs. Thus it was critical of a UGC decision to help Nottingham University purchase some privately owned buildings on its site which it accepted it would not require until its numbers exceeded 10,000, the largest student population that the UGC could envisage for it. (It now has over 25,000 students.) It was also critical, on an analogy with government departments, of universities building up financial reserves, even though as autonomous and legally independent bodies, it could be argued, and would have been a decade later, that they were only exercising reasonable managerial caution in an unstable financial climate. The UGC almost certainly over reacted to the criticisms on space use: one result was the instigation of a

comprehensive capacity survey of all university buildings – hugely complicated when applied to nineteenth-century ceremonial halls or, indeed, to
any pre-War buildings – and to the creation of a large UGC/institutional
bureaucracy in the regular updating of such surveys irrespective of whether
a new capital grant was requested. This was a sledgehammer to crack a nut
from which the university system was only relieved by the abolition of the
UGC.

The second major policy area which the PAC engaged with was the question of tenure. This first came to the fore in 1981 when the PAC was seeking
to raise the issue of the variation in staff:student ratios between universities
and subjects. The Chairman of the UGC responded firmly that this was a
matter for individual universities to decide on. But the PAC could not fail to
be drawn into the then current controversy of how universities were going to
be able to cope with the threatened budgetary reductions when their
academic staff salary costs were effectively fixed costs because the staff had
been appointed with tenure until retirement age subject only to a 'good
cause' clause in their statutes which was restricted to performance and behaviour. One vice-chancellor, Jack (later Lord) Butterworth, had taken coun-
sel's opinion on the contracts at his university and had been advised that the
compensation required to create an academic redundancy would be between
£40,000 and £150,000 depending on length of service. (In practice many of
the civic universities made appointments on a permanent basis but under
contracts which stated a three month notice period. However, in employment law it was deemed that custom and practice in such cases gave a guarantee of tenure equal to that in universities where the full acquisition of
tenure was acknowledged.) Parkes told the PAC that he expected that the
cuts would require a loss of 3,000 academic and 4,000 non-academic posts
and that the breaking of contracts might cost between £100m and £200m.
The PAC minuted 'We trust that in considering how best to solve the present
problems the UGC will bear in mind the desirability of introducing a greater
measure of flexibility into future contractual arrangements for academic
staff'.[9]

However, the UGC had no power to introduce flexibility into staff contracts
and, at a PAC hearing in 1982 on the costs of the additional resources that
the DES was now being asked to find to enable universities to make the
budget cuts required (the estimated cost had now risen to £250m), the DES
reported that the UGC had passed the problem to the CVCP. But the CVCP,
having exhausted attempts to devise new contracts which incorporated provision for redundancy on the grounds of financial exigency, were forced to
confess to the Secretary of State that 'the majority [of vice-chancellors] do
not believe their institutions could bring about the changes you envisage by
their own volition' within the timescale you have in mind'.[10]

By 1985 it was plain that neither the CVCP nor the UGC were able to act
effectively in the matter and the PAC expressed its pleasure that the DES
was moving towards legislation; in the light of the lack of communication
between the DES and the UGC over the likely redundancy costs arising from

the 1981 cuts, it urged the need for 'a more flexible demarcation of responsibility between the DES and the UGC'. The Committee looked to the newly created Croham Committee to produce a solution.[11] On the narrower point of tenure there is no doubt that the PAC demand for action, backed up by support from the Treasury, was critical in bringing about its abolition. Although the effect was mitigated by the House of Lords' insertion of safeguards for academic freedom into the 1988 legislation (Crequer 1989), the concept of academic tenure had been an essential element in the idea of a British university. In the new relationship with Government, its continuance was clearly anomalous but its removal was among many decisions which marked out the 1980s as a watershed in the changing position of the universities *vis-à-vis* the state.

The inability to solve the tenure issue was only one of the factors to make the PAC push for a clarification to the, in their view, ill-defined relationship between the DES, the UGC and the university system. Almost from the beginning the PAC had difficulty in reconciling itself to the convention, agreed in 1966, that while the Accounting Officer was the Permanent Secretary, communication and recommendations for changes of practice had to be addressed to the UGC which had few if any sanctions to impose them on autonomous universities. In 1973 the PAC, while giving the universities a clean bill of health after its first five years of auditing, sought to bring pressure on the UGC to be more active in encouraging the use of more 'economic', that is more 'modern', methods of management in universities. But the UGC replied, as it had done in 1970, that it regarded working within the constraints of the recurrent grant created a greater incentive for fiscal responsibility and the need to seek value for money than any other method the PAC could devise. Successive PACs clearly did not accept this approach which was anomalous to other public sector activities with which it had to deal, but in the absence of legislative reform and with the DES unable to exercise its Accounting Officer role except through the UGC, it had to restrict itself to pressurizing the UGC as best it could. Although the Jarratt Committee's recommendation that an examination of the role, structure and staffing of the UGC was quoted as the trigger for the Croham Review there is little evidence that the radical change in the legal status that was to emerge from the Review was in the Jarratt Committee's mind. The smoking gun was, in fact, the rapid descent into deficit at University College, Cardiff and the need, for the first time, for the Permanent Secretary to exercise his Accounting Officer's powers over the university system in the most extreme way by threatening to withdraw recurrent grant unless steps were taken to rectify the situation. The UGC's failure to grapple with the Cardiff problem at an early stage before it got out of hand played into the PAC's hands. The Committee's verdict:

> We believe strongly, however, that the UGC should have taken earlier and more positive action to identify, appraise and tackle the financial difficulties at Cardiff. They were well aware of the difficulties facing

universities as a result of grant levels; and indeed they assured our predecessors that they would be discussing with universities exactly the sort
of staffing problems that lay at the heart of Cardiff's troubles. We
consider that they took too passive a role in concluding that they were
unable to challenge the College's view that no staff reductions were
necessary and that there would be no consequent problems. Respect for
the independence of universities is important but this does not mean
that the UGC should have abjured sufficient control to be able to assure
themselves of competent financial performance by universities.[12]

reflected long held views about the ineffectiveness, from its standpoint, of
the UGC's respect for institutional autonomy and its reluctance to be drawn
into institutional management. The PAC went on to applaud the creation
and constitutional arrangements of the new UFC where the Chief Executive
was to become the Accounting Officer and a dominant lay element was introduced onto the membership of the Council. This solution was entirely
consistent with the Committee's criticisms of the UGC role over the years. It
followed this up with a second report in the same year in which it expressed
concern that 29 universities outside London had deficits on their income
and expenditure accounts at 31 July 1988. It called on the new Council to use
its new powers 'to act vigorously' and to ensure 'a high level of accountability
to Parliament for the financial control exercised over university expenditure
and the economic, efficient and effective use of resources'. It added a further
conclusion: 'We do not accept that university independence and autonomy,
although undoubtedly valuable in many respects, is a valid argument against
attempts to defend against shortcomings in realistic and effective management and control of the public funds on which universities are dependent'.[13]

This concluded an argument, begun in 1966, as to whether the UGC
system and its hands off relationship with universities could satisfy the
requirements of public accountability when that was extended to include
internal management practice and public service concepts of value for
money. In this sense the C and AG inspections, and the occasional incursions of the PAC, pushed universities into a management style that approxi-
mated much more closely to a public service model. Lord Murray, in the
evidence he gave in 1966, recognized that one effect of the introduction of
the C and AG would be to strengthen administration in universities and
'would almost inevitably decrease the responsibility of the academic side of
the university'.[14] This was not a convincing defence of the *status quo* to a body
concerned with the proper expenditure of public money but it did correctly
anticipate a cultural shift within many universities and fed later accusations
of managerialism. When internal audit, required to be introduced after
Cardiff, was added to external audit and C and AG audits, with academic
quality audits soon to be added, universities became one of the most audited
organizations in the land.

This is not to say that many of the criticisms of the C and AG staff
were inappropriate. There was considerable complaint about the PAC's

accusations about underuse of capacity in 1970 but a study conducted by the CVCP in 1967 had concluded that 'Some universities, for one reason or another, have no precise knowledge of their own levels of utilisation, and even less of how they compare with others'[15] and would seem amply to justify the PAC's concern. The establishment of regional O and M Units by consortia of universities met some of the criticisms but they failed to convince the PAC that universities were taking value for money seriously enough at the right levels, especially when the activities involved became enmeshed with questions of internal convenience. The philosophical issue remained. The UGC approach was to see itself as essentially an academic body, distributing resources on the basis of academic judgement to academic institutions which were legally independent and managing themselves autonomously. The discipline institutions were under was the level of grant received; how they spent it was essentially a matter for them and if there were inefficiencies they should be tolerated in the interest of preserving university autonomy. The PAC view was quite different: universities were publicly funded institutions and should accept the disciplines and accountability that went with that. A case could be made for their special 'unique' status but it could be exaggerated and policy and practice should not be permitted to deflect institutions from following the dictates of good practice in the expenditure of public money across the range of government activities. This latter view triumphed and the reforms embodied in the UFC, later reinforced in the legislation which brought the funding council system into being, were important in re-defining state-university relationships. The Accounting Officer was no longer a remote figure, from whom universities were 'buffered' by a benign UGC directed by fellow academics; the Accounting Officer was now the CEO of a funding body on which they were significantly dependent and on which the membership of the board was primarily lay.

From the C and AG's point of view the new accountability was a success. Although the National Audit Office (NAO) wrote a series of reports on individual breakdowns in institutional governance, the production of a Guide on Governance by the Committee of University Chairmen (CUC) gave it a template by which it could comment on individual difficulties, and the NAO did not find occasion to draw the PAC's attention to sector level failings. Indeed its Report some 20 years after its report referred to above, confirmed that HEFCE had been successful in delivering value for money. It noted that the sector was in surplus, although 9 per cent of institutions had had a deficit in two of the last three years but that only seven institutions fell into a high risk category. It also noted that HEFCE did not have the power to take over these institutions but 'works closely with [them] . . . attempting to resolve weaknesses through effective action from their governing bodies'.[16] Thus HEFCE appeared to have struck an effective working compromise between the UGC's unwillingness to cross the line of institutional autonomy and the need to lean on institutions to ensure that disasters were avoided. Significantly, however, in the worst case over this period at London Metropolitan University,

HEFCE had to threaten the same punitive action as the UGC had at Cardiff, the withdrawal of recurrent grant to achieve a solution.

Unlike the UGC, which was minimally staffed, the NAO Report pointed out that HEFCE's expenditure on regulating financial health was £2m per annum.[17] And this points up a critical change: the HEFCE (and the other funding councils) became not only the agent for the distribution of government funds in accordance with the Government's macro priorities for higher education but also the regulator of the system. It no longer described itself as a 'buffer' but as a 'broker' between the Government and the universities (HEFCE 2010). This again derived from the pressure exerted by the PAC. HEFCE did its best to preserve an arm's length relationship with institutions in financial matters but each individual institutional breakdown provided a precedent for more direct intervention culminating in the London Metropolitan affair. This resulted in further changes to the Financial Memorandum giving HEFCE the right to change the institutional accounting officer, in effect declaring no confidence in the vice-chancellor, potentially overriding the governing body. It created a direct relationship between HEFCE and the chair of the governing body, issued detailed guidance to governing bodies on their responsibilities and stated that both the chair and the head of the institution might be summoned to appear before the PAC (HEFCE 2010). Increasingly universities had become absorbed into a state accountability apparatus. This significantly rebalanced the nature of state-university relations.

Accountability for the quality of teaching

In September 1994 the Secretary of State, John Patten, wrote to the CVCP in the following terms: 'we need a rigorous assessment of the relative quality of teaching and learning to provide the necessary accountability for public funds'.[18] Patten was less than enthusiastic about the re-designation of the polytechnics and the origin of the letter was a visit to Singapore in January to address a higher education fair where he had been subject to a great deal of comment by the status conscious Singaporeans about the abolition of the binary line, and the tactics employed by British universities to attract international students. In April, addressing the HEFCE conference, he had stressed the importance the Government placed on achieving a 'broad comparability' of standards between institutions and charged the Higher Education Quality Council (HEQC) to give greater emphasis to this (Brown 2004: 50).

The Patten intervention marked the beginning of a new stage in the Government's campaign to impose external accountability on the conduct of university teaching. His concern, stimulated by the attitudes of the Singaporeans, which one suspects he shared, was that the demise of the CNAA removed an effective safeguard of the academic credibility of degree programmes in post-1992 universities in international markets and a control mechanism over their academic standards. Moreover, the rapid expansion of the public sector institutions from 1989, at marginal costs, under the influence of the PCFC funding model, was calculated to fuel doubts in Whitehall as well. A senior civil servant in an interview with Kogan said: 'Quality assurance was one example of government prescriptiveness . . . Once you got rid of the binary line it was inevitable and probably right'.[19] Part of the unspoken price for the merger of the sectors was the creation of some new quality mechanism, and reserve powers were written into the 1992 Act to ensure that, if necessary, it could be brought into existence.

Concern about the status of a university degree reached back, as we have seen, to disputes between the universities and local authority colleges about degree awarding powers in the 1950s, and the Robbins recommendation for the creation of the CNAA was always intended to provide a legitimization of degree level work in the colleges combined with an element of tutelage as to the breadth of work required for a degree. The CNAA process had worked well and in 1985 the Lindop Committee recommended that increasingly the polytechnics themselves should be given greater autonomy in self regulation. By 1992 all the polytechnics had become 'accredited' institutions and were subject only to periodic review: a transfer to full degree awarding powers represented a natural development. Meantime, in the university sector, Joseph had flagged up an interest in academic standards as early as 1983, initially as one of the questions on which he sought answers from the UGC. The CVCP immediately set up an Academic Standards Group under Philip Reynolds, the Vice-Chancellor of Lancaster. This Group produced three formal codes of practice on external examiners, postgraduate training and research degree examination appeals. In its 1984 response to the Secretary of State the UGC spoke approvingly of the first and, taking the view that prime responsibility for academic standards must rest with the institution, firmly rejected any idea of an external review organization (UGC 1984 para 6.8).

The Reynolds Group went on to produce codes for monitoring the content of courses and the quality of teaching, the training of academic staff and the validation of non-university programmes. However, this corpus of work did not satisfy Baker who called, as quoted above, for the universities to demonstrate more clearly to the public how their courses were monitored and regulated. In his address to the CVCP residential conference in September 1988 he expressed clear scepticism of universities' ability to monitor teaching – Reynolds lacked teeth.[20] In taking this issue up he made it clear that he had been influenced by the CIHE which had followed up its initial *Towards a Partnership* report (CIHE 1988), which had so influenced him in respect to student numbers, with a further document reporting companies' response to it. This contained the statement that companies were more interested in higher education's teaching than its research:

> A striking change . . . is the corporate concern, now widespread and often passionate in the process and output of teaching. We hope that level of interest will be translated into greater recognition of those

institutions and staff who stand at the forefront of the art of communi-
cating the world's knowledge to others. To enlarge the UK's capability
in the competitive practical world, the quality of the learning process is
central'.

(CIHE 1988 para 2.9)

The CVCP accepted that it needed to do more to fend off the DES and
accordingly set up an Academic Audit Unit (AAU) whose task was to scrutinize universities' quality control systems. But even at the beginning of the
Unit's life the civil servant in charge of higher education expressed his belief
to the newly appointed Director that the new machinery was too weak
because it was controlled by the universities themselves.[21] That was certainly
not the way individual universities which were audited saw it: to them the
AAU was as alien an organization as the QAA was to become, even though
the auditors were drawn from colleague institutions.

But the AAU had another doubter, the CDP, which argued that the
continuation of an audit process after the merger of the two sectors would
favour the old university sector and was in any case based on too narrow a
concept. As Stoddart argued, if CDP could not take over the CNAA it would
be better if a new organization altogether could be created which would be
sympathetic to the very different course structures in the polytechnics. The
Department's sympathies were with the CDP and, with CVCP acceptance,
support was achieved to set up a new organization, the HEQC, which was to
be owned and managed by the institutions but funded out of the income
saved by the closure of the CNAA. Giving up the AAU and the creation of
the HEQC was a direct product of the decision to merge the CDP into the
CVCP on the latter's terms and Stoddart's appointment as its chairman was
seen as balancing a pre-1992 university vice-chancellor remaining chair of
the CVCP.

Although the Department officially welcomed the initiative to establish the
HEQC the 1992 legislation contained reserve powers which enabled the
Department to set up its own quality organization. In September 1991, Alan
Howarth, the Minister for higher education, had told the CVCP that the
1992 Act would retain reserve powers for the Funding Councils to set up
their own quality organization in units attached to the Councils: 'The
taxpayer has a right to know what is being provided in return for
public funding. Prospective students and sponsors also have a right to know
the quality of courses on offer'.[22] Thus at the same time as the sector was
setting up, with Departmental support, a self regulating organization, the
Department was giving statutory powers to the funding councils to give assurance on academic standards. As Brown makes clear in his account of the
HEQC's life, the HEQC's view was 'that ultimately academic standards
were the institution's business. HEQC's aim throughout was to strengthen
the institutional capacity for self regulation by offering some benchmarks
and tools as a means for institutions to analyse, benchmark and strengthen
their provision' (Brown 2004: 69). The audit report was owned by the

institution audited and was couched in the unthreatening terms of 'points for commendation' and 'points for further consideration'. Later these two were listed in priority order as 'necessary', 'advisable' or 'desirable'. Deliberately, no overall judgement was offered, the aim being 'to provide a non-adversarial commentary on what the auditors saw as the strengths and weaknesses of each institution's arrangements' (Brown 2004: 51).

Meantime HEFCE (though not the Scottish Higher Education Funding Council which decided to establish its own unit linked to the QAA) having been given reserve powers, was pressed into activating them. This took the form of assessment rather than audit and was stated to be designed to ensure that education funded by HEFCE was of satisfactory quality or better (and to encourage speedy rectification of unsatisfactory quality), to encourage enhancement through the publication of the assessments, and to inform funding and reward excellence.[23] Assessment reports were to be categorized as 'excellent', 'satisfactory' or 'unsatisfactory'. In 1994, following Patten's address to the HEFCE conference, referred to above, the phraseology, 'informing funding' and 'rewarding excellence' was replaced by providing 'effective and accessible public information on the quality of information'.[24] A further change was the replacement of 'excellent', 'satisfactory' and 'unsatisfactory' with a numerical scoring approach where there were six cells, each scoring 1–4, giving a maximum score of 24. (This offered a gift from heaven to media created institutional ranking exercises.) The new scheme also offered an overall summative judgement of 'approved' or 'not approved'.

Instead of institutional assessments, the HEFCE Teaching Quality Assessments (TQA) addressed disciplines, 15 being addressed across 144 institutions in the period 1992–95 of which only 1.3 per cent were found to be 'unsatisfactory' (Cook quoted in Brown 2004). Out of over 3,311 TQA assessments, before the exercise was brought to an end, only 35 failures were actually established (Cook quoted in Brown 2004). As the outgoing Director of QAA put it in a lecture in 2009, between 1992 and 1997 the academic community was put under 'constant surveillance' by two different systems of quality assurance and reacted with 'loathing of what it considered to be the heedless and needless bureaucratic imposition' of the two systems (Williams 2009: 11; 8). Although the HEQC approach could not remotely be described as popular, within institutions it was not disliked as much as TQA which, with its numerical scoring approach, appeared to be blatantly competitive and simplistic. It also threw a considerable burden of preparatory stress on the departments assessed. A climax came when the Warwick Economics Department, a top ranked research department, having rehearsed their TQA performance to be confident they would be awarded 24 points out of 24 released their contempt for the process in a two page spread in the *Guardian* (Harrison *et al.* 2001).

By this time HEQC had been merged into the HEFCE unit and the QAA had taken over its functions. A number of other developments had also taken place: a new chief executive had been appointed to the QAA, John Randall, who had been Head of Professional Services at the Law Society. Randall was fully convinced of the universities' need to justify their performance to the public and early evidence of the QAA's approach was an extremely critical review of Thames Valley University conducted at the invitation of the University itself, which resulted in the vice-chancellor's resignation. Few doubted the accuracy of the QAA's criticisms in this case, although they had not been thrown up in previous HEQC audit reports of the University, but the impact of the review sent shock waves through the system (Brown 2004: 146). But discussions between CVCP (shortly to change its name to Universities UK) and HEFCE, with the Department acting as final arbiter, had established the concern throughout the whole sector about the overload on institutions of the quality inspection burden. This came to a head in March 2001 when Blunkett, the Secretary of State, announced without consultation with the QAA a 40 per cent reduction in the level of external review activity:

> We have invited HEFCE to discuss with QAA, Universities UK and SCOP [Standing Conference of Principals] ways to further reduce the subject review load while still providing reliable public information for students, employees and others. In broad terms, under the proposed university departments which have achieved good scores in the current round (at least three scores of 3 and three scores of 4 on the six factors assessed) will be exempt from external review in the next round – apart from a small proportion which would be sampled by agreement and would provide the necessary benchmarking of good practice. Taken with the planned further reduction in the average length of reviews, the aim is to secure a reduction of 40 per cent or more in the volume of review activity compared with existing arrangements.
>
> (Press Release quoted in Williams 2009)

There are two versions of why this step was taken. One is that Blunkett had been lobbied by Russell Group vice-chancellors, either directly or through the Prime Minister, and that an accommodation had been reached where vice-chancellors would reduce their campaign for 'top up' fees in return for a reduction in the burden of quality assurance. The other is that the decision reflected electoral considerations. A Liberal peer, Lord Norton of Louth, who held a chair at Hull, was due to open a debate in the House of Lords on 21 March (the day of the Blunkett announcement) in which he planned strong criticism of the heavily bureaucratic nature of the quality regime. Blunkett, anxious to avoid higher education becoming an issue in the 2001 General Election, took an instant decision, not even warning the Labour spokesman in the House of Lords who was due to reply on behalf of the Government, to diffuse the attack by, at the stroke of a pen, reducing the burden of the inspection regime. What both accounts – and both may be accurate – illustrate is the Government's deep involvement in policy determination in respect to the quality assurance regime (Brown 2004: 131; Williams 2009: 19).[25] The carefully negotiated terms relating to the legal independence of the QAA and the supposed academic control over its operations counted for little when the political chips were down. The degree of detail contained in the press release illustrated just how far the Department was involved in decision making. Randall resigned, complaining that the resulting changes left higher education facing too little scrutiny to ensure public confidence in standards (Brown 2004: 146).

Dearing and the standards agenda

The QAA was, in Williams' words, 'Dearing's child' (Williams 2009: 8). The AAU and the HEQC were formally owned by the universities and took as their key role to assist universities themselves in the task of maintaining and enhancing the quality of teaching and the learning process. We have seen, above, how a senior civil servant, right from the beginning, doubted the value of the process because he did not trust self regulation. It is not surprising, therefore, that the dice were loaded from the start in the Dearing Committee by the inclusion in its terms of reference, provided by the DES, that the Committee should have regard to the 'standards' of degrees and other qualifications and how they should be 'assured' (NCIHE 1997: 3).

The Committee seized on the phrases to express the view that existing arrangements for safeguarding standards were 'insufficiently clear to carry conviction with those who perceive present quality and standards to be unsatisfactory' (NCIHE 1997 para 10.2) but did not publish hard evidence of who the critics were nor, in any detailed way, what their criticisms were, except that in some areas professional bodies were expressing concern about 'present arrangements', and that franchising programmes had thrown up some issues of concern. The Committee's concern narrowed down to the need for 'threshold standards' and for consistency of standards across the system. The Report laid particular emphasis on the need for the QAA to develop a 'robust system of public information and assurance about the nature of higher education provision, as reflected in programme specifications and the arrangements for ensuring quality and standards' (NCIHE 1997 para 10.86) and envisaged an enhanced external examiner system where an appointed group of examiners who had been through a 'trainee/apprentice model' of training in order to achieve consistent standards (NCIHE 1997 para 10.94). It foresaw the QAA playing 'a key role in the safeguarding of quality and standards in higher education across the UK'; if the arrangements it recommended were not put in place 'pressure for increased and direct intervention from outside higher education would intensify' (NCIHE 1997 para 10.102).

Although it recognized, in one paragraph only, that 'each institution is responsible for its own standards' (NCIHE 1997 para 10.3) the thrust of the Report and its recommendations was to emphasize the establishment of a national framework which gave assurance to the public for the maintenance of standards. The mechanism which was to realize this, however, when it emerged, did not match up to the Committee's rhetoric; indeed it significantly watered it down. The new QAA, post Randall, followed an Academic Review process based on an institutional audit approach very close to that followed by the AAU and the HEQC. It emphasized that primary responsibility for standards and quality rested with the institutions themselves and that QAA reviews were to report on how well they met these responsibilities. The QAA specifically rejected any claim to be an inspector or regulator and was at pains to point out that it had no statutory responsibility to ensure that institutions acted on the recommendations it made. Its reports graded such recommendations as 'essential', 'advisable' or desirable', a ratcheting down from the TQA formula. Essentially the power of the Agency lay in the adverse publicity that could be created by a negative report, and in the prospect that recommendations identified as 'advisable' or 'desirable' would be likely to be enquired into again at the next review. Within higher education, the primary concern was the heavy administrative burden that the quality processes involved, the need to appoint 'quality managers' to ensure that quality processes were observed and the time, effort and bureaucracy that was expended on preparing for institutional audit visitations. Procedural reforms to achieve a 'lighter touch' rarely met their objective.

This tidy, if intensely bureaucratic, world was blown apart in 2009 by the hearings and Report entitled *Students and Universities* by the new Innovation, Universities, Science and Skills Select Committee (2009). This took as its key term of reference 'whether students [were] getting value for money out of higher education?' It concluded that:

> the system in England for safeguarding consistent national standards in higher education institutions is out of date, inadequate and in urgent need of replacement. The current arrangements with each university responsible for its own standards are no longer meeting the needs of a mass system of higher education in the 21st century with two million students. Given the amount of money that the tax payer puts into universities it is not acceptable, as we found during our inquiry, that vice-chancellors cannot give a straightforward answer to the simple question of whether students obtaining first class honours degrees at different universities had attained the same intellectual standards.
>
> The body that currently 'assures quality', . . . focuses almost entirely on processes, not standards. This needs to change. We call for the QAA to be transformed into an independent Quality and Standards Agency with a remit, statutory if necessary, to safeguard, monitor and report on standards.
>
> (Innovation, Universities and Skills Committee 2009: 5)

Within higher education the Report was seen as populist and simplistic but its impact on policy should not be minimized. Its opening words: 'The experience of the student is at the heart of higher education' provided the theme of the 2011 White Paper *Students at the Heart of the System* and its recommendations find much more than an echo in the revision of the QAA remit which, by 2011, was stating that its key responsibility was 'to safeguard the public interest in sound standards of higher education qualifications'; its operation had been overhauled to look specifically at institutions' provision of public information, to produce reports more quickly, and in clearer language aimed at a wide public audience, and to give a great deal more involvement to students. In particular, its reports would include a formal judgement on the quality of public information an institution had provided, and judgements on whether or not academic standards met UK expectations for threshold standards. Quality and enhancement would be graded as 'commended', meeting UK expectations for threshold standards, 'requires improvement to meet UK expectations' and 'does not meet those standards'.[26] Lying behind this carefully adjusted formula one can see a reversion to Dearing principles of explicit public accountability. The recommended change of title to Quality and Standards Agency had not been accepted and politically adroit drafting had sought to preserve the essence of the former QAA approach but a shift to becoming an agency that approved threshold standards in university degrees could not be avoided. The application of the new approach beginning in 2012–13 falls outside the period covered by this account; it will not, of course, apply to Scotland which remains wedded to a quality enhancement agenda, or in Wales.

Quality assurance and the political dimension

There can be little doubt that the various quality regimes imposed on higher education can be regarded as the greatest single unwelcome intrusion into academic life that has occurred since the 1980s. Henkel describes quality as 'a bureaucratic concept, reflecting bureaucratic values such as transparency, consistency, predictability, efficiency and equity and an administrative responsibility rather than a matter of academic concern' (Henkel 2007: 12) and argues that 'Setting up systems recording and paperwork often come to represent the definition of quality introduced by quality assurance policies' (Henkel 2000: 99). Tight provides implicit factual support for the criticism of the bureaucracy involved when he shows how an academic's working time spent on administration has risen from 19 per cent of a 50 hour week in 1969–70 to 33 per cent in 1994 (Tight 2010).

Williams, who as Director of the QAA up to 2009, was for the most part an apologist for the regime, agreed with Henkel's analysis:

> [Q]uality assurance took away the much prized status of academics as individuals accountable to little but their personal intellectual interest and integrity and forced them to answer questions from outside. They frequently felt disempowered and disinherited in consequence. There was resentment at this change . . . but not so much as when later developments seemed to take away their freedom of action as autonomous professionals and made them comply with externally imposed norms.
>
> (Williams 2009: 11)

He attributes the growth of a 'quality industry', especially to the period of TQA assessment which constituted, 'a new high stakes threat' to institutions. (Williams 2009: 13). This dates it from the Patten intervention of 1995. Fifteen or so years later the Select Committee was still referring back to the statutory powers exercised by the CNAA.

One might ask why the academic community itself did not resist the quality regime more robustly (except, of course, in the case of the Warwick economists). One answer might again come down to a breakdown of trust. King *et al.* undertook a survey of attitudes of members of QAA audit teams and found that rather than defend the process wholeheartedly they regarded it as 'a worthwhile price for avoiding provocation to government and inviting further intrusion that would lead to a more overbearing draconian and non-peer methodology based on external rules and "outsider" inspectors' (King *et al.* 2007). That this was not an idle fear can be judged by Williams' account of Margaret Hodge, the then Minister for Higher Education's outrage at the proposed reintroduction of an audit process and her feeling that universities should be subjected to Ofsted inspections like schools (Williams 2009: 20).

In practice the imposition of inspectors on universities after 1992 would have been politically difficult and the chief executive of HEFCE fought hard and successfully to avoid HMIs, who had been responsible for exercising limited powers in the polytechnics, being transferred into the quality unit in HEFCE not least because they lacked the intellectual stature to be effective in a university environment. It is worth asking, however, why Government, having accepted the polytechnics' case to be designated universities, should have sought to impose a quality regime of such intensity and to have continued to press for some explicit quality organization after 1988 in a way that it would have been impossible to imagine before 1980. There seemed to have been a number of policy drivers: a fear of loss of control, a concern about the effects of expansion, a feeling that a growing export market needed to be protected, a defence against criticism of increasing underfunding, and an ideological belief in the effectiveness of market forces but their need for regulation.

Loss of control The breakdown in respect for the universities began in Whitehall with the failure of universities to deal effectively with the student troubles of the late 1960s and early 1970s and was exacerbated by the CVCP's failure to recognize the economic realities which successive Governments were facing in the 1970s and early 1980s. By the mid-1980s the universities were sufficiently weakened to concede to pressure to set up the Reynolds' Group which they were forced to accept did an excellent job of tidying up procedures which in some institutions had become slack during the years of financial stringency. Academic audit was a natural progression and the creation of HEQC was part of the deal for the merger of the CVCP and the CDP. But the writing in of reserve powers for quality assurance under HEFCE reflected the Department's long held distrust of the effectiveness of self regulation under conditions of institutional autonomy, and residual doubts as to the ability of all the former polytechnics to match up to the expectations implied by re-designation as universities. The occurrence of a series of governance breakdowns within two years of the ending of the binary line did little to dispel this. The Department believed it must retain some levers of control. As Williams says: 'the structure and function of quality assurance are generally determined in order to satisfy political objectives, and both reflect, and help to consolidate, the ownership and control of higher education' (Williams 2009: 2).

The effects of expansion The merger of the two sectors occurred in the middle of the most rapid expansion seen in British higher education. Although this had been stimulated by Government funding policies, until restrained by the Treasury in 1994, the need for some reassertion of control over student numbers was inevitable. There may also have been a lurking 'more means worse' mentality. Amongst some policy makers the argument for TQA was to rebalance universities away from a concentration on the RAE. The recognition that Britain had embraced mass higher education was widely associated with doubts as to whether standards were being maintained.

Protection of an export market It was no accident that Patten's interest in quality assurance coincided with his attendance at a higher education fair in Singapore. No one had anticipated in 1980 that the removal of the subsidy for international students would lead to the creation of a valuable market in tuition fees for international students. This market became important first, simply as a source of non-government income for British universities and colleges, and then as a contribution to the British economy as a whole. Figure 5.1 shows just

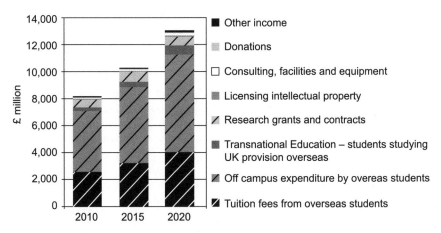

Figure 5.1 Higher education as an export industry

Source: BIS (2011a).

how important to the Government the protection of this market, through a constant iteration of rhetoric about the rigour of the quality assurance regime, has become. When the Director of the QAA incautiously criticized the reliability of the British degree classification system, which was then subject to review by the Burgess Committee, he was reprimanded by Ministers for potentially weakening Britain's market position abroad.[27] Sustaining the reputation of the QAA represents an important contribution to sustaining the British economy.

A defence against criticism of underfunding Figure 3.3 above sets out very clearly the reduction of the unit of resource over the period between 1976 and 1995. What it does not show is the differentiation of institutional funding between those universities that were funded for research as well as for teaching. In the debates in the CVCP in 1966 and in the decision to halt the decline in the unit of resource by the UGC in 1981, there was an implicit assumption that the retention of a favourable staff:student ratio was a key factor in maintaining a high quality university system. This position was, as we have seen, criticized by Baker who was ready to give higher priority to an expansion for its own sake than to the maintenance of an adequate resource base. The result was a rapid fall in staff:student ratios in the 1980s particularly in universities that did not recoup QR grant from the RAEs. It beggars belief that this did not have an impact on teaching. In an authoritative contribution to the quality debate, commissioned by the Higher Education Academy, Gibbs reviewed research evidence to find that higher funding can predict cohort size and that class size predicts student performance; that low staff:student ratios offer the potential for smaller class sizes and that large class sizes have negative effects on student performance and on the quality of student engagement; 'close contact with teachers is a good predictor of educational outcomes and close contact is more easily possible when there are not too many students for each teacher to make close contact with' (Gibbs 2010: 14–15). Brown's evidence from TQA scores suggested that one of the major reasons why higher TQA scores awarded to pre-1992 universities may have been their higher level of resources, including staff:student ratios, arising from their greater research funding. The discrepancies in funding have widened considerably since Brown was writing but the number of institutions and programmes failing to satisfy the QAA has remained tiny compared to the number of audits undertaken. The quality assurance process has, effectively, confirmed threshold standards across institutions that have very considerable differences in staff:student ratio levels and huge differences in their resource base. The judgemental definitions adopted by the QAA in 2011 seem calculated to ensure that this situation continues.

The ideology of the market Successive Conservative Secretaries of State were keen to give greater emphasis to market forces in the management of higher education. Partly this was because competition brought down costs, partly because they increasingly wished to put more of the levers of change in the hands of the consumer and partly because – and this was made explicit in the Browne Review – they thought it would drive up quality. All this fell naturally into the New Public Management model which the Labour Government developed further from its origins under the Conservatives. For higher education two consequences arose: the first was that for the market to work effectively students and their parents needed to be well informed; and the second was that there needed to be safety nets to safeguard the public interest from institutional failure. QAA represented a crucial element in the success of this approach: it promised to provide advance warning when things might be going wrong on the academic side and advice to the institution involved as to how to put them right. If it had followed the Dearing approach to the letter it would have provided an explicit guarantee that standards were being maintained even when market forces were driving the system but it did not go quite that far. The quality process represented an essential element in minimizing the high political risks of institutional fragility. There can be little doubt that the QAA performed this function well.

Where it was less successful was in its role of providing authorized market advice to the consumer through its institutional reports. A consultant's report, quoted in Brown, suggested in 1999 that only 12 per cent of respondents regarded QAA reports as the most important source of information and in the revised QAA approach reports are planned to be produced more quickly and to be more comprehensible to the public. (One doubts even then, whether they will replace the impact of league tables, institutional reputation and the student grapevine.) The latest QAA approach does, however, mark a new stage because it will provide explicit public guarantees about threshold standards, however loosely defined, in the name of public accountability which are supererogatory to the claims made by degree awarding institutions because they are to be made, in effect, under the legal authority of the state.

Accountability and autonomy

Accountability has been the Trojan horse which, by accident and sometimes by design, has imposed restrictions on institutional autonomy. The modern state in the hands of Thatcher and Blair became a major force for centralization and central direction in government. But in financial matters it was, in fact, Parliament, through the PAC, which drove a process of financial accountability in higher education which ultimately led to the abolition of the UGC and the creation of new structures of system governance. This, over time, led to the imposition of controls and regulation which encased institutional autonomy in a framework of Government bureaucracy which step by step has placed limits on operational autonomy. Events at Cardiff and at London Metropolitan University contributed to the process by providing examples as to why higher education had made itself vulnerable to the case for greater financial accountability.

But secure financial controls represented a safeguard for the academic community as well as for the public interest. The academic community has been much less sympathetic, however, to the Government's intrusion into the academic life of institutions through successive quality regimes. As described above, the quality industry has been prompted at each stage by ministerial or Departmental pressure. From a policy perspective, quality processes have provided a legitimation of reductions in public funding and a kite mark to protect the substantial growth of income deriving from international students. They have also provided a critical underpinning for a more marketized home, consumer driven, system. It has been very much in the state's interest to sustain a quality regime, and a reversion to a guarantee of threshold standards approach seems constructed to meet the state's requirements not the institutions'. The question needs to be asked as to whether such processes are an inevitable consequence of the march towards Trow's mass and then universal higher education? Trow himself, writing in 1994, saw the QAA as an example of 'the withdrawal of trust by government in the academic community, and in its capacity to critically assess its own activities and improve them'.[28] (He was, of course, writing just at the time when pressure from within the system had persuaded Blunkett to bring TQA to an end.) No other European country and certainly not the United States, has adopted such a draconian approach towards universities' powers of self regulation in respect to the standing of their degrees.

One is driven to the conclusion that the loss of the policing powers of the CNAA over the public sector institutions and continuing doubts about the impact of low cost expansion on them after re-designation played a significant part in the activation of the TQA regime and the thrust of the Dearing recommendations. The extraordinary defensiveness of university witnesses before a Select Committee, very obviously not sympathetic to higher education's values, tilted the quality regime back to the Dearing prescriptions. In doing so it suggested a serious limitation of institutional autonomy and corporate independence. Accountability for public funding to a public body was perhaps uncomfortable but not unacceptable; accountability to an external body for academic performance threatened the fundamental nature of what was traditionally seen as a generic characteristic of academic autonomy. The fragility of higher education's position can be judged by the following statement:

> We respect the autonomy of universities and colleges. It is the key to the success and resilience of higher education, but of course it comes with clear responsibilities and accountabilities. One of the clear roles of HEFCE is to work with the sector to achieve high standards of financial stewardship and the integrity of degree programmes provided by universities and colleges. Higher education has a very good story to tell.

However, we know that in the current climate public funding cannot be taken for granted. It will depend on being able to show that we are constantly striving for high standards through these difficult times.[29]

Written before the 2011 White Paper the statement is clear in its implication that autonomy is subject to performance as interpreted by external authorities.

6

Making policy at the institutional level

The capacity of universities, polytechnics and colleges to make policy has, throughout the period, been framed and constrained by national policy-making structures. Even when universities seemed to have the most institutional freedom, in the immediate post-War years, they were in practice constrained by commitments they had made in their quinquennial plans and by funding mechanisms imposed by the UGC. Paradoxically at a time when universities have been most constrained by limits on home student numbers and by the demands of accountability in its various guises, they have demonstrated the most entrepreneurial verve in establishing overseas campuses, international partnerships and recruitment strategies. Freedom to develop policy institutionally can be assessed on the basis of strategic policy, operational policy and academic or intellectual policy. The three categories are, of course, closely interlinked. The freedom to develop academic policy is, for example, significantly dependent on the degree to which an institution has operational autonomy, an argument which the universities deployed, without success, in relation to the administration of the teacher training colleges in the 1960s. However, in that case the absence of operational autonomy, while it inhibited them, did not extinguish the development of worthwhile academic policies in respect to curricula and validation arrangements. Institutional autonomy to make policy has always been bounded by the wider principal agent powers of the state, of funding bodies and of the local authorities in the case of the polytechnics and colleges, or even, in academic issues, by the CNAA or, in some disciplines, by bodies like the General Medical Council or the engineering institutions that control the award of professional qualifications. An important issue is how these three categories of policy making have changed over the period and how they have been constrained or otherwise by the centralization of policy in the various bureaucratic organs of the state.

The development of policy making machinery

In the nineteenth century the powers of the court (even then largely a rubber stamping body) and the council in non-Oxbridge universities were, in the words of Moodie and Eustace 'virtually unqualified' (Moodie and Eustace 1974: 34) but by 1945 significant changes had taken place in the distribution of *de facto* decision-making power within universities. In the 1920s and 30s, when universities and colleges on the UGC's grant list were only receiving about 30 per cent of their income from the state, the prime role of the lay governing body was to maintain institutional financial viability in particular fund raising and especially funds for capital expansion. Leeds, for example, launched eight separate public appeals in the 1920s (Brown 1953). By the 1930s, the economic downturn had very much reduced the prospect of significant capital gifts and vice-chancellors and senior academics began necessarily to play a much larger role. Ives *et al.* describe how in 1937 Priestley, the new vice-chancellor, had to take over the leadership of a fund raising drive for a new physics building at Birmingham, which foundered with the onset of War (Ives *et al.* 2000). The UGC in its dealings with university colleges which wanted to move to full chartered status or colleges wanting to come onto the grant list, always placed the ability to generate significant external funding and capital support high on its criteria for approval but it was also concerned to emphasize the importance of academic autonomy. In 1936 it refused an application for increased support from University College, Nottingham on the grounds that the College had not acceded to the Committee's reiterated request that academics should be given representation on the Council: 'What might be the overshadowing question at Nottingham relates not to finance, but to constitution . . . it is a university institution which does not enjoy that autonomous government which we regard as the special characteristic of the British university system'.[1] This was not the first time it had refused to support Nottingham's claim for full university status on these grounds.

During the War lay influence had continued to decline and, with the state's assumption of the major funding role in 1945, it declined yet further. Eric (later Lord) Ashby, a former vice-chancellor, writing in 1958 discussed university self government almost entirely in terms which reduced the governing body to a formal role. 'Major policy originates . . . at the level of departments and flows upwards to the Council as proposals to be approved: it never descends from the Council as directives to be obeyed' (Ashby 1958: 100). Self government was assured if the academic community had full control of admissions, curricula, examinations, the appointment of staff and the allocation of resources; if it did not 'academic freedom is insecure' (Ashby 1958: 102). Lay governance could exert influence 'not by originating policy and promulgating it as directives but by allowing it to originate at lower levels in the hierarchy and approving it, providing it does not conflict with the wider responsibilities of the university to the community' (Ashby 1958: 101). In other words, it was a long stop, not an originator of policy. Robbins saw the senate as being 'at the apex of academic government' and, while the Committee were 'in agreement with the principle of a majority of lay members on the council', added that 'a lay majority is only justifiable when it recognises a proper division of labour between itself and the senate' (Committee on Higher Education 1963 paras 662–6). Sir Robert Aitken, like Ashby a senior vice-chancellor, wrote three years after Robbins that 'custom and practice have established a firm division of responsibility between Council and Senate [at Birmingham] which makes Senate a partner rather than an agent of Council', and that the division of powers whereby the senate controlled all academic matters and could intervene in issues of financial control, the distribution of resources, building plans, investment and business and administrative affairs generally was 'entrenched as a principle; only in the gravest crisis would there be resort to Council to overrule Senate' (Aitken 1966: 11). At a discussion about university governance in 1970 Noel (later Lord) Annan presented a paper to the CVCP which asked:

> Is there a university in the country where [the governing body] is not a dignified rubber stamp? The true governing body is the senate . . . Even Council's Finance Committee does little more than set the stage for cutting the cake . . . We cannot and should not want to return to the days when Council really governed. We prefer self government by the academic staff.[2]

This was a period of maximum senate engagement. Senates were large and their membership was dominated by the professoriate. Vice-chancellors, although many of them were individually powerful and had driven substantial expansion programmes against internal opposition, remained *primus inter pares* and could be subject to robust dissent at senate meetings. Vice-chancellors were careful to canvas senate opinion on national issues before CVCP was permitted to make statements on the universities' behalf lest a senate should later express its disagreement with its vice-chancellor's reported views. However, vice-chancellors' positions were strengthened by the block grant system which gave them power over resources and by their ready access to the chairman of the UGC to plead special institutional cases. As chair of the senate a vice-chancellor was generally a very powerful figure in a university and did not need the later soubriquet of chief executive to secure assent to policies to which he or she was committed. Through the eyes of a young lecturer the senate could look remote and unrepresentative but to the outside world its pronouncements carried the full weight of academic autonomy. It was the power of the senate voice which led to universities failing to respond positively to the UGC's forecast of increased student demand in the early 1950s.

The situation was very different in local authority institutions where Jones and Kiloh (1987: 108) state that up to the late 1960s 'the standard pattern was to reserve to the authority and its officers all decisions affecting the college and its internal workings except, in practice, the day-to-day organisation of teaching'. Even after a Ministry initiative in 1959 when governing bodies began to be created (they became statutory requirements only in 1968) the meetings were serviced by a local authority officer and the principal was not necessarily a member. ' "In effect", they say, "all power resided at county hall" '(Jones and Kiloh 1987: 108). The academic programme was firmly under local authority control; no new course could be offered without authority approval. A system of Regional Advisory Councils (RACs) was introduced in 1947 to ensure that duplication of courses within regions did not occur, but these were themselves local authority run. (Even as late as 1980 a polytechnic wanting to introduce a new academic programme had to secure local authority, RAC, HMI and CNAA support before being able to do so.) Local authorities also had absolute control of resources, including matters to do with human resource management. The comment by the professor from Leeds to Tizard about the position of the Bradford and Huddersfield colleges, quoted above, almost certainly accurately reflects a wider picture of college/local authority relationships, at least as seen through university eyes. It was this contrast between the lack of academic autonomy in the colleges and the extensively academically controlled processes in the universities that lay at the heart of the UGC's resistance to degree awarding powers being granted to colleges in 1956 and to the Robbins recommendation for the creation of the CNAA in 1963.

The rejection of the Robbins recommendations in regard to the future of teacher training colleges and to the concentration of expansion in the universities brought some constitutional changes to public sector institutions. The teacher training colleges' concern about local authority controls led to the creation of the Weaver Study Group and to the establishment of college governing bodies and academic boards, the latter having powers to comment on strategy and resources. The polytechnics similarly were equipped with governing bodies and with academic boards. The colleges, because they had university representation on their governing bodies arising from the universities' validation role, seem to have had, in general, better relations with their local authorities than the polytechnics although in both cases their governing bodies were dominated by local authority members. The director of the polytechnic might have been formally recommended for appointment by the governors but the appointment was subject to local authority veto, and Jones and Kiloh took the view that in the local authorities' eyes the director was regarded as personally responsible to them for the management of the institution. One effect of this was to create tensions between academic boards and governors and directors, encouraging some academic boards to be strongly representative of trades union, mostly NATFHE, views. The absence of effective decision-making powers, even over new academic programmes which then had to be passed on to higher bodies outside the institution, did little to encourage a strong sense of collective responsibility. The comparison with the powers of a university senate which was able to approve and implement a new programme at a single meeting was very stark. When academic boards did seek to exercise collective responsibility as at the Lanchester Polytechnic in Coventry which chose to address the Secretary of State directly on an issue of a merger with the Coventry College of Education, the local authority decided to change the articles of government to reduce the board's role. The director may have been invested with very significant formal executive powers but could find his or her position severely squeezed between local authority and academic board imperatives. The local authority reaction to the growing national role of the polytechnics can be judged by their grudging attitude to the funding of a CDP secretariat in the early 1970s. Polytechnic directors played no role in the operation of the AFE/FE pooling arrangements; policy issues discussed within polytechnics were almost entirely local. It was only with the creation of NAB that polytechnic directors began to play a significant national role.

In the 1970s the senate dominance of policy issues within universities came under increasing pressure. During the 1960s, the expansion brought in waves of younger academic staff who wanted to see the 'democratization' of the universities by which they meant fewer permanent heads of departments and more non-professors given membership of the senate. This was followed by the student demand for membership of decision-making bodies. Senates were generally outflanked on this latter issue and wrong footed by students pursuing direct action in various forms and, when the CVCP struck a national accord with the National Union of Students in 1974, were happy to concede student membership of senates, councils and their committees as an easy price to pay for the disruption of sit ins and vain attempts to impose disciplinary regulations on student activists. The cumulative effect of these two sets of pressures, together with the impact of expansion generally, was to enlarge senates significantly. Pullen, for example, shows how the pressure for greater representation pushed the Manchester senate in its charter revision of 1973 up to 279 members, 209 professors *ex officio* and 67 elected members, which he describes as 'a flaccid body, little given to debating or voting' (Pullen with Abendstern 2004: 55). This was, of course, exceptional, reflecting the size of the university, but the 1970s gave universities in general a bumpy ride, with the oil crisis, the ending of the quinquennial system, the revision downwards of expansion targets and rising inflation. Senates were ill equipped to cope and, increasingly, smaller subsets of academics and administrators began to emerge, grouped round the vice-chancellor, to steer policy.

A particular change was the switch in resource allocation. In the period of rapid expansion, when UGC grant was tied to student number targets, university planning officers calculated the distribution of additional numbers between departments and resources followed. Following the cut backs of 1973–74, and even more so in 1981, student numbers became much less important than cash, a trend emphasized by the Treasury's own switch from volume to cash planning from 1976. A study of 12 universities in the period 1979–81 shows that while the universities did not interfere with the basic financial role of their council finance committee, they came to rely for academic resource allocation and for strategy on the following bodies: senate development committee (2), a development and estimates committee, a deans committee, resources and budget sub-committees of finance committees (2), a planning committee, an estimates and grants committee, a VC's advisory committee, a resources committee and an educational policy committee (Shattock and Rigby 1983). This paved the way for the establishment of central inner cabinets made up of senior university officers, deans and senior managers, what Clark was later to call 'the strengthened steering core' (Clark 1998) which, while formally committees of the senate, or occasionally joint committees of the council and senate, meeting usually weekly, steered policy for the university and took the critical strategic decisions. Sizer, in his very detailed account of how nine universities coped successfully with the 1981 cuts, drew three important conclusions: the first was that a vice-chancellor needed to build up a strong cohesive management team; the second was that, while not involving council actively in detailed decision making, it was important to ensure that it fully understood the role it had to play in supporting the vice-chancellor in ensuring that the institution faced up to 'the need to set priorities, make hard choices and develop an integrated financial and academic plan [and to] monitor its implementation and, if necessary, ensure appropriate action is taken' (Sizer 1987: 43). (Thus Sizer did not envisage shifting the responsibility to the governing body but making the key resource withdrawal decisions at a level somewhere within the academic structure.) His third conclusion was the need for academic involvement at all levels through 'a top down, bottom up, top down approach' where the final decision-making powers were held in the centre and not devolved to a faculty board level where 'there may be a reluctance to make hard choices and a preference for equal treatment and maintenance of the existing range of subjects' (Sizer 1987: 43). It is important to note, in the light of later views about academic self governance, that senate governance mostly coped quite effectively with the 1981 cuts, as can be seen from Table 3.3 above. Some senates, like Manchester, it is true, were simply unable to measure up to their own strategic rhetoric of concentrating on academic strengths and opted for equal misery across the board (Austin 1982) but this was more the exception than the rule.

The considerable media impact of the 1981 cuts together with the main findings of Sizer's study – which became available considerably before the eventual publication of his final report – suggested that universities could benefit from review under the Financial Management Initiative, which was taking place across Whitehall departments. At Swinnerton Dyer's suggestion, and in order to influence the PESC process, the CVCP bid to the Government for funding for such a review and the Chairman of the CVCP, Lord Flowers, approached Sir Alex Jarratt, formerly Chairman of Reed International, on the basis of a speech he had made on his installation as Chancellor of Birmingham, to be the chairman of the proposed Steering Committee on Efficiency Studies in Universities; Jarratt was not a Government nominee. Since the Committee's Report (CVCP 1985) and the linking of Jarratt's name with it has become symbolic, even a quarter of a century after

its publication, of the introduction of managerialism into universities it may
be useful to draw on some of the background. The main evidence is an
address that Jarratt gave to the CVCP in October 1985, after the Report's
publication,[3] and an interview recorded in the Hanney/Kogan Archive.[4] The
membership of the Committee was proposed by the CVCP, by Jarratt himself
or, in the case of Sir Robin Ibbs, the Prime Minister's Adviser on Efficiency,
by the Department, no doubt with an eye to winning support later for its
findings. It contained four institutional heads, a registrar, four industrialists,
including Jarratt himself, a leading academic who was the master of a
Cambridge college and Swinnerton Dyer, as chairman of the UGC, together
with Ibbs, who was on secondment from IBM. There were no DES assessors
and there appears to have been no DES pressure to reach certain conclusions. The inference of many critics of the Report, that it was following a
DES agenda, was not correct. The Committee's intention was to conduct
efficiency studies at six universities: Edinburgh, Essex, Loughborough,
Nottingham, Sheffield and UCL, and to use the results as evidence on which
to base recommendations. Keith Joseph and the Treasury were expecting a
Report devoted to cost savings and greater efficiency, although the individual
institutional studies provided no pressing examples of this, but the Committee
decided that wider issues were involved.

What Jarratt's speech to the CVCP and his later interview makes clear was
that an underlying theme, obscured by some of the detailed recommendations, was that universities were facing a period of rapid change, a position
they shared with big organizations and companies in the private sector.
Government needed to think through and specify more clearly what it
expected from universities and give them a longer planning horizon but
universities themselves needed to adjust their planning to be less reactive
and incremental and more strategic in their long term thinking. To do this
universities had to create planning and resource allocation units. Neither the
CVCP nor the UGC was fit for purpose in this context. Swinnerton Dyer,
who had chaired a long range planning committee at Cambridge and was
anxious to strengthen the UGC, was a major influence on the Committee's
thinking on these points and it was significant that the UGC was given
responsibility for monitoring the implementation of the Report.
Unfortunately these major themes were not what captured attention nor
were they headlined sufficiently in the Report. What critics focused on was
the designation of the vice-chancellor as 'chief executive', ignoring the
additional role quoted in the Report as 'academic leader', the invitation to
councils to 'reassert their responsibilities in governing their institutions'
and reverse the weakening in their role which was evident over the previous
30 years, and the idea that a degree of tension between senate and council
might be 'creative and beneficial in the long term' (CVCP 1985 paras 5.5
and 3.5). The question of the upgrading of the role of council had been
widely discussed in the Committee and had commanded academic support.
It is not surprising, however, that in the wider world without a more searching
assessment of the argument and the practical implications, it raised serious

concerns about the apparent relegation of the academic role in university governance. The Report captured most attention because of its designation of the vice-chancellor as the chief executive, a phrase introduced into the Report by the one registrar on the Committee, Geoffrey Lockwood (Jarratt himself used the phrase 'executive leader' in his address to the CVCP). At the time few vice-chancellors would have publicly claimed the designation and there is little sign that in the short run it did anything to change behaviour.

The Report included a range of recommendations on operational matters most of which were quickly adopted by universities. Many were already good practice in some universities. Equally, the recommendation for a planning and resources committee which included a senior lay element had already been anticipated in some institutions. (The recommendation was reinforced by the UGC's decision to require universities to provide five year financial and strategic plans.) Within universities, perhaps the most discussed recommendation was in respect of moving to a single cycle of meetings per term instead of two, though the Report was careful to warn against executive action becoming a substitute for due process through properly constructed committee systems. The Report also raised important issues about the devolution of decision making, giving training to develop management skills in vice-chancellors, pro-vice-chancellors, deans and heads of departments and the introduction of performance indicators, none of which were especially controversial, but on the larger strategic issues, the need for Government to provide long term strategic guidance and avoid imposing short term changes of direction, or the need to commission a review of the role, structure and staffing of the UGC, it failed. The Green Paper, published later in the year, was, in Jarratt's own words, 'a damp squib'[5] and the Croham Committee, driven by accountability issues did not tackle the issues which the Jarratt Committee would have hoped it would.

The Jarratt Report came to symbolize a central drive towards a new corporate management approach to the running of universities which heavily influenced future decisions about institutional management structures and the identification of governing bodies with company boards. In fact, the DES exercised no influence over the Report at either ministerial or official levels, and the new corporate structures in the polytechnics and the revitalization of governing bodies owed nothing to the Jarratt Report. The Report was a well intentioned stab at taking a long term view of the organization of universities 20 years after Robbins but it was not a Government blue print for a new approach to university management; it fed Joseph's obsession with the need for greater efficiency and value for money, both Treasury themes in the PESC dialogues, but it generated no response from him at all in regard to changes in the Government's approach to the university system. The real importance of the Jarratt Report lies in the fact that it urged a fundamental change in institutional self government brought about by the experience of coping with the 1981 cuts and by the experience, absorbed over the 1970s, that the state was no longer a funding partner that could be relied upon;

universities needed to construct new mechanisms of self government to confront a much more unstable future.

It was perhaps natural to see the Jarratt conclusions leading seamlessly to the 1988 polytechnic Higher Education Corporation (HEC) constitution, the strings being pulled by DES officials. Nothing, however, could have been further from the truth. The 1987 White Paper made it clear that freed from control of the local authorities the polytechnics and other transferred colleges would be given corporate status. They would be run by governing bodies to be appointed initially by the Government, whose membership would be strongly representative of local industry and commerce and the director would report only to them and not also to the local authority. The DES employed the management consulting firm, Tyzacks, to head hunt potential governors. It also proceeded to draw up a model set of articles for HECs which it discussed with the CDP and Standing Conference of Principals (SCOP). This was based on so-called 'Weaver principles' which dated back to the constitution drafted for the teacher training colleges by the Weaver Study Group in 1966. It assumed a governing body which was responsible for the educational character of the institution (a straight transfer of a power previously exercised by a local authority) and a director responsible for the management of the institution and for its internal discipline. But it also envisaged a directorate which would hold management responsibility in relation to the whole institution and not simply for one or more faculties or departments. (This last caveat was intended to ensure a strong central management team which did not disperse highly graded posts in academic positions.) It also proposed an academic board which 'shall have responsibilities for quality, planning and oversight of the polytechnic/college, including arrangements for the admission, assessment and examination of students and, where appropriate, the validation of courses'. The official responsible for the draft, Anthony Chamier, left open for discussion whether the academic board should be given 'executive powers'.[6] A minute of the CDP/SCOP meeting with DES officials recorded that the DES draft was intended 'to give an institution a degree of dignity and independence in common with universities, whilst providing a proper framework for an institution's conduct'. At a later meeting with the CDP alone, where there was criticism of the proposed position of the academic board, Richard Bird, the Deputy Secretary, argued that 'it was against the collegial tradition for such a major resource as the board to be marginalised', that is, by removing from it academic planning responsibilities.[7] DES officers, rather than seeking to extend the apparent thrust of the Jarratt Report, were offering the polytechnics and colleges a considerable liberalization of the former further education style constitution.

But this did not meet at all the interests of polytechnic directors. The CDP had already decided to set up, separately from the CDP/SCOP group, which had been sympathetic to the academic board proposals, a new much more hard nosed Hatfield Group, in whom it now entrusted its negotiations with DES officials. However, the most influential intervention in the process was a letter from Ken (later Sir Ken) Green, Director of Manchester Polytechnic, in March 1988 direct to Baker protesting that the Model Articles were 'a fudge' and arguing that people in industry would not be willing to commit themselves to be governors of polytechnics without a clear indication of what their roles might be. 'Is there an assumption' he asked 'that the academic board is responsible for academic policy? . . . If so where does that leave the director/principal for he/she certainly cannot be regarded by the governors as managing director/chief executive in the sense commonly understood in the business world unless he/she is responsible to them for all aspects of policy?' The present polytechnic constitution which made the governors ultimately responsible for policy and the academic board to the governors for the determination of academic policy and the place of research left the director only responsible for management. 'The reality is one of elaborate committee structures' with governing body debates dominated by separate constitutions. This left no place for leadership: 'institutions have increasingly become tired of "Weaverism", regarding it as costly, time wasting and irrelevant to the job to be done . . . The nonsense of the prevailing mode of direct responsibility of the academic board to the governing body for academic policy is that no one can be held accountable'; academic boards were 'mechanisms for procrastination and obstruction by vested interests'.[8] The Jarratt Report had 'failed to address head on why universities were ineffective in both a management and a policy making sense'.

This letter would certainly have resonated with Baker and strengthened the resolve of the Hatfield Group. When Bird met the full CDP in April 1988 he was told firmly that a much clearer remit for the CEO was required, that the use of the word 'Directorate' implied that the director was not in control or could be challenged or alternative views brought forward by senior colleagues and that academic planning was a management task and could not, therefore, be the ultimate responsibility of the academic board. By this time the Bill was already in draft and polytechnic directors had become powerful players in the consultation process. A second draft was issued in July with further amendments to be approved by the Secretary of State. The academic board was left with responsibility only for academic matters narrowly defined and thereafter its powers were advisory to the director. The director, from being a chief officer under the old constitution, became a chief executive under the new, with significant executive powers and sole power to make recommendations on the educational character of the institution to the governors; the governors became a unicameral body with powers encompassing all strategic and policy issues. The new HEC constitution passed unaltered into the post-1992 era. Henceforward, it was no longer the case that substantial *de jure* participation in governance by an academic body was a defining characteristic of a British university.

The new HEC constitution, once confirmed in legislation, became the constitution of choice for ministers and officials, and the next two decades saw a reinforcement of the responsibilities and authority of governing bodies at the expense of senates in the pre-1992 universities. A first step in this process was the emergence of the CUC. This began as a wholly informal gathering invited, or perhaps better described as summoned, to a meeting in 1986 in Oxford where a CVCP weekend conference had been held, to hear an address by the CVCP chairman. The tone of the address was apparently sufficiently patronizing to encourage a meeting of chairs the following year to discuss, on their own, how university councils might assist their universities in difficult times. Might lay chairs, who had perhaps held very senior posts in industry, be able to develop a separate and more useful conversation with a Conservative Government than the CVCP had yet achieved? In 1994, in the wake of the governance breakdown at Huddersfield and Portsmouth, the Committee was approached by the DES, to issue guidance on governance, by which in this context was meant the procedures of governing bodies, for the sector as a whole.

When the new governing bodies for the polytechnics took over in 1988, they were faced with the challenging role of keeping the institutions afloat without reserves, which had been retained by most of the local authorities, with considerable problems in respect to sites and maintenance backlogs, and uncertainty about student numbers. Their task was not at all unlike that faced by university councils in the 1920s and 30s; in consequence they adopted a much more hands on role than their colleagues in the universities were used to exercising in the 1980s. When the CUC expanded its membership to include the post-1992 universities it received an influx of much more pro-active members. The invitation to offer guidance on governance was followed by the issue of formal Guides on governance and, over time, by the creation of procedural regulations for the conduct of governing body business, the clarification of relations between the governing body and 'the executive' and the identification of institutional performance indicators by which the executive could be held to account. This marked a considerable shift in authority from the senate of the pre-1992 universities which had previously seen themselves as entirely responsible for academic outcomes but which was consonant with the unicameral responsibilities of the new universities. The process had meanwhile been given a significant push by the Dearing Committee's recommendations which were very much influenced by Dearing's own preference for the post-1992 university more business-like model (a brief experience as chairman of a pre-1992 university council had done absolutely nothing to ameliorate this). The Committee wanted smaller governing bodies with a maximum of 25 members, five yearly effectiveness reviews, annual reports on institutional performance and a governance code of practice. Governing bodies were to be responsible for the strategic direction of the institution. When the CUC issued a Code of Governance in 2004 it made no reference whatever to the role of a senate in the bicameral structures of the pre-1992 universities.

Two other reasons why the profile of governing bodies was raised was the growth of the accountability agenda and the movement for improved corporate governance in the private sector. The consequences of the Cardiff affair brought the creation of a new audit regime and the introduction of a

Financial Memorandum between the UFC/HEFCE and the institutions which made the governing body contractually responsible to HEFCE for the effective management of the institution's financial affairs. Later the liability of the chair of the governing body to be called to appear before the PAC to give evidence in a case of financial maladministration was added to the liability already imposed on the vice-chancellor as the institution's accounting officer. This further ratcheted up the governing body's need for a closer, more hands on role in the management of the university. The formalization of the role of governing bodies only mirrored developments in the private sector where the Cadbury Report 1992, the Hampel Report 1997 and the Higgs Report 2003 and the Combined Code on Corporate Governance (incorporating the Smith guidance on Audit and the Turnbull on risk) sought to impose structures more accountable to shareholders in companies and private enterprises. The DES, the Funding Councils and at times the CUC were encouraged to draw analogies between governing bodies and company boards of directors in spite of the fact that, except for the vice-chancellor, the membership of governing bodies was entirely non-executive and the structures were, therefore, much closer to that of large charities.

The result, at least in a presentational sense, was a complete reversal of the dominance of senate over council in the pre-1992 universities and a reassertion of governing body control in the post-1992. In practice, senates did not necessarily accept this changed position and governing bodies were rarely professional, cohesive and engaged enough to become the engine for accountability and strategy that formal documents claimed for them but the change in the balance of authority represented a decisive shift in the formal sources of university policy making. The HEFCE Financial Memorandum put the position unequivocally when it stated that the governing body 'is collectively responsible and has ultimate non-delegable responsibility for overseeing the institution's activities, determining its future direction and fostering an environment in which its mission is achieved' (HEFCE 2010 para 18).

A closer analogy to a company board of directors than a governing body might, in fact, be Clark's 'strengthened steering core'. This takes the form in many universities of an executive board chaired by the vice-chancellor, which may be accountable either to the senate/academic board and the governing body or to the governing body alone. It may either be made up of staff holding permanent management appointments, such as deputy and pro-vice-chancellors and take the form of a senior management team (like the directorate in the polytechnics) or of pro-vice-chancellors seconded into the centre from academic departments, deans and other senior academic and administrative figures, a structure more common in the pre-1992 universities. The essential features of such bodies is that they meet frequently, perhaps weekly, and act in a corporate sense to create policy, coordinate implementation, act to deal with pressure points and take executive actions. While the impact of the two kinds of bodies on organizational cultures is obviously considerable both represent a device to cope with institutional size, the increasing impact of central communications from the funding councils and other bodies and the pressures of accountability, competition and of the market place. Such bodies have tended to reduce yet further the role of senates, which meeting once or twice a term cannot hope to keep up with the pace of university business or, in the case of HECs, academic boards, where the dominance of the senior management team may inhibit debate and dissent. In the pre-1992 universities joint committees with council members and a substantial academic representation on council membership serve to ensure a continuing partnership between senate and council; in the HEC institutions the effect of the 1988 constitutional settlement tends to persist in a much more hierarchical approach to policy making. While in the pre-1992 universities the vestigial remnants of the Ashby bottom up: top down approach to governance have largely been replaced by the need to reach decisions centrally and speedily, in the HECs an even more top down managed environment obtains.

Managerialism

Institutional management in higher education has always tended to reflect the administrative/managerial style of its primary external funding bodies, what organizational theorists writing about post-1985 managerialism, call the neo-institutional/archetype phenomenon, where institutional isomorphism dictates that dominant cultural values, policy priorities and structural designs generate irresistible cultural pressures to conform to external organizational forms (Deem *et al.* 2007). The dominant model in the 1950s and 60s in the university sector was offered by Whitehall where ministers approved policies and civil servants implemented them. The Vice-Chancellor of Essex in his Reith Lectures referred to the need to develop 'an academic civil service' (Sloman 1963: 87) while the Franks Report on Oxford argued 'that the value of an efficient civil service in a university is that it makes possible, even with a complicated structure, to practise democratic control by academics of the policies which shape their environment' and went on to emphasize that like the Whitehall civil servant, the most senior professional administrators must be expected to exercise initiative in management issues (University of Oxford 1964 para 556). Universities, normally, had only one pro-vice-chancellor and a registrar, or registrar and secretary, who exercised a role not unlike that of a permanent secretary. University business was conducted through committees which were 'serviced' by administrators; senates and councils were the final arbiters of policy. The administrative culture was not just derivative from Whitehall; it was also a culture of choice which was integral to the academic role in governance.

Expansion was already changing the balance, however: the cost of administrative staffing between 1959–60 and 1964–65 more than doubled (Shattock 1970), exemplifying, though in a much more modest way, the 'managerial revolution' that was accompanying the very rapid expansion of universities in the USA (*c.f.* Rourke and Brooks 1966). The closing down of the colonies released a flood of recruits to university administration who reinforced the civil service ethic and, it was sometimes suggested, viewed university governance as just another form of 'indirect rule'. Three developments brought some change to this role: the first was the student revolt of the late 1960s/early 1970s where administrators found themselves on the front line, confronting sit ins, taking out injunctions and negotiating settlements with inflamed students' unions; the second was the need to confront repeated rounds of trades union activism in the 1970s; the third was the implementation of the 1981 cuts which placed heavy demands on the managerial and political rather than the administrative, character of some university administrations. It would nevertheless be true that although the number of pro-vice-chancellors per university had increased to around three, the essential features of the 'administration' remained largely unchanged into the 1980s.

The same principle of institutions taking their administrative/managerial culture from their dominant funding agency also applied in the public sector. Local authority control was handed down, with local government members and officers imposing managerial decisions on polytechnics; a significant element of institutional administration was carried out in city hall and was not at all influenced by institutional policy considerations. (It was only in London that the Inner London Education Authority (ILEA) gave its polytechnics independent company status which provided them with full responsibility for financial and estate management.) Polytechnics were permitted a full time post of assistant director, a hangover from the structure in further education, and as they grew the number of full time managerial assistant director posts grew (Jones and Kiloh 1987). Equally, as more business was devolved from city hall a polytechnic administration developed but the much more authoritative culture of the former local authority regime was transmitted to the internal management of the polytechnics where the committee 'servicing' function carried much less weight than in the university sector because the committees themselves carried much less authority. Assistant directors derived their authority not from the academic board or the governing body but from the director, and internal decision making was much more personal than in the universities: academics could be consulted on issues and could influence decisions but were not themselves decision makers except in the relatively narrow areas covered by the academic board. One consequence of this was a much greater willingness to contemplate an expansion of student numbers at marginal costs because the decision makers were more influenced by the managerial challenges and rewards involved than by the increased teaching loads and reduced time available for research. In other words in this, and in many other issues, a dominant underlying component of policy discussion was primarily the managerial rather than the academic interest. It could be argued that in the university sector the academic interest was sometimes too dominant, but in the public sector it was given too low a priority in decision making.

From the mid-1980s onwards the external framework within which higher education operated began to change: the UGC was swept away to be replaced by statutory bodies, the UFC and then the Funding Councils; the public sector was removed from local authority control and, from 1992, was transferred to the Funding Council model. Underlying these changes was a growing interest in both main political parties in public service reform, generally known as NPM. This has evoked a very large literature, admirably summarized in the first chapter of Deem *et al.'s Knowledge, Higher Education and the New Managerialism* (2007) and, addressed particularly towards higher education, in Shattock (2008). What emerges from this is the argument that the state's policy initiatives towards higher education have been driven by a cross-Government concern for public sector reform based on NPM approaches rather than by a distinctive higher education agenda and that the various individual policy initiatives have been derived from a quiver of public service reform ideas not from issues that grow directly out of higher education itself. This can be illustrated by Figure 6.1 which summarizes the Labour Government's approach to public service reform. This can be used to identify key policies which have also been applied in the higher education sector: top down performance management through the QAA and the RAE/REF, market incentives through variable tuition fees, shaping the service from below through the exercise of student choice based on better market information, the introduction of the National Student Satisfaction Survey and an improvement in capability and capacity through the efforts of organizations like the Leadership Foundation and the Higher Education Academy. These policies, which, of course, have been drivers for the Funding Councils, have led to a form of managerialism which Child calls 'cultural control' and which generates 'a detailed, intrusive and continuous regime of micro level "work control"!' (Child 2005 quoted in Deem *et al.* 2007).

One simple example of this is that while the UGC sent out no more than four or five circulars a year, but would have considerable correspondence with individual vice-chancellors, HEFCE issued on average 42 circulars over each of the five years 2006 to 2010. We do not have detailed information of the extent of the contact between HEFCE and DfES/DIUS/BIS but Taggart's account suggests it was very frequent in his period at HEFCE. Swinnerton Dyer said in 1991 that

> the UFC has suffered far more nitpicking interference from DES civil servants in the last few years than the UGC did in the previous five. Moreover the Financial Memorandum which regulates relations between the DES and the UFC manifests in every line that the DES is not prepared to rely on the UFC's competence and good sense. At least the latest version no longer claims for the DES, as earlier versions did, powers of interference with the affairs of universities that were plainly contrary to the law; but that is a matter on which universities need to remain vigilant.
>
> (Swinnerton Dyer 1991)

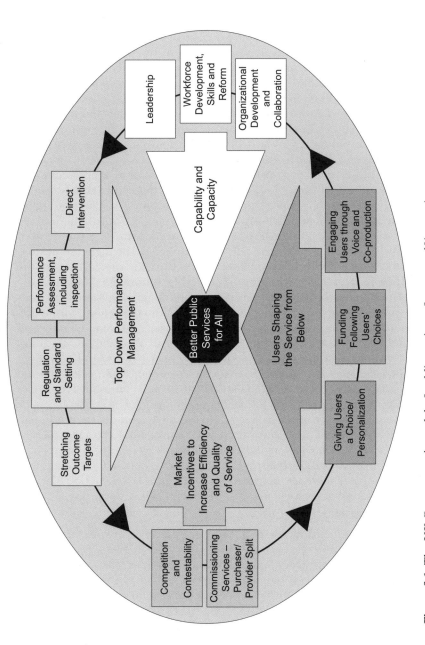

Figure 6.1 The UK Government's model of public service reform – a self-improving system

Source: Benington (2007).

One can conclude that micro-management of policy issues takes place at both Government to Funding Council and Funding Council to institution levels and that it is not surprising, therefore, to find it reproduced in management within universities.

The translation of management into managerialism was reinforced by the impact of the entry of the polytechnic management culture into the university system. Once established, the organizational culture developed from their local authority origins, was not changed by redesignation to university status. Indeed the challenges of institutional size, rationalization of sites and academic provision and financial stringency tended to encourage a commitment to a business style model. Thus De Montfort University's structure was described as compact with a small board of governors 'working closely with a Chief Executive . . . who really is the Chief Executive and has considerable delegated powers, . . . the Chief Executive runs the institution with the Senior Executive including four Pro-Vice-Chancellors, two Associate Vice-Chancellors, the Director of Finance, the Academic Registrar and the Director of Personnel' (University of Oxford, the North Report, 1997 Supplementary Volume: 60). This may have been a slightly extreme model, looking across the HECs as a whole, but it was no more than a realization of the model the CDP was striving for in 1988. As competition combined with financial stringency increased across higher education the managerial structures of the post-1992 universities began to seem increasingly attractive to some of the pre-1992 universities. Deem *et al.'s* research describes the rise in the pre-1992 universities of what they call 'the manager-academic', the pro-vice-chancellor or dean, who instead of continuing a part time academic commitment while taking on university wide duties takes a full time post in the centre of the university. Increasingly such posts are publicly advertised and appointments made for limited terms. Thus hybrid organizations are developed, with the HEC tradition of full time senior managers, usually but not exclusively, drawn from academic positions, mixed with a cadre of 'manager-academics' drawn from the ranks of the professoriate, some of whom might one day revert once again to academic positions. These latter appointees may wish to continue to work within a collegial culture but, cut off from an academic departmental base, find themselves increasingly involved in executive decision making and are invariably seen by their academic colleagues as solely part of the institution's executive management team.

The academic sense of working in an increasingly managed environment is enhanced by the growth of specialist branches within the central administration. Thus the demands of the QAA have led to the appointment of 'quality managers' whose task is to ensure that quality procedures are maintained and to prepare the institution for QAA visitations; the requirements of the RAE/REF demand the creation of a powerful research office both to assist with research grant applications and to manage the complex research assessment process; the growth in employment legislation has led to greatly enhanced human resource departments; while the competition for students has led to the development of marketing, schools liaison, widening participation and international offices all of whose activities are superimposed and sometimes supersede the academic responsibility for selection and admission. These offices represent both institutional responses to external pressures, but, more importantly, serve as portals through which external agendas are imposed on institutions. When combined with the characteristic 'business' practices of NPM: out sourcing, target setting, devolution of financial decision making and audit, the academic community could be forgiven for believing, even in the most collegial institutions, that its hold on strategy and policy formation had been seriously diluted. Unsurprisingly, the size of the managerial staff complement has continued to rise so that Whitchurch calculates that in 2010 it amounted to 20 per cent of the total higher education workforce (Whitchurch 2012). Indeed, Morgan, quoting HESA data estimates that the numbers of professional managers in higher education have risen by 30 per cent between 2004–05 and 2008–09.[9]

The make up and style of operation of the central body – variously called executive board, steering committee and senior management team – represents a key contribution to the organizational culture of an institution. Managerialism is inherently more likely to emanate from a senior management team made up exclusively of senior staff holding specialist executive briefs; more collegial styles can be expected from bodies where members retain academic links with their departments. A determining feature may be whether deans or heads of faculties/colleges are included or excluded from membership of the central body: the former ensures that academic issues are given equal weight to management issues in discussion, the latter tends to concentrate on the 'business' side of running the institution. But even the most academically orientated body cannot avoid grappling with an agenda which reflects the extent to which universities have been absorbed upward into a network of policy considerations which stem from a greatly more interventionist state. However much they ameliorate and interpret such issues for the benefit of their colleagues in the academic heartland of faculties and departments they cannot in the end protect them from their impact.

Academic policy making

A key, fundamental, policy area in British higher education has always been the first degree and the academic autonomy which is associated with degree awarding powers. Although more recently, and largely as a result of the demands of the RAE, research degrees have assumed a new importance, university status was defined up to 1992 by an institution's authority to confer a bachelor's degree. This stemmed from the historical position and powers of Oxbridge and the Ancient Scottish universities, which provided the model for the later civic universities. Traditionally institutions served an apprenticeship before being granted degree awarding powers, the exception being, as we have seen above, the 1960s New Universities founded under the auspices and close guidance of the UGC. An essential feature of the possession of degree awarding powers was the power to determine the curriculum. In the 1950s the universities sought to argue that operational autonomy and the right of academic self government constituted an essential element of degree awarding powers. This argument won the day in 1956 leaving the local authority colleges having to be satisfied with awarding the Dip.Tech. via the NCTA rather than a B.Tech. (but the universities' Achilles heel was always the existence of London's external degree system which permitted a college, however heavily controlled by a local authority, to register candidates for London degrees) and they were defeated in the argument over the assimilation of teacher training colleges into the university system in 1964. Up until 1999, when the Bolton Institute of Higher Education was given degree awarding powers, however, the legal right to award a degree was co-terminus with university status. In 2009 degree awarding powers for the Foundation Degree were extended to some further education colleges. What this process reflected was first, the gradual unravelling of the traditional university monopoly under the pressure of mass higher education and second, the state's concern that academic credentialing needed to be spread more widely than a grant of university status might allow. In particular, the decision to grant first degree awarding powers separately from university status indicated a recognition that without a national degree awarding agency like the CNAA some colleges could otherwise be permanently subordinated to degree validation by other institutions.

Unlike many continental European university systems where the state has retained final authority for the curriculum, in Britain degree awarding powers have always conferred autonomy in regard to what is taught and how it has been examined. The external examiner system, subjected to detailed scrutiny by the Reynolds Committee in the early 1980s, and by HEQC, has remained controlled by the institutions themselves, resisting an attempt by the Department to establish a national academy of external examiners which would have limited choice and imposed national regulation (Brown 2004). The first degree, therefore, has remained the responsibility of the degree awarding institutions and subject to the ebb and flow of academic/professional debate at departmental meetings, faculty boards and senates/academic boards rather than to a central national bureaucracy. This is not to say, however, that it has not been subject to pressures both from inside as well as outside the university system. In 1945, the university system in England and Wales inherited a single subject specialized degree system taught mostly within a mono-disciplinary department (with an alternative, general degree system, for students believed to be less academic, organized usually on a faculty basis). This came under severe challenge from two sources in the period up to Robbins. The first was generated, initially, by the radical new four year curriculum adopted at Keele, which emphasized breadth and inter-disciplinarity. The difficulties in launching the College and its slow growth inhibited the impact of the Keele break from tradition which only reached fruition in the 'new maps of learning' at Sussex. The syllabuses created in the

1960s New Universities left a permanent mark on the civic universities, the abandonment of general degrees, the extensive creation of joint degree programmes and, too, a breakdown of departmentalized academic silos into more diversified degree structures. The need to compete with the Sussex image at the time when the post Robbins expansion was driving up student recruitment created a powerful incentive for internal academic reform. (In Scotland, from which Lindsey had drawn much of his inspiration for the Keele syllabus, the continued commitment to four year degrees reduced the impact of these changes except at the single Scottish New University, founded after Robbins, at Stirling.)

The second challenge was the critique of the traditional university degree launched by Weaver, Robinson and Burgess which was an important element in the campaign for a separate, polytechnic-led, sector of higher education. Thus Robinson argued that 'the essential future of the polytechnic as an urban community university, as a people's university, must be its responsibility and responsiveness to the democracy rather than its insulation from it' (Robinson 1968: 39) reiterating, by implication, Crosland's criticisms of the university system as being insufficiently socially aware in his Woolwich speech. Pratt and Burgess, as we have seen above, saw an essential difference between the university and the public sector as being in who controlled the curriculum, the one pursuing an academic concern for knowledge for its own sake and the other, the more socially relevant community/vocational interest (Pratt and Burgess 1974: 9). Weaver said he 'had a prejudice against the dominance of academic criteria throughout the whole of education' (Weaver 1994) and was opposed to a university system whose 'social function is to concentrate on discipline-orientated analysis'.[10] As we have seen this attack had far reaching consequences for the structure of higher education. One curiosity is that while both challenges to the traditional university syllabus could be described as coming from the Left they proceeded from entirely different intellectual starting points. Tawney, a Labour appointee to the UGC, was a key proponent of the Stoke venture which was led locally by Labour Party figures; when launched, its leader was Lord Lindsey, very much a man of the Left. Yet there appear to be no philosophical overlaps with the Robinson, Burgess and Weaver group; Keele was planned quintessentially as a 'boarding school university' with maximum residential provision as compared to the Robinson ideal of the 'urban community university' (Robinson 1968: 15). Keele, with its high minded search for new intellectual coherences and its location on a walled country estate isolated from Stoke, was the antithesis of the downtown, mixed community setting of the North East London Polytechnic (NELP).

The Robinson, Burgess and Weaver views had considerable impact on policy in regard to the binary line but there is no evidence to suggest they influenced curricula thinking about professional/vocational education within polytechnics or within the CNAA. The Report of the Committee of Inquiry into the Engineering Profession (the Finniston Report) 1980 drew no distinction in recommending a greater element of practical work and industrial experience between universities and polytechnics. The polytechnic idea may have been more designedly vocational but in engineering, at least, it tended to follow a common professional model. On the other hand, Burgess's School of Independent Studies at NELP and its support for the sub-degree Dip.HE, itself a direct forerunner of the Foundation Degree, offered a creative alternative to the traditional A level entry and made what was, numerically, a modest contribution to the issue of widening participation while contributing considerably to new curricula approaches.

Two other national initiatives sought to change first degree structures. The first was the Enterprise in Higher Education (EHE) programme, launched in 1987 from the Department of Employment on the initiative of Lord Young, a close associate of Keith Joseph. The project, which aimed to embed the concept of enterprise and transferable skills into higher education syllabuses, was to some extent a natural follow up to the Green Paper's appeal to higher education to adjust its courses more to the needs of industry. (Both Burgess and Weaver served on EHE committees.) The project offered funding worth £1m per institution for 56 institutions over a period of five years. Its aim was explicitly to change the culture of higher education but it was careful not to try to impose change but relied on institutions themselves to pick up the baton. The project could not be described as a success. The final report concluded that teaching orientated and vocational institutions were much more sympathetic to the aims of the project and that in others there were sometimes 'fears that "enterprise" would impose entrepreneurial and commercial ideologies to the detriment of academic autonomy and values' (Burniston *et al.* 1999). It said that the RAE had diverted attention and resources away from the EHE agenda and that the embedding of EHE across the sector was uneven and could only be achieved by changes in the mainstream funding methodology (Burniston *et al.* 1999). This was rather less than a ringing endorsement: a decade after the end of the programme in 1996 it would have been hard to find any traceable impact; when the funding stopped the impetus evaporated and staff in post-1992 universities turned to seeking new resources through the RAE.

The second national initiative was launched in October 1990 at a conference at the University of Kent to introduce the concepts of modularization and semesterization to British universities. This had already been discussed in general terms in the university sector in the context of the burst of expansion in student numbers in the late 1980s which seemed to confirm the transition to mass higher education: questions had been raised as to whether the time was not ripe to overhaul the traditional single subject degree and adopt the US model which had been designed, it was said, to reflect a wider student clientele; a significant number of polytechnics had already moved in this direction. The October conference stressed the advantages of modularization for the introduction of a Credit Accumulation and Transfer System (CATS) and of semesterization for introducing a third summer semester, as in the US, for students who wished to follow the CATS route to a degree. Enthusiasm was such that a follow up conference was held in April 1991 when the benefits of modularization were spelled out as being more flexible course design, better use of staff time, more student choice, more opportunity for credit accumulation, equality for full and part time study and offering a platform for re-thinking objectives, learning strategies and assessment methods. By this time a momentum had been generated. In June 1991 the CVCP issued a paper 'Modular Curriculum and Structure'[11] which asserted the following advantages of the system:

- It encouraged a review of educational objectives, learning strategies and assessment methods.
- It improved the quality/economy of teaching/learning flexibility to accommodate an increasing diversity of entrant.
- It accommodated off campus student placement.
- It enabled part time study.
- It increased the number of pathways through the total provision of an institution.
- It facilitated transfer between institutions.
- It identified new inter-disciplinary pathways.
- It spread the examination load.

The CVCP's Academic Advisory Committee recommended that all universities adopt a two semester academic year. In September, at the CVCP residential conference Alan Howarth, the Minister of State for higher education pointed out that the age participation rate had risen from 1:8 in 1980 to 1:5 in 1990 and might be expected to rise to 1:3 by 2000. The central issue for the 1990s, he said, would be how to increase productivity while maintaining quality. He went on to confirm the DES's support for modularity and semesterization as offering ways of achieving economies and of widening participation. Vice-chancellors returned to their universities convinced, and in a significant number of institutions, forced the change.[12]

Subsequent experience has shown that not only was there no research which confirmed the effectiveness of the recommended new structures (Shattock 2003) but that none of the advantages presented in the CVCP paper were actually realized: the numbers of students taking advantage of CATS points was minimal, third semester programmes failed to attract students, part time numbers did not increase, the examination load actually increased, 'bite' sized modular courses were not seen as academically as satisfying as courses that stretched over a whole year and there was no evidence that modularity and semesterization, as such, was better suited to the interests of the imagined new student clientele, nor that teaching under the new structure was more economical. Why then did so many universities adopt the new system? The first and most obvious answer was that vice-chancellors, destabilized by the 1991 White Paper were seriously concerned about being outflanked by the polytechnics which, for the time being, seemed to command more of ministers' attention. But perhaps a deeper reason was that universities themselves had lost confidence. What was surprising was the docile way in which senates gave up long held academic practice without much debate for what was essentially an unproven system. Yet, Henkel's finding was that:

> Modulerisation of the curriculum was frequently seen as compounding the difficulties consequent on massification. It signified a transfer of power from academics and departments to the institution in the name of extrinsic values and interests . . . most academics felt that modulerisation had been imposed on them by the senior management of their universities and for political and administrative, rather than educational reasons.
>
> (Henkel 2000: 227)

None of the universities at the top of the RAE league table adopted modular structures or changed from a three term academic year; all the post-1992 institutions, on the other hand, could be described as modular and semesterized.

Although many pre-1992 universities found ways to adapt modularity to pre-existing academic course structures the changes were symptomatic of wider uncertainties. Hogan has demonstrated the extent to which universities embarked on academic re-organizations in the 1990s and early 2000 period: between 1993 and 2002 out of 81 universities included in one survey, 60 had undertaken at least one significant re-organization and only two of the post-1992 universities in the study had not done so. There was no apparent pattern to these re-organizations: 18 reduced the number of faculties and departments, 11 reduced the number of faculties/schools of study, three increased the number of faculties/schools but reduced the number of departments and three more removed faculties altogether and replaced them with schools formed out of merged departments. In a separate analysis 51 out of 68 universities between 1994 and 2002 had changed their academic structure of faculties or schools, 26 reducing the number of faculties, 12 replacing faculties with schools and 11 increasing the number of faculties or schools. Reviewing the rationale for these changes there seems to be little consensus – the arrival of a new vice-chancellor, looking for greater efficiency, obtaining better communication, establishing a structure better equipped either to compete in the RAE or to provide inter-disciplinary in teaching. Hogan concludes that 'managerial rather than academic concerns have been dominant factors behind most re-organizations' (Hogan 2005: 54).

The managerial revolution that has occurred at the most senior levels of university governance has reached down into the academic heartland. Pro-vice-chancellorships dedicated to quality or research or the student experience have been replicated at lower levels by executive deanships, by the grouping of departments into colleges where the college head has executive powers, or by the creation of interdisciplinary schools where school heads have subsumed the powers of mono-disciplinary departments. Such changes are partly a symptom of a wider uncertainty of how institutions should respond to external pressures but also to some loss of faith in the community's powers to respond quickly and effectively to them. The result has been a reversion to a more executive, less participative, style of academic policy making. How far this has impacted on organizational cultures is not clear. The answer seems to lie in the extent of a university's commitment to a research agenda: more hierarchical structures, operating under senior management teams that exercise direct executive power tend to abound in institutions where research has a lower priority and the importance of student recruitment and retention is paramount; more participative structures where central decision-making bodies have a strong non-executive academic component tend to flourish in research active institutions. Such differentiation is rooted in institutional histories as well as in a commitment to a particular kind of mission. But even in the most executively driven institution there is little inclination to try to reach down to dictate the style and content of what is taught and how it is taught. Academic policy at the grass roots level remains substantially more bottom up than top down.

Institutional autonomy

A distinctive feature of British universities, as compared to their continental European counterparts, has been their autonomy: historical in origin, this has been preserved by Government as a matter of policy. When the nineteenth-century English university colleges were given full university status their charters gave them a level of autonomy that paralleled Oxford, Cambridge, London, Aberdeen, Edinburgh, Glasgow and St Andrews. British universities were not founded by the state (at least until Keele and the 1960s New Universities) but by a range of private interests, religious and secular. Even after the Government committed itself to continuous recurrent funding in 1919 it was only on a deficiency basis and one of the main responsibilities of the UGC was to provide assurance to the Treasury that institutions made appropriate efforts to generate resources of their own. As we have seen above, all this was to change in 1945 but the concept of legal autonomy and the sense that universities required autonomy to function as universities was by this time engrained in Government thinking, and the UGC's continued and strengthened intermediary role was the result.

Nearly 70 years later the European Universities Association (EUA) carried out a survey of university autonomy across Europe under the headings organizational autonomy, financial autonomy, staffing autonomy and academic autonomy and produced a scorecard which clearly showed the British university system to be the most autonomous in Europe (Esterman *et al.* 2011). The very fact that such a report has been produced reflects the concern in the European Commission, as well as in the EUA, about a lack of autonomy in European universities and the effect this may have both in global competition in university league tables and in their economic contribution through innovation. For many European university systems movement in the direction of greater autonomy has meant a devolution of resource allocation powers from central government bureaucracies, the transfer of powers to enable new academic posts to be created, the empowerment of universities to become their own employers with their own staff conditions of service, the endowment of universities with the site and buildings which they use and the state's abandonment of powers to exercise final control over course syllabuses and examinations. The flow has essentially been downward from the state to the individual university.

By contrast British universities were always separate legal identities, allocating the resources they had available to them according to their own priorities, were always empowered to create or abolish posts and to employ staff on their own conditions of service, were owners of their own property and other assets and had the power to award their own degrees. In Britain, it can be argued, the movement in the flow of power has been in the opposite direction to the rest of Europe with the state becoming increasingly concerned to involve itself in operational detail in order to ensure the achievement of national policy objectives. Examples might be the retrospective decision to reward differentially academic departments receiving the scores in the top categories in the 2001 and 2008 RAEs, the decision in 2007 by John Denham, then Secretary of State, to withdraw resources from universities in respect to students undertaking equivalent or lower qualifications (ELQs), thereby requiring students wishing to take a second first degree level qualification in a new field to pay full cost tuition fees, or the decision by OFFA to require universities to exercise control over the level of tuition fees they may charge dependent on their satisfying the Office on their access plans and performance in recruiting students from economically disadvantaged backgrounds. In their own way each example illustrated an exercise of arbitrary Government power, the first, the determination to override HEFCE advice to increase differentiation in research funding, the second, an unthinking budgetary decision required by the Treasury which effectively eliminated a whole category of their intake from the Open University and Birkbeck College and the third, an intervention imposed by the need to meet the conflicting objectives of the two partners of the Coalition Government. But what is surprising about these examples is that there have not been many more. It is certainly the case that institutional autonomy has narrowed since 1945 but it is also the case that autonomy has been an intrinsic characteristic of the British university system which it has been an important element of state policy to preserve. At a formal level, institutional autonomy was protected by the Privy Council through individual institutional statutes and by the definition, until 2008, of universities' eleemosynary charitable status. But ever since the nineteenth century, academic freedom and university autonomy have been linked as part of society's unwritten cultural constitution.

University autonomy was, of course, constrained by the demands of the state between 1939 and 1945. A return to previous levels of freedom was very much part of the agenda for reform generated by Bruce Truscot (Truscot

1943). Responsibility for translating this into bureaucratic practice rested with the immediate post-War generation of university leaders. As we have seen earlier the all too easy subordination of the previously much admired German university system to Nazism and the failure of university communities in Germany to protest against the treatment of Jewish academics, emphasized in Britain the importance of recognizing the value of universities as centres of independent thought. Moreover, the contribution of science to the War effort, fostered by the freedom of scientific inquiry in British universities in the inter-War years, had been fully recognized both by the public and in Whitehall, even though the most striking contribution, at Bletchley, remained a secret until much later. The threats to university independence in the immediate post-War years were considerable: the university system had had to accept full state funding and the manpower demands of post-War reconstruction in professional fields were insatiable. University figures like Hetherington from Glasgow were only too well aware of the dangers of the degree of financial dependence on the Government to which universities had had to subscribe (Illingworth 1971). The solution was the reconstruction of the UGC as the body which acted as the bulwark against Government interference and as the body which also advised Government on university priorities. The fact that the UGC was responsible to the Treasury, which professed no expertise in educational policy, rather than the Board of Education, gave it great authority to act in a quasi ministerial fashion. This suited the Government. There was little confidence in the Board of Education and if the targets for scientific and technological manpower were to be met, as spelled out by the Barlow Committee and later by the Advisory Council on Science Policy, a reinvigorated UGC seemed to be the most effective instrument. The extremely close links between the CVCP and the UGC and the UGC and the Treasury established forms of bureaucratic practice which managed to preserve a respect for institutional autonomy within a funding framework which could otherwise have provided a vehicle for extensive state direction.

Robbins captured the essence of the argument in the following:

> We believe that a system that aims at the maximum of independence compatible with the necessary degree of public control is good in itself as reflecting the ultimate values of a free society. We believe that a multiplicity of centres of initiative safeguards spontaneity and variety, and therefore provides the surest guarantee of intellectual progress and moral responsibility. We do not regard such freedom as a privilege but rather as a necessary condition for the proper discharge of the higher academic functions as we conceive them.
>
> (Committee on Higher Education 1963 para 709)

Only a year before this statement was published the Treasury had successfully defended the universities' immunity from inspection from the Comptroller and Auditor General. The Robbins Report made it clear that it attached 'great importance to this immunity . . . [and was] glad that the Treasury has successfully upheld it' (para 754) but three years later the decision was over-turned. However, the effect of the PAC decision was to confirm the principle of institutional autonomy as set out by Robbins, above, and to cast it in concrete for the future. The most sensitive issue was always the independ-ence of the UGC in its relations with the DES. The PAC had lined up a series of the most eminent witnesses drawn from the House of Lords including Lord Butler, a previous Chancellor of the Exchequer. Lord Bowden, the Principal of UMIST, Lord James, Vice-Chancellor of York, Lord Franks, Master of Worcester College, Oxford and a former Permanent Secretary, Lord Heyworth, Lord Murray and Lord Robbins himself. All of them spoke with convincing vehemence about the need to preserve university autonomy, though with more nuanced views about the universities' immunity from inspection, with the result that the PAC's eventual decision went out of its way to set at rest any fears that the C and AG would be a threat 'to proper academic freedom' and that no harm should come to 'the proper autonomy of the UGC and the universities' (PAC 1967 para 29). University autonomy had become entrenched in Parliamentary thinking.

But institutional autonomy seems to have been less welcome in the DES. Weaver in his Joseph Payne Lecture in 1973 was critical of the Robbins proposed structure for higher education for suggesting that such a high proportion of students should be educated 'in the autonomous institutions' and drew a distinction between autonomous institutions and those that were 'socially controlled', claiming that the decisions of 1965 and 1966 regarding the polytechnics ensured that 'a proper balance was held between the claims of academic freedom and social responsiveness' (Weaver 1973: 10). Both Crosland and Weaver used the phrase 'the autonomous sector' pejoratively; Crosland told Kogan that he had 'insisted' that the universities be made subject to the C and AG (Kogan 1971: 196). It is arguable that if the reinforcement of the binary line had not taken place university autonomy might have been severely tested by Weaver/Crosland attempts to make them more subject to an ideologically inspired social agenda: the binary line, as indeed Weaver claimed, was a protection for universities against Government intrusion.

This 'protection' survived until the merger of the two systems in 1992 when, in the changed position of the 1992 Act it was also extended to the new universities. However, this was no longer seen by officials, as it was in 1963–65, as offering the potential for a loss of state control. Developments in the second half of the 1980s, an age of increasing financial transparency, had demonstrated that funding incentives in a period of falling unit costs, changes in funding formulae and the creation of separate competi-tive streams for new initiatives, plus accountability, could override the exist-ence of legal guarantees of autonomy. Steering the system could become much more a matter of modelling funding formulae than high profile ministerial pronouncements that were difficult to implement. In addition, the traditional university autonomy was already narrowing: formula fund-ing, the introduction of the Financial Memorandum, the new regulations and audit arrangements, the idea of a contract for funding student numbers, the amendment of university statutes to end tenured appointments and the provisions for a quality organization in addition to the HEQC, all represented restrictions on universities' freedom. Moreover, the Thatcherite prejudice against producer-led organizations offered a significant counter argument to the virtues of institutional autonomy which, under this line of thinking, was interpreted as control by the academic community.

One approach was to stimulate internal governance reform by strengthening the powers of lay governors *vis-à-vis* those of the senate as had been achieved in the constitutional changes to the governing bodies of polytechnics in the 1988 Act. Laymen, it was thought would be more sympathetic to Government priorities and more open to external social or economic pressures. In practice, there was little evidence that this was the case. A second approach was the utilization of NPM approaches that had been applied in other public services, such as the NHS, which were specifically designed to unpick producer-led services and make them more efficient and socially responsive. University autonomy represented a natural target for such reforms. At the same time, Government was also cognisant of the fact that institutional autonomy provided a vehicle for what Robbins described as 'that scope for individual and institutional initiative that British tradition has always held to be one of the main essentials of intellectual and spiritual health' (Committee on Higher Education 1963 para 9). Individual and institutional initiative were also part of the pantheon of Thatcherite, and later Blairite virtues, and in research, at least, came to be seen as essential adjuncts to a successful economy. For the next 20 years the Government was to steer a zigzag course between these two approaches.

There is no doubt that the introduction of the idea of a market and of greater inter-institutional competition, key elements of the 1992 reforms, were designed in part to unlock the negative or defensive attitudes that Conservative Ministers saw as the consequence of institutional autonomy. But within two years of the legislation being passed the rapid expansion of student numbers brought the termination of a market in student numbers and the imposition, under Treasury instruction to HEFCE, of rigid controls on student numbers, buttressed by fines for overshoots (later to be further tightened by the requirement to repay the Funding Council in respect to undershoots). Greater marketization could, of course, offer more freedom to exercise autonomy, as the Browne Report (2010) argued, but once again the idea of full marketization proved to be unrealistic in the light of public expenditure demands.

The period between 1992 and 2006 saw attempts to impose a full range of NPM techniques on higher education – quality, efficiency, performance indicators, competition, customer responsiveness, marketization and audit – with variable results but too often their effectiveness was compromised by the workings of institutional autonomy, itself a key component of NPM as in the creation of Foundation Trust Hospitals and Academies. The employment of NPM measures resulted in greater Government intervention. Swinnerton Dyer's comments were quoted above on DES 'nitpicking'. Such micro management was to increase in the 1990s and in the noughties at a time when, paradoxically, universities' dependence on state funding was in rapid decline. But in spite of the increasing level of intrusion the principle of institutional autonomy was never publicly questioned. When the Dearing Committee issued a set of prescriptive recommendations on the behaviour of governing bodies, suggesting that the Funding Council should impose sanctions on institutions failing to implement them, the Government was persuaded to ignore them. Indeed, in one area of institutional activity, the recruitment of international students who could pay full cost tuition fees, autonomy thrived. No one in 1980 when the decision was taken to remove the subsidy for overseas students fees, least of all, Mark Carlisle, the apologetic Secretary of State, could have envisaged the explosion of entrepreneurial activity which it released, from overseas agents, to overseas offices to overseas campuses, with large international offices negotiating substantial agreements in countries where the British Government might have key economic and political interests. Thus while limits have been placed on institutions' independence from the state, the sense of institutional autonomy, of self direction and operational independence has, if anything, been enhanced.

The Robbins Committee spelled out what it believed were the essential components of university autonomy: freedom to make academic appointments without external constraints and to decide on salaries, gradings and titles; freedom to create and control the curriculum and maintain academic standards (including the freedom to appoint its own external examiners); freedom to select students for admission providing equity was observed, and to set entrance requirements; freedom to decide the balance between teaching and research; and freedom to decide its own path of institutional development subject to the state's responsibility (because it was the major source of finance) to coordinate the system through the operation of a UGC (Committee on Higher Education 1963 paras 711–31). A check list 50 years later would qualify some of these components: appointments with tenure can no longer be made but as a result of Lord Jenkins' academic freedom amendment to the 1988 Bill the major protection provided by tenure has been retained; the assumption of the right to maintain its own academic standards has been challenged by the existence of the QAA but in only one case (Thames Valley University) has a QAA review precipitated serious consequences for an institution, although the new and as yet untested QAA formula for assessing threshold standards could threaten this; the right to select students for admission has been put under pressure as a result of successive Governments' wish to broaden access to higher education (a wish shared, it should be added, by the institutions) and by the Coalition Government's attempt to link growth and fee levels to qualification levels, but the process has been one of incentivization rather than fiat; decisions on the balance of teaching and research have been heavily qualified by a succession of RAEs but selectivity in some form was an inevitable consequence of the trend to mass and universal higher education, and, as we have seen above, the motivation to undertake research, even in institutions primarily funded for teaching, remains undimmed. The most significant change in the final component, the loss of the UGC as the body, rather than the Department, to be responsible for the coordination of the university system was again the natural consequence of the growth of the higher education system but the principle of an intermediary body, though one very much changed by the funding arrangements introduced in 2012, has been retained. Institutional autonomy has survived as a characteristic of the British higher education system through the vicissitudes of changes of government, the centralization of policy machinery and the increasing pressure on public finance; its vitality remains an important component in the interlocking mosaic of decision-making centres that comprise higher education's policy framework.

But it must be recognized, in spite of the EUA's rating quoted above, that the concept of institutional autonomy has been narrowed by constant Government intervention through financial regulation, most notably through the increasing specificity of the Financial Memorandum, policy-led changes in funding arrangements and by the activities of the QAA. Moreover the ability to exercise institutional autonomy is not evenly spread: an institution substantially dependent on home student tuition fee income and with little balancing research income is irredeemably more vulnerable to external intervention than an institution flush with research funding and a guaranteed market in international students. What is true for universities in the Russell Group is not necessarily true for less advantaged institutions. Generalized statements about autonomy must be qualified by a differentiation amongst institutions in their ability to sustain it.

7

Higher education and making policy

A review of policy making in British higher education from the end of the Second World War to the publication of the 2011 White Paper *Higher Education, Students at the Heart of the System* has the merit of covering a coherent phase in the funding of higher education and in state-higher education relations. It also covers a period when the age participation rate grew from around 3 per cent to over 43 per cent, and may be about to stabilize at somewhere around the latter figure. Quoting these two developments in this way suggests that the policies that delivered such significant changes were pursued consistently towards desired ends – nothing could be further from the truth. Policy on these issues, and others described in the book, was episodic and inconsistent, generated by a range of forces and events, economic, political, and social, more often external to higher education than driven from within. Even when the state grew more dominant in decision making, policy emerged out of interaction and bargaining between a number of bodies rather than from a single source. Ideology played a part, as for example in the Woolwich speech or the adoption of a public choice approach to decision making, but it was always leavened by 'low' politics and by pragmatism; political parties unconsciously adopted policies that were more bipartisan than polarized by Party manifestos or political programmes.

Another advantage in taking a view of higher education over such a long period is that it offers the opportunity to establish what might be some of the characteristics of policy making in the British higher education environment. One of these is the apparent paradox of higher education's close integration with the state's policy apparatus and the continued explicit and implicit acceptance of the principle of institutional autonomy. Examples can be quoted where lines have been crossed but the fact that this has been so infrequent is a testimony to the extent to which the principle is embedded in the working of the system. A second characteristic is the absence of a clearly definable focus for policy making: it might have appeared at times to lie in the hands of a secretary of state but in practice it was more likely to have been generated from multiple sources inside and outside government, including within higher education itself. A third is that policy change has generally been reactive not pro-active, the product of rising numbers, financial shortfalls or changes in the environment rather than of endogenous pressures for reform. In one sense this has provided stability through a period of very substantial economic and societal change but in another it has rendered higher education liable to constant adjustment and readjustment to external events over which it has had no control. Policy making has always been something of a bumpy ride.

Financial decision making and policy

Throughout the period, policy was framed by two relentless drivers, the growth in demand for higher education and the cost implications of meeting that demand. Until 1962, when the age participation rate had reached 8.5 per cent (4 per cent in the universities) the growth in demand had been absorbed by the Treasury or by local authority budgets. Local authority expenditure on higher education was to remain uncapped until 1981 except in so far as local authority expenditure as a whole was subject to Treasury control. For the universities, any politics that were involved in financing expansion in this period were largely contained within the narrow focus of UGC-Treasury relations and were not exposed to the cold winds of wider competition. Once the PESC process was in place, however, this was to change and the university interest had to fight its corner in a government wide competition for public funds. In a governance system which gave a single department, the Treasury, so much power as the arbiter of public expenditure planning, it was inevitable that it would play a profound, if arm's length, role in the determination of policy because it authorized the expenditure limits within which policy could be made, as well as, on occasion, forcing policy change to contain expenditure within planned limits. The various technical changes in the process from volume planning to cash limits to cash planning, the abolition of the quinquennial funding system and the variations in the spending review periods all had additional impacts on shorter term development questions, as did the fluctuations of Government public expenditure policy, as for example in the 1980 to 1983 period, the continued restraint on public expenditure in the later 1980s and the 1990s, and in the 2010 comprehensive spending review. The Treasury's ultimate responsibility under the PES process was to balance the nation's public expenditure books; it was professionally not sympathetic to bids based on unquantifiable claims of long term future investment and this, very often, was the only card higher education had to play.

Over the period, among many examples of financial decision making, four stand out as critical to the shape of higher education as we see it at the end of the period. The first was the decision of the Robbins Committee, uncritically followed by the Cabinet, to base its recommendations for a growth in numbers on an estimate of a 4 per cent growth in the economy rather than the 2.5 per cent forecast by Treasury officials. Since the Cabinet paper was in the name of the Chief Secretary to the Treasury it must be regarded as the official Treasury view although it can also be seen as a political gloss because the Conservative Government recognized that it had no choice politically but to accept the Robbins' student number forecasts. But had the lower figure of 2.5 per cent been used the implications for government priorities would have had to have been addressed more sharply and issues such as tuition fees, loan policies and the cost of international students, all of which featured in the drafts of Treasury papers to Robbins, would have had to have been thought about in a more fundamental way than they were, for example, in the Shirley Williams 13 Points only six years later. It is hard to believe that Lord Robbins, himself a distinguished economist and government financial adviser, could have accepted the NEDC 4 per cent growth rate without question. The main tasks of his Committee were to forecast the rate of growth in student numbers and the structure of institutions it required not how government should pay for it but Chapter XIV of the Committee's Report was undoubtedly helpful to a Government politically committed to reversing the image it had created for itself in 1962 only twelve months earlier.

The second critical decision was the removal of what in a *post hoc* rationalization was described as the fee subsidy for international students in 1980. Famously criticized at the Commonwealth Prime Ministers' Conference, where Margaret Thatcher was attacked by third world Commonwealth leaders over the decision, no higher education related decision could have had a greater unintended consequence. Conceived as a Treasury-led budget cut, the income deriving from international student tuition fees not only enabled the system to survive the financial stringencies of the next decade or so but fuelled a spirit of self help in universities which had not been apparent in the immediate post Robbins era of the 1970s. (It also encouraged a commercialism which pushed some institutions into ethically and academically dubious ventures with consequences for the reputation of the system as a whole.) Globalization opened new possibilities for universities both academically and as mixed economy institutions.

The third decision was taken by Kenneth Baker, reversing the unpopularity of his predecessor's Green Paper to commit the Government to expansion, but to abandon tying numbers to a fixed unit of resource thus opening the way to expansion at marginal costs. Reading John Major's account of his negotiations over expenditure when, as Chief Secretary, he controlled the PES process, it is clear that the Treasury would have permitted no other decision to be reached. Not only were the academic implications of this in universities and polytechnics considerable but the longer term policy issue about how to pay for expansion was solved, from the Treasury's point of view, for a decade until the joint CVCP/CDP working group found itself forced to call for 'top up' fees. The consequence of over rapid expansion to meet income targets followed by the post-1992 rationalization of unit costs across the two sectors had a permanent impact on staff:student ratios across the system.

The last of the decisions, in many ways a natural consequence of the Baker policy, was the introduction of tuition fees for home students backed by income contingent loans, taking effect in 2006, a decision which was not followed in Scotland. Unlike the first three, this was driven initially from within higher education itself through UUK and the Russell Group, which saw it as the only politically possible solution to breaking the impasse on funding, but would only have been possible with the active commitment of the Government, of the Prime Minister himself, and ultimately, on the basis of a narrow vote, of Parliament. It was, as described above, the outcome of an intensely political process within the Government itself. But the seeds of the decision reached back to the mid-1980s and Keith Joseph's defeat when, supported by the Treasury, he had tried to introduce means testing for tuition fees. Perhaps the most significant feature of the 2004 decision was that it prepared the ground for the more extreme decision on tuition fees in 2010. In a little over a decade from the Dearing Report, which first recommended the introduction of a student paid tuition fee, the ground rules for funding higher education had changed almost completely. Certainly the 2010 decision was driven by New Public Management theories and by public choice economics but in terms of political decision making it is impossible to see it as anything other than a direct outcome of a Government fiscal crisis where the Treasury's role was paramount. It is too early to say whether the new policy is sustainable.

The officials' role in policy making

Treasury influence was always indirect, even before it relinquished control of the universities to a spending department, but was powerful and could be decisive because of its dominant position in the PESC process. From the start, therefore, the powers of the spending department (from 1964 the DES) were qualified, and, in practice, were limited further by the existence both of an intermediary body which, in the case of the UGC, was specifically seen as a 'buffer' between the Department and the institutions, and by the institutions' representative bodies, primarily the CVCP and, later, the CDP. It was natural, therefore, that Departmental policies derived from officials, who managed the interfaces between the various bodies, rather than ministers, where the turnover was generally rapid.

In 1964, when it took over control of the university sector, the Ministry of Education already had a track record of restructuring from its decisions in 1956 to identify colleges for a concentration of advanced work, from the establishment of the CATs as an elite group and from their subsequent withdrawal from local authority control in 1961. As a Ministry it had been divided in its thinking but when Anthony Part left to be the Permanent Secretary of the new Ministry of Technology, the leading voice amongst the officials was Toby Weaver's. Under Weaver, the officials' views were strong enough to convince both Conservative and Labour Ministers to reject core

Robbins recommendations both on the transfer of teacher training colleges to university control and on the philosophy of a unitary university system to which colleges would be promoted from below. In doing so both ideological considerations and long term relationships and alliances with the local authorities played a part. Officials must also have been influenced by the conservative attitudes which universities displayed towards any concession of their monopoly of degree awarding powers and in respect to qualifications to be awarded in the teacher training colleges, as well as by their public resistance to the issue of a transfer of control from the Treasury to the Ministry in the evidence they submitted to Robbins.

But attitudes were to change in the Department: after the political turmoil of the 1970s it is not surprising that the close relationship between the Department's officials and the local authorities had changed. Once again it was the officials who were driving policy as the THES leak of the Government's draft response to the Select Committee's 1980 Report makes clear and it was the officials, rather than ministers, who were the true begetters of NAB. The NAB turned out to be uncomfortable for ministers and the Government's general hostility towards the local authorities ensured that ministers, notably Baker, took a leading role in the decision to remove local authority control from the public sector of higher education. The officials had always seen NAB as a temporary solution and ministers, officials and the CDP found themselves, therefore, in support of a common objective. In 1990–91 it was again the officials who made the proposals for the merger of the two sectors and Clarke, the Secretary of State who merely endorsed them, but by this time the CVCP had joined the CDP in regarding the abolition of the binary line as inevitable. This was, of course, welcome to the Treasury because it enabled a rationalization of costs across the two sectors, a necessary step in Treasury eyes in the light of the cost of the rapid growth in student numbers in the 1989 to 1994 period.

Personalities and the policy process

With the notable exceptions of Joseph, as a conceptual thinker, and Baker, as prompted by CIHE, as the advocate of a return to expansion, it was therefore the civil servants who were the real architects of policy in regard to the system and the structure of higher education. This was less true, however, in the creation of policy in respect to research, which itself had an increasing impact on structure. Baker's decision to ignore arguments about the maintenance of a given unit of resource or the preservation of staff:student ratios reduced for a while the priority of cost as a driver (until the onset of the 'top up' fees debate). This coincided with the arrival of a third policy driver, that of research: research as a contributor to innovation and national economic progress where, it was said, success depended on concentration into fewer sites, and research as a potential restructuring agent which drove the differentiation of the system and facilitated high positions in international league tables. Once again the Treasury played a role in the emergence of policy with its questions about how research was coordinated across government and its identification of a 'black hole' in the UGC's funding mechanism for research. But in this case it was the initiative of a single individual, Swinnerton Dyer, who devised a new funding model, created the RAE process and, as Chairman, led his UGC colleagues into agreeing to it, which established a mechanism that came to play a dominant role not only in the direction of the system itself but in institutional policy making and in the professional lives of the academic community. Subsequent efforts to intensify the process in 2003 and by Gordon Brown, as Chancellor, to give greater emphasis to relevance were essentially only refinements which sought to exploit, for Government purposes, what was in effect a revolutionary reversal of the Robbins structure: where the Robbins approach was to equalize universities up to the level of the leading institutions, the RAE encouraged increasing differentiation in favour of the leading institutions. This was itself a reaction against the costliness of the Robbins vision. When the public sector entered the RAE it served to confirm a research hierarchy in British higher education which lent itself easily to translation into league tables.

Institutional autonomy

From the granting of university charters to the nineteenth-century university colleges, autonomy for universities had been hard wired into the British political and intellectual mindset, and it was reinforced by the reform of the UGC and the actions of the CVCP in the immediate aftermath of the Second World War, as well as by the protection it was offered by the Treasury. But the unspoken pact of the retention of absolute independence with full state funding did not last and brought another policy player into the system, Parliament. The loss of exemption from scrutiny by the Comptroller and Auditor General and by the PAC was an inevitable consequence of the decision to accept full funding from the state in 1945–46 coupled with the growth of student numbers. PAC interventions thereafter were mostly bureaucratic and tiresome to universities but, except for the pressure to remove tenure, not fundamental to the British model of university autonomy. However, the ambiguities built into the 1966 compromise whereby the UGC, even though lacking statutory powers, should be the guardian of financial propriety and the public purse, were exploded by the financial mismanagement at Cardiff. Here the intervention of the PAC was decisive and, occurring simultaneously with the DES's decision to remove public sector higher education from local authority control, provided the opportunity, seized with both hands by DES officials, to radically change the governance of the university system as well as that of the public sector. Without the issue of Cardiff reaching No 10 and the PAC the Croham Committee would probably have contented itself with recommending a strengthening of UGC powers, which was what Jarratt, under the influence of Swinnerton Dyer, had intended; in fact it precipitated the most fundamental change in the governance of higher education since the transfer of responsibility for the universities to the DES.

Superficially the creation of the funding council system enhanced autonomy – the funding councils were, it was asserted, funding not planning bodies; in a competitive market universities could be more, not less, independent. But within two years, as a result of a Treasury intervention to control expansion, restrictions on institutional freedom to admit home students above target had been rigorously imposed, the binary line appeared to have been reintroduced by the third RAE and the QAA was rampant across the enlarged sector. As the decade proceeded the restrictions imposed by the Financial Memorandum increased: by 2011 it ran to 49 pages of regulation and appendices. The attempt to marketize higher education had been frustrated by the state itself. Institutional strategies for development tended to revolve around technical funding issues, and internal reorganizations aimed at achieving better internal management or at improving RAE performance. In practice fundamental change came slowly and incrementally.

Institutional autonomy remained a key article of faith but it was exercised on a much narrower front. In the period 1945 to 1972 the quinquennial planning system, often seen primarily as being of most benefit because it provided a secure financial platform, offered institutions the opportunity to propose new developments, new departments and new degree programmes: it positively encouraged new ideas. Not all might be accepted by the UGC but the possibility of bottom up innovation was healthy for the system. The 1972 to 1977 planning, based on the 1972 White Paper forecast of numbers, was foreclosed both by a slow down in demand and by the worsening national financial situation. When calls for strategic plans were resumed in the 1990s they were filed for reference only by HEFCE (HEFCE had only invited them to encourage universities to undertake strategic planning). HEFCE was restricted to calling for bids for new initiatives for which approval had been obtained from the DES. This was innovation top down and encouraged multiple bidding by institutions for small pots of money to be spent on ideas which the institutions did not originate themselves. Instead of calling for bold new academic ventures universities were more likely to be engaged in promoting peripheral 'third stream' activities or new initiatives to generate international student fee income. The tendency to move to more authoritarian structures was a reflection of a more top down system.

The tightening of central government control might have been attributed to the dependence of higher education on the public purse but in fact by the 1990s many universities had been successful in diversifying their income base. The introduction of tuition fees for home students in 2006 might have been expected to give an added fillip to institutional independence but paradoxically it seemed that the more institutions raised the proportion of their income which came from non-state sources the tighter the regulatory regime of state control became. The state welcomed the injection of non-state funds, including the post-2006 new home tuition fee funding, but was unwilling to follow the logic that a transfer to a market approach implied. In this higher education was not alone: one of the problems of the application of NPM methodology throughout the public sector of the economy has been the extent to which it lends itself to top down interpretations of the implications of public choice.

Autonomy and academic standards

One area where autonomy was seriously threatened was in respect to academic standards. The source of the threat was ideological rather than based on evidence-based practical concerns. In the 1950s universities had successfully defended their degree awarding monopoly but the creation of the CNAA not only greatly extended degree awarding powers but provided a national guarantee of their standing. Influenced by public choice economic theory and by his own (and Margaret Thatcher's) doubts about the content of some university teaching (sociology, for example, at the Open University, Peace Studies at Bradford) Joseph leaned heavily towards some form of national accountability. The Reynolds group and HEQC represented attempts to meet the political demand but to keep the machinery in university hands. Civil servants, however, shared politicians' doubts: nothing could illustrate better the breakdown of a common culture than the doubts expressed by a senior civil servant at the ability of the Academic Audit Unit to police the university system (see p. 361). The decision to write a new quality organization into the 1992 legislation reflects such doubts as well as the general attitude in Whitehall towards the post-1992 institutions. The fact that so few adverse reports have been made (except on some international franchising operations) does not suggest that the enormous bureaucratic effort involved has been cost effective. Yet the evident political interest in both major political parties in intervention in the question of academic standards points to the fact that a critical area of institutional autonomy may be subject to renewed challenge in the future.

The impact of high level policy reviews

If we accept that policy making in higher education was mostly reactive, rather than pro-active and that 'disjointed incrementalism' offers the best general description of its development, an unanswered question lies in why major policy reviews were not more successful in significantly altering the fundamental dynamics of the system or in achieving real paradigm change. The Robbins Committee, certainly the most powerful and well resourced review, was successful in its forecast of demand, but in this it did not do much more than extend the projections already arrived at by the UGC. It signally failed to anticipate accurately the financial consequences, and its domination by senior university figures rendered it insufficiently sensitive to the aspirations of local authority leaders so that its structural recommendations were holed below the waterline by Harold Shearman's Note of Reservation to the Report. The 1980 Select Committee review and the Leverhulme funded Inquiry of 1981–83 were effective in informing debate about the future of higher education, but the Select Committee recommendation for a public sector funding body apart, neither produced policy recommendations that were implemented. The Dearing Committee delivered on its primary task, which was to propose a new and workable funding system but its recommendations were undermined by commitments made to the NUS by the new Secretary of State and by the Government's decision to adhere to the budgetary constraints imposed by the previous Government's expenditure review. The Committee's commitment to lifelong learning achieved little traction with a Government that might have been expected to have been sympathetic to it; many other of its recommendations had the effect of increasing bureaucracy without producing tangible change. Its most significant contribution was to argue the case for treating the 1992 merger of the two sectors as creating a unified system which had its own particular needs, but this was contradicted from the outset by the Government's ratcheting up of successive RAEs which served to increase the historic differentiation between institutions. Finally, the 2003 review conducted directly by the Secretary of State, while it solved the long running funding problem in the short term saw the funding mechanism, which it so controversially recommended, overturned within four years by the Browne Review, the recommendations of which were then neutered by the 2010 Comprehensive Spending Review.

The answer seems to be that the resolution of higher education policy issues was almost always better addressed piecemeal. The most powerful drivers of change have not been the considered views of high level 'blue ribbon' reviews but the year to year momentum provided by the pressures of growth, the development of the knowledge economy and its structural implications for institutions, and the impact of political change. The political process has not been able to adjust itself to paradigmic change.

The 'inside out' and the 'outside in' thesis

When higher education was small, policy both in student numbers and in cost (at one stage in the 1950s the egg subsidy alone exceeded the total cost of the universities; Clayton 1988) was largely driven internally, in the university sector by the universities themselves and by the UGC, and in the public sector at local levels with institutions closely integrated with local authorities. The universities clearly won the battle with the NACEIC and the Board of Education in 1953 for additional resources for the expansion of applied science and technology but, in 1964–65, lost the argument to implement the Robbins recommendations to create a unitary, university-led, higher education system. But even after the Woolwich speech and the establishment of the binary line, the sense of a self driven university sector, the so-called 'autonomous sector', continued up to 1979–80 when the impact of reductions in public expenditure created crises on both sides of the binary line. The UGC sought to solve the issues which the cuts raised for the universities by drawing on the traditional values of the sector, restoring the unit of resource at the expense of cutting student numbers and protecting excellence at the expense of other considerations. These values, however, no longer commanded support in the external political environment and a new Secretary of State, Keith Joseph, made it clear that henceforward major issues of policy would be the prerogative of Government. In the public sector the capping of the 'pool' and the creation of NAB sounded the end of uncontrolled funded expansion outside the universities. The 'inside out' approach to policy making had been brought to an end. Neither organizational structure was to survive and by 1992 the funding council system was in place (and devolved to Scotland and Wales), a structure much more adjusted to Conservative party ideology and to successive Governments' desire to steer the system to fit with Government priorities.

The more layers that appeared in the state system of supervision or control the more irrational (in higher education terms) and the less higher education orientated, policy changes became. Policy became much more 'outside in' (Shattock 2006). When, in the university sector, the top layer was the UGC which was closely interconnected with the universities themselves, policy, even when not necessarily to their liking, was consistent and comprehensible. Once PESC entered the decision-making arena, and later when the Department became influential in policy making, with the funding council acting as an active intermediary, policy decisions had a tendency to be fractured, inconsistent and unrelated to higher education realities on the ground. Moreover, the more the framework within which higher education worked – the universities under the UGC, the polytechnics under NAB – was loose, the more institutions could pilot their own development, but the more, after 1992, the framework tightened under the funding council system the more institutions were constrained. Policy shifts at the top, such as the ELQ decision, could have sharp and unlooked for effects on the ground. But, while policy options could be said to have narrowed over the last two decades on the home front, they have undoubtedly widened internationally so that within the same institution decision makers may be at once working within a highly restricted 'home'policy environment, and at the same time in a world of opportunity, internationally. This dichotomy is unhelpful in designing an institutional strategy and can be fraught with risk.

One effect of the position which the universities occupied pre-Robbins, and indeed until 1979–80, was that afterwards the CVCP was always on the defensive arguing for a return to better times. The CDP, however, was on an upward trajectory with every step of their advance, membership of NAB, freedom from the local authorities, conferment of university titles, representing a step away from the arbitrary controls exercised by town halls. In the 1980s, when the universities were on the backfoot, deeply resentful of the cuts, the polytechnics were moving forward and developing close links with DES officials which were to pay off handsomely in the 1987 and 1991 White

Papers. It was always said that Conservative politicians were more sympathetic to polytechnic directors because they displayed more positive attitudes than vice-chancellors but it may be just that they had more to be positive about. The warm relationship did not extend much beyond 1992.

The distinctiveness of British higher education policy making

British higher education is distinctive within Europe and in the wider international community because in a centralized state system it is nevertheless difficult to identify a single centralized locus for policy formulation: policy making is distributed over a wide range of bodies. As the opening paragraphs of this chapter demonstrate particular policy changes have been driven from the Treasury via PES, from the Department (or Departments), from the Cabinet Office itself, from the UGC/NAB/UFC/PCFC, and the funding councils, from the CVCP/CDP/UUK/Russell Group and from the institutions themselves. Policy changes came about much more from these bodies, or subsets of these bodies, interacting with one another, and emerging from a policy web of connected interests, than from clear expressions of the need for policy change, as, for example, from specially commissioned high level external reviews. (Even devolution, which was expected to encourage significant regional variation in policy, has, the tuition fee issue apart, produced only marginal differentiations from approaches adopted in Westminster.) This is not to say that the policy process has not also been driven by personalities: among politicians previous chapters suggest that Joseph, Baker and Blair were exceptional in launching game changing policies while amongst other figures, Murray (UGC), Weaver (DES), Parkes (UGC), Swinnerton Dyer (UGC) and Stoddart (CDP) played critical roles in driving policy change.

An additional distinctive feature has been the role of the Treasury. The Treasury has never been just a Ministry of Finance but has always exercised a wide ranging policy role across departments, augmented in the years 1997 to 2007 by Brown's overlordship of domestic policy in the Blair Government. The Treasury's role was exemplified in the operation of PESC/PES and the fiscal, economic and political values which were intrinsic to the evaluation of departmental bids: the higher education interest was made to compete explicitly with other national priorities in a way that could determine policy at a considerable distance from the point of impact. Under Blair, the Cabinet Office, with its interest in NPM approaches, sought to compete with the Treasury in influence but the 2010 Comprehensive Spending Review decisions might be said to have given the Treasury the last word in higher education policy for the time being. The close involvement of the Treasury, through its role in controlling public expenditure, has had the effect of making higher education policy making more dependent, than in many countries, on the ebb and flow of government policies. It may also have protected it from what might have been more ideological approaches to policy making if policy had resided under the control of a single government department or had been subject to major influence by one or other of the leading political parties.

The higher education community may like to think that it ought to develop its own policies tailored to its own interests but in fact, since 1945, higher education has always been closely integrated with government itself and its interests. What changed was the tone of the relationship. In the earlier period a common culture existed between the university world (but not AFE) and Whitehall. The meeting at UCL in 1969 in which Shirley Williams and her senior officials held a day long meeting with selected members of the UGC, CVCP and the scientific community to explore how to face up to the prospective funding demands of an expanding sector represents a good example of an open discussion between colleagues and equals to find solutions to what were seen as a common problem. But this common culture did not survive the financial traumas of the beginning of the 1980s. It may not have been coincidental that this was the point at which the age participation rate reached around 15 per cent, the figure at which, in Trow's categorization, a system moved from elite to mass higher education. Relations with Whitehall became more distant; with NAB in existence officials had to be even handed in their relations with the two sectors; the funding system encouraged an arm's length relationship. Mass higher education increasingly signalled an increase in state control; with the merger of the two sectors in 1992, universities were no longer special in the way they had been before 1981.

However, the historically held view of institutional autonomy was retained and extended to the new universities. Under local authority control the public sector institutions had had a measure of operational autonomy but lacked the independence of the university sector and were always open to local political intervention. But the 1992 decisions gave with one hand and took away with another. The polytechnics, and later a second generation of higher education colleges, gained autonomy but the enforcement of a research agenda reopened the question of significant institutional differentiation. This was re-emphasized in the 2003 and 2011 White Papers. Institutional autonomy has been a key concept in British higher education and, as the EUA survey demonstrates, represents a further example of British higher education's distinctiveness. Whether it can be sustained, or perhaps sustained in equal measure, however, across all institutions in the face of the pressures imposed by the modern state remains an important policy issue for the future.

Notes

1 Higher education and the policy process

1 Hanney/Kogan Archive, Kogan interview 14 June 1995.

2 Determining the structure of higher education

1 CVCP Archive, Minutes 7 March 1936 Vol 4, MSS 399/1/1/3, Modern Records Centre, University of Warwick.
2 NA, UGC 5/15 quoted in Gosden, P. H. J. (1976) *Education in the Second World War*. London: Methuen.
3 CVCP Archive, Minutes 5 June 1943 Vol 3, MSS 399/1/1/3.
4 CVCP Archive (1945) Memorandum to the Chancellor 'Parliamentary grant to the Universities and University Colleges, Financial Year 1945–46' Vol 4, MSS 399/1/1/4.
5 *Ibid.*
6 *Ibid.*
7 CVCP Archive, *A Note on University Policy and Finance in the Decennium 1946–56* 6 July Vol 4, MSS 399/1/1/4, p. 2.
8 *Ibid.*, p. 14.
9 *Ibid.*, p. 15.
10 *Ibid.*, p. 14.
11 CVCP Archive, Minutes 31 March 1944 Vol 4, MSS 399/1/1/4.
12 NA, UGC 2/24 quoted in Gosden 1976, *op cit.*
13 NA, Ed 136/816 quoted in Benn, R. and Fieldhouse, R. 'Government policies on university expansion and wider access: 1945–51 and 1985–313 compared', *Studies in Higher Education*, 18(3): 297–313.
14 NA, Ed 136/716 quoted in Benn and Fieldhouse, *ibid.*
15 Walsh papers (Walsh, J. J.), interview with Sir James Mountford 13 Sept 1978, MS 1774 Box 1, Leeds University Library.
16 CVCP Archive *A Note on University Policy and Finance in the Decennium 1946–56* 6 July Vol 4, MSS 399/1/1/4 paras 44–6.
17 NA, Ed 136/560 1943 quoted in Gosden 1976, *op cit.*

18 CVCP Archive, Minutes 25 October 1941 Vol 3, MSS 399/1/1/3.
19 NA, Cab 132/1 6 July 1946 quoted in Dean, D. W. (1986) 'Planning for a post war generation: Ellen Wilkinson and George Tomlinson at the Ministry of Education 1945–51', *History of Education*, 15(2): 95–117.
20 CVCP Archive, Minutes 26 October 1944 Vol 4, MSS 399/1/1/4.
21 CVCP Archive, Minutes 27 January 1950 quoting AUT evidence Vol 6, MSS 399/1/1/6.
22 CVCP Archive, 26 October 1944 Vol 4, MSS 399/1/1/4.
23 CVCP Archive, Minutes 22 February 1946 Vol 4, MSS 399/1/1/4.
24 *Ibid.*
25 NA, UGC 1/2 papers of UGC Technological Sub Committee 1950.
26 NA, UGC 7/867 27 March 1952, quoted in Walsh, J. J. (1996) 'Higher Technological Education in Britain: the case of Manchester Municipal College of Technology', *Minerva*, XXXIV(3): 219–57.
27 NA, UGC 1/3 Report on Higher Technological Education 19 March 1953.
28 CVCP Archive, letter from H. V. Lowry *Times Educational Supplement* 5 May 1950 Vol 7, MSS 399/1/1/7.
29 Walsh papers, interview with Sir Anthony Part 1977.
30 *Ibid.*, p. 49.
31 CVCP Archive, Report of a meeting with the Financial Secretary to the Treasury 22 November 1956 Vol 12, MSS 399/1/1/12.
32 CVCP Archive, Report of a meeting with the Financial Secretary to the Treasury 25 January 1962 Vol 17, MSS 399/1/1/17.
33 NA, UGC 7/872 30 April 1953 quoted in Walsh 1996, *op cit.*
34 CVCP Archive, Minutes 26 July 1944 Vol 4, MSS 399/1/1/4.
35 CVCP Archive, Minutes 26 October 1944 Vol 4, MSS 399/1/1/4.
36 NACTST oral evidence to the Robbins Committee, Robbins Report, Evidence Part 1 Vol F para 1822 27 June 1962.
37 CVCP evidence to the Robbins Committee, Evidence Part 1 Vol D 10 November 1961.
38 Ministry of Education evidence to the Robbins Committee, Evidence Part 1 Vol F para 144.
39 *Ibid.*, para 177.
40 *Ibid.*, para 147.
41 CVCP Archive, Minutes 13 December 1963 Vol 20, MSS 399/1/1/20.
42 CVCP Archive, Minutes 13 December 1963 Vol 20, MSS 399/1/1/20.
43 CVCP Archive, Alexander quoted in Minutes 6 February 1964 Vol 20, MSS 399/1/1/2.
44 McConnell papers (McConnell, T. R.), BANC, MSS 89/3c Bancroft Library, Berkeley.
45 NA, Ed 136/955 quoted in Godwin, C. D. (1998) 'The origin of the binary system', *History of Education*, 27(2): 171–91.
46 NA, UGC 7/295 UGC Minutes 21 May 1964 quoted in Godwin 1998, *ibid.*
47 Walsh papers, Lord Murray interview (tape) Box 2.
48 NA, UGC 1/2 Minutes of the main Committee April 1945.
49 CVCP Archive *A Note on University Policy and Finance in the Decennium 1946–56* 6 July Vol 4, MSS 399/1/1/4.
50 CVCP Archive, Minutes 31 January 1947 Vol 4, MSS 399/1/1/4.
51 CVCP Archive, Minutes 28 March 1947 Vol 4, MSS 399/1/1/4.
52 CVCP Archive, Minutes 30 April 1948 Vol 5, MSS 399/1/1/5.

53 CVCP Archive, UGC Minute quoted in CVCP Minute 30 April 1948 Vol 5, MSS 399/1/1/5.

54 Walsh papers, interview with Albert Sloman.

55 Walsh papers, letter from Sir Edward Hale 24 August 1978 Box 3.

56 CVCP Archive, Minutes of meetings on 28 October and 7 December 1955 Vol 11, MSS 399/1/1/11.

57 Walsh papers, Richard Griffiths interview.

58 CVCP Archive, Minutes 23 October 1959 Vol 14, MSS 399/1/1/14.

59 NA, UGC 1/8 Minutes 16 June 1960.

60 NA, UGC 1/8 Minutes 17 November 1960.

61 NA, UGC 1/8 Minutes 26 January 1961.

62 Walsh papers, Lord Murray interview (tape) Box 2.

63 Walsh papers, Richard Griffiths interview.

64 Walsh papers, Lord Morris interview.

65 NA, Cab129/100 24 February 1960, quoted in Hennessey, P. (2006) *Having It So Good: Britain in the Fifties.* London: Allen Lane.

66 Walsh papers, interview with Sir Anthony Part 1977.

67 NA, UGC 1/8 Minutes 26 February 1961.

68 NA, UGC 7/169 New Universities file 14 October 1959, quoted in Shattock, M. L. (1994) *The UGC and the Management of British Universities.* Buckingham: Open University Press, p. 78.

69 NA, UGC 7/169 1959, quoted in Shattock, *ibid.*

70 McConnell papers, interview with Richard Crossman, MP, 31 July 1964.

71 Robinson, E., personal communication.

72 NA, Ed 86/472 paper SSG (64) 1 1964 quoted in Godwin 1998, *op cit.*

73 NA, Ed 86/406 1965 quoted in Godwin 1998, *op cit.*

74 Weaver, Sir T (1979) 'What Future for Higher Education?' The Earl Grey Memorial lecture, University of Newcastle, 3 May 1979, Leeds University Library.

75 *Ibid.*

76 Britton, E. (1964) 'The Future of the Regional Colleges' WUMRC, ATTI Higher Education Advisory Panel, Document 250, 19 November, quoted in Sharp, P. R. (1987) *The Creation of the Local Authority Sector of Higher Education.* London: Falmer Press.

77 Personal interview 1 October 2010.

78 Walsh papers, interview with Sir Herbert Andrew 1977.

79 Walsh papers, Geoffrey Caston interview.

80 Walsh papers, interview with Sir Herbert Andrews 1977.

81 Association of Education Committees A 317 Mr Prentice's advisory group on higher education, Paper no. 5 November 1965, quoted in Gosden 1983.

82 Personal interview 1 October 2010.

83 Walsh papers, interview with Lord Ashby.

84 *Ibid.*

85 CDP Archive, Minutes 13 July 1970, MSS 326/1/1 Box 28. Modern Records Centre, University of Warwick.

86 CVCP Archive, Minutes 11 November 1966 Vol 24, MSS 399/1/1/24.

87 Walsh papers, Geoffrey Caston interview.

88 Department of Education and Science (1965) Note of a meeting between Coventry LEA and Crosland, Lord Bowden, Weaver and Copleston, Secretary of the UGC, quoted in Shattock 1994, *op cit.*

89 CDP Archive, address by Sir William Pile to CDP conference, Coombe Lodge 8–10 April 1974, MSS 326/1/21.

90 CDP Archive, meeting with CLEA 10 January 1975, MSS 326/1/21.
91 CDP Archive, meeting with representatives of the Headmasters' Conference 22 November 1974, MSS 326/1/21.
92 CDP Archive, Professor Terence Miller, CDP Annual Conference at Coombe Lodge 1979, MSS 326/1/23.
93 CDP Archive, meeting with Edward Simpson, 3 February 1976, MSS 326/1/23.
94 *Times Higher Education Supplement* (1981) 30 January.
95 *Ibid.*, 2 February.
96 CDP Archive, paper for meeting on 2 June 1981, MSS 326/1/24.
97 *Education* (1981) 16 October, p. 308.
98 Hanney/Kogan Archive, Kogan interview, 14 June 1995.
99 Hanney/Kogan Archive, Hanney interview, 7 March 1995.
100 Hanney/Kogan Archive, Hanney interview, 7 March 1995.
101 Personal interview, 1 October 2010.
102 *THES* (1981) 30 January; 2 February.
103 CDP Archive, Minutes 3 October 1986, MSS 326/1/55.
104 CDP Archive, Minutes 11 February 1987, MSS 326/1/56.
105 Hanney/Kogan Archive, Hanney interview 27 March 1995.
106 CVCP Files, Address by Secretary of State to CVCP Residential Conference, September 1990.
107 CDP Archive, paper by Laing Barden 25 July 1987, MSS 326/1/57.
108 CVCP Files, paper by Sir Eric Ash, Residential Conference, September 1990.
109 CDP Archive, Address by John McGregor, Secretary of State at Portsmouth Polytechnic 6 June 1990, MSS 326/1/68.
110 CVCP Files, Report of the Joint CVCP, CDP Working Group on Funding Mechanisms 17 August 1990.
111 CDP Archive, Address by John Stoddart to CDP 12 September 1990, MSS 326/1/68.
112 CVCP Files, Minutes of CVCP Council 25 January 1991, report on a dinner between CVCP and CDP 24 January.
113 Hanney/Kogan Archive, Hanney interview 23 April 1997; Personal interview, 8 December 2010.
114 Hanney/Kogan Archive, Hanney interview 23 April 1997.
115 Personal interview, 8 December 2010.
116 CDP Archive, paper by M. Lewis 18 July 1988, MSS 326/1/61.
117 CVCP Archive, CVCP meeting with Crosland 11 November 1966 Vol 24, MSS 399/1/1/24.
118 CDP Archive, Pratt and Locke briefing papers January 1991, MSS 326/1/69.
119 CVCP Archive, Minutes 26 February 1954 Vol 10, MSS 399/1/1/10.
120 McConnell papers, interviews 20 October 1970 and, undated, 1973.
121 NA Treasury files T227/1768 1961.
122 NA Treasury files T227/1772 1961.
123 Ministry of Education evidence to Robbins Committee, Evidence Part 1 Vol F paras 177 and 180.
124 Robbins Report (Committee on Higher Education 1963) Evidence Part 1 Volume D, written and oral evidence. CVCP Memorandum on Relations between Universities and Government para 5.
125 Robbins Report (*ibid.*) Evidence Part 1 Volume D, written and oral evidence, p. 1164.
126 CVCP Archive, reported at meeting 23 September 1986 Vol 46, MSS 399/1/1/46.

127 Hanney/Kogan Archive, Kogan interview 4 April 1995.
128 CVCP Files, Review of the CVCP (the Flowers Report) 9 February 1988.
129 CDP Archive, Minutes of CDP Management Committee 5 May 1992, MSS 326/5/2.
130 Personal information.
131 Personal interview with senior civil servant, 18 March 2011.

3 The financial drivers of higher education policy

1 CVCP Files, Address by Secretary of State to the CVCP Residential Conference, 23 September 1986.
2 Personal interview evidence, 8 December 2010 and 18 March 2011.
3 CVCP Archive, Minutes 17 February 1984 Vol 43, MSS 399/1/1/43.
4 Personal interview evidence, 13 December 2010.
5 Personal interview evidence, 13 December 2010.
6 NA, UGC 1/10 Minutes 17 January 1962.
7 NA, UGC 1/8 Minutes 17 November 1960.
8 NA, UGC 1/10 Minutes 17 January 1962.
9 CVCP Archive, CVCP Statement 26 March 1962 Vol 18, MSS 399/1/1/18.
10 McConnell Papers, interview with Lord Murray 27 May 1976.
11 NA, UGC 1/10 Minutes 21 September 1962.
12 Personel communication.
13 McConnell Papers, interview with Sir Kenneth Berrill 19 September 1973.
14 CVCP Archive, Minutes 25 September 1969 Vol 29 Pt 1, MSS 399/1/1/29a.
15 CVCP Archive, Office Paper VC/74/101 27/28 September 1974 Vol 34, MSS 399/1/1/34.
16 CVCP Archive, Address by Sir Edward Parkes, Chairman of the UGC to the CVCP 24 October 1980 Vol 40, MSS 399/1/1/40.
17 CVCP Archive, Letter from Secretary of State to Chairman of UGC 1 September 1983 Vol 43, MSS 399/1/1/43.
18 CVCP Archive, 3 July 1984 Vol 43, MSS 399/1/1/43.
19 CVCP Archive, *ibid.*
20 CVCP Archive, Report of the Group on Alternative Funding 19 August 1988 Vol 47, MSS 399/1/1/47.
21 CVCP Files, Address by Secretary of State to CVCP Residential Conference 28 September 1988.
22 CVCP Files, Report of the Joint CVCP, CDP Working Group on Funding Mechanisms 17 August 1990.
23 CVCP Files, record of a meeting with the Prime Minister 2 December 1991.
24 CVCP Files, Additional Funding – Progress report, January 1995.
25 CVCP Files, Minutes 2 February 1996.
26 NA Treasury files, draft of evidence to the Robbins Committee, T 227/1768, 1961.
27 Boyd Carpenter, J. A. (1963) The Robbins Report, Memorandum by the Chief Secretary to the Treasury and Paymaster General C (63) 173, para 8. (I am grateful to Professor Gareth Williams for showing me this document.)
28 *Ibid.*, para 13.
29 CVCP Archive, Minutes 17 June 1966 Vol 23, MSS 399/1/1/23.
30 CVCP Archive, Minutes, CVCP Residential Conference 23/25 September 1966 Vol 24, MSS 399/1/1/24.

31 CVCP Archive, Minutes 25 September1969 Vol 29 Pt 1, MSS 399/1/1/29a; Institute of Education, Weaver Archive, WVR 3/39 1969.
32 CVCP Archive, Speech by William Waldegrave, Minister for Higher Education, Westfield College, 17 November 1982 Vol 42, MSS 399/1/1/42.
33 Hanney/Kogan Archive, Hanney interview 13 March 1995.
34 CVCP Archive, Paper VC/70/24 20 February 1970 Vol 29 Pt 2, MSS 399/1/1/29b.
35 CVCP Archive, Minutes 20 February 1970 Vol 29 Pt 2, MSS 399/1/1/29b.
36 McConnell Papers, interview with Sir William Pyle, 2 November 1971.
37 CVCP Archive, Address by Secretary of State to CVCP Residential Conference 23 September 1986 Vol 46, MSS 399/1/1/46.
38 Personal communication from someone present at the Lancaster speech.
39 Hanney/Kogan Archive, Hanney Interview 7 June 1995.
40 CVCP Files, Minutes of CVCP Council meeting 19 January 1990.
41 CVCP Files, CVCP Press Statement 25 October 1990.
42 CDP Archive, Officers and Chairmen meeting 18 November 1987, MSS 326/2/29.
43 CDP Archive, paper by Roger Brown, Secretary of CDP, 9 July 1990, MSS 326/1/68.
44 CVCP Archive, Minutes 27 February 1953 Vol 9, MSS 399/1/1/9.
45 CVCP Archive, Minutes 16 December 1965 Vol 23, MSS 399/1/1/23.
46 Walsh Papers, interview with Sir Herbert Andrews.
47 CVCP Archive, Minutes 28 February and 6 March 1967 Vol 24, MSS 399/1/1/24.
48 CVCP Archive, Minutes 2 January 1970 Vol 29 Pt 2, MSS 399/1/1/29b.
49 CVCP Archive, 26 March 1976 Vol 35, MSS 399/1/1/35.
50 Hanney/Kogan Archive, Kogan interview 4 April 1995.
51 CVCP Archive, Meeting with the Secretary of State 15 October 1979 Vol 39, MSS 399/1/1/39.
52 Personal interview evidence 4 December 2010.
53 Personal interview evidence 13 December 2010.

4 Research and policy

1 CVCP Archive, Evidence to Trend Committee, 22 February 1963 Vol 19, MSS 399/1/1/19.
2 CVCP Archive, Minutes of Special Meeting, 2–3 October 1970 Vol 30 Pt 1, MSS 399 1/1/30a.
3 Ministry of Education (1946) Circular 81, 8 April para 1.
4 CVCP Archive, Address by the Chairman of the UGC to CVCP 24 October 1980 Vol 40, MSS 399/1/1/40, original emphasis.
5 CVCP Archive, Minutes 17 February 1984 Vol 43, MSS 399/1/1/43.
6 CVCP Archive, Minutes 17 February 1984 Vol 43, MSS 399/1/1/43, original emphasis.
7 CVCP Archive, Speech by Sir Keith Joseph at an SRHE/*THES* Conference 9 July 1985 Vol 43, MSS 399/1/1/43.
8 UGC Letter to universities, *Planning for the Late 1980s: The Resource Allocation Process*, 19 November 1985.
9 *The Government's Response to the Lambert Review 2004 Science and Innovation Investment 2004–2014* p. 176.
10 HEFCE *Funding Higher Education in England* 2007/20 July.

11 Royal Society, *The Royal Society's Response to the White Paper, The Future of Higher Education* 2003.
12 HEFCE *RAE 2008: the outcome RAE* 01/2008 18 December.

5 The politics of accountability

1 CVCP Archive, Speech by Sir Keith Joseph at an SRHE/*THES* conference 9 July 1985 Vol 43, MSS 399/1/1/43.
2 CVCP Archive, Minutes 15 January 1988 Vol 47, MSS 399/1/1/47.
3 PAC *Third Report 1948–49* London: HMSO HC 233.
4 Select Committee on Estimates, *Fifth Report 1951–52* London: HMSO HC 163, quoted in Shinn, C. H. (1986) *Paying the Piper.* Lewes: Falmer Press.
5 NA, Treasury files T227/1768 1961.
6 PAC Report, *Parliament and the Control of University Expenditure*, Session 1966–67 London: HMSO HC 290 20 January 1967, UGC oral evidence para 1037.
7 PAC 21st Report Session 1993–95 *The Financial Health of Institutions in England* HC 139 May 1995.
8 PAC *Third Report, Use of Capacity*, Session 1969–70, London: HMSO HC 297 29 April 1970.
9 PAC *Tenth Report, Assessment of Universities' Grant Needs and Staff: Student Ratios* Session 1980–81, London: HMSO HC 233 June 1981, para 10.
10 CVCP Archive, Letter to the Secretary of State, 10 July 1984 Vol 43, MSS 399/1/1/43.
11 PAC *41st Report, Redundancy Payments to University Staff* Session 1985–86 London: HMSO HC 179 30 June 1986, paras 24 and 25.
12 PAC *1st Report, Financial Problems in Universities* Session 1989–90 London: HMSO HC 136 January 1990, para 2(d).
13 PAC *36th Report, Restructuring and Finances of Universities* Session 1989–90 London: HMSO HC 258 11 July 1990 Recommendations (i) and (IX).
14 PAC Report, *Parliament and the Control of University Expenditure* Session 1966–67 London: HMSO HC 290 20 January 1967, Lord Murray oral evidence para 782.
15 CVCP Archive, *Use of University Capacity*, A study by K. S. Davies, 1967 Vol 25, MSS 399/1/1/25.
16 PAC *36th Report, Regulating Financial Sustainability in Higher Education* Session 2010–11 London: SO HC 914 June 2011, para 11.
17 *Ibid.*
18 CVCP Files, Letter from the Secretary of State, John Patten, to the Chairman of the CVCP 21 September 1994.
19 Hanney/Kogan Archive, Kogan interview 23 April 1997.
20 CVCP files, 28 September 1988.
21 Personal interview 3 March 2011.
22 CVCP files, 25 September 1991.
23 HEFCE, *Assessment of the Quality of Education* February 3/93 1993.
24 HEFCE, *The Quality Assessment Method from April 1995* December 39/94 1994 quoted in Brown 2004.
25 Personal interview, senior civil servant, 4 December 2010.

26 QAA 2011 www.qaa.ac.uk/about us, and institutional review.
27 Personal interview 3 March 2011.
28 Trow, M. (1994) 'Managerialism and the academic profession: quality control', *Higher Education Report* 2, Quality Control Centre, quoted in Brown, 2004 p. 88.
29 HEFCE (2009) Strategic Plan 2006–2011, updated, HEFCE 2009/21.

6 Making policy at the institutional level

1 UGC 1936 Letter from Secretary of UGC to Nottingham University College, quoted in Shinn, C. H. (1986) *Paying the Piper: The Development of the University Grants Committee 1919–1946*. London: Falmer Press, p.125.
2 CVCP Archive, paper by Lord Annan, CVCP special meeting 2–3 October 1970 Vol 30, MSS 399/1/1/30.
3 CVCP Archive, Address by Sir Alex Jarratt to CVCP, 29 October 1985 Vol 45, MSS 399/1/1/45.
4 Hanney/Kogan Archive, Hanney interview 28 April 1994.
5 *Ibid.*
6 CDP Archive, Minutes 22 December 1987 Vol 47, MSS 399/1/1/47.
7 CDP Archive, Minutes of meeting 11–13 April 1988, MSS 326/1/61.
8 CDP Archive, Letter from Kenneth Green to Secretary of State, 28 March 1988, MSS 326/1/61.
9 Morgan, J. *Times Higher Education*, 7 October 2010.
10 Institute of Education Archive, DC/WVR 1/1.77 Weaver, Sir Toby, Address to polytechnic directors at Blagdon, 9 December 1969.
11 CVCP files, 'Modular Curriculum and Structure' CVCP June 1991.
12 CVCP files, 25 September 1991.

References

ABRC (Advisory Board of the Research Councils) (1987) *A Strategy for the Science Base.* London: HMSO.

Advisory Council for Applied Research and Development (1983) *Improving Research Links between Higher Education and Industry.* London: HMSO.

Aitken, R. (1966) *Administration of a University.* London: University of London Press.

Aldritch, R. (2002) *The Institute of Education 1902–2002.* London: Institute of Education, University of London.

Alexander, Sir W. M. (1964) Editorial: Training College Prospects, *Education*, 18 December.

Annan, Lord (1987) The Reform of Higher Education in 1986, *History of Education*, 16(3): 217–26.

Ashby, E. (1958) *Technology and the Academics.* London: Macmillan.

Association of Universities of the British Commonwealth (1958) *Home Universities Conference, Report of Proceedings.* London: Association of Universities of the British Commonwealth.

Austin, D. (1982) Salva sit universitas nostra: a memoir, *Government and Opposition*, 17: 469–89.

AUT (Association of University Teachers) (1944) *Report on University Development Pt 1*, AUT March.

AUT (Association of University Teachers) (1958) *Report on a Policy for University Expansion.* London: AUT.

Baker, Lord (1993) *The Turbulent Years: My Life in Politics.* London: Faber and Faber.

Baker, Lord (2010) The Queen's shilling is no sovereign remedy for a world class sector, *Times Higher Education*, 9 September.

Ball, Sir Christopher (1990) *More Means Different.* London: RSA.

Barnett, C. (1986) *The Audit of War.* London: Macmillan.

Benington, J. (ed.) (2007) *Reforming Public Services.* TSO National School of Government.

Berdahl, R. O. (1959) *British Universities and the State.* Berkeley, CA: University of California Press.

Berdahl, R. O. (1962) University–state relations re-examined, *Keele Sociological Review*, 15–29.

Bird, R. (1994) Reflections on the British Government and higher education in the 1980s, *Higher Education Quarterly*, 48(2): 73–85.

BIS (Department of Business, Innovation and Skills) (2011a) *Estimating the Value to the UK of Education Exports.* Research paper no. 46.

BIS (2011b) *Higher Education: Students at the Heart of the System,* CM 8122 June. London: Stationery Office.

Blair, Tony (2010) *A Journey.* London: Hutchinson.

Bocock, J., Baston, L., Scott, P. and Smith, D. (2003) American Influence on British higher education: science, technology and the problem of university expansion, *Minerva,* XLI(4): 327–46.

Booth, Sir Clive (1983) DES and Treasury, in A. Morris and J. Sizer (eds) *Resources and Higher Education.* Guildford: SRHE.

Booth, Sir Clive (1999) The rise of the New Universities in Britain, in D. Smith and A. K. Langslow (eds) *The Idea of a University.* London: Jessica Kingsley.

Boyle, Lord (1979) *Government, Parliament and the Robbins Report,* Joseph Payne Memorial lecture 1979, Series of the College of Preceptors, 31 March. London: College of Preceptors, Bloomsbury House.

Boyson, R. (1995) *Speaking My Mind.* London: Peter Owen.

Briggs, Lord (1991) A founding father reflects, *Higher Education Quarterly,* 45(4): 311–32.

Brown, E. J. (1953) *Private Donors in the History of the University of Leeds,* University of Leeds.

Brown, R. (2004) *Quality Assurance in Higher Education: The UK Experience Since 1992.* London: Routledge.

Browne, J. D. (1979) *Teachers of Teachers: A History of the Association of Teachers in Colleges and Departments of Education.* London: Hodder and Stoughton.

Browne Report (2010) *Securing a Sustainable Future for Higher Education* www.independent.gov.uk 12 October (accessed 17 May 2012).

Burgess, T. (2005) Obituary of Sir Edward Britton, *Guardian,* 7 January.

Burgess, T. (2001) Obituary of Sir Toby Weaver, *Guardian,* 13 June.

Burniston, S., Rogers, J. and Brass, J. (1999) *Enterprise in Higher Education: Changing the Mindset.* London: DfEE Research brief No 117.

Cabinet Office (1987) *Civil Research and Development: Government Response to the First Report of the House of Lords Select Committee on Science and Technology 1986–87 Session* CM 185. London: HMSO.

Campbell, J. (2000) *Margaret Thatcher: Vol 1 The Grocer's Daughter.* London: Pimlico.

Carswell, J. (1985) *Government and the Universities.* Cambridge: Cambridge University Press.

CIHE (Council for Industry and Higher Education) (1987) *Towards a Partnership, Higher Education-Government-Industry.* London: CIHE.

CIHE (1988) *Towards a Partnership: The Company Response.* London: CIHE.

Clark, B. R. (1998) *Creating Entrepreneurial Universities.* Oxford: Pergamon.

Clayton, K. (1988) Recent developments in the funding of university research, *Higher Education Quarterly,* 42(1): 20–7.

Collingwood, R. G. (1993) *The Idea of History* (ed. T. M. Knox). New York: Oxford University Press.

Committee on Higher Education (the Robbins Report) (1963) *Higher Education: A Report* Cmnd 2154. London: HMSO.

Committee on Scientific Manpower (the Barlow Report) (1946) *Report* Cmnd 6824. London: HMSO.

CPRS (Central Policy Review Staff) (1977) *Population and the Social Services: Report.* London: HMSO.

Crequer, N. (1989) The passing of the Education Reform Act, *Higher Education Quarterly*, 43(1): 3–19.

Crosland, Susan (1982) *Tony Crosland*. London: Jonathan Cape.

Crossman, R. (1975) *Diaries of a Cabinet Minister* Vol 1. London: Hamish Hamilton and Jonathan Cape.

Crowther Hunt, Lord (1983) Policy making and accountability in higher education, in M. L. Shattock (ed.) *The Structure and Governance of Higher Education*. Guildford: SRHE.

CVCP (Committee of Vice Chancellors and Principals) (1970) *University Development in the 1970s*. London: CVCP.

CVCP (1972) *Report of the Inquiry into the Use of Academic Staff Time*. London: CVCP.

CVCP (the Jarratt Report) (1985) *Report of the Steering Committee for Efficiency Studies in Universities*. London: CVCP.

Dahrendorf, R. (1995) *A History of the London School of Economics and Political Science 1895–1995*. Oxford: OUP.

Daiches, D. (1964) *The Idea of a New University*. London: Andre Deutsch.

Darling, A. (2010) The love of common sense, a review of Blair's *The Journey*, *Guardian*, 11 September.

Darling, A. (2011) *Back from the Brink*. London: Atlantic Books.

Dean, D. W. (1986) Planning for a post war generation: Ellen Wilkinson and George Tomlinson at the Ministry of Education 1945–51, *History of Education*, 15(2): 95–117.

Deem, R., Hillyard, S. and Reed, M. (2007) *Knowledge, Higher Education and the New Managerialism*. Oxford: OUP.

Denham, A. and Garnett, M. (2001) *Keith Joseph*. Chesham: Acumen.

DES (Department of Education and Science) (1965) *Secretary of State's Speech at Woolwich Polytechnic 27 April 1965*. Admin. Memo 7/65.

DES (1966a) *A Plan for Polytechnics and other Colleges*, Cmnd 3006. London: HMSO.

DES (1966b) *The Government of Colleges of Education, Report of the Study Group*. London: HMSO.

DES (1970) *Student Numbers in Higher Education in England and Wales, Planning Paper No 2*. London: HMSO.

DES (1972a) *Education: A Framework for Expansion*, Cmnd 5174. London: HMSO.

DES (the James Report) (1972b) *Teacher Education and Training*. London: HMSO.

DES (1981) *Higher Education in England Outside the Universities: Policy, Funding and Management*. London: DES.

DES (1985) *The Development of Higher Education into the 1990s*, Cmnd 9524. London: HMSO.

DES (1987) *Higher Education: Meeting the Challenge*, Cmnd 114. London: HMSO.

DES (1991) *Higher Education: A New Framework*, Cmnd 1541. London: HMSO.

DES/SED (Department of Education and Science/Scottish Education Department) (1978) *Higher Education into the 1990s: A Discussion Document*. London: DES.

DfES (Department for Education and Skills) (2000) Grant letter from the Secretary of State to the Chairman of HEFCE, 29 November.

DfES (2003) *The Future of Higher Education*, Cm 5735. London: HMSO.

Dodds, H. W., Hacker, L. M. and Rogers, L. (1952) *Government Assistance to Universities in Great Britain*. Memoranda submitted to the Commission on Financing Higher Education. New York: Columbia.

Donoughue, Lord B. (1986) *Prime Minister: The Conduct of Policy Under Harold Wilson and James Callaghan*. London: Jonathan Cape.

DSIR (1965) *Report of the Research Council for the Year, 1964*, Cmnd 2394. London: HMSO.

DTI, HM Treasury and DfES (2002) *Investing in Innovation: A Strategy for Science, Engineering and Technology*. London: SO.

Editor, *The Times* (1992) 14 October.

Education (1965) Editorial, *Education*, 2 April p. 659.

Esterman, T., Nokkala, T. and Steinal, M. (2011) *University Autonomy in Europe 11*. Brussels: European Universities Association.

Flexner, A. (1930) *Universities, American, English and German*. Oxford: OUP.

Gallie, W. B. (1960) *A New University: A.D. Lindsay and the Keele Experiment*. London: Chatto and Windus.

Gardner, J. (2011) *The Blitz*. London: Harper Collins.

Gibbs, G. (2010) *Dimensions of Quality*. The Higher Education Academy.

Gladstone, W. E. (1850) UK Parliament *Hansard Third Series* Vol 112 p. 1495.

Glennester, H. (1990) Social policy since the Second World War, in J. Hills, (ed.) *The Welfare State in Britain since 1974*. Oxford: Clarendon Press.

Glennester, H. and Low, W. (1990) Education and the Welfare State, in J. Hills (ed.) *The Welfare State in Britain since 1974*. Oxford: Clarendon Press.

Godwin, C. D. (1998) The origin of the binary system, *History of Education*, 27 (2): 171–91.

Gosden, P. H. J. (1976) *Education in the Second World War*. London: Methuen.

Gosden, P. H. J. (1983) *The Education System Since 1944*. Oxford: Martin Robertson.

Halsey, A. H. (1992) *Decline of Donnish Dominion*. Oxford: Clarendon Press.

Halsey, A. H. (1996) *No Discouragement: An Autobiography*. Macmillan: Palgrave.

Harrison, M., Lockwood, B. Miller, M. et al. (2001) Higher education: trial by ordeal, *Guardian*, 30 January.

Harte, N. (1986) *The University of London 1836–1986*. London: Athlone Press.

Heclo, H. and Wildavsky, A. (1981) *The Private Governance of Public Money*. London: Macmillan.

HEFCE (Higher Education Funding Council for England) (2010) Model Financial Memorandum between HEFCE and institutions, HEFCE 2010/19 July.

Henkel, M. (2000) *Academic Identities and Policy Change in Higher Education*. London: Jessica Kingsley.

Henkel, M. (2007) Changes in the governance and management of the university: the role of governments and third party agencies, in *Changing Governance in Higher Education: Incorporation, Marketization and other Reforms – A Comparative Study*. Hiroshima: COE Publications, Hiroshima Research Institute of Higher Education.

Hennessey, P. (1990) *Whitehall*. London: Harper Collins, Fontana Press.

Hennessey, P. (1992) *Never Again: Britain 1945–51*. London: Penguin.

Hennessey, P. (2006) *Having It So Good: Britain in the Fifties*. London: Allen Lane.

HEPI (Higher Education Policy Institute) (2011) *Higher Education: Students at the Heart of the System – An Analysis of the Higher Education White Paper*. Oxford: HEPI.

HM Treasury (the Plowden Report) (1961) *Control of Public Expenditure*, Cmnd 1432. London: HMSO.

HM Treasury (1970) *Reorganisation of Central Government*, Cmnd 4506. London: HMSO.

HM Treasury (1976) *Cash Limits on Expenditure*, Cmnd 6440. London: HMSO.

HM Treasury (1980) *The Government's Expenditure Plans 1980–81*, Cmnd 7746. London: HMSO.

Hogan, J. (2005) Should form follow function? Changing academic structures in UK universities, *Perspectives*, 19(2): 49–57.

Hutchins, R. M. (1952) *The Higher Learning in America*. New Haven: Yale University Press.

Illingworth, Sir C. (1971) *University Statesman: The Story of Sir Hector Hetherington*. Glasgow: George Outram & Co. Ltd.

Innovation, Universities Science and Skills Select Committee (2009) *Students and Universities, Eleventh Report of Session 2008–09*, HC170–1 Vol 1. London: SO.

Ives, E., Drummond, D. and Schwarz, L. (2000) *The First Civic University: Birmingham 1880–1980*. Birmingham: University of Birmingham.

Jeffries, K. (1999) *Anthony Crosland*. London: Metro Books.

Jenkins, S. (2006) *Thatcher and Sons: A Revolution in Three Acts*. London: Allen and Lane.

Johnstone, B. and Marlucci, P. N. (2010) *Financing Higher Education Worldwide, Who Pays? Who Should Pay?* Baltimore, CA: Johns Hopkins Press.

Jones, S. and Kiloh, G. (1987) The management of polytechnics and colleges, in T. Becher (ed.) *British Higher Education*. London: Allen and Unwin.

Joseph, Sir K. (1982) Letter to the Chairman of the UGC, 17 July.

Jump, P. (2011) Poacher who rather enjoys game keeping, *THE*, 27 October.

Kelsall, K. K. (1957) *Report on an Inquiry into Applications for Admission to Universities*. London: Association of Universities of the British Commonwealth.

King, R., Griffiths, P. and Williams, R. (2007) Regulating intermediation and quality assurance in higher education: the case of the auditors, *Oxford Review of Education*, 33(2): 161–74.

Knight, P. (2007) After the storm, a brighter era dawned, *Guardian*, 20 March.

Kogan, M. (1971) *The Politics of Education*. London: Penguin Books.

Kogan, M. and Hanney, S. (2000) *Reforming Higher Education*. London: Jessica Kingsley.

Kolbert, J. M. (2000) *Keele, The First Fifty Years*. Keele: Melandrium Books.

Labour Party (1962) *The Years of Crisis, Report of the Labour Party's Study Group on Higher Education*. London: Labour Party.

Lawler, J. (writing as James Dundonald) (1968) Advice to an Alderman, in J. Lawler (ed.) *The New University*. London: Routledge and Kegan Paul.

Lawson, N. (1992) *The View from No 11*. London: Boston.

Lee, M. (1998) Overseas students in Britain: How their presence was politicised in 1966–67, *Minerva*, XXXVI (4):305–21.

Lindblom, C. E. (1965) *The Intelligence of Democracy*. New York: Free Press.

Lowe, R. (1988) *Education in the Post War Years: A Social History*. London: Routledge.

Major, J. (1999) *The Autobiography*. London: Harper Collins.

Mandleson, P. (2010) *The Third Man*. London: Harper Collins.

March, J. G. and Olsen, J. P. (1996) Institutional perspectives on political institutions, *Governance*, 9(3): 248–64.

Merrison Report (1982) *Report of a Joint Working Party on the Support of University Scientific Research*, Cmnd 8567. London: HMSO.

Middleton, R. (1996) *Government Versus the Market*. Cheltenham: Edward Elgar.

Ministry of Education (the McNair Report) (1944) *Committee on Teachers and Youth Leaders, Report*. London: Ministry of Education.

Ministry of Education (the Percy Report) (1945) *Special Committee on Higher Technological Education, Report*. London: HMSO Ministry of Education.

Ministry of Education (1951) *Higher Technological Education*, Cmnd 8357. London: HMSO.

Ministry of Education (1956) *Technical Education*, Cmnd 9703. London: HMSO.

Minogue, M. (1983) Theory and practice in public policy and administration, *Policy and Politics*, 11: 63–85.

Moberly, W. (1949) *The Crisis in the University*. London: SCM Press Ltd.

Moodie, G. C. and Eustace, R. B. (1974) *Power and Authority in British Universities*. London: Allen and Unwin.

Morris, A. and Sizer, J. (eds) (1983) *Resources and Higher Education*. Milton Keynes: SRHE/Open University Press.

Mountford, Sir James (1972) *Keele, A Historical Critique*. London: Routledge and Kegan Paul.

Mullin, C. (2009) *A View from the Foothills*. London: Profile Books.

NAB (National Advisory Body for Public Sector higher Education) (1983) *Strategy for Public Sector Higher Education into the 1990s*. NAB, February.

NAB (National Advisory Body for Public Sector Higher Education) (1987) *Management for a Purpose*. London: NAB.

National Advisory Council on Education for Industry and Commerce (1950) *The Future Development of Higher Technological Education*. London: HMSO, 14 November.

NCIHE (National Committee of Inquiry into Higher Education) (the Dearing Report) (1997) *Higher Education in the Learning Society*. London: HMSO.

NEDC (National Economic Development Committee) (1963) *Growth of the United Kingdom Economy up to 1966*. London: HMSO.

NEDC (1963) *Conditions Favourable to Foster Growth*. London: HMSO.

OECD (1975) *Education Development Strategy in England and Wales*. Paris: OECD.

PAC (Public Accounts Committee) (1967) *Parliament and the Control of University Expenditure*. London: HMSO, HC 290.

PAC (Public Accounts Committee) (1982) *11th Report*: Assessment of universities' grant needs. Oral evidence. London: HMSO, HC 175 31 March.

PAC (Public Accounts Committee) (1990) *Financial Problems of Universities: First Report* HC 136 Session 1989–90. London: HMSO.

Palfreyman, D. P. (2012) Bring back Lord Robbins, *Perspectives*, 16(3): 98–102.

Parkes, Sir Edward (1982) Evidence to the Public Accounts Committee, *Eleventh Report Session 1981–82*. London: HMSO, HC 175 3 February.

Perkin, H. J. (1970) *New Universities in the United Kingdom, Case Studies in Innovation*. Paris: OECD.

Peston, M. (1976) The education of vice chancellors, *New Universities Quarterly*, 30(2): 177–87.

Pratt, J. (1997) *The Polytechnic Experiment 1965–1992*. Buckingham: Open University Press.

Pratt, J. (1999) Policy and policy making in the unification of higher education, *Journal of Education Policy*, 14(3): 257–69.

Pratt, J. and Burgess, T. (1974) *The Polytechnics: A Report*. London: Pitman.

Pullen, B. with Abendstern, M. (2004) *A History of the University of Manchester 1973–1990*. Manchester: Manchester University Press.

Rawnsley, A. (2010) *The End of the Party, the Rise and Fall of New Labour*. London: Viking, Penguin Books.

Robbins, Lord and Ford, B. (1965) Report on Robbins, *Universities Quarterly*, 20(1): 5–16.

Robbins, L. (1966) *The University in the Modern World*. London: Macmillan.

Robinson, E. (1968) *The New Polytechnics*. London: Cornmarket.

Rourke, F. E. and Brooks, G. E. (1966) *Managerial Revolution in Higher Education*. Baltimore, MD: Johns Hopkins University Press.

Sabatier, P. A. (1986) Top-down and bottom-up processes to implementation research: a critical analysis and suggested synthesis, *Journal of Public Policy*, 6: 21–48.

Salter, B. and Tapper, T. (1994) *The State and Higher Education*. Ilford: Woburn Press.

Scott, P. (1995) *The Meaning of Mass Higher Education*. Buckingham: Open University Press.

Scottish Tertiary Education Advisory Committee (1985) *Future Strategy for Higher Education in Scotland*, Cmnd 9676. London: HMSO.

Select Committee on Education, Science and Arts (1980a) *Interim Report on Overseas Students' Fees* London: HMSO, HC552–1, 16 April.

Select Committee on Education, Science and Arts (1980b) *The Funding and Organisation of Courses in Higher Education, Volume 1, Report* and *Volume 11, Minutes of Evidence*. London: HMSO, HC 787–1, September.

Select Committee on Education, Science and Arts (1981) Evidence from Sir Edward Parkes, 23 July.

Sharp, P. R. (1987) *The Creation of the Local Authority Sector of Higher Education*. London: Falmer Press.

Shattock, M. L. (1970) A changing pattern of university administration, *Universities Quarterly*, 24(3): 310–20.

Shattock, M. L. (1988) Financial management in universities: the lessons from University College, Cardiff, *Financial Accountability and Management*, 4(2): 99–112.

Shattock, M. L. (1994) *The UGC and the Management of British Universities*. Buckingham: Open University Press.

Shattock, M. L. (2003) Research, administration and university management: what can research contribute to policy?, in R. Begg (ed.) *The Dialogue between Higher Education Research and Practice*. Dordrecht: Kluwer Academic Publishers.

Shattock, M. L. (2006) Policy drivers in UK higher education in historical perspective: 'inside out' and 'outside in' and the contribution of research, *Higher Education Quarterly*, 60(1): 115–30.

Shattock, M. L. (2008) The change from private to public governance of British higher education: its consequences for higher education policy making 1980–2006, *Higher Education Quarterly*, 62(3): 181–208.

Shattock, M. L. (2012) Parallel worlds, the California Master Plan and the development of British higher education, in S. Rothblatt (ed.) *Clark Kerr's World of Higher Education Reaches the 21st Century*. Dordrecht: Springer.

Shattock, M. L. and Rigby, G. (eds) (1983) *Resource Allocation in British Universities*. Guildford: SRHE.

Simon, E. (1946) The Universities and Government, *Universities Quarterly*, 1: 79–95.

Sizer, J. (1987) *Institutional Responses to Financial Reductions in the University Sector: Report of a Research Project*. London: DES.

Sloman, A. (1963) *A University in the Making*. London: BBC.

Smith, G. and May, D. (1980) The artificial debate between rationalist and incrementalist models of decision making, *Policy and Politics*, 8: 147–61.

Snow, C. P. (1934) *The Search*. London: Victor Gollancz.

Snow, C. P. (1962) *Science and Government*. New York: The New American Library.

SRC (Science Research Council) (1970) *Selectivity and Concentration in the Support of Research*. London: HMSO.

Stewart, W. A. C. (1989) *Higher Education in Post War Britain*. Basingstoke: Macmillan.

Stoddart, J. (1992) *Direct* CDP No 4 July–August.

Swinnerton Dyer, P. (1991) Policy on higher education and research, *Higher Education Quarterly*, 45(3): 204–18.

Taggart, G. J. (2004) *A critical review of the role of the English Funding Body for Higher Education in the relationship between the State and Higher Education in the period 1945–2003*. ED thesis, Bristol.

Tapper, T. (2007) *The Governance of British Higher Education*. Dordrecht: Springer.

Thain, C. and Wright, M. (1995) *The Treasury and Whitehall: The Planning and Control of Public Expenditure 1976–93*. Oxford: Clarendon Press.

Thatcher, M. (1995) *The Path to Power*. London: Harper Collins.

Tight, M. (2010) Are academic work loads increasing? The post war survey evidence in the UK, *Higher Education Quarterly*, 64(2): 200–16.

Trend Committee (1963) *Committee of Enquiry into the Organisation of Civil Science*, Cmnd 2171. London: HMSO.

Trow, M. (1963) Robbins: a question of size, *Universities Quarterly*, 18: 136–52.

Truscot, B. (1943) *Red Brick University*. London: Faber and Faber.

Truscot, B. (1945) *Red Brick and these Vital Days*. London: Faber and Faber.

Truscot, B. (1951) *Red Brick University*. Harmondsworth: Penguin.

UGC (University Grants Committee) (1948) *University Development from 1936–1947*. London: HMSO.

UGC (1950) *A Note on Technology in Universities*. London: UGC.

UGC (1958) *University Development 1952–57*. London: HMSO.

UGC (1964) *University Development 1957–62*, Cmnd 2267. London: HMSO.

UGC (1968) *University Development*, Cmnd 532. London: HMSO.

UGC (1979) *Report on Russian and Russian Studies in British Universities*. London: UGC HMSO.

UGC (1984) *A Strategy for Higher Education into the 1990s*. London: UGC.

UGC (1985) *UGC's response to the Green Paper on Higher Education*. London: UGC.

UGC (the Oxburgh Report) (1987) *Strengthening University Earth Sciences*. London: HMSO UGC.

Universities Bureau of the British Empire (1946) *Conference of Home Universities 1946, Report of Proceedings*. London: University Bureau of the British Empire.

Universities Bureau of the British Empire (1955) *Conference of Home Universities 1955, Report of Proceedings*. London: Universities' Bureau of the British Empire.

University of Oxford (the Franks Report) (1964) *Report of a Commission of Inquiry under the Chairmanship of Lord Franks*. Oxford: University of Oxford.

University of Oxford (the North Report) (1997) *Commission of Inquiry, Supplementary Volume*. Oxford: OUP.

Venables, Sir P. (1978) *Higher Education Development: The Technological Universities 1956–76*. London: Faber.

Walden, G. (1996) *We Should Know Better: Solving the Education Crisis*. London: Fourth Estate.

Walsh, J. J. (1996) Higher Technological Education in Britain: the case of Manchester Municipal College of Technology, *Minerva*, XXXIV(3): 219–57.

Watson, D. and Amoah, M. (2007) *The Dearing Report Ten Years On*. London: Institute of Education, Bedford Way Papers.

Watson, D. and Bowden, R. (1999) Why did they do it? The Conservatives and mass higher education, *Journal of Education Policy*, 14(3): 243–56.

Weaver, T. (1965) Higher education and local government, *Education*, 20 August.

Weaver, T. (1973) *Higher Education and the Polytechnics*, The Joseph Payne Memorial Lecture 1973–4 of the College of Preceptors. London: College of Preceptors, Bloomsbury House.

Weaver, Sir T. (1994) Knowledge gets you nowhere, *Capability*, 1(1): 6–12.

Whitburn, J., Mealing, M. and Cox, C. (1976) *People in Polytechnics*. Guildford: SRHE.

Whitchurch, C. (2012) *Reconstructing Identities in Higher Education: The Rise of 'Third Space' Professionals*. London: Routledge.

Whitehead, A. N. (1929) *The Aims of Education and Other Essays*. New York: Free Press.

Wiener, M. (1981) *English Culture and the Decline of the Industrial Spirit*. Cambridge: Cambridge University Press.

Williams, G. L. (2004) The Higher Education Market in the United Kingdom, in P. Teixira, B. Jongbloed, D. Dill and A. Amaral (eds) *Markets in Higher Education*. Dordrecht: Kluwer Academic Publishers.

Williams, P. (2009) *The Result of Intelligent Effort: Two Decades in the Quality Assurance of Higher Education*. London: Institute of Education.

Williams, R. (1997) Reflections on Cornford's Cambridge and the present dilemmas of British higher education, *Minerva*, 34: 63–72.

Index

Locators shown in *italics* refer to figures and tables.
The term higher education has been abbreviated to HE throughout this index.

Dundee Institute of Art and
Technology, 28
Dundee University, 184
Dundonald, J., 52
Durrand, 73
Durham University, 19, 20, 26, 36, 99,
129

Eccles, D., 27–8
Economic and Social Research Council
(ESRC), 173
economy, national
feature and importance at time of
Robbins expansion, 137, 140–41,
140
impact as driver of HE funding,
103–17, 104, 107, 112–13
impact of institutional differentiation,
180–83
see also expenditure, public
Edinburgh University, 100, *129*, 219,
236
education, further
Hankey report on, 11, 12, 17
education, schools of
proposed development within
universities, 32, 33–5
see also colleges of education
education, teacher
evolution of university policy
involvement, 31–43
James report on, 42–3, 68
role of local education authorities,
19, 23, 24, 27–8, 29, 30–31,
31–43
role of Ministry in changing
governance structures, 89, 93–4
see also colleges of education
education, technical
debates, policies and structuring of
early post-war, 19–31
research as an objective of technical
colleges, 171
role of local education authorities, 19,
23, 24, 27–8, 29, 30–31
White Paper on Technical Education
1956, 27, 47–8, 89
education, technology
role of local education authorities, 19,
23, 24, 27–8, 29, 30–31

education, vocational
approach to in post war debates, 9–10
as an argument for the introduction
of binary line, 57, 60
East Anglia University rejection of, 53
problems of perception and university
status, 20–22
decline in the proportion of
vocational studies in polytechnics,
84
Education: a Framework for Expansion
(1972), 68, 69, 146–7
Education, Science and Arts Select
Committee, 71, 76, 126, 160
Education (journal), 66
Education Act (1944), 13, 22, 31
Education Reform Act (1988), 79, 98
efficiency, economic
impact as driver of HE funding,
103–17, 104, 107, 112–13
*Efficiency Studies in Universities Steering
Committee Report* (Jarratt, 1985), 106,
115, 220–21, 222
EHE (Enterprise in Higher Education)
programme, 233
elitism, higher education
criticism by Robinson and Weaver, 57
transformation from to mass HE,
68–87, 76
Equivalent or Lower Qualifications
(ELQs), 237
Elvin, L., 35
engineering
Finniston report on profession of,
232–3
*English Culture and the Decline of the
Industrial Spirit* (Wiener), 96
Enterprise in Higher Education (EHE)
programme, 233
entry, university
evidence of falling standards, 47
ESRC (Economic and Social Research
Council), 173
Essex University, 46, *49*, 50, 122, 193–4,
219
esteem, parity of
failure of binary line wish for, 84–5
Esterman, T., 236
European Universities Association
(EUA), 236–7, 242, 254

HE structures and, 9, 11, 13, 15, 16, 18, 24–5, 26, 27, 28, 30, 31, 34, 38, 47, 48, 50, 51, 64, 66, 70, 71, 74, 78, 81, 82, 88, 89, 90–91, 92, 93, 102
institutional level policy making and, 217, 219, 220, 236, 237, 238, 239–40
players and institutions in policy process and, 244–5, 246, 247, 248, 249, 253
politics of accountability and, 189–90, 191, 192–3, 196, 208
research and policy and, 174, 180, 183
see also Public Expenditure Survey Committee (PESC) process; Public Expenditure Surveys; Jarratt Committee report; University Grants Committee (UGC)
Trend, B., 91
Trend Committee report (1963), 170, 172–3
Trevelyan, C., 56
Tribe, 9
Trow, M., 172
Trueman, A., 30
Truscot, B., 9–10, 17, 21, 237–8
tuition fees, 2, 3, 5, 6, 80, 100, 108, 103, 116, 117, 130–4, 153, 161–4, 166, 203, 245, 247
criticality of for HE policy, 246
philosophy, history and debates behind policies for, 155–68
Turner, F., 62

UCAS (Universities and Colleges Admission Service), *135*
UCCA (Universities Central Council on Admissions), 87, 117, 134
UCL (University College London), 11, 99, 163, 184, 219, 254
UFC (Universities Funding Council), 1, 6, 64, 77–8, 79, 82, 83, 97, 101, 106, 115, 132–3, 149, 153–4, 166, 179, 182, 187, 193, 197, 198, 224, 227, 253
UGC *see* University Grants Committee
UK Council for Overseas Students Affairs (UKCOSA), 158
UMIST (Manchester Institute of Science and Technology), *128*, 184

unit of resource *see* student unit of resource
unitary system of higher education
move towards a unitary system, 68–87, 76
creation of binary line, 54–68
universities
as beneficiary of investment in technological education early post-war, 29–30
autonomy of, 210–12, 230–6, 236–42, 248–50
debates surrounding early post-war function, 9–10
impact of 1981 cuts on work of, 125–9, 127, 128–9
Jarratt report on efficiency studies in, 106, 115, 220–21, 222
moves from binary line in 1970s and 1980s, 68–87, 76
recommendations of NACEIC for technology in, 24
role in changing policy-making structures, 88–102
role of PAC in policy-making for, 193–9
strengths, features and threats to autonomy of, 236–4
see also accommodations, academic; accommodation, university; committees, university; degrees; facilities, university; funding; governance; investment, university
see also influences and pressures e.g. expansion, higher education; government and civil service; policies and policy-making; status, university; standards, academic
see also role e.g. research; colleges of education
see also specific e.g. Warwick University; York University
Universities Bureau of the British Empire, 47
Universities Central Council on Admissions (UCCA), 87, 117, 134
Universities Funding Council (UFC), 1, 6, 64, 77–8, 79, 82, 83, 97, 101, 106, 115, 132–3, 149, 153–4, 166, 179,

**TEACHING FOR QUALITY
LEARNING AT UNIVERSITY
Fourth Edition**

John Biggs and Catherine Tang

9780335242757 (Paperback)
September 2011

eBook also available

Teaching for Quality Learning at University, now in its fourth edition, is a bestselling book for higher education teachers and administrators interested in assuring effective teaching. The authors outline the constructive alignment of outcomes based teaching, including how to implement it and why it is a good idea to do so. Clearly organized and written, with practical examples, the new edition is thoroughly updated.

Key features:

- Each chapter includes tasks that offer a 'how-to' manual to implement constructive alignment in your own teaching practices
- Aids staff developers in providing support for teachers
- Provides a framework for administrators interested in quality assurance and enhancement of teaching across the whole university

www.openup.co.uk

 **OPEN UNIVERSITY PRESS**
McGraw - Hill Education

INSPIRING ACADEMICS
Learning with the World's
Great University Teachers

Iain Hay (Ed)

9780335237425 (Paperback)
2011

eBook also available

Inspiring Academics draws on the experience and expertise of award-winning university teachers to illuminate exemplary teaching practice. It is structured around five core themes: inspiring learning, command of the field, assessment for independent learning, student development and scholarship.

Key features:

- Brings together the work of top academics from around the world
- Highlights practical ways to improve university teaching
- Openly discusses what does not work, as well as what does

www.openup.co.uk

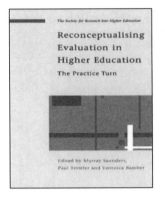

RECONCEPTUALISING EVALUATION IN HIGHER EDUCATION
The Practice Turn

Murray Saunders, Paul Trowler
and Veronica Bamber

9780335241613 (Paperback)
2011

eBook also available

This book seeks to dismantle traditional boundaries in approaches to evaluation, assessing how value and worth is attributed to activities in higher education. It looks at evaluative practice in Higher Education rather than the evaluation of Higher Education.

Key features:

- Conceptualizes, theorizes, and gives empirical examples of evaluative practices across the HE sector
- Considers both the UK and, comparatively, diverse international contexts
- Evaluates the impact of projects to improve teaching and learning in HE

www.openup.co.uk

Managing Successful Universities
Second Edition

Michael Shattock

9780335237432 (Paperback)
2010

eBook also available

This bestselling book defines good management in a university context and how it can contribute to university success. Extensively updated to reflect political, financial and social developments since the first edition, it includes a new chapter on the management of teaching and research and gives in-depth coverage to managing retrenchment and the importance of human resource management.

Key features:

- Describes the holistic characteristics of university management
- The need to be outward looking and entrepreneurial in management style
- The ways successful universities utilize the market to reinforce academic excellence

www.openup.co.uk

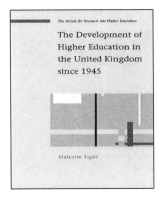

THE DEVELOPMENT OF HIGHER EDUCATION IN THE UNITED KINGDOM SINCE 1945

Malcolm Tight

9780335216420 (Hardback)
2009

eBook also available

Essential reading for all higher education policy makers, managers, administrators and academics, this book provides an authoritative account of the development of higher education in the UK since 1945. The changes in the system have been far-reaching and numerous, affecting a wide range of people beyond those who work or study in universities or colleges, including parents, employers and policy makers.

Key features:

- An overview of the history of higher education in the UK up until 1945
- A detailed tabular summary of post-war higher education developments
- A list of current UK universities and their origins

www.openup.co.uk